AF521889

1998

THE ONE SHOW
VOLUME 20

JUDGED TO BE ADVERTISING'S BEST PRINT, RADIO, TV

A Presentation of
THE ONE CLUB FOR ART & COPY

BOB BARRIE
President

MARY WARLICK
Executive Director

GRAHAM CLIFFORD
Creative Director

EDWIN LAGUERRE
Designer

MARY WARLICK
Editor

AMY ROY
Assistant Editor

MARIA HASSEL
Editorial Assistant

Cover Concept

GRAHAM CLIFFORD
Art Director

MATT SHERRING
Writer

CD-ROM

KEVIN SWANEPOEL
Programming and production

TODD GAFFNEY
Production
ONE CLUB INTERACTIVE

ROGER HORROCKS
ALAN ALSTON
Programming
ARMADILLO INTERACTIVE

Some comments in the *Gold on Gold* section originally appeared in *one. a magazine* volume II, issue I

Published and Distributed by
ROTOVISION S.A.
Sales Office: Sheridan House
112-116a Western Road
Hove, East Sussex, BN3 1DD
United Kingdom
Telephone: +44 (0) 1273 727268
Fax: +44 (0) 1273 727269

In Association with
THE ONE CLUB
FOR ART & COPY
32 East 21 Street
New York, NY 10010
Telephone: 212-979-1900
Fax: 212-979-5006
e-mail: oneclub@inch.com
web site: www.oneclub.com

First Printing
ISBN 0-929837-12-6

Production and Separation by
ProVision/Singapore
Telephone: 65-334-7720 Fax: 65-334-7721

Printed in Singapore

TABLE OF CONTENTS

BOARD OF DIRECTORS

PRESIDENT'S MESSAGE

1998 was a year of change and transition for The One Club for Art and Copy.

We hosted the first One Show Interactive competition, which was, by all accounts, an unqualified success.

We saw *one*, the club's superbly designed and edited magazine, secure the position as the "must-read" for the thinking creative person.

We benefited from the arrival of active new board members Lee Clow, Helayne Spivak, Mark Fenske, Tracy Wong, Jeff Goodby and Mark Johnson. And our first board member from an interactive agency, Tim Smith.

We witnessed The One Club's renewed commitment to exposing more minority students to advertising as a potential career, with programs initiated by Mr. Fenske.

We added some significant changes to the Show itself for next year that I think you'll find exciting.

And we saw the exhausted Gary Goldsmith hand over the presidency of The One Club to yours truly. If I have only a fraction of the impact Gary had in his three-year term, I'll die a happy man.

Oh, and we also saw a presidential commitment to bigger hors d'oeuvres at the One Show.

But, in one area of the club, we celebrated a significant *lack* of change. You see, August brought the tenth anniversary of our Executive Director, Mary Warlick. Many other clubs and shows today seem to be struggling with a search for identity, changes in ownership, financial problems and a general cynicism over the proliferation of awards forums. Through all this, The One Club for Art and Copy perseveres, its reputation solid and its ranking in the minds of creatives worldwide intact. Make no mistake, an overwhelming portion of the credit for this success goes to Ms. Warlick and her dedication to our club.

The next time you see her, wish her a happy anniversary. And thank her.

Enjoy the annual.

BOB BARRIE
August 1998

JUDGES AND
ONE CLUB MEMBERS

1998 ONE SHOW JUDGES

JAMIE BARRETT
Wieden & Kennedy

BRUCE BILDSTEN
Fallon McElligott

HARRY COCCIOLO
Leagas Delaney

SAL DEVITO
DeVito/Verdi

BILL HEATER
Heater Advertising

JELLY HELM
The Martin Agency

SALLY HOGSHEAD
Robaire and Hogshead

BOB KUPERMAN
TBWA Chiat/Day

CHUCK MCBRIDE
Wieden & Kennedy

RISA MICKENBERG

JIM MOUNTJOY
Loeffler Ketchum Mountjoy

DAVE O'HARE
Hal Riney & Partners

ERNIE SCHENCK
Hill Holliday Connors Cosmopulos

MIKE SHINE
Butler Shine & Stern

ROB SILTANEN
TBWA Chiat/Day

STEVE SIMPSON
Goodby Silverstein & Partners

LUKE SULLIVAN
Fallon McElligott

JOHN VITRO
VitroRobertson

LYLE WEDERMEYER
Martin/Williams Advertising

JAY WILLIAMS
Arnold Communications

ONE CLUB MEMBERS

MIKE **A**BADI
HY ABADY
JEFFREY ABBOTT
DAVID ABBOTT
DOUG ADKINS
EMMELINE AGUIRRE
YASMIN AHMAD
DANIEL AKESSON
DARIUS EDWARD ALAIE
JOE ALEXANDER
CARL ALLY
PASCAL ALOUIDOR
AIMEE ALPERT
DAVID ALTSCHILLER
OLIVIA ALTSCHULER
PATRICIA ALVEY
SHARON AMATO
MARTIN AMBA
GIDEON AMICHAY
MATTHEW AMMIRATI
RALPH AMMIRATI
JOHN AMODEO
BRUCE ANASTON
AUDREY ANDERSON
RON ANDERSON
STEPHANIE ANDERSON
TRUDY ANDERSON
DAVID ANGELO
ADRIANA ANGOTTI
ANTHONY ANGOTTI
FRANK ANSELMO
FRANK ANTON
J.P. APPELBAUM
JILL APPLEBAUM
MARCELO S.S. ARAGAO
STEPHANIE ARCULLI
PICHAYEN ARI
ARNOLD ARLOW
DAVID ARNOLD
RON ARNOLD
STEPHANIE ARNOLD
LORRAINE ARROLL
SAM ASH
JIMMY ASHWORTH
CRAIG ASTLER
ENRIQUE ASTUY
JAYSON ATIENZA
CHINNAWUT AWAKUL
RUTH AYERS
ROSEANNE AZARIAN
DOMINICK **B**ACCOLLO
DANIEL C. BACHMANN
KRISTINA BACKLUND
RONALD BACSA
TOM BAGOT
CHRIS BAIER
LARRY BAISDEN
SANDRA BALBOA
MICHELLE BANKS
MARK BARBER
CHRISTOPHE BARDOT
SHANNON-MEGAN BARRECA
BOB BARRIE
LAUREN BARROCAS
DANIEL BARRY
GARY BASSELL
STEVE BAUTISTA
JEFF BAXTER
ESENGUL BAYKAL
TIM BAYLESS
JENNIFER BAYNE
TOYGAR BAZARKAYA
CLIFFORD BEACH
ALLAN BEAVER
WENDY BECK
WENDY BECKER
ELIZABETH BEKESZ
DOUG BELL
BRIAN BELLANCA
JARETT BELLUCCI
GREGG BENEDIKT
JACQUELINE BENITEZ
GORDON BENNETT
ROGER BENTLEY
AMANDA K. BERGER
DANIELLE BERGER
MARCI BERGMAN
PAUL BERNASCONI
DAVID BERNSTEIN
PETER BERTA
FRED BERTINO
WAYNE BEST
DANA BETGILAN
MICHAEL BETTS
DOMINIQUE BIGER KAHN
ARTHUR BIJUR
BRUCE BILDSTEN
PAT BILGER
CHARLES A. BLACK
CLAY BLACK
CHARLES BLACKWELL
BRENDON BLAKE
LAURA BLOCK
STEVEN BLOCK
SUZANNE N. BLOCK
ALEX BOGUSKY
JOHN BOONE
NICOLE BOTKIER
ALIX BOTWIN
MARGARET BOYD
RICK BOYKO
MARK BRADY
SCOTT BRENNAN
JIM BRODIE
BILL BROKAW
MICHAEL BRONOWITZ
DARA BROOKS
CARL BROSCIOUS, JR.
GEORGE BROWN
KETURAH E. BROWN
MARK BROWN
SHAMEKA M. BROWN
TIM BRUNELLE
GAIL SCHOEN BRUNN
SARAH BRUNS
JANE BRYSON
MARTIN BUCHANAN
ROB BUCK
CAROL BUETTNER
RON BURKHARDT
ERIC BURNARD
PAT BURNHAM
ALLISON BURTON
JOHN BUTLER
KEVIN BUTLER
LARRY **C**ADMAN
ANDREW M. CAHILL
STEVE CALLEN
CATHIE CAMPBELL
LORI CAMPBELL
PAUL CAPPELLI
ROB CARDUCCI
DAVID CARLIN
GRETCHEN CARSWELL
JASON CARTER
CINDY CASARES
MARK CATALINA
TODD CATHER
CHAD CHADWICK
SUSANNE CHAMP
WILSON CHAN
ANN TING CHANG
JACK CHANG
JONATHAN CHANG
JOSEPH CHANG
LINDA CHANG
MARIA CHANG
ERIN CHEESEMAN
KENNY CHEN
CHUNG-MAU CHENG
JAY CHIAT
VINCENT CHIECO
CHIN CHUL CHOI
LOUIE CHOW
MARVIN CHOW
CHRIS CHURCHILL
KIRK CITRON
AMY CLARK
MARK CLARK
ROSSER CLARK
TIM CLARKE
BART CLEVELAND
CINDY CLEVENGER
LEE CLOW
KARL CLUCK
HENRY COCHRAN
DANIEL COHEN
GARY COHEN
JOSH COHEN
STEVE CONNELLY
JUDY CONNER
PAUL CONNORS
DOUG COOK
DIANE COOK-TENCH
MARTY COOKE
COLIN COSTELLO
SHARLA COSTELLO
MARK HENRY COUSIN
MICHAEL COX
ROBERT COX
ROB CRAMER
JEFF CRAMP
COURT CRANDALL
STEVE CRANE
JUAN CRAVERO
RICHARD CREAN
LOURDES CRESPO
JACK CRIFASI
PETER CROSBY
GREG CROSSLEY
KEVIN CRUICKSHANK
PHYLISS CUNNINGHAM
JOE CUPANI
GREG CURRAN
STEPHEN CURRY
MICHAEL CZAKO
BILL **D**'AMBROSIO
JOANNA D'AVANZO
MARGUERITE D'ESPOSITO
CHRIS D'ROZARIO
SHARON DANG
MICHAEL DANKO
KEITH DARBY
PATRICIA DARCEY
PHILIP DAVIDSON
PHIL DEARMAN
IZZY DEBELLIS
ANTHONY DECAROLIS
VICTOR DECASTRO
JAY DEEGAN
TONY DEGREGORIO
STEVE DEITERS
JERRY DELLA FEMINA
CHARLES DEMARCO
JOSH DENBERG
JAYNE DESESA
JOHN DEVITO
SAL DEVITO
KELVIN A. DICKERSON
STEVE DILDARIAN
GREG DINOTO
TONY DIPIETRO
PATRICK DISTASIO
ANGELA DOMINGUEZ
MARTY DONOHUE
STEVE DOPPELT
TOM DOUD
SEAN DOUGHERTY
ROB DOW
JAMES B. DOWNER
RALEIGH DRENNON
DANIEL J. DREXLER
JOE DUFFY
ROSALYN DUNHAM
MICHAEL L.C. DUNN
LAURENCE DUNST
JIM DURFEE
SUSAN DURO
SUSAN DWYER
LISA CIOCCI **E**GAN
SHANNON EDWARDS
MICHAEL EILPERIN
EINAR GUNNAR EINARSSON
ARTHUR EINSTEIN
PRISCA EKKENS
STUART ELLIOTT
KEVIN ENDRES
GARY ENNIS
PATRICIA LYNN EPSTEIN
MARCELO ERMELINDO
ERIC ESSIG
PAUL EVANS
ERIK **F**AHRENKOPF
JOHN FAHY
MICHAEL FARKAS
SARAH FELDMAN
STEVEN FELDMAN
MARK R. FENSKE
SCOTT FERGUSON
JOSEPH FERRAZANO
MICHAEL FETSKO
KERRY FEUERMAN
CARLOS FIGUEIREDO
MICHAEL FINE
BENJAMIN FINKEL
SYLVIA FINZI
NIRA FIRESTONE
ANN FISHER
TIM FISHER
PETER FITZ
BOB FITZGERALD
CORA FLASTER
MIKE FLEGLE
KATHERINE FLYNN
NICOLE FORTE
GINA FORTUNATO
LISA FRANCILIA
SELA FRANCIS
CLIFF FREEMAN
ROBERT FREMGEN
DAVID M. FRIEBERG
JOHN FUNCK
JERRY FURY
TYE FUSSELL
DAMASO CRESPO FUSTER
TOM **G**ABRIEL
BRYAN GAFFIN
BOB GAGE
TOM GALATI
BRIAN GALLAGHER
NICHOLAS GAMMA
MARK GANTON
BERTRAND GARBASSI
GERY GARCIA
SALVADOR GARCIA
CARLOS GONZALEZ GARCIA
DAVID GARDINER
BETH GARDNER
TOM GARDNER
LEE GARFINKEL
AMIL GARGANO
LISA GARRONE
GIANINA GAUCI
DEAN GEMMELL
JOHN GEORGE
RICHARD GERDES

HAROLD GERMAN
IAN HENDRIK GESCHKE
STEVEN GIAMARINO
GEORGE GIER
CARLA GIGANTE
ANTHONY GILL
BRAD GILMORE
DAVID A. GILMOUR
FRANK GINSBERG
GUDBJORG GISSURARD
JASON GLASSMAN
KENNETH GLEASON
MAX GODSIL
GEORGE GOETZ
RHODESSA GOINGS
BRIAN GOLD
LINA GOLDENBERG
DAN GOLDGEIER
DAVID GOLDOFF
CHRIS GOLDSCHMIDT
ALEXANDRA GOLDSMITH
ZAKIMA GOLDSMITH
DAVID GOLDSTEIN
MARK GOLDSTEIN
MITCH GORDON
DOUG GRABOWSKI
ROY GRACE
STELLA GRAFAKOS
DIANNE D. GRAHAM
DAVID GRAY
JEFF GRAYBILL
ROSALIND GREENE
STEPHANIE GREENE
NORM GREY
DICK GRIDER
LYNN GRIFFES
JEFF GRIFFITH
PHILIP GROWICK
ROLAND GRYBAUSKAS
MICHAEL GUARINI
KURT GUENTHER
KATHLEEN GUIDICE
GINA GUIFFRIDA
LORI **H**ABAS
DEB HAGAN
JIM HAGAR
JAMES HAINIS
ALYSON HALLBERG
MATTHEW HALLOCK
TRACE HALLOWELL
ADA HALOFSKY
MARK HALSKI
BILL HAMILTON
THOMAS C. HANSEN
WAYNE HANSON
NICK HARDY
KEITH HARMWEYER
CABELL HARRIS
ERICH HARTMANN
JACKIE HATHIRAMANI
JIM HAYMAN
THOMAS HAYO
BLAISE HAYWARD
BRENT HEINDL
CHERYL HELLER
ALEXIS HEMPHILL
BRADLEY HENSEN
ROY HERBERT
MAUREEN HERCHE
ELANA HERSHMAN
RONY HERZ
KENNETH HERZOG
LEE HESTER
RALF HEUEL
DAWN HIBBARD
BILL HILLSMAN
WOODY HINKLE
ANDREW HIRSCH
PETER HIRSCH
JUSTIN HLUBOKY
MICHELLE HOAGLAND
KARI HOERCHLER
AMY HOFFAR
SIGAL HOFSHI
SALLY HOGSHEAD
ANNIE HOLDSWORTH
BARRY HOLLAND
ROBERT S. HOLLANDER
BILL HOLLISTER
DAVE HOLLOWAY
JENINE HOLMES
SANDRA HOLTZMAN
JIM HORD
LAURENCE HORVITZ
RYAN HOSE
HUGH HOUGH
BRIAN HOWLETT
MARK HRICIGA
JONATHAN HUDSON
DION HUGHES
MIKE HUGHES
CHEN HUI-FANG
SHAYNE-ALEXIS HUMPHREY
KATHY HUNTER
AMANDA HUNTZINGER
LISA HURWITZ PERETZ
JOHN HYNES
PAUL **I**ANNUZZO
MAURICIO MORI IKEZAKI
NICOLE INFANTE
AKI INOUE
MICHELLE ISHAY
MARA IUTCOVICH
DICK **J**ACKSON
JUDI JACOB
ADRIANNA JACOBS
CHRIS JACOBS
HARRY M. JACOBS, JR.
PER ROBERT JACOBSON
JOHN JAECKEL
HOLLY JAFFE
JAYDEE JANA
CROCKETT JEFFERS
ADRIAN JEFFERY
MICKEY JENKINS
DAVID JENSEN
ANDREW JESKE
CHRIS JETKO
MARGARITA OLIVA JIMINEZ
ANTHONY A. JOHNSON
MARCUS JOHNSON
RAYMOND JOHNSON
STEVE JULIUSSON
JEFFREY JUREVIC
TAL **K**AGAN
BRIAN KALINA
RIC KALLAHER
DAN KAN
CHARLES KANE
DANIEL KANE
MELINDA KANIPE
PETER KAPLAN
SCOTT KAPLAN
LINUS KARLSSON
MARSHALL KARP
YOSHIKO KASUGA
LISA KAUFMAN
RICHARD KAUFMAN
LESLIE KAY
WOODY KAY
ELIZABETH KEANE
ROBERT L. KELLY
JOEY KILRAIN
JOANNE KIM
ELIZABETH KING
KERRY KINNEY
JEFF KIRSCHNER
RICHARD KIRSHENBAUM
LEON KISLOWSKI
KRISTI KLAMER
JOE KNEZIC
LINDA KNIGHT
ANDREW KNIPE
CYNTHIA KNOX
NICOLE KOBELI
LESLIE HERMAN KOLK
KLARISA KONSTANTINOVSKY
BENIER KORANACHE
RENEE KORUS
JEFF KOSLOSKI
MARIA KOSTYK-PETRO
SAADI KOUALTI
JUDY KOZUCK
BARRY KRAUSE
STEPHEN KRAUSS
DAVID KREWINGHAUS
KEN KRIMSTEIN
NEAL KROUSE
STEWART KRULL
PRADEEP KUMAR
KUANG-CHUN KUO
KIM KWANG-KYU
ROBERT **L**ABARGE
JACQUELINE X.S. LAGANA
MASSIEL LAGO
BEN LAGUNAS
STEPHEN LAND
STEVEN LANDSBERG
ANDY LANGER
ANTHONY LAPETRI
EDUARDO LARIOS
CAROLE LARSON
KEVIN LASKOFF
GARY BONILLA LATONI
STACY LAVENDAR
JOE LEAHY
HO JONG LEE
JANE LEE
JENNIE LEE
NEIL LEINWOHL
DANY LEE LENNON
DICK LEONARD
JODIE LEOPOLD
ELIZABETH LERNER
MIKE LESCARBEAU
SHARON LESSER
CHIK WAN LEUNG
PETER LEVATHES
ROBERT LEVENSON
KATE LEVIN
WARREN LEWIS
TOM LICHTENHELD
SUSAN LIEBER
ADRIAN LIM
MARJORIE MORRIS LIPAN
LISA LIPKIN-BALSER
WALLACE LITTMAN
STEVEN LIU
DEBORAH LIVINGSTON
ALBERTO LLAURADOR
DAVID LOEW
GEORGE LOIS
ANA CARMEN
RIVABEN LONGOBARDI
CARLOS LOPEZ
EYRA LOPEZ
CARSON LORD
KIMBERLEY LOWE
BEIRNE LOWRY
HSIAN-FU LU
PETER LUBALIN
DAVID LUBARS
JOHN LUDWIG
FRANCESCA LUM
LISA LURIE
JOHN LUTTER
MICHAEL LYONS
SARAH LYONS
MIKE **M**ACCARONIO
TONY MACCHIA
MARCELO MACHADO
SAM MACLAY
SHYAM MADIRAJU
PREETHI MAHADEVIAH
MADHU MALHAN
KAREN MALLIA
PAUL MALMSTROM
PETER MALONEY
BRADLEY MANIER
JOHN MANNION
BETSY MANSFIELD
JENNIFER MANTZ
BRIAN MARABELLO
KAREN MARCHETTI
LEE MARGOLIS
GABITASHVILI MARINA
LOUIS MARINO
KENNETH MARKEY
LAWRENCE MARKS
RHODA MARSHALL
DAVE MARTIN
ARNOLD MARZAN
DIANE MASAL
MICHAEL MAURER
RICHARD MAY
MICHAEL MAYES
SAM MAZUR
JAMES MAZZOLA
SCOTT MCAFEE
ED MCCABE
TED MCCAGG
CLEM MCCARTHY
KERRY MCCARTHY
BRIAN MCDERMOTT
FRANK MCGOVERN
KEVIN MCKEON
DON MCKINNEY
M.K. MCMULLEN
NED MCNEILAGE
ROB MCPHERSON
LENA MEDINA
MICHAEL MEDINA
HEATHER MEE
LYNNE MEENA
ROBERT MELLETT
MARK MENDELIS
FRANK MEO
TOM MERRICK
JUSTO GUIJARRO MESA
LUIS MIGUEL MESSIANU
MARIO G. MESSINA
LYLE METZDORF
TERRI MEYER
GREG MEYERS
BETHANN MIALE
JEANINE MICHNA
MARK MILLAR
CHRISTOPHER MILLER
DON MILLER
REID MILLER
SARAH MILLER
JONATHAN L. MINDELL
BRETT MINIERI
BILL MITCHELL
STEVE MITCHELL
STEVEN MITSCH
MARISE MIZRAHI
RONALD MODICA
TY MONTAGUE
PABLO MONZON
ISRAEL MORALES
MELVIN MORGAN
CASSIO MORON
DAWN MORRIS
JACOB MORRIS
TREVOR MORRIS
DEBORAH MORRISON
MARCO MORSELLA
AARON MOSHER
JIM MOUNTJOY
TOM MOYER
ZAK MROUEH
MARY MUELLER
WILLIAM MUNCH, JR.
SIBILA MUNOZ
VINNY MURATORE
KYLE C. MURPHY
LEXIE MURRAY
MARIA ELENA MYRKA
TRACY **N**ADER
THOMAS NATHAN
ROBERT S. NEEDLEMAN
TED NELSON
ARUN K. NEMALI
JOSEPH NEY
THU NGUYEN
STEVE NICHOLAS
KRIS NICHOLS
AMY NICHOLSON
JENNIFER NOBLE
SUSAN NOBLES
OLLE NORDELL
CHRIS NOTT
DICK **O**'BRIEN
JAMES O'BRIEN
MICK O'BRIEN
KELLY O'KEEFE
JOE O'NEILL

DAVID OAKLEY
BILL OBERLANDER
RIP ODELL
DAVID OGILVY
VICKY OLIVER
ALEX OLMSTED
SONJA OLSON
CAROLYN OPPENHEIM
PETER ORAVETZ
MARTIN ORZIO
MIKIO OSAKI
KWASI OSEI
SEYMON OSTILLY
CELE OTNES
ANGELA OTTOMANELLI
ALVARO **P**AEZ
CAROLYN PAGLIUCA
JOHN PAINTER
JACK PALANCIO
MARINA PALMER
SHARYN PANAGIDES
JENNIFER PAPPALARDO
MICHAEL PARENT
SAM PARK
JAMES D. PARKER
WARD PARKER
DAVID PARSON
KIMBERLY PAUL
ALIDO PAVAN
MICHAEL PAVONE
MICHAEL PAYER
ROGER B. PE
JASON PEARSON
JON PEASE
DOUG PEDERSEN
STEPHEN PEDERSON
JOYCE PEDRETTI
RICHARD PELS
JUDY PENNY
ALEXANDRE PERALTA
RICKY PERKINS
ELLEN PERLESS
DAVID PETERS
DAVID PIATKOWSKI
MIKE PILATO
DONNA PILCH
JEREMY PIPPINGER
BILLY PITTARD
TERRY PLAYER
JONATHAN PLAZONJA
CHRIS POLLOCK
SHIRLEY POLYKOFF
CHRIS POULIN
STAN POULOS
DAVE PRAGER
ED PRENTISS
TIM PRICE
BRYAN J. PRINDIVILLE
JEFFREY PROPPER
KEVIN S. PROUDFOOT
ERIK PROULX
TONY PUCCA
KAY COLMAR PULLEN
AMY PUTMAN
NAZNEEN **Q**AZI
KEITH QUESENBERRY
ALDO QUEVEDO
MICHAEL **R**ACKLEY
LYNDA RAIHOFER
KAREN RAJCIC
FARIA RAJI
APARNA RAMAN
CLAUDIA RAMIREZ
RENE RAMIREZ
ANSELMO RAMOS
JEFFREY RANBOM
ALISSA RANDALL
MICHAEL RAPPAPORT
KIM RASMUSSEN
JAMIE RAUDENBUSCH
JOHN REA
MIKAL REICH
STEVE REICH
IAN REICHENTHAL
BRANDON REIF
DAVE REMER
LIANA RICCARDI
JOSEPH RICCI
NANCY RICE
ROB RICH
ALLEN RICHARDSON
KIMBALL RICHMOND
HAL RINEY
JOHN ROBERTSON
MARK ROBERTSON
MICHAEL ROBERTSON
SCOTT ROCKWOOD
ALEXIS RODRIGUEZ
JASON B. ROGERS
MIKE ROGERS
GAD ROMANN
KATHERINE ROSE
JONATHAN ROSEN
ROB ROSENTHAL
BERNIE ROSNER
TOM ROST
ROSANNE ROTENBERG
MELISSA ROTH
MARK ROTHENBERG
CAROLYN AMOROSI ROTHSEID
JOSHUA RUBIN
JONATHAN RUBY
JOHN RUSSO
NAT RUSSO
ROCCO RUSSO
MEL RUSTOM
NANCY RYBCZYNSKI
NORA RYDER
TED **S**ABARESE
STEVE SAGE
VINNY SAINATO
SALOMON SAINVIL
EVELYN C. SALAZAR
JEFFREY SALGADO
RUSTAM SALMZIANOV
JAMES SALZANO
RAJIV SAMVATSAR
EARLE SANDBERG
DAVID SANDOR
ROBYN SANDS
DAVID SANTIAGO
EMMANUEL SANTOS
CINDY SARGENT
CARL SASTRAM
ARIEL SAULOG
ROBERT SAXON
JOANNE SCANNELLO
MAISIE SCHAROLD
ERNIE SCHENCK
SANDRA SCHER
DAVID SCHERMER
GLENN SCHEUER
DENNIS SCHEYER
CHRISTOPHER SCHIFANDO
MARK SCHIMMEL
CHRIS SCHLEGEL
TIMOTHY SCHLEIF
PAUL SCHMIDT
MICHAEL SCHREIER
JILL SCHROEDER
ERIC SCHUTTE
MICHAEL SCHWABENLAND
HEINZ SCHWEGLER
JEAN J. SCHWENZNER
KEITH M. SCOTT
JOHN SCULLY
DANIELLE SEARLES
LEE SEIDENBERG
TOD SEISSER
LIAM A. SHANNON
BILL SHEA
BOB SHEA
MIKE SHEEHAN
ZHONG SHEN SHEN
HILLARY SHENK
LORI SHEPPARD
MATTHEW SHERRING
BRETT SHEVACK
EDWARD SHIEH
LORI SIBAL
TIM SIEDELL
FRED SIEGEL
MARK SILVEIRA
TONIA SIMON
JENNIFER SIMON
JON SISENWEIN
MARK SIVERTSEN
DEBORAH SKALER
STEVE SKIBBA
MARCUS SLAVEN
MIKE SLOSBERG
ROBERT SLOSBERG
DAVID A. SMITH
DAVID A. SMITH, JR.
GARY S. SMITH
JASON A. SMITH
KIM SMITH
NANCY SMITH
PETE SMITH
ADRIANA SOLER
PEDRO SOLER
MAGGIE SOLOMON
MO SOLOMON
RICHARD SOLOMON
HARI SONITIS
OTTO SOONTARODOM
CHERI SOUKUP
MARK SPECTOR
JOHN SPITERI
DOUGLAS SPITZER
HELAYNE SPIVAK
AMY SPIZZO
AARON KILLIAN SPRATT
KASH SREE
LEE ST. JAMES
GABRIEL ST. JOHN
JOHN STAFFEN
JOSEPH STALUPPI
TODD STANTON
CHRIS STAPLES
STEVEN STARK
NANCY STARKEY-COHEN
SCOTT STEFAN
DEAN STEFANIDES
MICHAEL STELZER
ROGER STEPHENS
JONATHAN STERN
GLENN STEVENS
CHRIS STOLTZ
KATHLEEN STOLTZFUS
ELIZABETH STONE
ROB STRASBERG
DENZIL STRICKLAND
BOB SULLIVAN
MICHAEL SULLIVAN
TUSSANEE SUNTIVIPARNON
LESLIE SUPER
JACK SUPPLE
MARC SURCHIN
NICK SUSTANA
MICK SUTTER
KIMBERLY SWANSON
STEVE SWARTZ
JOE SWEET
LESLIE SWEET
RICH SWIETEK
JOHN SZALAY
DEAN SZOSTCZUK
NORMAN **T**ANEN
WILLIE TANG
DONNA TARIGO
MATTHEW TARULLI
C. DOW TATE
KEVIN TEEVENS
RODOLFO TERRADA
MIKE TESCH
MARY ANN TESTERMAN
KEVIN THOEM
GREG THOMAS
BENJAMIN THOMPSON
DAVID THOMPSON
JIM THOMPSON
ERIC TILFORD
TODD TILFORD
JOHN P. TOPACIO
MARK TOWNSLEY
ROY TRIMBLE
MATTHEW TRUMINO
STAZ TSIAVOS
ROMAN TSUKERMAN
AITI TU
AMY TURIEL
MILES TURPIN
RODNEY **U**NDERWOOD
TOM UNGAR
VICTOR **V**ALADEZ
VASSIL S. VALKOV
PETER VAN BLOEM
FRANCINE VAN KOOLBERGEN
JAN VAN MESDAG
NANCY VECILLA
PAUL VENABLES
DANIEL VENDRAMIN
JESSICA VENEGAS
THERESA VENEZIA
AMY VENSEL
STEPHEN VERSANDI
MATTHEW VESCOVO
CAROL VICK
MEGAN E. VILSAK
LARRY VINE
MICHAEL VITIELLO
JOHN VITRO
JOSEPH VOLPICELLI
LEILA VUORENMAA
ELAINE **W**AGNER
JUDY WALD
DEBORAH WALDMAN
MARVIN WALDMAN
THOMAS WALKER
YA-LI WANG
ADAM WARD
BOB WARREN
TRICIA WARREN
DEB WARRENFELTZ
SHANE WATSON
PETER WATT
JAMES WEBB
DEACON WEBSTER
LYLE WEDEMEYER
KAREN WEECH
JOY WEEENG
IWAN WEIDMANN
LES WEINER
ERIC WEISBERG
MARTY WEISS
WENDY WENDLAND
LAWRENCE G. WERNER
ROBERT SHAW WEST
BILL WESTBROOK
NAT WHITTEN
ENBRUCE WHOU
CHRIS WIGERT
SCOTT WILD
RICHARD WILDE
CLAY WILLIAMS
JAY WILLIAMS
STEVE WILLIAMS
TIM WILLIAMS
CLAIRE WILLMS
GREG WILSON
STEWART WINTER
SILKE WINTER
CHRIS WOJDA
DAVID WOJDYLA
STEFEN WOJNAROWSKI
DAVID WOLFF
ALAN WOLK
DAVID A. WONG
JUDY WONG
RENA WONG
BRIAN WOODRUFF
LAURA B. WOODS
ANNIE WU
SEIJI **Y**AMASAKI
BETSY YAMAZAKI
C.Y. YANG
RICHARD YELLAND
JUNG HWAN YOON
LYNETTE **Z**ATOR
JEFFREY ZELDMAN
CAROLE ZESCH
RAINER ZIERER
MARK ZITO
MAT ZUCKER

GOLD, SILVER
& BRONZE

GOLD AWARD
newspaper over 600 lines
single

art director
NEIL DAWSON
writer
CLIVE PICKERING
client
VOLKSWAGEN GROUP UK
agency
BMP DDB/LONDON

WE ARE WITHHOLDING A VOLKSWAGEN
'SURPRISINGLY ORDINARY PRICES' ADVERTISEMENT
UNTIL WE RECEIVE CONFIRMATION THAT
A VOLKSWAGEN POLO L DOES INDEED COST £7990.

SILVER AWARD
newspaper over 600 lines
single

art director
PAUL BELFORD

writer
NIGEL ROBERTS

photographers
GLEN ERLER
LAURIE HASKELL

client
WATERSTONE'S
BOOKSELLERS

agency
BDDP.GGT/LONDON

BRONZE AWARD
newspaper over 600 lines
single

art directors
JOHN DOYLE
JOHN EMMERT

writer
KARA GOODRICH

photographer
GEOFF STEIN

client
SHREVE CRUMP & LOW

agency
DOYLE INC/WESTON

Since 1796
Authoring moments for over 200 years.

Oysters produce pearls when they're irritated. These must have been furious.

SHREVE, CRUMP & LOW
Two floors. And who knows how many stories.

GOLD AWARD
newspaper over 600 lines
campaign

art director
PAUL BELFORD

writer
NIGEL ROBERTS

photographers
LAURIE HASKELL
JAMES NACHTWEY
GLEN ERLER
JOEL-PETER WITKIN

client
WATERSTONE'S
BOOKSELLERS

agency
BDDP.GGT/LONDON

SILVER AWARD
/spaper over 600 lines
campaign

art directors
JOHN DOYLE
MICHELLE CARACCIA
JOHN EMMERT
MARY AVERY

writer
KARA GOODRICH

photographer
GEOFF STEIN

client
SHREVE CRUMP & LOW

agency
DOYLE INC/WESTON

Decidedly not the week to renounce all worldly goods.

Oh, no, not now, not this week, not ever. How impregnable would the human heart need to be to resist the beauty and charm of a piece from the Damiani Collection? Far more unbreachable than your own.

It is marvelous, is it not? The sparkle of myriad diamonds conjoined within 18k white gold ringlets of 18k white gold balls. Ultimately destined to encircle your wrist and heart, not necessarily in that order. Then there are the earrings. It would be a shame to break up a perfectly matched set. Which leads us naturally to the bold and singular ring. It is a vexing but glorious predicament.

Casa Damiani has been the source of the finest precious gem jewelry for over 40 years. Craftsmen, trained under the tutelage of Damiano Grassi himself, carry on the Italian tradition of goldsmithing harking back to the crowded Pontevecchio. Housed in a Palace in Milan (how appropriate) are masterworks in progress that will do no less than advance the art of jewelrymaking. They have the International awards to prove it. Yet, more importantly, Damiani has a following of zealous devotees who share one goal: Increasing their own personal prized collections. That can be done. Exclusively at Shreve, Crump & Low in New England. Eschew romance novels. Give up Rocky Road ice cream. Even forgo the temptation of sun worship. Just stop yourself short of disavowing your passion for wearing beautiful jewelry. At least for this week.

SHREVE, CRUMP & LOW

Two floors. And who knows how many stories.

Wise men come bearing gifts.

You have heard it before. "I have everything I could ever want." "I don't require a thing but you." Need we admonish you only a fool would dare heed those words. At this festive time of year, it is your heartfelt obligation to produce the perfect gift. Thus we most graciously offer our assistance.

The fine offering on this page should assuage any feelings of inadequacy you may harbor. Dilaro jewelry makes the perfect and much adored gift.

The new Symphony Collection from Dilaro is a veritable wish list of diamonds, rubies, sapphires and 18k gold or platinum, even 18k gold and platinum. Whether it be a stylish linked necklace and bracelet or the whimsy of precious gem-studded butterflies and bees, the recipient, eyes open wide, will meet each with protestations of "You shouldn't have," as she quickly slips it on. You could always cover all your proverbial bases and purchase a combination of the above. Dilaro jewelry is thoughtfully designed to be stacked and worn collectively. And, owing to an informal elegance that encourages everyday wear, they may rarely grace the inside of her jewelry box. Isn't that pleasant testimony to your gift-giving prowess? Come to the exclusive source of Dilaro's marvelous collection. Shreve, Crump & Low, also known as, sanctuary for many an earnest but befuddled gift-seeker. She'll never even miss the frankincense and myrrh.

SHREVE, CRUMP & LOW

Two floors. And who knows how many stories.

The holidays are over. It's months until your birthday. Think. Think.

You want it. There. That's reason enough to purchase yourself something from the Dilaro jewelry collection. And what woman wouldn't want something this collection has to offer? There are huggie earrings sprinkled liberally with diamonds. A Roman drop pendant suitable for an emperor's wife. Matte 18k gold finish rings with Rhodolite garnets, sapphires and diamonds. These are stackable rings which complement the stackable gemstone bracelets. (And, no, two does not constitute a stack.)

Designer John Apel, the master craftsman of Dilaro, has once again utilized precious metals and stones to artfully express the relationship between art and nature. Let the gold come in waves and let the stones create small rock piles in your jewelry box. Better still, his concept translates to jewelry that is appropriate for almost any occasion and surprisingly affordable. And, in Massachusetts, this amazing collection is exclusive to Shreve, Crump & Low. South Dakota's Statehood Day? National Tuba Day? Grover Cleveland's Birthday? (Actual or observed?) Never mind. Justification really is such a nag. Instead just select a special piece from the Dilaro Collection and then mark the day with bright red ink on your calendar. And, next year you can celebrate the occasion in the customary way: by purchasing another.

SHREVE, CRUMP & LOW

Two floors. And who knows how many stories.

Oysters produce pearls when they're irritated. These must have been furious.

What exactly do you do to incite an oyster to produce pearls this voluptuous and beautiful? Is it possible that a tiny grain of sand could be irksome enough to elicit this kind of reaction. Or is there more? Fortunately, Mikimoto is the chosen safekeeper of the profound secret to coaxing perfection from these hypersensitive mollusks.

In 1893, Kokichi Mikimoto cultivated the world's first pearl. Today, over 100 years later, cultured pearl purchasers still use 'Mikimoto' and the word 'best' interchangeably. In point of fact, only five of every 100 pearls brought up from the sea are deemed worthy of a Mikimoto necklace, bracelet, or earrings. Examine then, the case of the Black-lipped Tahitian Oyster. After all, it takes years for an oyster to produce enough nacre to form a pearl of any respectable quality. About two years for just 0.5mm of nacre. The size of black pearls averages 10 to 15mm. Not handy at math? Suffice to say, a dozen or more excellent harvest years are required to collect enough black pearls that match in size, shape and color to create one necklace. Add to that the pickiness of Mikimoto and you have got a necklace that is definitely worthy of a little modest pleading.

We cordially invite you to come to Shreve, Crump & Low and drown yourself in our astounding South Seas collection exclusively from Mikimoto. It will certainly give you pause to wonder why everyone can not respond to little irritations as graciously as the oyster does.

SHREVE, CRUMP & LOW

Two floors. And who knows how many stories.

SILVER AWARD
newspaper 600 lines or less single

art director
PAUL HIRSCH
writer
JOSH DENBERG
client
PORSCHE
agency
GOODBY SILVERSTEIN & PARTNERS/ SAN FRANCISCO

Your dog may stick his head out the window. But only once.

The new 911 can go 0 to 60 in 5.3 seconds with a top speed of 171 MPH.

To avoid a stop at the vet, we suggest you leave the windows up.

911 from Porsche. There is no substitute.

BRONZE AWARD
newspaper 600 lines or less single

art director
CINDY COHEN
writer
ROB STRASBERG
photographer
KEN GRIFFITHS
client
LAND ROVER NORTH AMERICA
agency
GRACE & ROTHSCHILD/ NEW YORK

Our return policy is simple. You will return.

SILVER AWARD
newspaper 600 lines or less
campaign

art director
MICHAEL COHEN
writers
CURTIS SMITH
MIKE DUCKWORTH
photographer
PAT STAUB
client
MOON PIE
agency
LOEFFLER KETCHUM
MOUNTJOY/CHARLOTTE

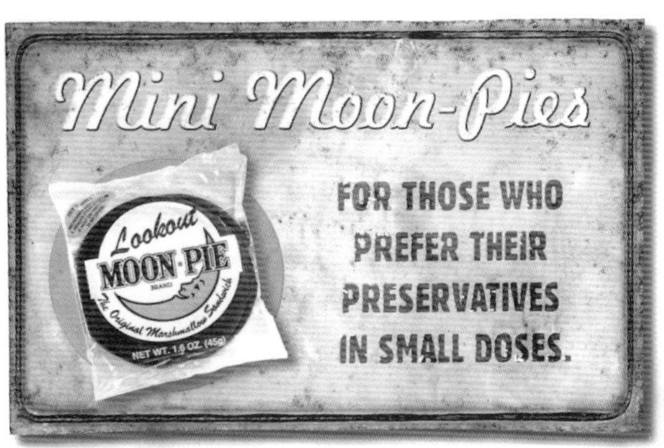

BRONZE AWARD
newspaper 600 lines or less
campaign

art director
DOUG MICKSCHL
writer
TROY LONGIE
photographer
STUART BLOCK
client
REYNOLD GUITAR LESSONS
agency
PERISCOPE/MINNEAPOLIS

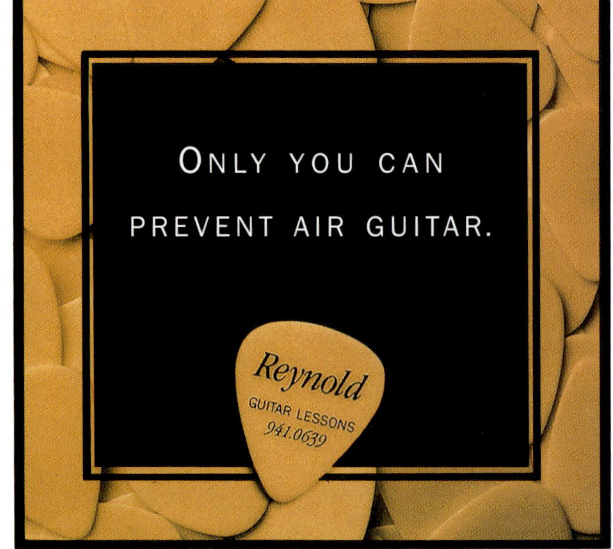

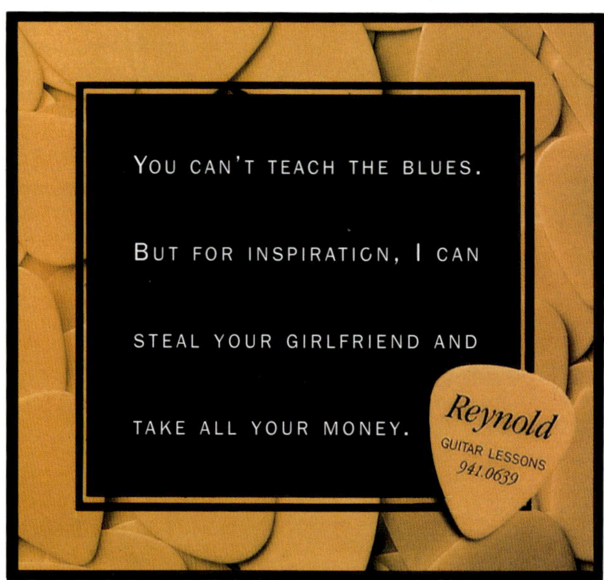

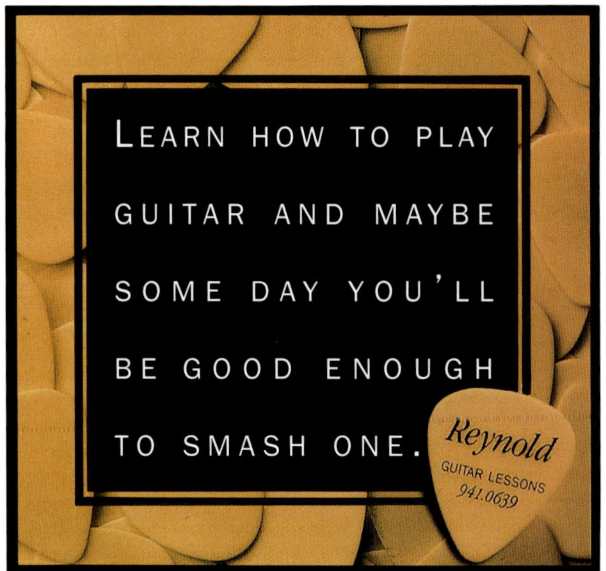

GOLD AWARD
magazine color
full page or spread
single

art directors
MATT PETERSON
MIKE PROCTOR

writers
IAN COHEN
GRANT HOLLAND

photographer
BOB PETERSON

client
SIMS SNOWBOARDS

agency
HAMMERQUIST SAFFEL
& HALVERSON/SEATTLE

SILVER AWARD
magazine color
full page or spread
single

art director
STEVE MAPP

writer
SCOTT WILD

photographers
DAN ESCOBAR
SIMON BRUTY

client
ADIDAS AMERICA

agency
LEAGAS DELANEY/
SAN FRANCISCO

BRONZE AWARD
magazine color
full page or spread
single

art director
JOHN VITRO
writer
JOHN ROBERTSON
photographers
CHRIS WIMPEY
STOCK
client
TAYLOR GUITARS
agency
VITROROBERTSON/
SAN DIEGO

Ross Powell and his wife were driving back from a vacation in the mountains.

Ross saw a sign for a guitar shop, pulled over and said, "I'll be right out."

He went inside and fell in love with a Taylor.

In Ross' words, he "talked about that guitar all the way home."

Which was 195 miles.

Finally, after talking about it all the next week, he drove back to the same store to buy it. Which was almost 400 miles round trip.

If you ever get a chance to pull over and try a Taylor, we hope you will.

It'll give you something to chat about for the next three or four hundred miles.

GOLD AWARD
magazine color
full page or spread
campaign

art director
JOE KAYSER
writers
STEVE SILVER
TOM BAGOT
illustrator
JEFF ALEXANDER
photographers
HUNTER FREEMAN
BOB MIZONO
client
BRODERBUND SOFTWARE
agency
SAATCHI & SAATCHI/
SAN FRANCISCO

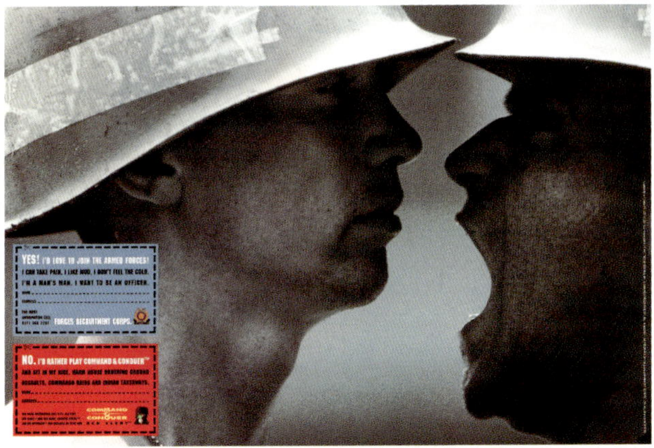

SILVER AWARD
magazine color
full page or spread
campaign

art director
ROB FLETCHER

writer
DAVID ALEXANDER

photographers
ZED NELSON
JOE SATORE
THOMAS HOEPKER

client
VIRGIN INTERACTIVE
ENTERTAINMENT

agency
BANKS HOGGINS
O'SHEA/LONDON

BRONZE AWARD
magazine color
full page or spread
campaign

art director
KELLY BECK
writer
JOHN ROBERTSON
photographer
BRETT COLVIN
client
ODYSSEY GOLF
agency
VITROROBERTSON/
SAN DIEGO

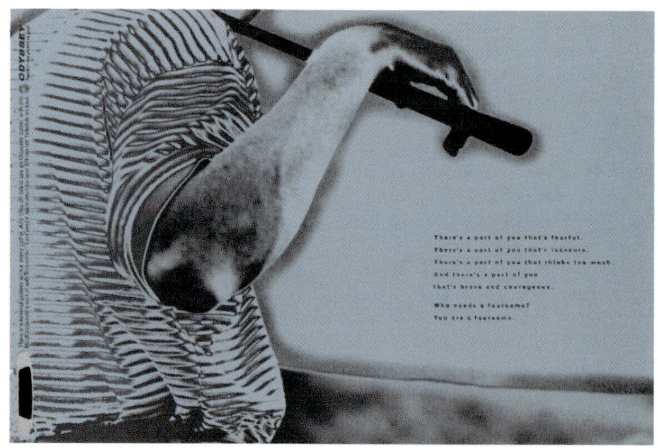

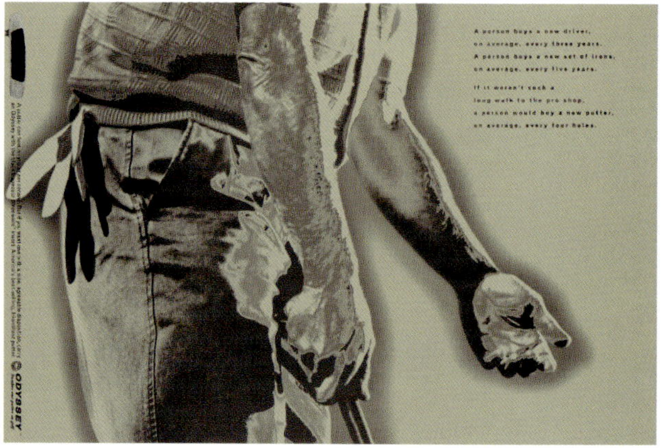

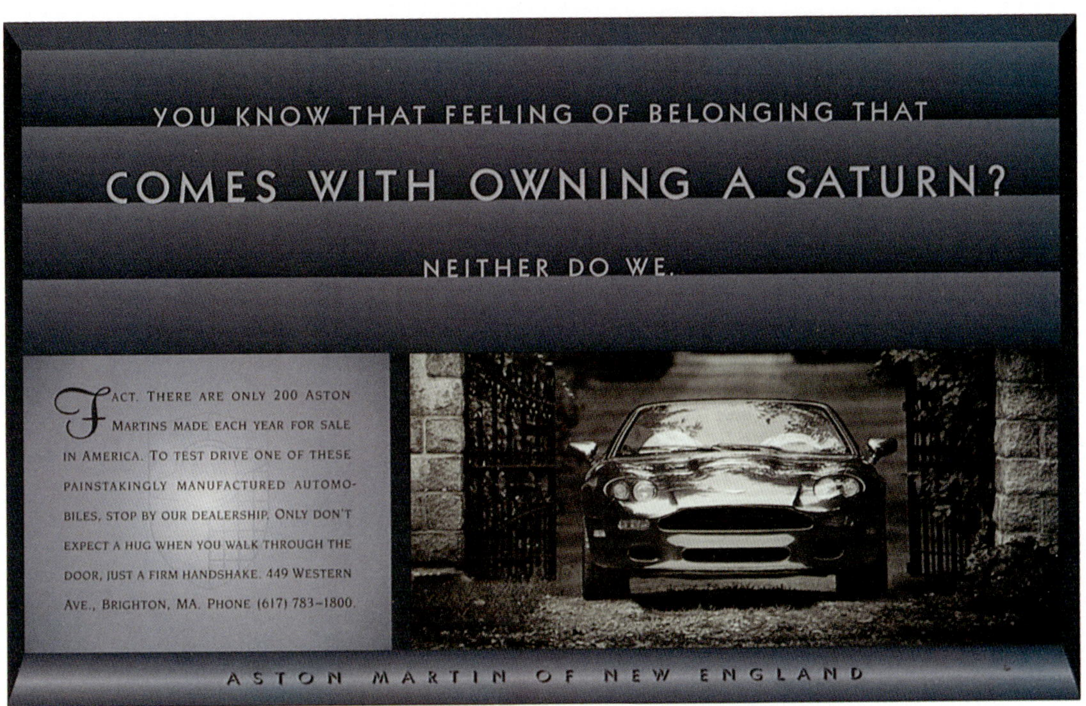

BRONZE AWARD
magazine less than a page
b/w or color
single

art director
SEAN FARRELL
writer
CHRIS DECARLO
photographer
JIM FLYNN
client
ASTON MARTIN
agency
INGALLS ADVERTISING/
BOSTON

THE PERFECT TIME FOR COCKTAILS?
BETWEEN 1922 AND 1928.

GUESTS will be forgiven for wondering what year it is. For old Phnom Penh is alive and well and living at Hotel Le Royal. The preferred address of writers and adventurers fond of absorbing a drink as well as the culture of the Kingdom of Cambodia. Jointly restored with Grand Hotel d'Angkor in Siem Reap, the splendour of an ancient civilisation is now just a hotel room away.

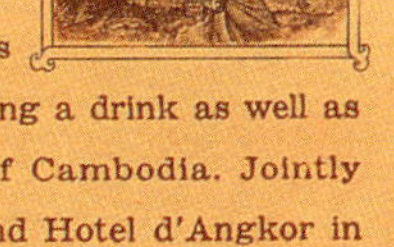

Hotel Le Royal, 68 Monivong Boulevard, Phnom Penh, Kingdom of Cambodia. Fax (855) 23-368-118 or e-mail raffles grand royal@cm17.com. A member of Small Luxury Hotels of the World.

BRONZE AWARD
magazine less than a page
b/w or color
single

art director
TED ROYER
writer
ROWAN CHANEN
illustrators
TED ROYER
POK CHENG HAI
client
RAFFLES
INTERNATIONAL
agency
SAATCHI & SAATCHI/
SINGAPORE

SILVER AWARD
magazine less than a page
campaign b/w or color

art director
TED ROYER

writer
ROWAN CHANEN

illustrators
TED ROYER
POK CHENG HAI

client
RAFFLES INTERNATIONAL

agency
SAATCHI & SAATCHI/
SINGAPORE

Grand Hotel d'Angkor,
Kingdom of Cambodia

On our walls are pictures
of 12th century Cambodia.
They're called windows.

Though the mystery of the surrounding temples has always been open to debate, the question of where to stay has not. Since 1929, a visit to Grand Hotel d'Angkor has been synonymous with a visit to the Kingdom of Cambodia. Now restored along with the celebrated Hotel Le Royal in Phnom Penh, the treasure of an ancient civilisation is just a hotel room away.

Hotel Le Royal
Grand Hotel d'Angkor

For reservations fax (855) 23-368-118, e-mail raffles.grand.royal@cm17.com or write to 68 Monivong Boulevard, Phnom Penh, Kingdom of Cambodia. A member of Small Luxury Hotels of the World.

Angkor Wat,
Kingdom of Cambodia

On a clear day
you can see for 800 years.

Amongst temples to the gods, a shrine to mortals. Since 1929, Grand Hotel d'Angkor has been as much a legend as the celebrated ruins that surround it. No adventurer worth his elephant and porter would have stayed anywhere else in the Kingdom of Cambodia. Now restored along with Hotel Le Royal in Phnom Penh, the treasure of an ancient civilisation is just a hotel room away.

Hotel Le Royal
Grand Hotel d'Angkor

For reservations fax (855) 23-368-118, e-mail raffles.grand.royal@cm17.com or write to 68 Monivong Boulevard, Phnom Penh, Kingdom of Cambodia. A member of Small Luxury Hotels of the World.

Hotel Le Royal,
Cambodia

The perfect time for cocktails?
Between 1922 and 1928.

Guests will be forgiven for wondering what year it is. For old Phnom Penh is alive and well and living at Hotel Le Royal. The preferred address of writers and adventurers fond of absorbing a drink as well as the culture of the Kingdom of Cambodia. Jointly restored with Grand Hotel d'Angkor in Siem Reap, the splendour of an ancient civilisation is now just a hotel room away.

Hotel Le Royal
Grand Hotel d'Angkor

Hotel Le Royal, 68 Monivong Boulevard, Phnom Penh, Kingdom of Cambodia. Fax (855) 23-368-118 or e-mail raffles.grand.royal@cm17.com. A member of Small Luxury Hotels of the World.

BRONZE AWARD
magazine less than a page
b/w or color
campaign

art director
SEAN FARRELL
writer
CHRIS DECARLO
photographer
JIM FLYNN
client
ASTON MARTIN
agency
INGALLS ADVERTISING/
BOSTON

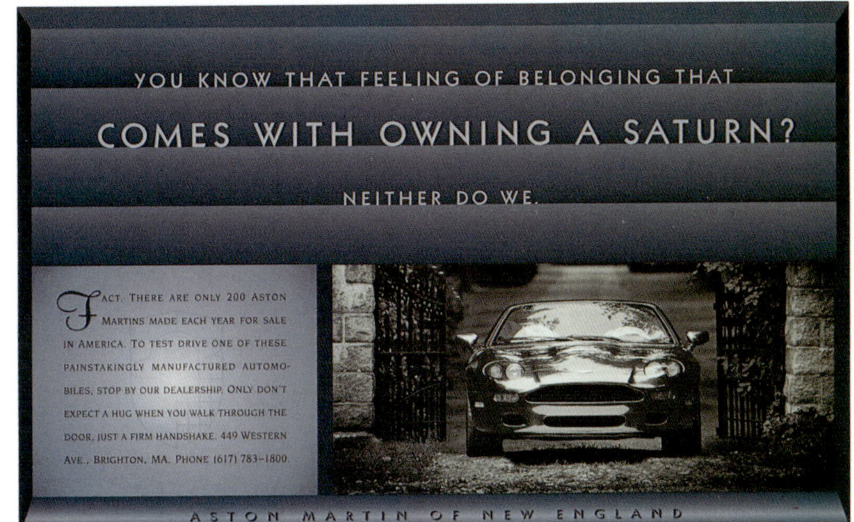

GOLD AWARD
outdoor: single

art director
VALERIE ANG-POWELL
writer
BLAKE DALEY
illustrator
JEAN PERRAMON
photographer
HUNTER FREEMAN
client
CALIFORNIA FLUID MILK PROCESSORS
agency
GOODBY SILVERSTEIN & PARTNERS/ SAN FRANCISCO

SILVER AWARD
outdoor: single

art director
VALERIE ANG-POWELL

writer
BLAKE DALEY

photographer
JOHN E. BARRETT

client
CALIFORNIA FLUID
MILK PROCESSORS

agency
GOODBY SILVERSTEIN
& PARTNERS/
SAN FRANCISCO

BRONZE AWARD
outdoor: single

art directors
MARK FAULKNER
NOEL HAAN

writer
STEFFAN POSTAER

photographer
TONY D'ORIO

client
CALLARD & BOWSER-
SUCHARD/ALTOIDS

agency
LEO BURNETT COMPANY/
CHICAGO

GOLD AWARD
outdoor: campaign

art directors
LEE CLOW
JESSICA SCHULMAN

writers
CRAIG TANIMOTO
ERIC GRUNBAUM

photographers
MAGNUM PHOTO
CORBIS BETTMAN
BETTMAN ARCHIVE

client
APPLE COMPUTER

agency
TBWA CHIAT/DAY/
VENICE

SILVER AWARD
outdoor: campaign

art director
IAN GRAIS

writer
ALAN RUSSELL

photographer
HANS SIPMA

client
PLAYLAND

agency
PALMER JARVIS DDB/
VANCOUVER

BRONZE AWARD
outdoor: campaign

art directors
JEFF CURRY
FRANK FUSCO

writers
TOM CHRISTMANN
BOB HAVLENA

photographers
STEWART FERREBE
IMA USA/PHOTONICA
THE IMAGE BANK
GRACE HUANG

client
TARGET

agency
KIRSHENBAUM BOND &
PARTNERS/NEW YORK

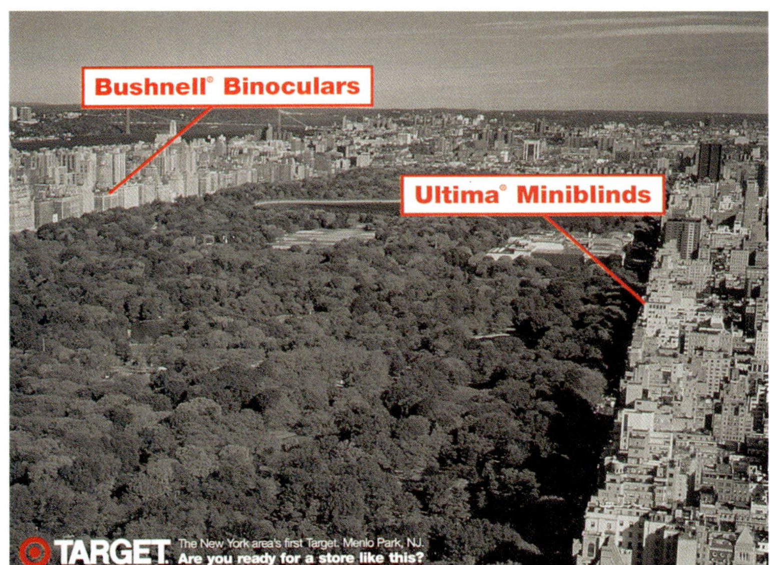

GOLD AWARD
trade color
full page or spread
single

art director
BOB BARRIE

writer
DEAN BUCKHORN

photographer
L'OSSER VATORE
ROMANO PHOTO SERVICE

client
TIME MAGAZINE

agency
FALLON MCELLIGOTT/
MINNEAPOLIS

If you think watching a volcano
in a movie is frightening, imagine
watching one in a rearview mirror.

The world's most interesting magazine.

SILVER AWARD
trade color
full page or spread
single

art director
RALPH WATSON

writer
JOHN SIMPSON

photographers
JIM APPLETON
PAUL CLANCY

client
POLAROID

agency
LEONARD/MONAHAN/
FOXBOROUGH

BRONZE AWARD
trade color
full page or spread
single

art director
DARREN LIM

writer
ALEX LANGE

photographer
NORA SCARLETT

client
NICKELODEON

agency
MAD DOGS & ENGLISHMEN/
NEW YORK

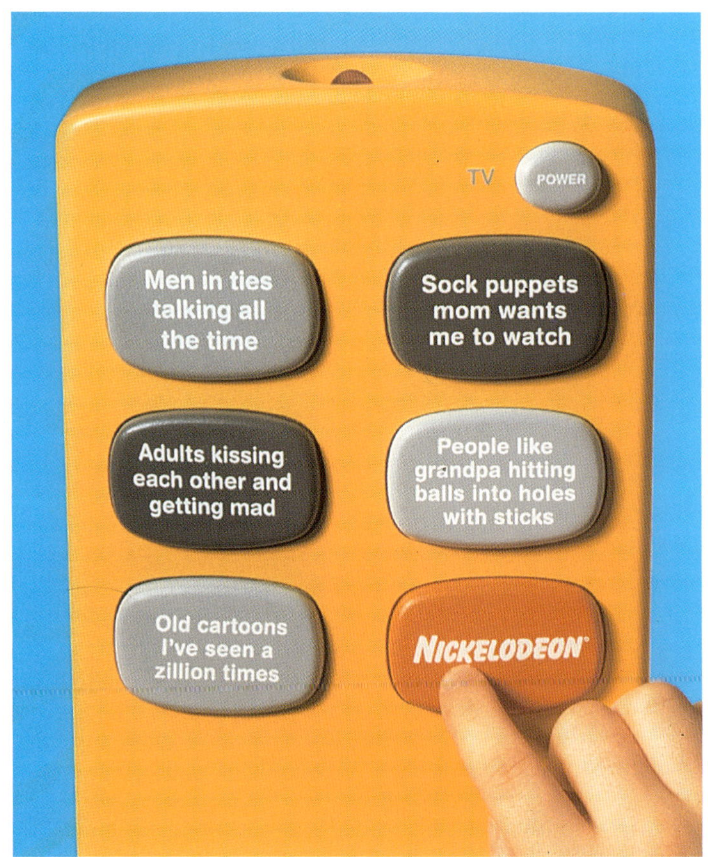

SILVER AWARD
trade b/w or color campaign

art director
GUY SHELMERDINE

writer
STEVE O'BRIEN

photographer
WILLIAM HOWARD

client
ESPN/ESPN 2

agency
GROUND ZERO/
SANTA MONICA

BRONZE AWARD
trade b/w or color campaign

art director
JOHN DAMES

writers
TODD MITCHELL
WADE PASCHALL

photographer
MICHAEL EASTMAN

client
MONSANTO PROTIVA

agency
CORE/ST LOUIS

GOLD AWARD
collateral: brochures

art directors
STANLEY WONG
JASON STUART

writers
BRIAN COOPER
TODD WALDRON

designers
STANLEY WONG
JENSEN TSOI CHEN SHUN

photographer
PLATON OF HAMILTON PHOTOGRAPHER

client
LEVI STRAUSS & CO JAPAN

agency
BARTLE BOGLE HEGARTY/SINGAPORE

GOLD AWARD
collateral: point of purchase and in-store

art director
GARY GOLDSMITH

writer
DEAN HACOHEN

photographer
STOCK

client
SONY ELECTRONICS

agency
LOWE & PARTNERS/ SMS/NEW YORK

SILVER AWARD
collateral: point of purchase and in-store

art director
ANDREW CLARKE

writer
ANDREW CLARKE

illustrator
PROCOLOR

photographer
SHAUN PETTIGREW

client
BURGER KING

agency
SAATCHI & SAATCHI/ SINGAPORE

GOLD AWARD
public service/political
newspaper or magazine
single

art director
DOUG PEDERSEN

writers
CURTIS SMITH
MIKE DUCKWORTH

photographer
JIM ARNDT

client
OUTWARD BOUND

agency
LOEFFLER KETCHUM
MOUNTJOY/CHARLOTTE

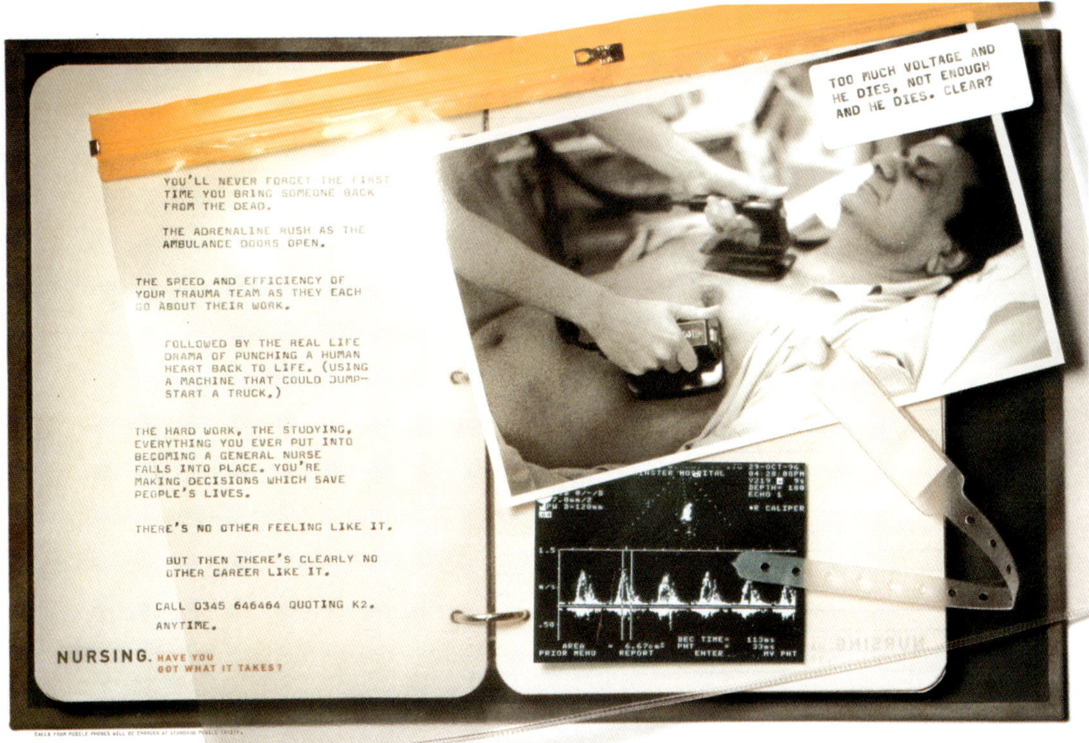

SILVER AWARD
public service/political
newspaper or magazine
single

art directors
JOHN MESSUM
COLIN JONES

writer
MIKE MCKENNA

photographer
GRAHAM CORNTHWAITE

typographer
ROGER KENNEDY

client
DEPARTMENT OF
HEALTH/COI

agency
SAATCHI & SAATCHI/
LONDON

BRONZE AWARD
public service/political
newspaper or magazine
single

art director
CHRISTOPHER GYORGY

writer
CHRIS JACOBS

photographer
THE NEGRO LEAGUES BASEBALL MUSEUM

client
THE NEGRO LEAGUES BASEBALL MUSEUM

agency
THE MARTIN AGENCY/ RICHMOND

420 FEET IS 420 FEET

NO MATTER WHAT COLOR YOUR SKIN IS

Take this little test. Name the five all-time greatest hitters in baseball history. Done? Okay, now let's check your answers. Did Josh Gibson or Roy Campenella make the cut? If not, why not?

Unfortunately, the truth is that many of baseball's best players are often overlooked when it comes to the "greatest" lists. And the reason is simple. They spent their careers in the Negro Leagues.

But the fact is, it was no easier to smack a ball over the center field wall in the Negro Leagues than it was in the major leagues. In the major leagues batters had to face great pitchers like Dizzy Dean. In the Negro Leagues they had to face great pitchers like Satchel Paige.

Actually, if anything, it was even harder to hit a home run in the Negro Leagues. You see, while the rules in the Negro Leagues were the same as in the majors, they weren't exactly strictly enforced. Pitchers could throw pretty much anything they wanted. Spitballs, emery balls, even those dreaded shineballs. They would cover the ball in Crisco if they thought they could get away with it.

As Roy Campanella said, "I never knew what the ball would do once it left the pitcher's hand."

But, despite it all, the great Negro League hitters still managed to knock more than a few out of the park. Buck O'Neil, Oscar Charleston, John Henry Lloyd, and Cumberland "Cum" Posey could rip the hide off a ball as well as any of the white legends. (Okay, Babe Ruth aside.)

Of course, speaking of Babe Ruth, that brings us to Josh Gibson – the "black Babe Ruth." In 1931 alone, he hit 72 home runs. It's even said his lifetime home run tally may have reached 1,000. And make no mistake, these homers weren't just hit in small baseball fields out in the countryside. Supposedly, Josh Gibson is credited with the longest home runs ever hit in Cincinnati's Crosley Field, Pittsburgh's Forbes Field, and "The House That Babe Built," Yankee Stadium.

Negro League teams won approximately 300 of the more than 400 exhibition games against white teams.

Hall of Famer Oscar Charleston, Pablo Mesa and Alejandro Oms of the 1927 Cuban Stars. The Stars were a Cuban team that often played in the Negro Leagues.

"What is the matter with baseball? The answer is plain prejudice, that's all."
—*The Chicago Defender, 1938*

NEGRO LEAGUES BASEBALL MUSEUM

★ GRAND OPENING NOVEMBER 1 ★

From the Civil War all the way through the 1950s, the Negro Leagues had a profound effect on our country. They were responsible for not only integrating baseball, but also American society as a whole.

The Negro Leagues Baseball Museum is dedicated to keeping that rich history alive. Our new 10,000 square-foot facility, at 18th and Vine, is filled with the stories, memorabilia, and photographs of the more than 2,600 African-Americans who played baseball in the Negro Leagues.

Join us at Bartle Hall on Saturday night, November 1st, as we host a gala dinner to celebrate the grand opening of our new facility in Kansas City. There will be dinner and dancing, as well as a number of big names to rub elbows with. Larry King. Danny Glover. Rachel Robinson (Jackie's widow). And even Bob Costas, who's slated to be MC.

Tickets are still available at $125 per person. For more information or to make reservations, please call (816) 221-1920. You can also check out our Web site at www.negroleaguesmuseum.com.

SEPARATE BUT EQUAL? OR SEPARATE BUT BETTER?

Negro League teams often traveled all night on buses, only to get off and play four games in one day.

Negro League players had to face inequalities just about everywhere they went. In the South, as well as in the North, black ballplayers were denied access to restaurants, hotels, and even gas station rest rooms. As Double Duty Radcliffe of the Chicago American Giants said, "We didn't get a chance sometimes to take a bath for three or four days because they wouldn't let us."

There was one place, however, Negro Leaguers could stand on equal ground. The baseball field.

While white and black players weren't allowed to play each other in the same league, they still managed to get together for a few exhibition games.

The final tally? Of the more than 400 exhibition games, blacks won over 300.

Now, we're not implying that the Negro Leaguers were three times better than white players. There were great white ball clubs. There were great black ball clubs. But the truth is, blacks were just a lot more motivated.

For the white players, these games were just another way to pick up a paycheck. For the Negro Leaguers, they were a great deal more than that. These games were their only chance to prove to the world that they were serious players. That they could not only hang with the white major league teams, but they could beat them time and again.

Of course, after winning over 300 exhibition games, you could certainly say they proved their point.

"We were trying to prove to the world that we were as good or better."
— Buck O'Neil

SATCHEL DIDN'T NEED A RELIEF PITCHER. THE BATTERS DID.

In the Negro Leagues, pitchers played a full game, every game. As Riley Stewart said, "We didn't have no relief pitcher. You go out there, you go for nine. That's it. You were paid for nine and that's the way they wanted you to pitch. Nine innings."

No sweat for Satchel Paige. He'd throw nine innings on Friday, then do it again on Saturday and Sunday. The more games he played, the more money he made. And if there's one thing Satchel loved as much as winning, it was the Almighty Dollar.

Of course, Satchel on the mound for nine innings was not exactly a comforting thought to opposing hitters. That meant nine long innings of trying to hit Satchel's jump ball, trouble ball, bee-ball, hesitation pitch, Long Tom, Little Tom, four-day creeper, and midnight rider.

Hack Wilson, one of the National League's best home run hitters, had this to say about Satchel's pitching: "It starts out as a baseball, but when it gets to the plate it looks like a marble." Upon hearing that comment, Satchel responded, "You must be talking about my slowball. My fastball looks like a fish egg."

"I never threw an illegal pitch. Trouble is, once in a while I toss one that ain't been seen by this generation."
— Satchel Paige

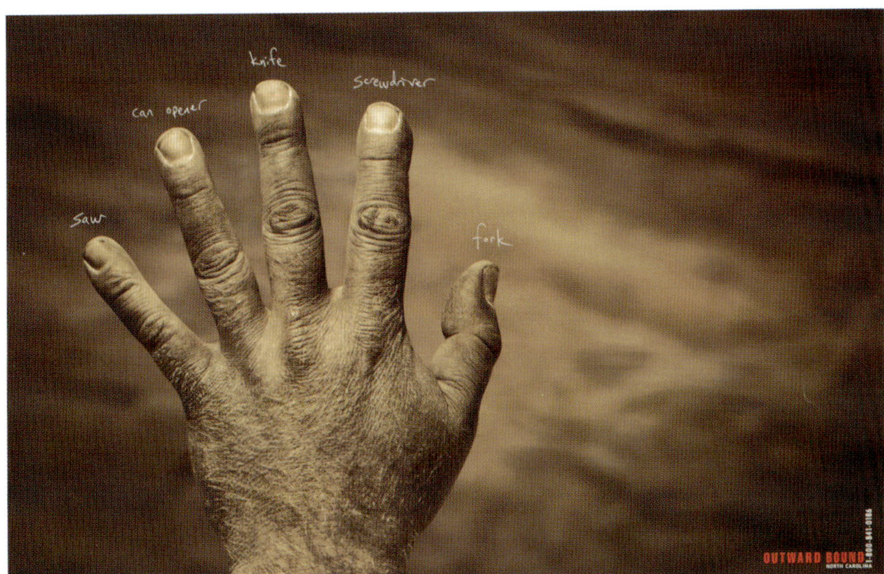

GOLD AWARD
public service/political
newspaper or magazine
campaign

art director
DOUG PEDERSEN

writers
CURTIS SMITH
MIKE DUCKWORTH

photographer
JIM ARNDT

client
OUTWARD BOUND

agency
LOEFFLER KETCHUM
MOUNTJOY/CHARLOTTE

SILVER AWARD
public service/political newspaper or magazine campaign

art directors
JOHN MESSUM
COLIN JONES

writer
MIKE MCKENNA

photographer
GRAHAM CORNTHWAITE

typographer
ROGER KENNEDY

client
DEPARTMENT OF HEALTH/COI

agency
SAATCHI & SAATCHI/LONDON

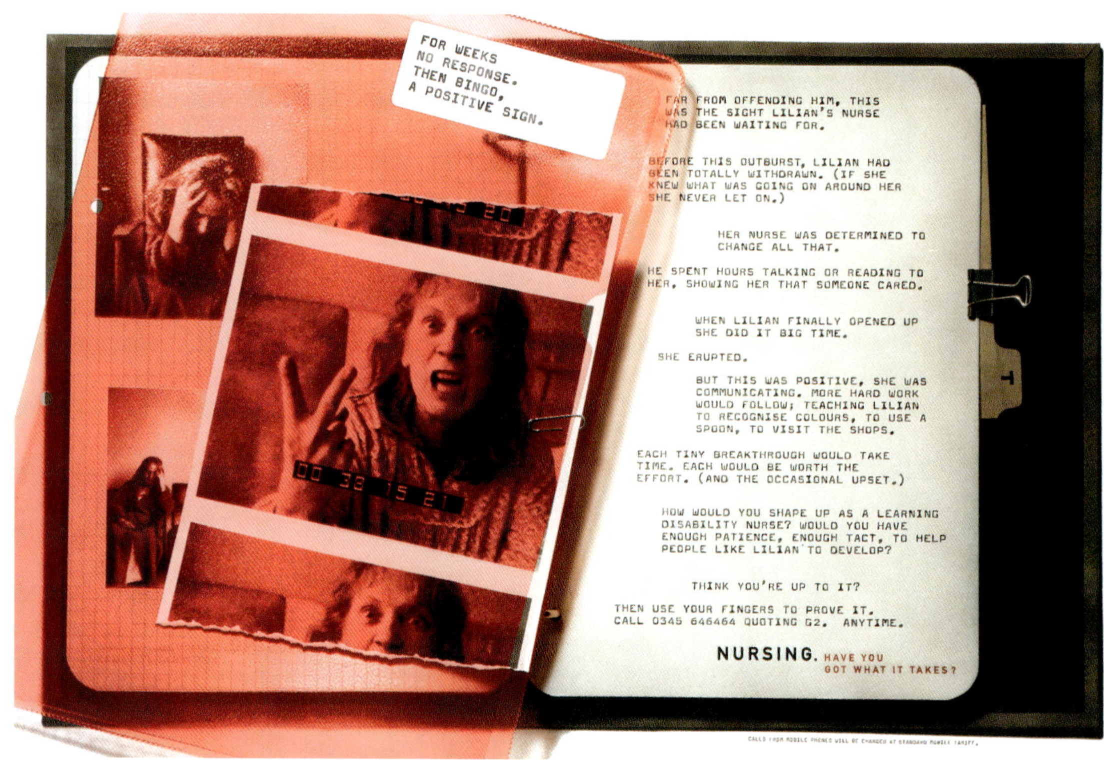

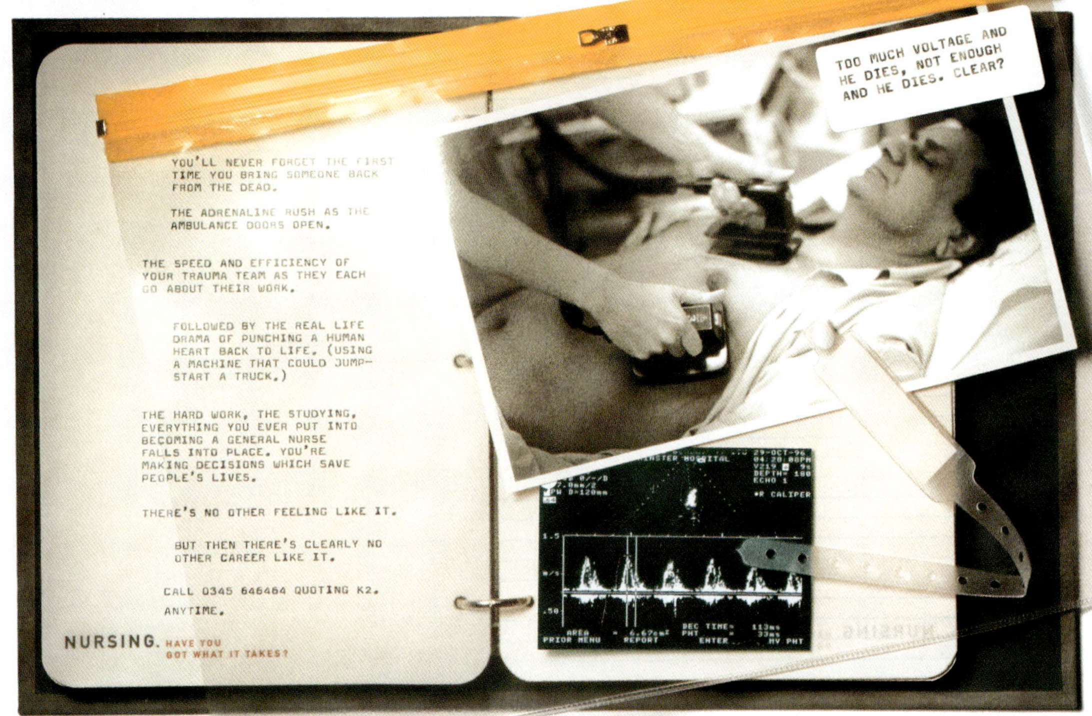

THE FIRST THING YOU DO TO SOMEONE HEARING VOICES, IS TO PERSUADE THEM TO LISTEN ONLY TO THE MORE REASONABLE ONES.

You are evil, scrape away the evil with a knife, hurt yourself, you're useless. End your life no-one likes you why fight it, you are worthless you are the devil himself go to hell.

CAROL WAS NEVER COMPLETELY ALONE. THERE WERE ALWAYS HER 'VOICES' TO KEEP HER COMPANY.

SHE HEARD THEM SO OFTEN THAT EVENTUALLY SHE FOUND IT DIFFICULT TO DISTINGUISH BETWEEN WHAT WAS REAL AND WHAT WAS IMAGINED.

WHEN CAROL COULDN'T HANDLE THE TAUNTS AND COMMANDS ANY LONGER SHE SOUGHT HELP. SHE WAS INTRODUCED TO A MENTAL HEALTH NURSE.

THE NURSE ENCOURAGED HER TO LISTEN ONLY TO THE MORE REASONABLE 'VOICES'.

SLOWLY, AND WITH MORE GENTLE COAXING, CAROL BEGAN TO TALK LESS ABOUT THE WHISPERING IN HER HEAD AND MORE ABOUT THE WORLD AROUND HER.

SHE WAS STARTING TO RECOVER.

THE NEED FOR MENTAL HEALTH NURSES, LIKE CAROL'S, HAS NEVER BEEN GREATER.

BUT IT TAKES A SPECIAL KIND OF PERSON TO MAKE IT IN THIS CAREER.

THEY'RE PATIENT, RESOURCEFUL; BLESSED WITH AN ABUNDANCE OF TACT, SENSITIVITY, AND COMPASSION. AND THE COURAGE TO MAKE A PHONE CALL.

CALL 0345 646464 QUOTING BS.

ANYTIME.

00 30 48 10

NURSING. HAVE YOU GOT WHAT IT TAKES?

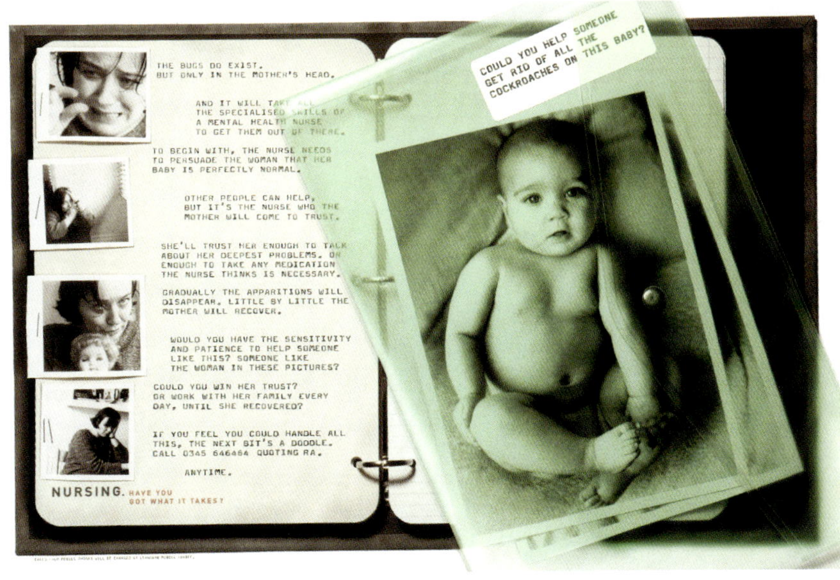

BRONZE AWARD
public service/political newspaper or magazine campaign

art director
CHRISTOPHER GYORGY

writer
CHRIS JACOBS

photographer
THE NEGRO LEAGUES BASEBALL MUSEUM

client
THE NEGRO LEAGUES BASEBALL MUSEUM

agency
THE MARTIN AGENCY/ RICHMOND

GOLD AWARD
public service/political
outdoor and posters

art director
NANCY STEINMAN
writer
JEFF BOSSIN
photographer
MYRON BECK
client
CALIFORNIA DEPARTMENT OF HEALTH SERVICES
agency
ASHER & PARTNERS/
LOS ANGELES

You've just had your leg
blown off!

There's a 50% chance you will die within minutes. Landmines kill or maim someone every 20 seconds. Almost all the victims are civilians, not soldiers. In Cambodia alone one in every 236 people is an amputee. Over 110 million unexploded landmines lie just beneath the surface in 62 countries. Take a stand. Give all you can to fund mine clearance operations and help the victims. Support a total worldwide ban. Call 1300 303 440, or write to GPO Box 9944, Melbourne, 3001.

GENEROUSLY DONATED BY YOUNG & RUBICAM MATTINGLY ADVERTISING, GUNN & TAYLOR PRINTING AND SPICERS PAPER. PLEASE DISPOSE OF THOUGHTFULLY.

SILVER AWARD
public service/political
outdoor and posters

art director
GRANT RUTHERFORD
writer
RICHARD MUNTZ
client
INTERNATIONAL CAMPAIGN TO BAN LANDMINES
agency
YOUNG & RUBICAM/
MATTINGLY, AUSTRALIA

BRONZE AWARD
public service/political
outdoor and posters

art director
CARLA MOONEY
writer
DYLAN LEE
client
MOTHERS AGAINST
DRUNK DRIVING
agency
PAGANO SCHENCK
& KAY/BOSTON

CURB YOUR DOG

Failure to do so is a $50 fine. Which is more severe than the punishment given to a drunk driver who smashed into Julia Coppola and her two daughters. The drunk driver went home without a fine. Julia's daughters went home without a mother.

Mothers Against Drunk Driving It's a serious crime. Let's treat it that way.

SILVER AWARD
public service/political
collateral brochures
& direct mail

art director
DOUG PEDERSEN
writers
CURTIS SMITH
MIKE DUCKWORTH
photographer
JIM ARNDT
client
OUTWARD BOUND
agency
LOEFFLER KETCHUM
MOUNTJOY/CHARLOTTE

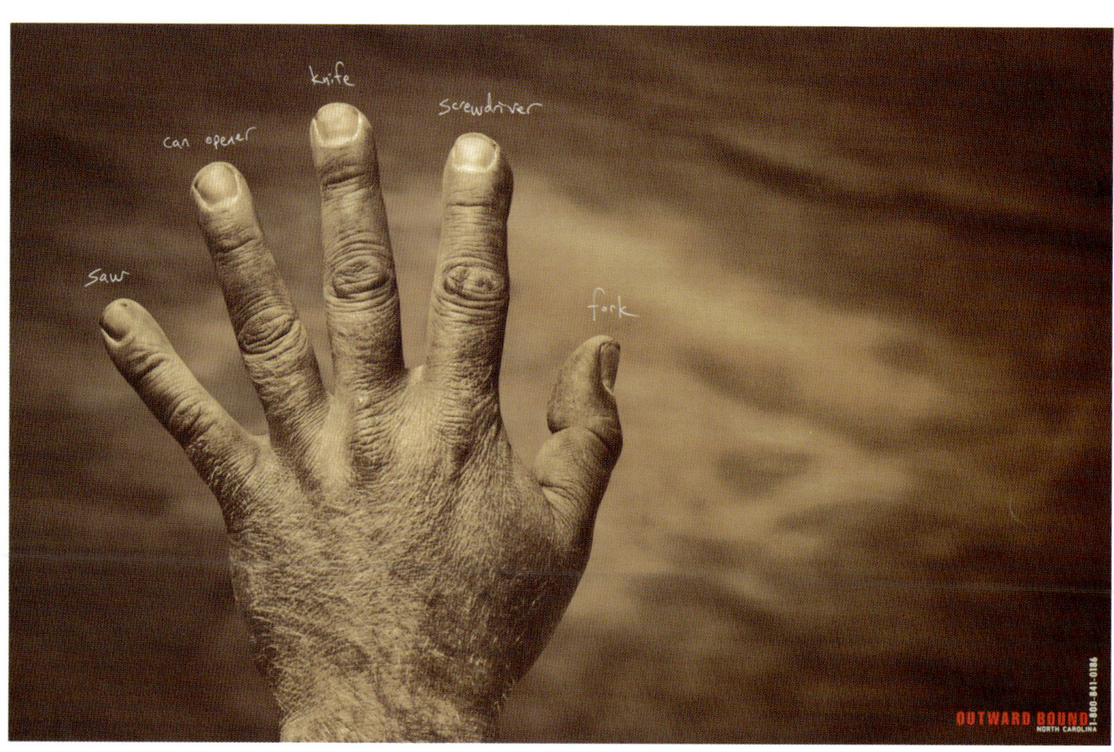

MUSIC: Born Free
SUPER: That's the great thing about pets. They really don't care. Adopt today. Companion Animal Placement.

GOLD AWARD
public service/political television: single

art directors
ERIC ARONIN
DAVE LADEN
JOHN WAGNER

writer
ERIC ARONIN

production company
@RADICAL.MEDIA

directors
STEVE MILLER
RICK LEMOINE

client
COMPANION ANIMAL PLACEMENT

agency
SUBURBAN ADVERTISING/ JERSEY CITY

CD1 #1

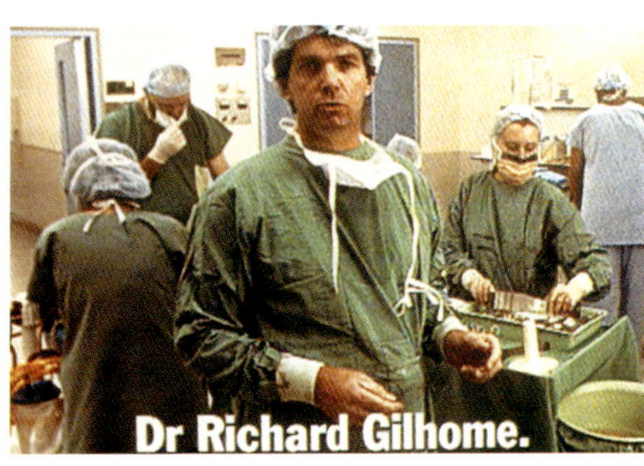

SFX: Screeching brakes.
SUPER: Dr. Richard Gilhome.
GILHOME: I'm a trauma surgeon and I want to reconstruct what happens to the human body in less than 2/10ths of a second, when hit by a car braking from 70 kph, over a braking distance of 50 meters. Even in a car equipped with ABS. The first impact will occur around 46k's. The bumper shatters the knee joint, tearing flesh and ligaments. The full weight of the head smashes through the windscreen. The neck snaps. The skull shatters and the pedestrian's brain is turned into pulp. Within 2/10ths of a second the pedestrian's body will hit the road. With a seventy percent chance of being dead. And had you been braking from 60k's not 70 there's a good chance you could have stopped in time and the pedestrian would have suffered nothing worse than a severe fright.
Think about it.
SUPER: 10kph less will save lives. TAC

SILVER AWARD
public service/political television: single

art director
ROB DOW

writer
GREG HARPER

agency producer
ROMANCA JASINSKI

production company
RENEGADE FILMS

director
COLIN SKYBA

client
TRANSPORT ACCIDENT COMMISSION

agency
GREY ADVERTISING/ MELBOURNE

CD1 #2

BRONZE AWARD
public service/political
television: single

art director
ERICH FUNKE
writers
WENDY MOORCROFT
MICHELLE KATZ
agency producer
HELENA WOODFINE
production company
VELOCITY AFRIKA
director
KEITH ROSE
client
REACH FOR A DREAM
agency
TBWA HUNT LASCARIS/
JOHANNESBURG

CD1 #3

SFX: Music under throughout
ANNOUNCER: Last year, Sam found out that he had leukemia. At Reach For A Dream, we help children with life-threatening diseases, by giving them the encouragement to face their illnesses. Because children like Sam need hope and support. And all the friends they can get.
SFX: Boys cheering.
SUPER: Reach For A Dream

GOLD AWARD
consumer radio: single

writer
BRYANT MARCUM
agency producer
BRYANT MARCUM
client
UTAH TRANSIT
AUTHORITY
agency
FJCN/W&R/
SALT LAKE CITY

CD2 #R1

MUSIC: Piano driven public service-type.
TEEN: (unintelligible) I'be-looind-ry-rife.
FEMALE INTERPRETER: I've ruined my life.
TEEN: (frustrated) I-ast-ry-budder-fo-a-wide-to-duh-mawl-atty-ted-no-bay-deeb.
INTERPRETER: I asked my brother for a ride to the mall and he said, "No way, dweeb."
TEEN: (emotional) I-fel-twapt.
INTERPRETER: I felt trapped.
TEEN: (more emotional) So-o-poob-by-ireperense-Iperstry-riss-n-pur-dis-irenwing-tro-dem.
INTERPRETER: So to prove my independence, I pierced my lips and put this iron ring through them.
TEEN: (losing it) Naw-et-hurs-do-tauk.
INTERPRETER: Now it hurts to talk.
TEEN: Ad-by-rom-is-rakeen-be-wer-id-duh-ho-sumuh.
INTERPRETER: And mom is making me wear it the whole summer.
TEEN: Fogus!
INTERPRETER: Bogus!
PSA STYLE ANNOUNCER: Please, teenagers. Piercing body parts is no way to prove your independence. Buy a UTA Summer Youth Pass. It's a rippin' dog tag you wear around your neck. And a Summer Youth Pass gets you around without help from mom or your gomer brother.
TEEN: (under control again) Sukin-denah-troo-a-sraw-boes.
INTERPRETER: Sucking dinner through a straw blows.
ANNOUNCER: Kids seventeen and under can purchase one for twenty-five dollars, two or more for twenty each. Call BUS-INFO for details.
TEEN: (emotional again) Den-dere's-my-navel-wing.

SILVER AWARD
consumer radio: single

writer
ANN COYLE
agency producer
ANN COYLE
client
ANHEUSER-BUSCH
agency
DDB NEEDHAM/
CHICAGO

CD2 #R2

SFX: Music up.
HESTON: Today I would like to talk to you on a very serious note. Because this is the story of a man overcoming monumental physical pain and suffering to make it a Bud Light. There is nothing funny about what you are about to hear.
GUY: Well, actually it is kinda funny.
HESTON: Work with me, son.
GUY: Okay, I was at a ballgame.
HESTON: HE WAS AT THE BALLGAME!
GUY: Yep. And so I like when I saw the Bud Light vendor I went to raise my arm so he'd see me.
HESTON: HIS ARM AROSE!
GUY: Exactly. But I hit my funny bone on the seat next to me.
HESTON: (sobbing) NO! NO! NO!
GUY: Yeah. So I just raised my other arm and, ya know, got his attention and the Bud Light.
HESTON: He got the Bud Light. Young man, do you ever look back and wonder what would have happened if you'd have just given up? If you hadn't followed your dream of making it a Bud Light?
GUY: Uh, not really.
HESTON: Probably a wise idea. So for the great taste that won't fill you up and never lets you down, make it a Bud Light. Anheuser-Busch, St. Louis, Missouri.

BRONZE AWARD
consumer radio: single

writer
STEVE DILDARIAN
agency producer
DEBRA KING
client
ANHEUSER-BUSCH
agency
GOODBY SILVERSTEIN
& PARTNERS/
SAN FRANCISCO

CD2 #R3

FROGS: Bud...weis...er (under throughout).
SFX: Swamp sounds.
LOUIE: Frankie?
FRANK: Yeah, Louie?
LOUIE: I don't know how much longer I can listen to this.
FRANK: Oh, come on, put it behind you. The frogs got the part...it's over.
LOUIE: No, no, no, this is far from over. You know, I think there might be room for me in this campaign.
FRANK: Look, they're a very popular trio of frogs. You're a lizard.
LOUIE: Umm-hmm. I mean I know they're popular, but what if something were to happen to one of them? Something horrible.
FRANK: What's going to happen to them?
LOUIE: I don't know...uh, uh...a large branch falls at an inopportune moment...ahh, ohh! One of them eats a tainted fly...how awful!
FRANK: I don't like the way you're talking.
LOUIE: Oh yeah, you know sometimes on these TV shoots...you know what...a lily pad could malfunction and zzztt electrocute one of them.
FRANK: Stop it.
LOUIE: That would be awful. I'm just looking out for the frogs.
FRANK: No, you're not.
LOUIE: I'm not threatening anyone.
FRANK: Yes you are.
LOUIE: No, no, all I'm saying is they should look into a good insurance policy.
FRANK: Would you listen to yourself?
LOUIE: Don't read anything into that.
FROGS: Bud...weis...er.
ANNOUNCER: Anheuser-Busch, St. Louis, Missouri.

GOLD AWARD
consumer radio
campaign

writer
ANN COYLE
agency producer
ANN COYLE
client
ANHEUSER-BUSCH
agency
DDB NEEDHAM/
CHICAGO

CD2 #R4

SFX: Music up.
HESTON: Today I would like to talk to you on a very serious note. Because this is the story of a man overcoming monumental physical pain and suffering to make it a Bud Light. There is nothing funny about what you are about to hear.
GUY: Well, actually it is kinda funny.
HESTON: Work with me, son.
GUY: Okay, I was at a ballgame.
HESTON: HE WAS AT THE BALLGAME!
GUY: Yep. And so I like when I saw the Bud Light vendor I went to raise my arm so he'd see me.
HESTON: HIS ARM AROSE!
GUY: Exactly. But I hit my funny bone on the seat next to me.
HESTON: (sobbing) NO! NO! NO!
GUY: Yeah. So I just raised my other arm and, ya know, got his attention and the Bud Light.
HESTON: He got the Bud Light. Young man, do you ever look back and wonder what would have happened if you'd have just given up? If you hadn't followed your dream of making it a Bud Light?
GUY: Uh, not really.
HESTON: Probably a wise idea. So for the great taste that won't fill you up and never lets you down, make it a Bud Light. Anheuser-Busch, St. Louis, Missouri.

SFX: Music Up.
HESTON: I understand some of you have been turning to self-help books and motivational speakers as a source of inspiration. Well, not me. My inspiration comes from the common man and what he must do to make it a Bud Light.
GUY: Well, me and my wife were shopping for groceries. We go once a week.
HESTON: THEY GO SHOPPING ONCE A WEEK!
GUY: So we get to the beer case and I get a six-pack of Bud Light. Well, she tells me to put it back.
HESTON: SHE TELLS HIM TO PUT IT BACK!
GUY: She says she's sick of me picking the beer. She wants to pick it.
HESTON: SHE WANTS TO PICK IT!
GUY: So I said fine, go ahead. So she picks up the Bud Light and puts it in the cart.
HESTON: SHE PUTS THE BUD LIGHT IN THE CART!
GUY: Yeah, she wanted the Bud Light the whole time. It's like she was playing with my mind or something.
HESTON: Playing with your mind, was she? Well, it's obvious who won that little round of emotional warfare.
GUY: Who?
HESTON: So, for the great taste that won't fill you up and never lets you down, make it a Bud Light.
GUY: No, seriously, who?
HESTON: Anheuser-Busch, St. Louis, Missouri.

SFX: Music Up.
HESTON: In this cold, often contentious world, we can forget that we are all people...people who need people. But not this man who extended the hand of good fellowship, and made it a Bud Light...
GUY: I'm in my backyard, you know, just minding my own business.
HESTON: JUST MINDING HIS OWN BUSINESS!
GUY: And my neighbor sticks his head over the fence and says, "hey, c'mon over, and have a beer!"
HESTON: COME...JOIN ME...TAKE A LOAD OFF, COMPADRE.
GUY: Well, I really don't like the guy. But he's got Bud Light, so I'm torn.
HESTON: TORN...TORN LIKE AN OLD SWEATER!
GUY: Kinda, yeah. So what the hey, I figure why hold a grudge? So I go over and have a Bud Light.
HESTON: HE HAS A BUD LIGHT! Sir, you're building bridges, you're making friends.
GUY: Yeah, well, he's also got a pool.
HESTON: You've got moxie, and don't let anyone ever take that away from you.
GUY: I won't.
HESTON: So for the great taste that won't fill you and never lets you down, make it a Bud Light. Anheuser-Busch, St. Louis, Missouri.

SILVER AWARD
consumer radio campaign

writer
AARON STERN
agency producer
ROB SONDIK
client
POWER BAR
agency
CITRON HALIGMAN BEDECARRE/ SAN FRANCISCO

CD2 #R5

WOMAN: Good evening. Your Florist.
MAN: Hi. What time do you guys close tonight?
WOMAN: Eight.
MAN: And you're up in Mesquite, right?
WOMAN: Uh-huh.
MAN: Okay, I'm leaving work now in downtown Dallas and wanted to pick up some roses.
WOMAN: Alright.
MAN: The thing is, I wanted to get some direction from you.
WOMAN: Oh gosh. Hold on...does anyone know how to get... Central which way...
MAN: Ma'am?
WOMAN: Yes?
MAN: I'm actually on a bicycle so I can't get on the highway.
WOMAN: He's on a bicycle...You're on a bicycle?
MAN: Yeah. I'm gonna have a PowerBar and ride up there. I need to get some flowers for my girlfriend.
WOMAN: You're riding your bicycle all the way here for your girlfriend?
MAN: Yeah. We kind of had a fight and she took the car. But I should be okay. I'm just gonna eat a PowerBar and hop on my bike. So you close at eight?
WOMAN: We do, but you're on a bicycle?
MAN: Yeah, but the PowerBar should give me plenty of energy to get there. Can you just write, "I'm sorry, I know I was wrong" on the card?
WOMAN: Okay?
MAN: I'll see you in a little while?
WOMAN: Bye.
ANNOUNCER: PowerBar energy bars. Balanced nutrition and lasting energy for everyday life...and then some. Power on.

BRONZE AWARD
consumer radio campaign

writer
STEVE DILDARIAN
agency producer
DEBRA KING
client
ANHEUSER-BUSCH
agency
GOODBY SILVERSTEIN & PARTNERS/ SAN FRANCISCO

CD2 #R6

FROGS: Bud...weis...er (under throughout).
SFX: Swamp sounds.
LOUIE: Oh, come on, will they give it a rest already.
FRANK: What's the matter Louie?
LOUIE: The frogs have been going at it all day.
FRANK: Yeah, well ya know, they gotta rehearse.
LOUIE: They gotta rehearse? Give me a break, it's not a monologue. They've got one line.
FRANK: Well, ya know, frogs are workaholics.
LOUIE: Hey, I could have that down in five minutes. Bud-weis-er. That's a wrap, take five, thank you.
FRANK: Louie, it's all in the inflection, you know that.
LOUIE: What?
FRANK: The nuances are everything.
LOUIE: Nuances...where are you lookin' up this stuff...don't lecture me.
FRANK: You could say "weis", or you could say *"weis"*... you hear that? Two completely different schools of comedy.
LOUIE: Schools of comedy...what are you reading, books?! Frank, they are not rehearsing, they are mocking us.
FRANK: I disagree...I think you are going out of your mind.
LOUIE: I'm going out of my mind? Huh? Huh? Look at them, look at them. They're mocking me, they're mocking you, the birds, the ferrets—everyone who didn't get the part.
FRANK: You're the only one I see getting upset about it.
LOUIE: I've got more talent on the underside of my tongue than those frogs have in their entire body. Look at them...look at the one on the left. He, in particular, is mocking you, my friend, and he's mocking you badly.
FROGS: Bud...
LOUIE: You stink!
ANNOUNCER: Anheuser-Busch, St. Louis, Missouri.

GOLD AWARD
consumer television
over :30 single

art director
KILPATRICK ANDERSON
writer
JAMES LEMAITRE
agency producer
LISA JAKANOVICH
production company
X-RAY
director
JESSE PERETZ
client
NIKE
agency
WIEDEN & KENNEDY/
PORTLAND

CD1 #4

MODERATOR: People make fun of you because you're fast, because you wear Zoom Air. Well, let's turn the tables, let's pretend that I'm slow. I want you to insult me. Come on, Michael?
MICHAEL JOHNSON: You Turtle.
MODERATOR: Uh...Oh! Ouch! (laughing) Gary?
GARY PAYTON: Slow Poke.
MODERATOR: Good, only you can help you people..Okay, Al, I'm slow.
AL Unser, Jr.: Ketchup Bottle.
MODERATOR: Very good. Come on. Let out the aggression.
MICHAEL JOHNSON: Mr. Slow Pants.
MODERATOR: Okay, that's great!
GAIL DEVERS: Hey, Molasses!
MODERATOR: That kind of hit BOINNNNGGG, right between the eyes. Isn't this fun? Michael, come on, I can take it!
MICHAEL JOHNSON: Mrs. Butterworth.
MODERATOR: Mrs. Butterworth! She's slow! (laughing).
GARY PAYTON: Jerk.
MODERATOR: Okay, you said that with conviction, but I can take it 'cause I'm a professional.
SUPER: Thin, light, responsive Zoom Air.

SILVER AWARD
consumer television
over :30 single

art director
JON SOTO
writer
ALBERT KELLY
agency producer
KRISTIN LOUDIS
production company
TATE & PARTNERS
director
BAKER SMITH
client
NIKE
agency
GOODBY SILVERSTEIN
& PARTNERS/
SAN FRANCISCO

CD1 #5

RUNNER 1: All we want to do is just run, man.
RUNNER 2: We're regular guys.
RUNNER 2: As soon as we do this...we're criminals.
RUNNER 2: People get so freaked out!
WOMAN WITH BABY: Do you have to do that here?
BLACK MAN: You crazy people!
MAN IN CAR: (honking horn) Get outta the road man!
YOUNG WOMAN: I used to run...when I was eight! She almost hit that lady.
RUNNER 2: Yeah, there's runners everywhere.
RUNNER 2: Good runners too.
RUNNER 2:They all go through the same thing.
RUNNER 2: Runners aren't criminals.
RUNNER 2: Running's not a crime.
RUNNER 1: Ya know, I wanna run. I wanna run, I just wanna run.
SUPER: What if we treated all athletes the way we treat skateboarders?

MUSIC: Da-Da-Da.
ANNOUNCER: The German-engineered Volkswagen Golf. It fits your life, or your complete lack thereof.
ANNOUNCER: On the road of life there are passengers and there are drivers. Drivers wanted.

BRONZE AWARD
consumer television
over :30 single

art director
ALAN PAFENBACH
writer
LANCE JENSEN
agency producer
KEITH DEZEN
production company
TATE & PARTNERS
director
BAKER SMITH
client
VOLKSWAGEN
agency
ARNOLD COMMUNICATIONS/ BOSTON

CD1 #6

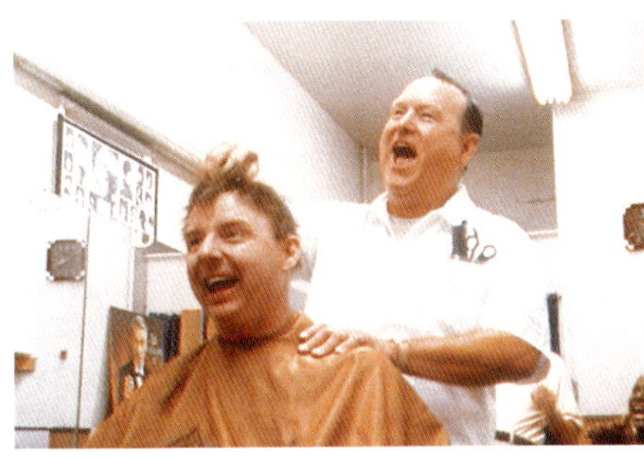

MUSIC: Hank Williams – Hey Good Looking.
RADIO ANNOUNCER: In Merrit County High School Basketball, the Tylerville Tigers lost their sixth consecutive game.
NICK: Hey, guys.
WAITRESS: Hey, Nick.
GUY 1: How'd you bowl last night?
NICK: Should have been there. Seven-ten split. I nailed it.
GUY 2: It's against the law of physics.
GUY 3: You know gravity.
GUY 4: Lucky.
GUY 5: Hmm.
FATHER: So Mr. Ferguson says to me, Bucky, how do the words regional assistant manager sound to you?
SON: Way to go, Pop!
GUY 1: So the traveling salesman says, pig schmig, I think I'm engaged (laughs).
GUY 2: I don't get it.
BAILIFF: All rise.
JUDGE: This court will come to order.
GIRL 1: Oh my gosh.
GIRL 2: He's so cute.
COACH: You're not picking up the passes, you're missing the free throws, what are you thinking about? Dropping the ball. You kids look like a bunch of clowns out there.
SFX: Sound of electric razor.
CHRIS ROCK: Two brothers talk, right. And the first brother says, hey pig schmig, I think I'm engaged.
SUPER: Carl the Barber. HBO subscriber since 1976.
SUPER: It's not TV. It's HBO.
WOMAN: He never looked so good.

BRONZE AWARD
consumer television
over :30 single

art director
DON SCHNEIDER
writer
MICHAEL PATTI
agency producers
REGINA EBEL
BECKY FRIEDMAN
RANI VAZ
production company
PYTKA
director
JOE PYTKA
client
HBO
agency
BBDO/NEW YORK

CD1 #7

GOLD AWARD
consumer television
over :30 campaign

art director
FRANK CLARK
writer
DEAN SALING
agency producer
JOYCE SCHMIDTBAUER
production company
OBERLENZ FILMS
director
TONY OBER
client
SEATTLE SUPERSONICS
agency
WONGDOODY/SEATTLE

CD1 #8

SUPER: The Sonics are coming to your home.
SAM: Just knock on the door?
CREW GUY: Just knock on the door.
MOM: Oh my goodness!
SAM: Wassup!
MOM: Nice to meet you!
SAM: You too.
DAD: Say hi to Big Smooth!
JORDAN: You wanna see my Chicago Bulls jersey?
SAM: Yeah. This is...this is what he has. We gonna wash this. We gonna wash this in here, okay?
JORDAN: No!
SAM: You the man!
JORDAN: Yeah–gimme the ball!
SAM: C'mon, be the man!
SAM: Oh, they ran a play on you! Where you at, man?
JORDAN: (giggles)
SAM: Okay, a little low-five, then!
JORDAN: Um, Sam? Did you bring your pajamas?
SAM: Hmm?
JORDAN: Did you bring your pajamas? I wanna be on TV!
SAM: Yeah...whatever.
SUPER: See them in your home.
MOM: Okay, time to go to bed! Sam, stop that! In the bed, now!
SUPER: 56 games on free TV.
JORDAN: Go Sonics!

SUPER: The Sonics are coming to your home.
GARY: How y'all doin'?
RESIDENTS: Fine!
GARY: Huh? Oh, okay.
WOMAN 1: I always thought you were awfully thin.
WOMAN 2: Put your thread in back.
GARY: Put the thread in back? Like that?
WOMAN 3: Nooo...
GARY: Y-you own it. No...nobody own it. You wanna buy it? Okay, that's $400. You can have it now.
WOMAN 4: She's kinda tight with her money.
SUPER: See them in your home.
GARY: Ohhh...You been practicin'! (laughs).
SUPER: 56 games on free TV.
MAN: Go Sonics!

SUPER: The Sonics are coming to your home.
NATE: I heard there was a Tupperware party going on here!
TUPPERWARE LADY: There is a Tupperware party!
NATE: Am I a little late? My name is Nate McMillan and my favorite piece of Tupperware is the Cake Taker. I love making cakes.
TUPPERWARE LADY: And you push and you'll hear a burp. Are you ready? And the thing about the Modular Mate containers is that...
TUPPERWARE LADY: Yes?
NATE: Can you wash these in the dishwasher?
TUPPERWARE LADY: Yes, you can. Thank you for asking.
NATE: Oh, great!
TUPPERWARE LADY: And what's really great about the Remarkabowl is that the outside of it is rubberized. And it feels like a basketball that's been used on the cement.
NATE: Mmm...That's pretty good!
WOMAN: And you play quarterback, right?
NATE: (surprised) I play q...what?
SUPER: See them in your home.
NATE: I appreciate you having me. I really did enjoy myself. I did. Do you have a box or something for me?
SUPER: 56 games on free TV.
TUPPERWARE LADY: Go Sonics!

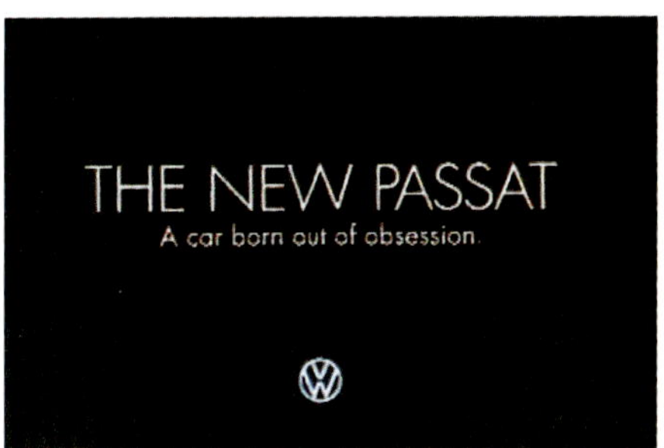

WALTER: (attempting to speak), Thursday...
SFX: Bursts of the sound of electrical equipment.
WALTER: 3rd of April, pump adjustable seats completed. Fan-shaped water-jets, which reduce water consumption, therefore the water bottles can be smaller, which helps to reduce the weight of the car.
MUSIC: Loud "oompah" music.
SFX: Lock clicking.
SFX: Light clapping.
SUPER: The New Passat. A car born out of obsession.

SILVER AWARD
consumer television
over :30 campaign

art director
RICHARD FLINTHAM

writers
ANDY MCLEOD
NICK GILL

agency producer
HOWARD SPIVEY

production company
PRODUKTION

director
DOMINIC MURPHY

client
VOLKSWAGEN
GROUP UK

agency
BMP DDB/LONDON

CD1 #9

BRONZE AWARD
consumer television
over :30 campaign

art directors
KIM SCHOEN
SEAN MULLENS
writers
SUZANNE FINNAMORE
SUSAN TREACY
CHRIS LISICK
agency producer
STEVE NEELY
production company
@RADICAL.MEDIA
director
TARSEM
client
LEVI STRAUSS & CO
agency
FOOTE CONE & BELDING/
SAN FRANCISCO

CD1 #10

BAGGER: Can I carry this out to your car?
RANDY: So...Wanna take this baby...for a spin?
YOUNG GIRL: Sure. Mind sitting in the back seat?
SFX: Randy hitting the car hood, laughs.
RANDY: No problem. You wouldn't believe the leg room back here...It's like...a plush couch.
SFX: Car brakes screeching. Car horn.
RANDY: You can't do that...with anti-lock brakes.
SFX: Car door opening. Squealing tires. Door slamming shut.
YOUNG GIRL: Hey.
YOUNG GUY: Hey...So...so who's the guy in the back?
YOUNG GIRL: That's just...Randy.
YOUNG GUY: Hey.
RANDY: How ya doin'?
RANDY: Good lookin' kid.
YOUNG GUY: Uh...What are we doing?
RANDY: What are we doing? We're cruising in on the smoothest V8's ever made.
YOUNG GUY: You look very pretty.
RANDY: Hey, you two ever think of having kids? Child-proof locks.
SFX: Car door locking.
RANDY: You start, you know, let me know.
YOUNG GIRL: Hi!
HOSTESS: Hi! Two?
YOUNG GIRL: Three.
SUPER: Levi's. They go on. www.levi.com.

GOLD AWARD
consumer television
:30 single

art director
JON SOTO
writer
ALBERT KELLY
agency producer
KRISTIN LOUDIS
production company
TATE & PARTNERS
director
BAKER SMITH
client
NIKE
agency
GOODBY SILVERSTEIN
& PARTNERS/
SAN FRANCISCO

CD1 #11

SECURITY GUARD: Excuse me!
TENNIS PLAYER MAN 1: Ah, nuts!
SECURITY GUARD: Hold your horses there, McEnroe. Do you see the sign?
TENNIS PLAYER MAN 2: What sign?
SECURITY GUARD: I've seen you guys playing tennis here before.
TENNIS PLAYER MAN 1: Look we're not from around here.
SECURITY GUARD: I'm just trying to my job, understand that. I'm trying to help you out here.
TENNIS PLAYER MAN 1: Run, Ashley, run!
SECURITY GUARD: Hey! Hey, hey, hey, hey, hey hey. HEY! Off the fence! Couple o' monkeys up there.
SUPER: What if we treated all athletes the way we treat skateboarders?
SECURITY GUARD: Game over. The night's done. Jackasses.

SILVER AWARD
consumer television
:30 single

art director
MICHAEL OUWELEEN
writer
MICHAEL OUWELEEN
agency producer
JENNIFER DAVIDSON
production company
TAYLORMADE
director
BRUCE HURWIT
client
CARTOON NETWORK
agency
CARTOON NETWORK/
ATLANTA

CD1 #12

GUY: Got a guy ran off a ledge...alright sir...sir keep running–keep running alright, but don't look down.
GUY: You looked down? (pause) Well now you're gonna fall.
GUY: Sir, you're gonna make a hole in the ground in the shape of your body. (more to himself than the person on the other end of the line) And hopefully, you'll make an accordion noise.
GUY: (quiet, proud) You're gonna be all right.
SUPER: Welcome to Cartoon Network.
DAFFY: Screwy, ain't it?

BRONZE AWARD
consumer television
:30 single

art director
ANDREW FRASER
writer
ANDREW FRASER
agency producer
HOWARD SPIVEY
production company
OUTSIDER
director
PAUL GAY
client
VOLKSWAGEN
GROUP UK
agency
BMP DDB/LONDON

CD1 #13

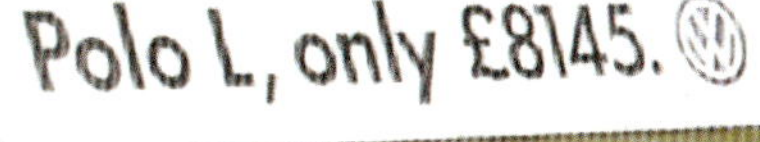

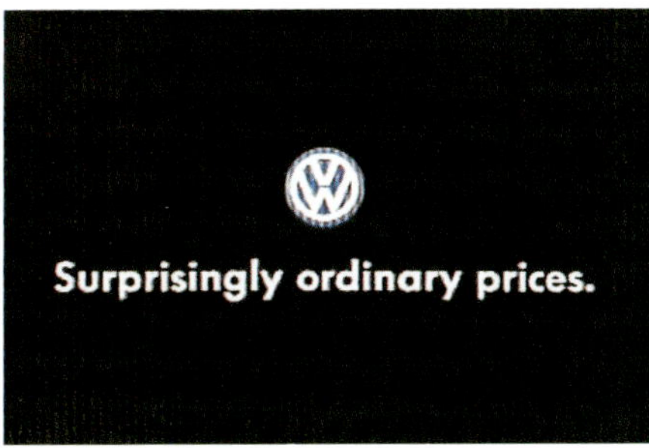

SFX: Tennis match sounds.
SUPER: Volkswagen.
Surprisingly ordinary prices.

BRONZE AWARD
consumer television
:30 single

art director
ANDREW FRASER
writer
ANDREW FRASER
agency producer
HOWARD SPIVEY
production company
OUTSIDER
director
PAUL GAY
client
VOLKWAGEN GROUP UK
agency
BMP DDB/LONDON

CD1 #14

GOLD AWARD
consumer television
:30 campaign

art director
ANDREW FRASER
writer
ANDREW FRASER
agency producer
HOWARD SPIVEY
production company
OUTSIDER
director
PAUL GAY
client
VOLKWAGEN GROUP UK
agency
BMP DDB/LONDON

CD1 #15
Best of Show

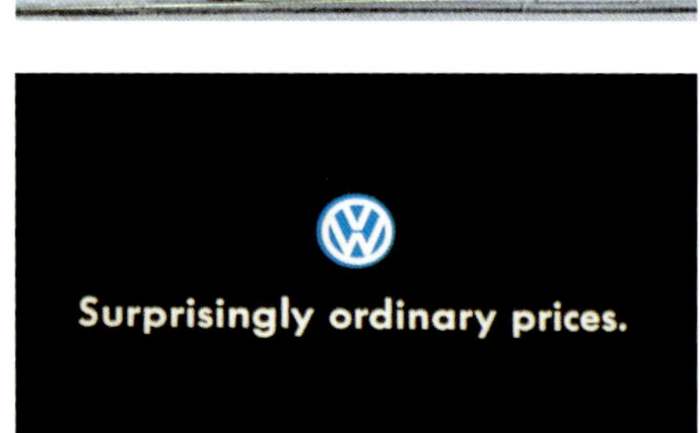
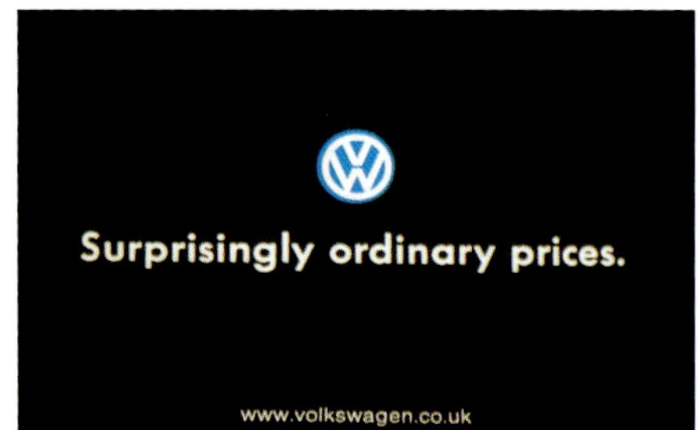
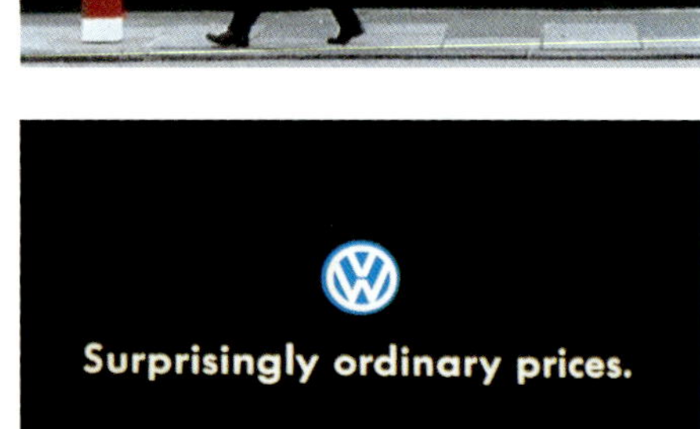

SUPER: Volkswagen.
Surprisingly ordinary prices.

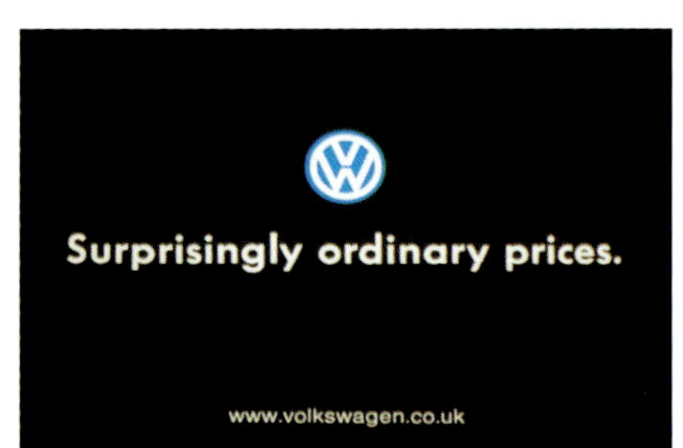

SUPER: Volkswagen.
Surprisingly ordinary prices.

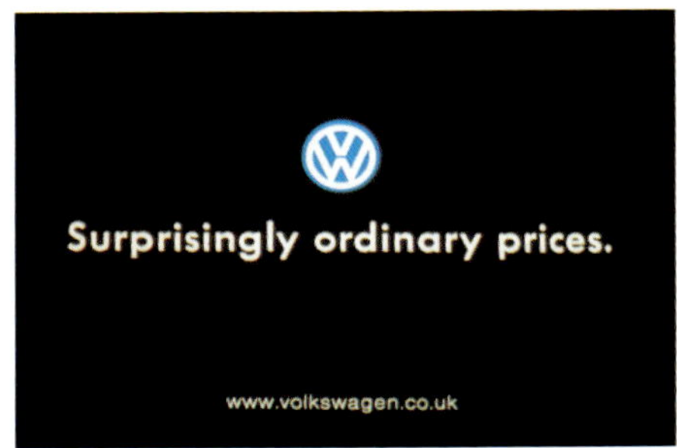

SUPER: Volkswagen.
Surprisingly ordinary prices.

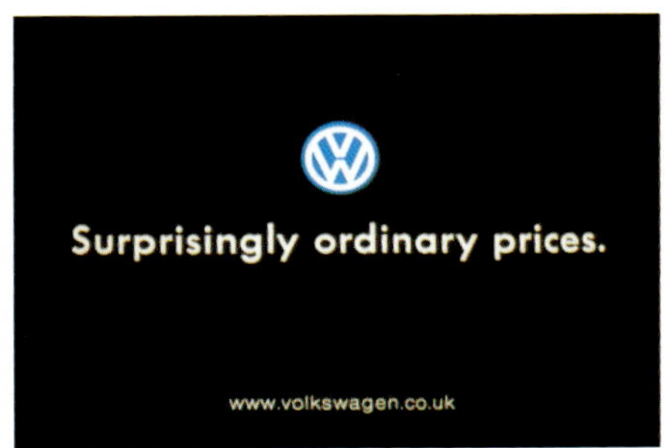

SUPER: Volkswagen.
Surprisingly ordinary prices.

GOLD AWARD
consumer television
:30 campaign

art director
MICHAEL OUWELEEN
writer
MICHAEL OUWELEEN
agency producer
JENNIFER DAVIDSON
production company
TAYLORMADE
director
BRUCE HURWIT
client
CARTOON NETWORK
agency
CARTOON NETWORK/
ATLANTA

CD1 #16

WOMAN: Hello–I need you to get out of there RIGHT NOW! I want you jump up in the air, and hang there...DON'T ARGUE WITH ME, JUST HANG THERE!... Spin your legs very fast...until your legs are making a wheel...Now, come down, hit the ground–and zip out of there.
SUPER: Welcome to Cartoon Network.
DAFFY: Screwy, ain't it?

SFX: Phone rings.
WOMAN: (pause) A man's pointing a gun at you? No, don't hang up! No–what I want you to do is reach behind your back. No, I know you don't have anything behind your back. You're just gonna reach behind your back and when you pull your hand out, you're gonna have a reeeally big mallet. Did that work?
DAFFY: Yeth.
SUPER: Welcome to Cartoon Network.
DAFFY: Screwy, ain't it?

GUY: Got a guy who needs to hide, fast! Let's move! Let's move! Alright! Sir, you gotta stop screaming. Now listen, I need you to look around...is there a rock...a building...a car...anything to hide behind there. Sir?
COMPUTER GUY: What's he got?
GUY: One skinny tree. No, we are going to get you out of there, you hold on. Now sir, for this to work, you're gonna have to tippy- toe behind that tree. And you will disappear.
SUPER: Welcome to the Cartoon Network.
DAFFY: Screwy, ain't it?

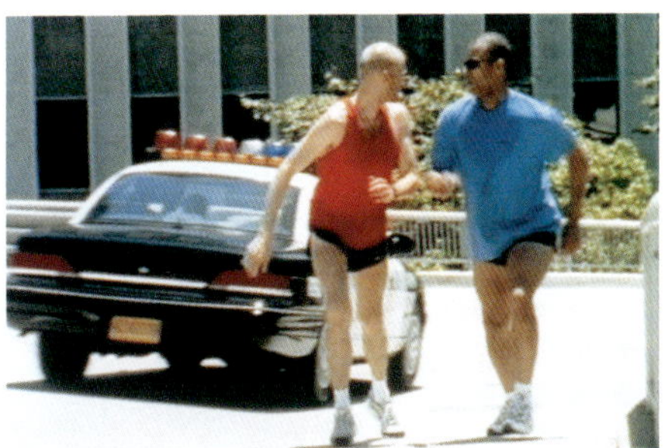

RUNNER 1: All we want to do is just run, man.
RUNNER 2: We're regular guys.
RUNNER 2: As soon as we do this...we're criminals.
RUNNER 2: People get so freaked out!
WOMAN WITH BABY: Do you have to do that here?
BLACK MAN: You crazy people!
MAN IN CAR: (honking horn) Get outta the road man!
YOUNG WOMAN: I used to run...when I was eight! She almost hit that lady.
RUNNER 2: Yeah, there's runners everywhere.
RUNNER 2: Good runners too.
RUNNER 2:They all go through the same thing.
RUNNER 2: Runners aren't criminals.
RUNNER 2: Running's not a crime.
RUNNER 1: Ya know, I wanna run. I wanna run, I just wanna run.
SUPER: What if we treated all athletes the way we treat skateboarders?

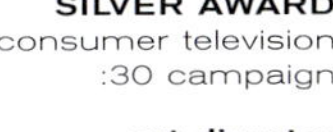

SILVER AWARD
consumer television
:30 campaign

art director
JON SOTO
writer
ALBERT KELLY
agency producer
KRISTIN LOUDIS
production company
TATE & PARTNERS
director
BAKER SMITH
client
NIKE
agency
GOODBY SILVERSTEIN
& PARTNERS/
SAN FRANCISCO

CD1 #17

SILVER AWARD
consumer television
:20 and under: single

art director
TODD GRANT
writer
STEVE DILDARIAN
agency producer
KHRISANA MAYFIELD
production company
@RADICAL.MEDIA
directors
BRYAN BUCKLEY
FRANK TODARO
client
ANHEUSER-BUSCH
agency
GOODBY SILVERSTEIN
& PARTNERS/
SAN FRANCISCO

CD1 #18

LOUIE: Ohhhh, if I could swim...I would swim over there and I would go up and I would say, "Hello, I'm Louie. How are you? Nice to meet you." I would grab their heads and I would hold them under the water like this, like this. That's right.
FRANK: Louie, you are one sick lizard.

BRONZE AWARD
consumer television
:20 and under: single

art director
TODD GALLENTINE
writers
CHERYL VAN OOYEN
MARK MENDELIS
agency producer
CHERI ANDERSON
production company
TOOL OF NORTH
AMERICA
director
CHRIS HOOPER
client
IKEA NORTH AMERICA
agency
DEUTSCH/NEW YORK

CD1 #19

SFX: Alarm sounding.
ANNOUNCER: Curtains. And everything else for your bed and bath. At IKEA's Bedroom Event.

SILVER AWARD
consumer television
:20 and under: campaign

art director
HAL CURTIS
writers
JERRY CRONIN
JEFF BITSACK
SHAWN PRESTON
agency producer
DAN DUFFY
production company
@RADICAL.MEDIA
directors
FRANK TODARO
BRYAN BUCKLEY
client
ESPN
agency
WIEDEN & KENNEDY/
PORTLAND

CD1 #20

SUPER: NHL Equipment Managers.
MAN 1: A little too much curve?
MAN 2: (Getting up) Yeah.

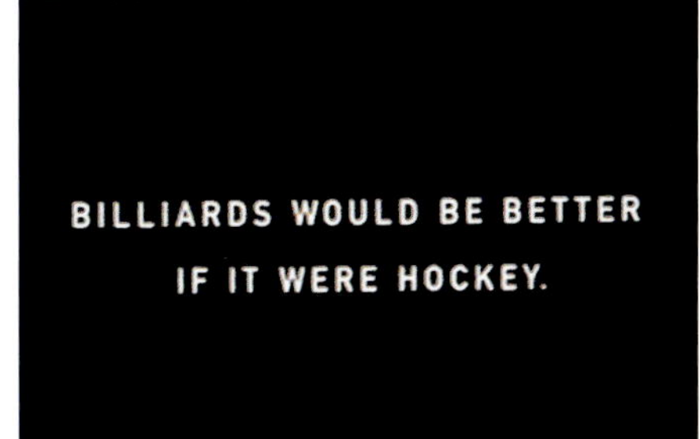

ANNOUNCER 1: Well, he's sweating over there, but not because he's losing. Dan Malloy is leading five to three.
ANNOUNCER 2: He's got to come back up and, hopefully, shoot the five in the same pocket.
ANNOUNCER 1: Well, that shouldn't be a problem. I think that was the toughest thing. It would appear now...uh...the rack is his for the taking. And there it is.
ANNOUNCER 2: Notice the cue ball, center of the table.
SUPER: Billiards would be better if it were hockey. NHL on Fox.
ANNOUNCER 2: Bing.
ANNOUNCER 1: Roddy's lucky to avoid a slashing call. And, as you can see there's some action on table number one.

BRONZE AWARD
consumer television
:20 and under: campaign

art director
ROGER CAMP
writers
ERIC SILVER
JEFF BITSACK
agency producer
LIZ GRAVES
production company
MOXIE PICTURES
director
CHRISTOPHER GUEST
client
FOX NETWORK
agency
CLIFF FREEMAN
& PARTNERS/
NEW YORK

CD1 #21

GOLD AWARD
consumer television
varying lengths campaign

art director
KILPATRICK ANDERSON
writer
JAMES LEMAITRE
agency producer
LISA JAKANOVICH
production company
X-RAY
director
JESSE PERETZ
client
NIKE
agency
WIEDEN & KENNEDY/
PORTLAND

CD1 #22

MODERATOR: Gail, I believe it was your week to write something.
GAIL DEVERS: A faraway land by Gail Devers. Once upon a time there was a far away land. A land where everyone was equal. Where people, fast and slow, could join hands and sing in harmony. Where you were judged by the size of your heart, not the size of your lead. Where people looked past the Zoom Air in your shoes and saw the real you. The end.
MODERATOR: Words can be powerful. Michael, hold my hand.
SUPER: Thin, light, responsive Zoom Air.

MODERATOR: You all wear Zoom Air. You're all aware that it's thin, light and responsive. So how do you feel about having to wear shoes that make you even faster? Gary? Conflicting emotions?
GARY PAYTON: I keep telling myself I'm doing it for the team. They need me to be explosive. But sometimes that's not enough. The hardest part is putting them on. When I'm lacing them up, I try to think about happy things. Like ice cream. Or puppies.
CHEF KOJI: Or shrimp.
MODERATOR: Gary, you are one sweet guy. Did everyone hear the puppy part?
SUPER: Thin, light, responsive Zoom Air.

MODERATOR: People make fun of you because you're fast, because you wear Zoom Air. Well, let's turn the tables, let's pretend that I'm slow. I want you to insult me. Come on, Michael?
MICHAEL JOHNSON: You Turtle.
MODERATOR: Uh...Oh! Ouch! (laughing) Gary?
GARY PAYTON: Slow Poke.
MODERATOR: Good, only you can help you people..Okay, Al, I'm slow.
AL UNSER, JR.: Ketchup Bottle.
MODERATOR: Very good. Come on. Let out the aggression.
MICHAEL JOHNSON: Mr. Slow Pants.
MODERATOR: Okay, that's great!
GAIL DEVERS: Hey, Molasses!
MODERATOR: That kind of hit BOINNNNGGG, right between the eyes. Isn't this fun? Michael, come on, I can take it!
MICHAEL JOHNSON: Mrs. Butterworth.
MODERATOR: Mrs. Butterworth! She's slow! (laughing).
GARY PAYTON: Jerk.
MODERATOR: Okay, you said that with conviction, but I can take it 'cause I'm a professional.
SUPER: Thin, light, responsive Zoom Air.

SILVER AWARD
consumer television
varying lengths campaign

art directors
DON SCHNEIDER
DONNA WEINHEIM
writers
MICHAEL PATTI
JEFF WATZMAN
agency producers
LISA GROSSMAN
REGINA EBE
BECKY FRIEDMAN
production companies
HOUSE OF USHER
PYTKA
directors
KINKA USHER
JOE PYTKA
client
HBO
agency
BBDO/NEW YORK

CD1 #23

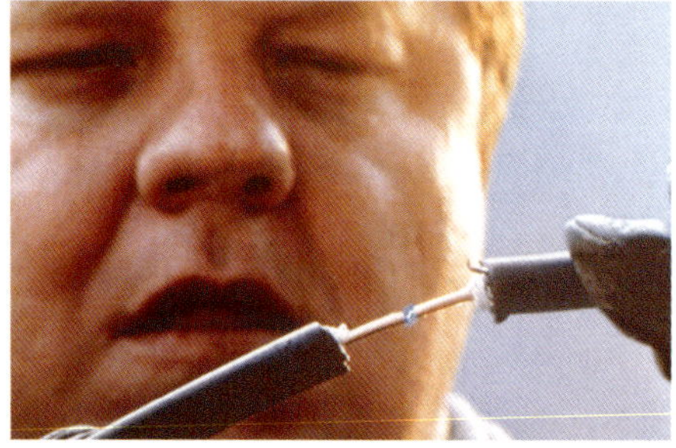

MAN: Oh!!!...Yee hee!!
CROWD 1: Oh!!!...Yeah!!!
CROWD 2: Oh!!!...Yeah!!!
CROWD 3: Oh!!!...Yeah!!!
CROWD 4: Oh!!!...Yeah!!!
SFX: Static.
CROWD: Yeah!!!
SFX: Static.
CROWD: Oh!!!!
SFX: Static.
CROWD: Yeah!!!
CABLE GUY 1: Riley, you're one sick, sadistic puppy.
SFX: Static.
CROWD: Oh!!!
CABLE GUY 2: Heh-heh...
ANNOUNCER: It's not TV. It's HBO.

BRONZE AWARD
consumer television
varying lengths campaign

art director
TODD GRANT
writer
STEVE DILDARIAN
agency producers
CINDY EPPS
KHRISANA MAYFIELD
production company
@RADICAL.MEDIA
directors
BRYAN BUCKLEY
FRANK TODARO
client
ANHEUSER-BUSCH
agency
GOODBY SILVERSTEIN
& PARTNERS/
SAN FRANCISCO

CD1 #24

SFX: Crickets chirping in the background.
FROGS: Bud...weis...er. (repeating throughout)
LOUIE: I can't believe they went with the frogs.
LIZARD II: Louie.
LOUIE: Our audition was flawless.
LIZARD II: Louie.
LOUIE: We did the look. Heh?...we did the tongue thing...
LIZARD II: Um-hum.
LOUIE: That was great.
LIZARD II: Louie, frogs sell beer.
LOUIE: Ehh.
LIZARD II: That's it, man, the number one rule of marketing.
LOUIE: The Budweiser Lizards. We could have been huge.
LIZARD II: Hey, there will be other auditions.
LOUIE: Oh yeah, for what. This was Budweiser, buddy. This was big.
SFX: Tongue catching a bug.
LOUIE: Those frogs are gonna pay.
LIZARD II: Let it go, Louie, let it go.

GOLD AWARD
consumer television
under $50,000 budget
single

art director
FRANK CLARK
writer
DEAN SALING
agency producer
JOYCE SCHMIDTBAUER
production company
OBERLENZ FILMS
director
TONY OBER
client
SEATTLE
SUPERSONICS
agency
WONGDOODY/SEATTLE

CD1 #25

SUPER: The Sonics are coming to your home.
SAM: Just knock on the door?
CREW GUY: Just knock on the door.
MOM: Oh my goodness!
SAM: Wassup!
MOM: Nice to meet you!
SAM: You too.
DAD: Say hi to Big Smooth!
JORDAN: You wanna see my Chicago Bulls jersey?
SAM: Yeah. This is...this is what he has. We gonna wash this. We gonna wash this in here, okay?
JORDAN: No!
SAM: You the man!
JORDAN: Yeah–gimme the ball!
SAM: C'mon, be the man!
SAM: Oh, they ran a play on you! Where you at, man?
JORDAN: (giggles)
SAM: Okay, a little low-five, then!
JORDAN: Um, Sam? Did you bring your pajamas?
SAM: Hmm?
JORDAN: Did you bring your pajamas? I wanna be on TV!
SAM: Yeah...whatever.
SUPER: See them in your home.
MOM: Okay, time to go to bed! Sam, stop that! In the bed, now!
SUPER: 56 games on free TV.
JORDAN: Go Sonics!

SILVER AWARD
consumer television
under $50,000 budget
single

art director
KEVIN MACNAMARA
writers
DANNY SEARLE
JASON HODGES
agency producer
DI WILLSON
production companies
PRODIGY
GREAT SOUTHERN FILMS
ADELAIDE
director
DAVID GADDIE
client
MITSUBISHI MOTORS
AUSTRALIA
agency
YOUNG & RUBICAM/
ADELAIDE

CD1 #26

ANNOUNCER: The Mitsubishi Express has loading doors...on both sides. The competition...doesn't. The Mitsubishi Express. Working man's best friend.
SUPER: Man's best friend.

BRONZE AWARD
consumer television
under $50,000 budget
single

art director
TOM GIANFAGNA
writer
AMY BORKOWSKY
agency producers
DIANE JEREMIAS
SUSAN DULEPSKI
production company
FIVE UNION SQUARE
director
TOM SCHILLER
client
COURTYARD BY
MARRIOTT
agency
LOWE & PARTNERS/
SMS/NEW YORK

CD1 #27

NEVER UNDERESTIMATE
THE IMPORTANCE OF
A GOOD NIGHT'S REST.

THE HOTEL DESIGNED

BY BUSINESS TRAVELERS®
Call 800-321-2211

SUPER: National Science Symposium, Williman Center.
HOST: Our keynote speaker holds a Ph.D. in chemistry and serves as Director of our North American Facility. Please join me in welcoming Dr. James Dalrymple.
SUPER: Never underestimate the importance of a good night's rest.
SFX: Applause continues.
DALRYMPLE: Thank you. Thank you very much.
SUPER: Courtyard by Marriott.

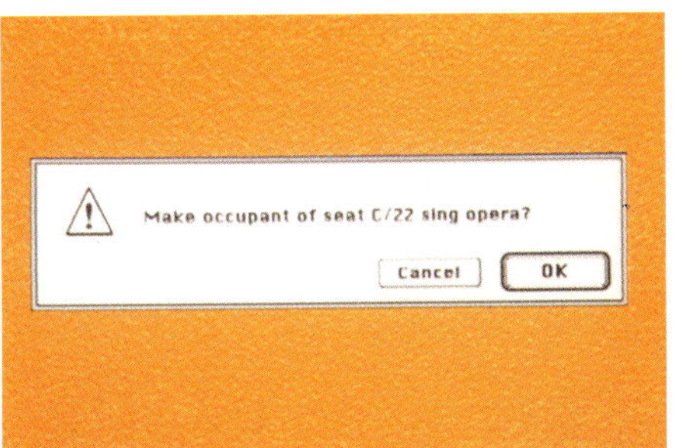

MULTIMEDIA DIALOGUE BOX: Play music? (OK/Cancel). OK selected.
SFX: Music track played.
DIALOGUE BOX: Left cinema speaker only? (OK/Cancel). OK selected.
SFX: Music and soundtrack is now played through left speaker only.
DIALOGUE BOX: Right cinema speaker only? (OK/Cancel). OK selected.
SFX: Music and soundtrack is now played through right speaker only.
DIALOGUE BOX: Stereo? (OK/Cancel). OK selected.
SFX: Music played in stereo again.
DIALOGUE BOX: Lights on? (OK/Cancel). OK selected. Lights go on.
DIALOGUE BOX: Light off? (OK/Cancel). OK selected. Lights go off.
DIALOGUE BOX: Lights on? (OK/Cancel). Ok selected. Lights go on.
DIALOGUE BOX: There are 9 cellular phones in the theater. Shall I make them ring? (OK/Cancel). Ok selected.
SFX: 9 cellular phones ring.
DIALOGUE BOX: Stop phones ringing? (OK/Cancel). OK selected.
SFX: Phones all stop ringing at once.
DIALOGUE BOX: Make occupant of seat C-15 sing opera? (OK/Cancel). OK selected.
SFX: Person in seat gets up and sings opera at top of voice.
DIALOGUE BOX: He sounds terrible. Shall I make him leave? (OK/Cancel). OK selected.
DIALOGUE BOX: Shut down? (OK/Cancel). OK selected. The Apple Rocketbook shuts down.
SUPER: The Apple Rocketbook. So much power, anything is possible.

GOLD AWARD
non-broadcast
cinema

art director
MIKE O'SULLIVAN
writers
RICHARD MADDOCKS
MURRAY WATT
agency producer
JACKIE CLARK
production company
MOJO PARTNERS/
AUCKLAND
directors
RICHARD MADDOCKS
MIKE O'SULLIVAN
client
APPLE COMPUTER
agency
MOJO PARTNERS/
AUCKLAND

CD1 #28

SILVER AWARD
non-broadcast
cinema

art director
NOEL HASSON
writer
JOHN COOK
agency producer
JOHN DORIS
production company
GLASSWORKS
director
ALASTAIR HEARSUM
client
GALLAHER
agency
CDP/LONDON

CD1 #29

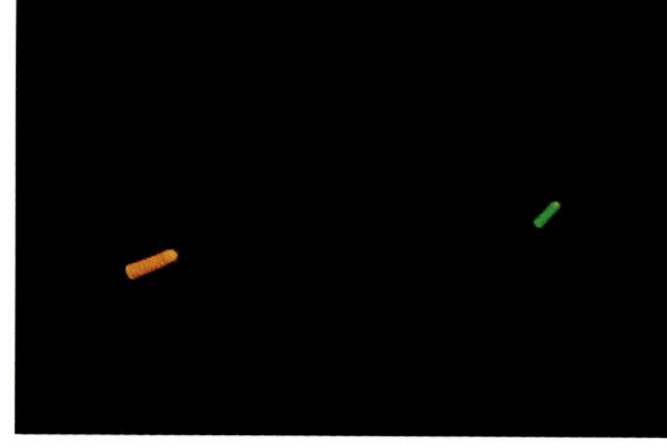

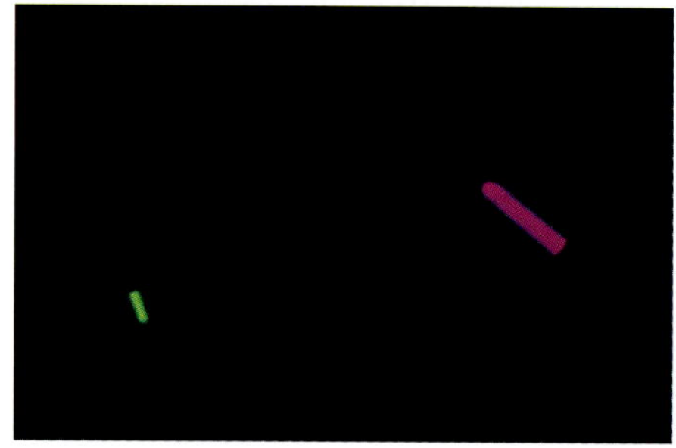

MAN: Hi, babes.
WOMAN: Oh, hi.
MAN: Ah, you're in bed already.
WOMAN: Yeah.
MAN: Well, all right. Leave the light off. I've got a surprise for you.
SFX: Bedroom door opens, closes.
MAN: I bet you haven't seen one of these before.
WOMAN: Uh! A luminous condom–Ooh-er-no (nervous laugh).
MAN: Oomph–ouch! What's all these clothes doing on the floor?
SFX: Wardrobe doors slowly creak open.
MAN: Hold on a minute, what's going on here?
SFX: Neigh of horse and sound of hooves.
MUSIC: Air on a G-String.
ANNOUNCER: Hamlet Extra Mild, for Extra Happiness.

BRONZE AWARD
non-broadcast
cinema

art director
IAN DUCKER
writer
WILL FARQUHAR
agency producer
JULIA METHOLD
production company
BBC
STEVE KELYNACK
director
GREGORY ROOD
client
BBC
agency
THE LEAGAS DELANEY PARTNERSHIP/LONDON

CD1 #30

LOU: Just a perfect day...Drink sangria in the park.
BONO: And then later when it gets dark.
SKY: We go home.
BOWIE: Just a perfect day.
SUZANNE: Feed animals in the zoo.
ELTON: Then later a movie too, and then home.
BOYZONE: Oh! It's such a perfect day.
LESLEY: I'm glad I spent it with you.
BURNING SPEAR: Oh! such a perfect day.
BONO: You just keep me hanging on.
HEATHER: Just a perfect day.
EMMYLOU: Problems all left alone.
TAMMY: Weekenders on our own.
SHANE: It's such fun.
DR. JOHN: Just a perfect day.
BOWIE: You made me forget myself.
ROBERT: I thought I was someone else.
HUEY: Someone good. Yeah.
IAN BROUDIE: Oh! It's such a perfect day.
GABRIELLE: I'm glad I spent it with you.
DR. JOHN: Oh! Such a perfect day.
EVAN: You just keep me hanging on.
BRETT: You're going to reap just what you sow.
CHOIR: Reap. Reap. Reap.
JOAN: You're going to reap
LAURIE: Just what you sow.
HEATHER: You're going to reap just what you sow.
SUPER: Whatever your musical taste. It is catered to by BBC Radio and Television.
SUPER: This is only possible thanks to the unique way the BBC is paid for by you.
LOU: Oh, what a perfect day.
SUPER: BBC. You make it what it is.

GOLD AWARD
foreign language
commerical: television

art director
MARCELLO SERPA
writer
EUGENIO MOHALLEM
agency producer
MARIA DO SOCORRO GOES
production company
ANDREAS HEINIGER
director
ANDREAS HEINIGER
client
ALPARGTAS SA
agency
ALMAP/BBDO/
SÃO PAULO

CD1 #31

ANNOUNCER: Nike versus Mizuno. The acid test. On the left foot, Nike. And on the right foot, Mizuno.
SFX: The starting gun.
ANNOUNCER: Mizuno in the lead! Nike in the lead! Mizuno in the lead! Nike in the lead! Mizuno in the lead! Mizuno is the winner! Nike is last.
SUPER: Mizuno. Serious performance.

BRONZE AWARD
foreign language
commerical: television

writers
OSCAR ASKELÖF
FILIP NILSSON
agency producer
MARIA BERGKVIST
production company
TRAKTOR
director
TRAKTOR
client
VOLVO PB
SVERIGE/VOLVO S40 T4
agency
FORSMAN BODENFORS/
GOTHENBURG

CD1 #32

SUPER: The new Volvo V40 T4.
Zero to100 in 7.3 seconds.

GOLD AWARD
multi-media campaign

client
VOLKSWAGEN GROUP UK

agency
BMP DDB/LONDON

print

art directors
NEIL DAWSON
ANDREW FRASER

writers
CLIVE PICKERING
ANDREW FRASER

typographers
KEVIN CLARKE
DAVE WAKEFIELD

broadcast

art director
ANDREW FRASER

writer
ANDREW FRASER

agency producer
HOWARD SPIVEY

production company
OUTSIDER

director
PAUL GAY

CD1 #15

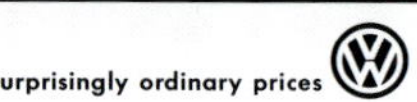

SUPER: Volkswagen.
Surprisingly ordinary prices.

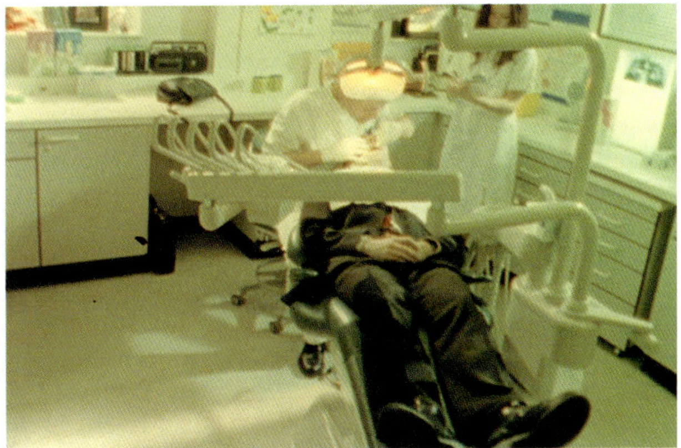

SUPER: Volkswagen.
Surprisingly ordinary prices.

SILVER AWARD
multi-media campaign

client
APPLE COMPUTER
agency
MOJO PARTNERS/
AUCKLAND

print

art director
MIKE O'SULLIVAN
writers
RICHARD MADDOCKS
MURRAY WATT
typographer
GLEN CHAPMAN

broadcast

art director
MIKE O'SULLIVAN
writers
RICHARD MADDOCKS
MURRAY WATT
agency producer
JACKIE CLARK
production company
MOJO PARTNERS
AUCKLAND
directors
MIKE O'SULLIVAN
RICHARD MADDOCKS

CD1 #28

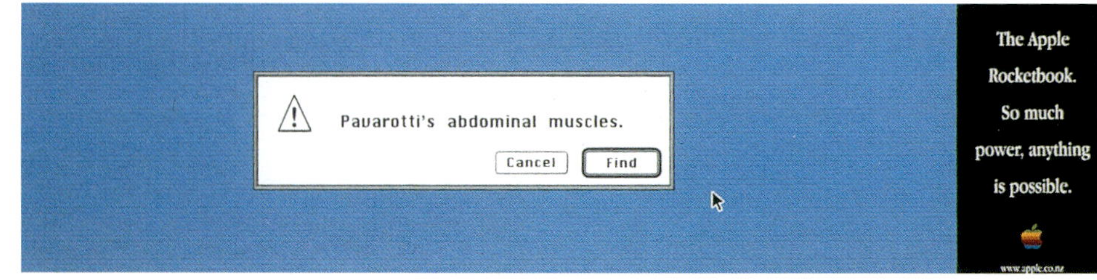

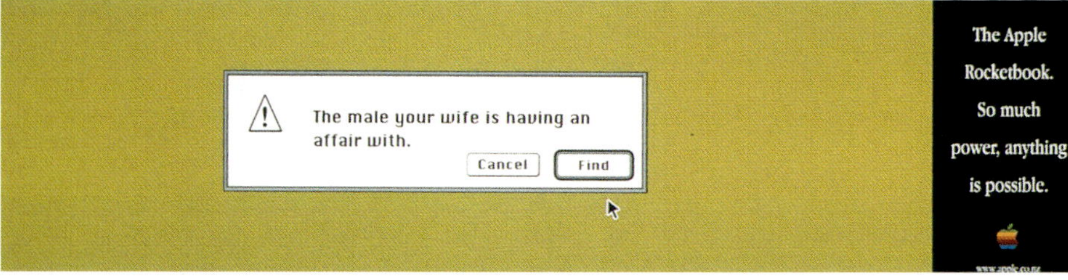

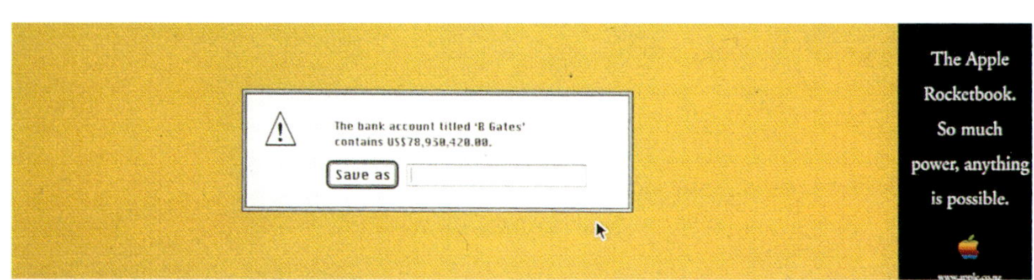

There are 9 cellular phones in the theatre.
Shall I make them ring?
Cancel
OK

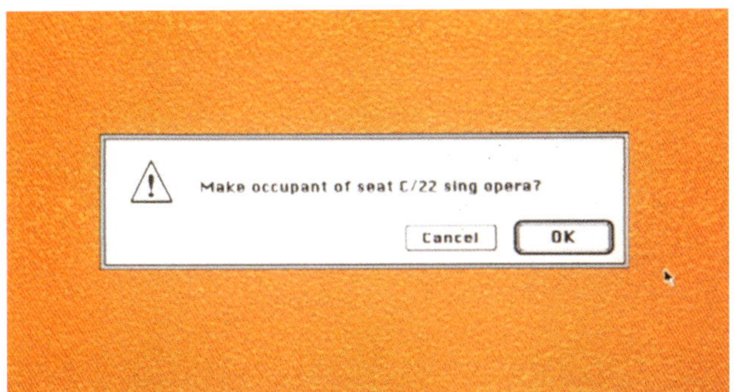
Make occupant of seat C/22 sing opera?
Cancel
OK

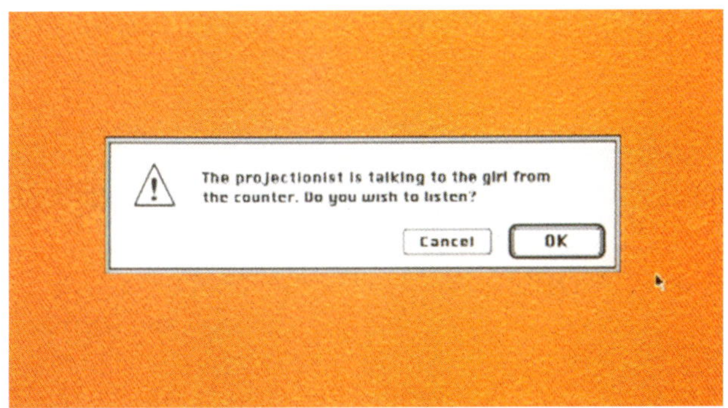
The projectionist is talking to the girl from
the counter. Do you wish to listen?
Cancel
OK

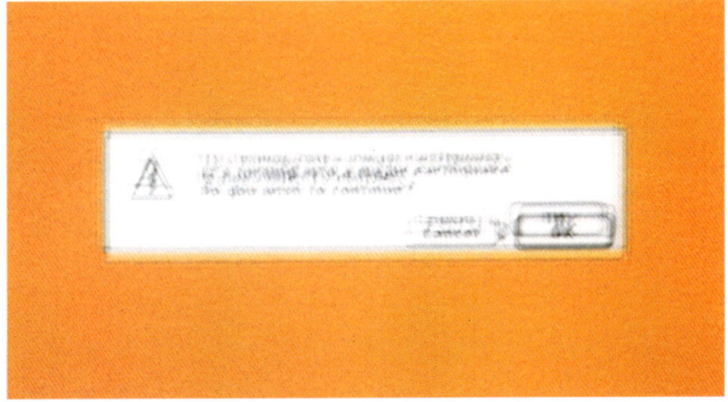

The Apple Rocketbook.
So much power, anything is possible.

GOLD, SILVER & BRONZE

BRONZE AWARD
multi-media campaign

client
ESPN/ESPNEWS

agency
GROUND ZERO/
SANTA MONICA

print

art director
GUY SHELMERDINE

writer
STEVE O'BRIEN

photographer
CRAIG SARUWATARI

broadcast

art director
GUY SHELMERDINE

writer
STEVE O'BRIEN

agency producer
AMY LANEY

CD1 #33

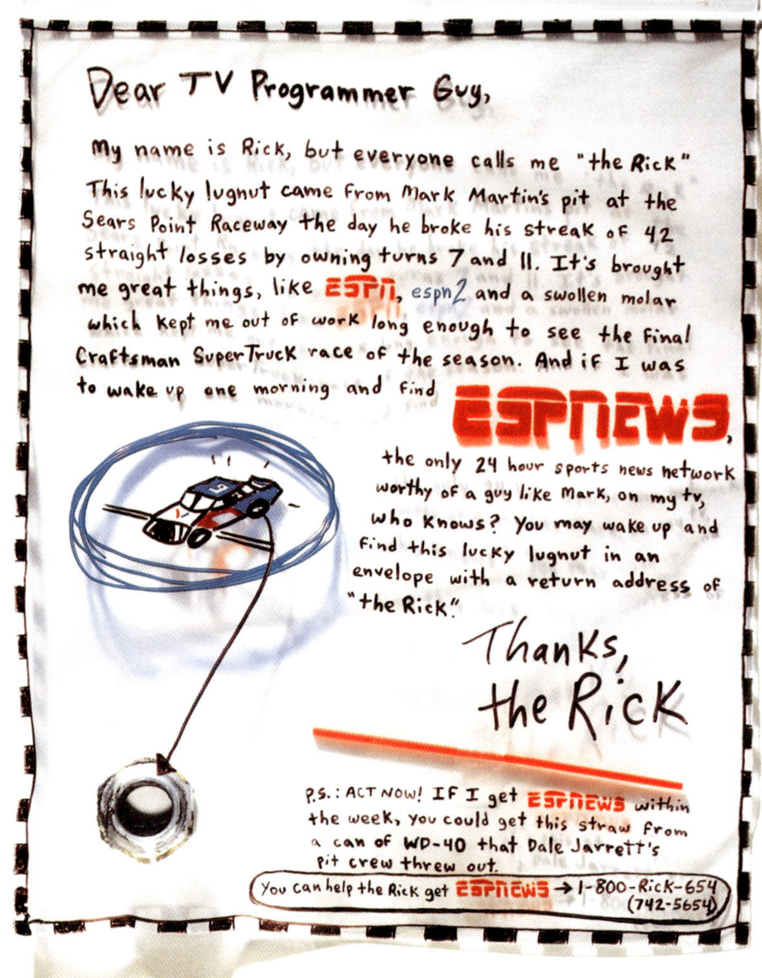

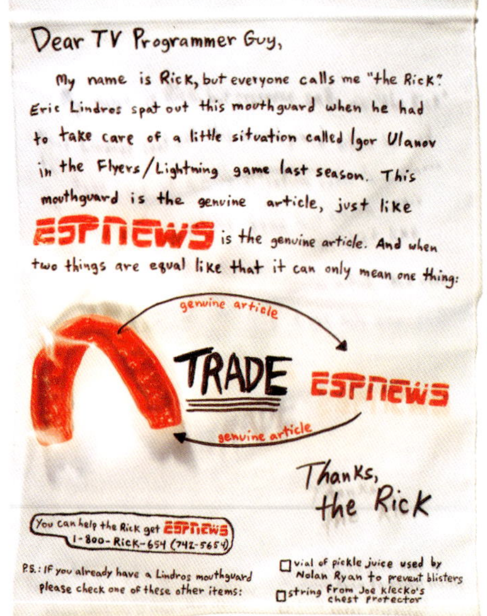

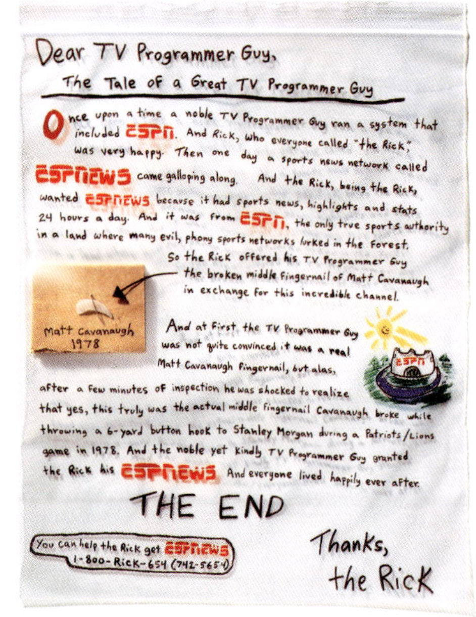

THE RICK: Hi my name is Rick, but everyone calls me "the Rick." These are my sports figurines. Now a lot of people call these dolls. They're not dolls, they're sports figurines. And I just want to get that straight. They're not toys and they're not dolls. They're figurines. Hey, Curtis. It's Curtis Martin, Patriots...grrrr.

GOLD AWARD
college competition

art directors
MATT STEIN
KEVIN PROUDFOOT

writers
MATT STEIN
KEVIN PROUDFOOT

college
VCU ADCENTER/
RICHMOND

Assignment: Pastamatic - automatic pasta machine campaign

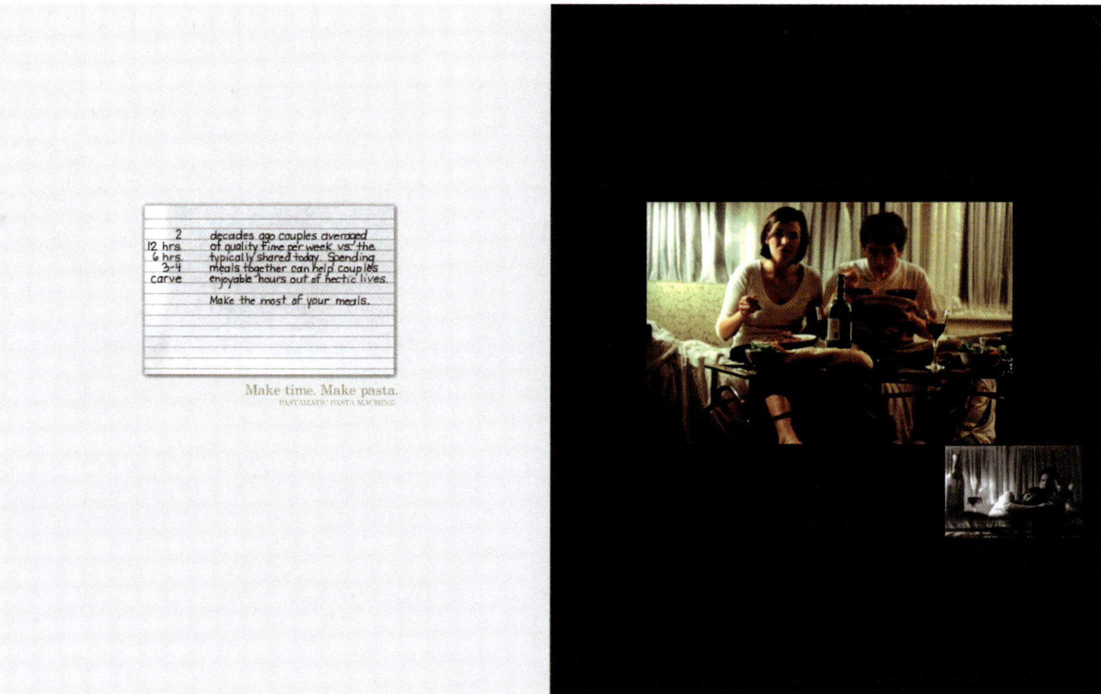

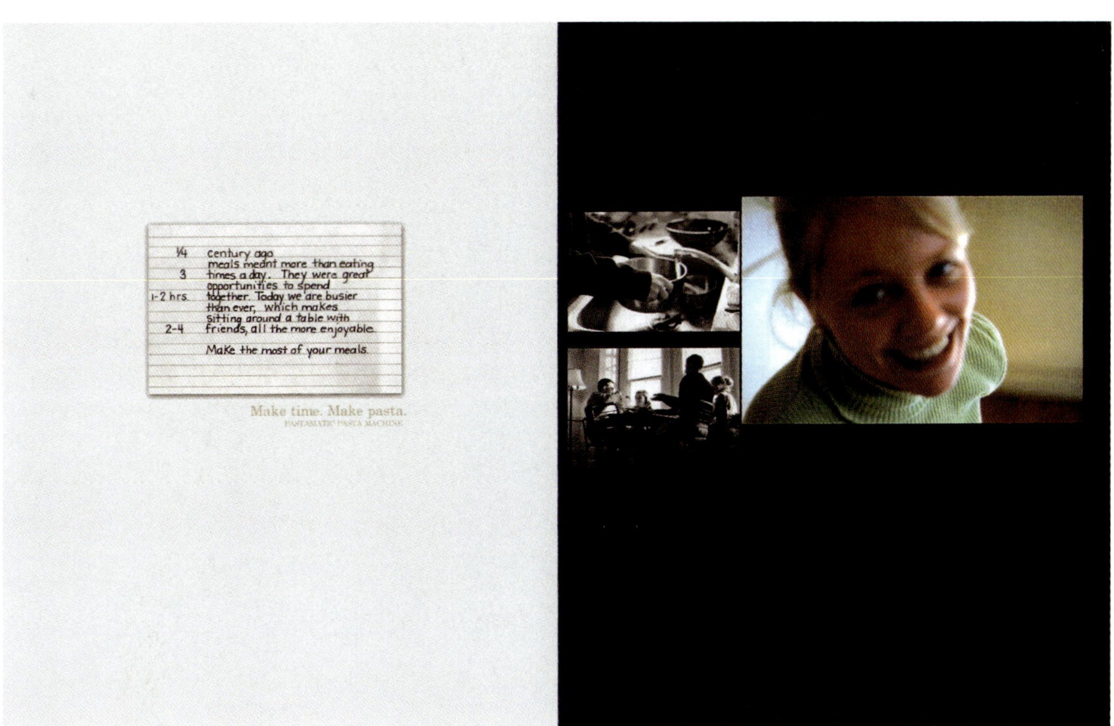
1/4 century ago
meals meant more than eating
3 times a day. They were great
opportunities to spend
1-2 hrs. together. Today we are busier
than ever, which makes
sitting around a table with
2-4 friends, all the more enjoyable.
Make the most of your meals.
Make time. Make pasta.
PASTAMATIC PASTA MACHINE

SILVER AWARD
college competition

art director
GREG THOMAS

writers
JOHN FIEBKE
BRAD GILMORE

college
VCU ADCENTER/
RICHMOND

Assignment: Pastamatic - automatic pasta machine campaign

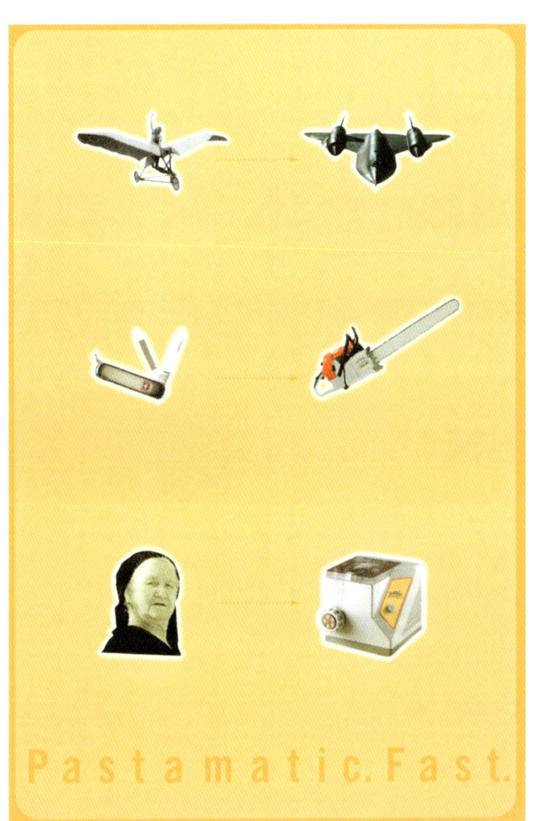

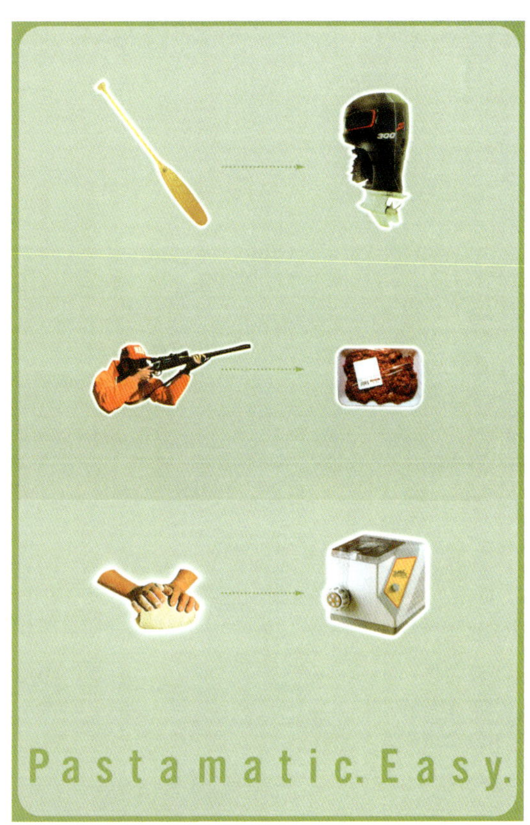

BRONZE AWARD
college competition

art director
CLAIBORNE WINTER

writer
STEPHEN LUNDBERG

college
VCU ADCENTER/
RICHMOND

Assignment: Pastamatic - automatic pasta machine campaign

BEST OF SHOW

BEST OF SHOW

BEST OF SHOW AWARD
consumer television
:30 campaign

art director
ANDREW FRASER
writer
ANDREW FRASER
agency producer
HOWARD SPIVEY
production company
OUTSIDER
director
PAUL GAY
client
VOLKSWAGEN
GROUP UK
agency
BMP DDB/LONDON

CD1 #15

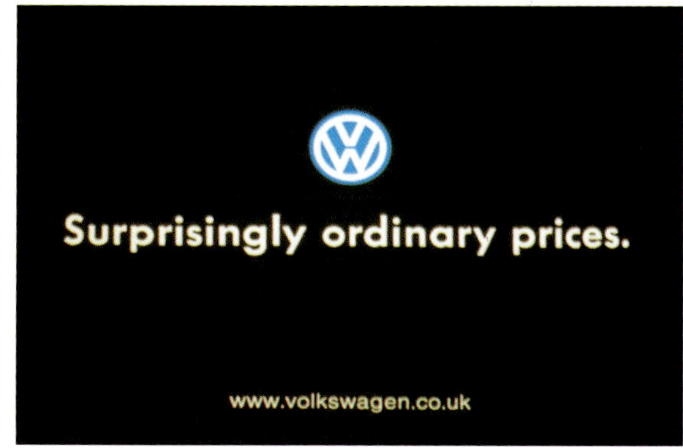

SUPER: Volkswagen.
Surprisingly ordinary prices.

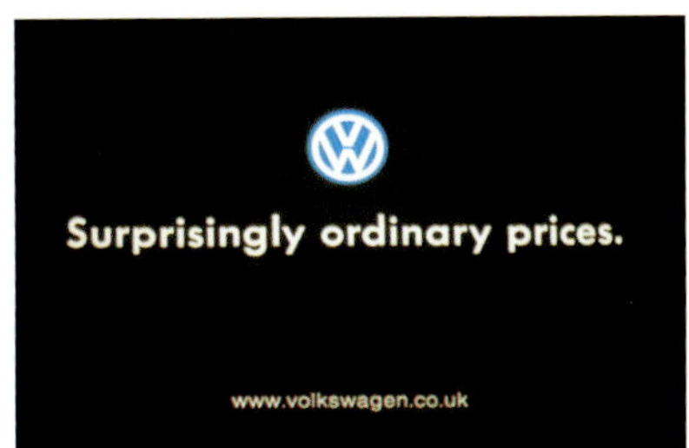

SUPER: Volkswagen.
Surprisingly ordinary prices.

SUPER: Volkswagen.
Surprisingly ordinary prices.

GOLD ON GOLD

GOLD AWARD
foreign language
commercial

client
SÃO PAULO ALPARGTAS

agency
ALMAP/BBDO/
SÃO PAULO

CD1 #31

After ten hours of television commercials one could come to the conclusion that our entire society has been built around the worship of athletes.

BRUCE BILDSTEN
One Show Judge

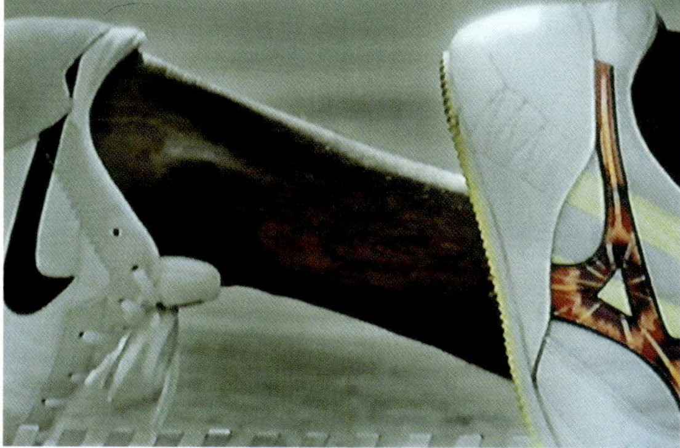

ANNOUNCER: Nike versus Mizuno. The acid test. On the left foot, Nike. And on the right foot, Mizuno.
SFX: The starting gun.
ANNOUNCER: Mizuno in the lead! Nike in the lead! Mizuno in the lead! Nike in the lead! Mizuno in the lead! Mizuno is the winner! Nike is last.
SUPER: Mizuno. Serious performance.

What to do against a brand that is the standard in its category? What to do against a competitor who has the world's best athletes under contract? What to do with just 80 thousand dollars against a budget of 1 to 2 million dollars per spot?

We decided to pray.

And since we are not as Catholic as we used to be, we decided to take a look at the Supreme Creative Annual – the Bible.

And suddenly, the Almighty guided our hands to the right page.

Everything became clear, and when we read that simple tale, we felt we were in the presence of a miracle, and that all we had to do was to switch roles.

Mizuno was David. Nike was Goliath. And the idea was the stone.

We were saved if God (the client) approved.

Amen.

MARCELLO SERPA
EUGENIO MOHALLEM

GOLD AWARD
public service/political
outdoor and posters

client
CALIFORNIA DEPARTMENT OF HEALTH SERVICES

agency
ASHER & PARTNERS/
LOS ANGELES

Basically, they told us to "de-glamorize" smoking via an outdoor board. We thought it would be a great idea to use the ubiquitous nature of cigarette advertising against itself. Have the viewer think for just a moment that they were looking at a couple of Marlboro men. But, between those picturesque poses, what might those guys really be saying?

Anyway, we presented it to the client and they not only loved it, but they had the guts to run it (after a calvary of lawyers said we wouldn't get sued, but what the hell, give 'em credit anyway). Then we found the two best pseudo-Marlboro men we could find and shot it. Helllooo One Show!

NANCY STEINMAN
JEFF BOSSIN

Print campaigns were great. Tables full of great campaigns. One after another. I was amazed.

LUKE SULLIVAN
One Show Judge

GOLD AWARD
collateral: brochures

client
LEVI STRAUSS & CO.
JAPAN

agency
BARTLE BOGLE
HEGARTY/SINGAPORE

What makes this award very meaningful is the acknowledgement of a successful collaboration of creative efforts between the West (London's creative team) and the East (Asia's design team), that resulted in a recognized piece of work for a Japanese client.

It puts beyond doubt the validity and truth of BBH's belief; namely, the attitudes of teenagers are pretty similar all over the world, and that values of a brand like Levi's appeals to youth markets everywhere. Based on this belief, we had created campaigns out of both London and Singapore that build on the similarities of these teenagers. These have resonated well across the globe.

Also, the award proves that below the line, even if it is just a piece of sticker, is as crucial as a great TV or print campaign, when it comes to brand building.

In developing the work, top of mind is the need to demonstrate or showcase values of Levi's and particular to this campaign, that of individuality. The challenge is for us to translate the print concept of "No Two Pairs of Levi's Are the Same" into a different medium, in this instance a 2-D consumer magazine. To reinforce the idea, each consumer magazine is coded with a different serial number, thus "No Two Levi's Books are the Same."

STANLEY WONG

GOLD AWARD
newspaper over 600 lines
single

client
VOLKSWAGEN
GROUP UK

agency
BMP DDB/LONDON

WE ARE WITHHOLDING A VOLKSWAGEN
'SURPRISINGLY ORDINARY PRICES' ADVERTISEMENT
UNTIL WE RECEIVE CONFIRMATION THAT
A VOLKSWAGEN POLO L DOES INDEED COST £7990.

Press, as anyone will tell you, is far more difficult than TV. So while we didn't quite get the Best of Show – the moral victory was ours. Sod off, Andrew.

CLIVE PICKERING
NEIL DAWSON

GOLD AWARD
consumer television
:30 campaign

client
VOLKSWAGEN
GROUP UK

agency
BMP DDB/LONDON

CD1 #14 & #15

GOLD AWARD
multimedia campaign

client
VOLKSWAGEN
GROUP UK

agency
BMP DDB/LONDON

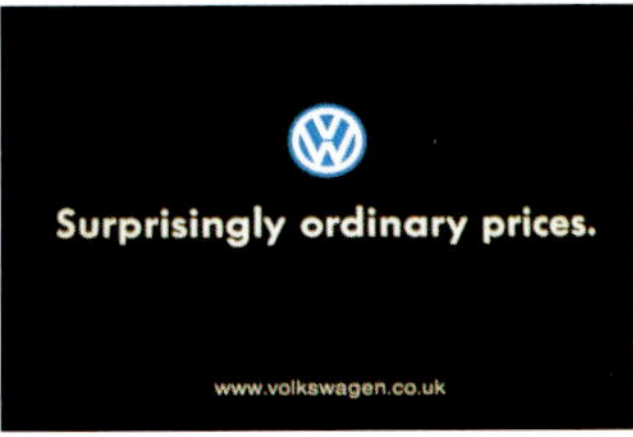

SUPER: Volkswagen.
Surprisingly ordinary prices.

A copywriter in London is suffering from hiccups. He gets on a plane, flies to New York, and takes his seat at the One Show Awards. Two hours later the hiccups are cured.

ANDREW FRASER

The brief was to change the public perception that the Polo is expensive, while also fitting in with the rest of Volkswagen's understated advertising. Much of the campaign's success has been due to this subtle approach and simple idea. It stood out from other car ads, which relied more on techniques, locations, soundtracks, huge budgets. It confirms the maxim, "When everyone else shouts, whisper."

one. a magazine, vol. II issue i

GOLD AWARD
consumer television
:30 campaign

client
CARTOON NETWORK

agency
CARTOON
NETWORK/ATLANTA

CD1 #16

WOMAN: Hello–I need you to get out of there RIGHT NOW! I want you to jump up in the air, and hang there...DON'T ARGUE WITH ME, JUST HANG THERE!... Spin your legs very fast...until your legs are making a wheel...Now, come down, hit the ground–and zip out of there.
SUPER: Welcome to Cartoon Network.
DAFFY: Screwy, ain't it?

SFX: Phone rings.
WOMAN: (pause) A man's pointing a gun at you? No, don't hang up! No–what I want you to do is reach behind your back. No, I know you don't have anything behind your back. You're just gonna reach behind your back and when you pull your hand out, you're gonna have a reeeally big mallet. Did that work?
DAFFY: Yeth.
SUPER: Welcome to Cartoon Network.
DAFFY: Screwy, ain't it?

GOLD ON GOLD

A positive trend that I saw was the desire to make great concepts simpler. People seem to be spending more time editing their idea down to its most effective state. Fewer moving parts. Less ad decoration.

JIM MOUNTJOY
One Show Judge

GUY: Got a guy who needs to hide, fast! Let's move! Let's move! Alright! Sir, you gotta stop screaming. Now listen, I need you to look around...is there a rock...a building...a car...anything to hide behind there. Sir?
COMPUTER GUY: What's he got?
GUY: One skinny tree. No, we are going to get you out of there, you hold on. Now sir, for this to work, you're gonna have to tippy-toe behind that tree. And you will disappear.
SUPER: Welcome to Cartoon Network.
DAFFY: Screwy, ain't it?

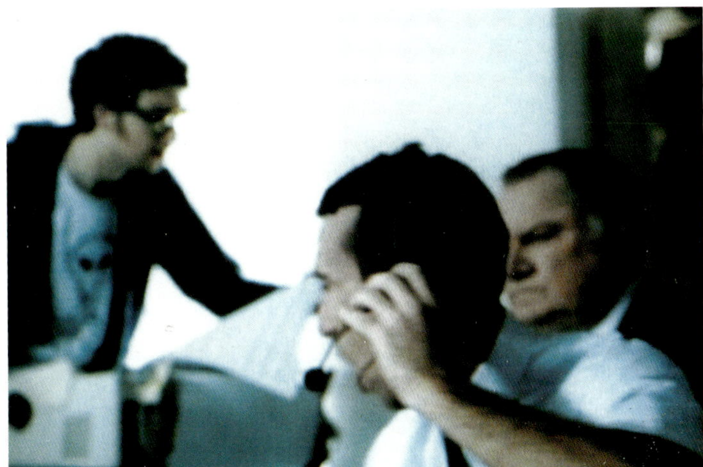

The best cartoons ever made – the '40s and '50s, Warner Brothers – were essentially made to amuse the 4 or 5 guys in the room at the time. The only audience they were writing for was themselves, because they simply didn't know who would be in the theaters when one of their cartoons ran. There were, of course, no focus groups. And "Management" didn't ever bother with them, because the studio couldn't care less. "Management" thought they did Mickey Mouse, even.

Now. Our only chance at doing work that's nearly as good as their cartoons–because they were geniuses, see – is to recreate their environment. Which we're trying to do.

Sure, everyone around here has to wear white short sleeve shirts and skinny black ties. But nothing gets tested, second-guessed or run past a pack of MBAs around a conference table, either. It's a trade-off.

Who wants a job?

MICHAEL OUWELEEN

I believe in cartoons, which are the most bizarrely concentrated form of humor on the planet. They have this amazing visual language that we all know the grammar of.

one. a magazine, vol. II issue i

GOLD AWARD
trade: color
full page or spread
single

client
TIME MAGAZINE

agency
FALLON MCELLIGOTT/
MINNEAPOLIS

If you think watching a volcano in a movie is frightening, imagine watching one in a rearview mirror.

The world's most interesting magazine.

We wish we could take more credit for these ads.

But frankly, we're writing about the most amazing product in the world.

The world.

DEAN BUCKHORN
BOB BARRIE

"Volcano" had to adhere to rules dictated by the client, and by the nature of the business. We almost always use photos that have appeared in *Time*, so we have access to some of the world's greatest photography. The campaign itself is constantly evolving...Plus we're dealing with recent news events, so the work always feels fresh to us.

one. a magazine, vol. II issue i

GOLD AWARD
consumer radio: single

client
UTAH TRANSIT AUTHORITY

agency
FJCN/W&R/
SALT LAKE CITY

CD2 #R1

We accomplished our goal with this spot. Lip ring usage among Salt Lake teens is down 34%. Belly rings are down 27%. And we have yet to see anyone walking around with nipple piercings. Because of "Lip Ring," Salt Lake City is becoming the unsullied, wholesome place of yesteryear. And if summer bus pass sales went up 21% in the process, so be it.

Thanks to Andy, a great client, whose first question after we present concepts is, "Can we do all of them?" Thanks to Randy, the art director. And thanks to the One Show judges. I like the pencil. I showed it to my wife. She said, "It must be good, because it's heavy."

BRYANT MARCUM

MUSIC: Piano driven public service-type.
TEEN: (unintelligible) I'be-looind-ry-rife.
FEMALE INTERPRETER: I've ruined my life.
TEEN: (frustrated) I-ast-ry-budder-fo-a-wide-to-duh-mawl-atty-ted-no-bay-deeb.
INTERPRETER: I asked my brother for a ride to the mall and he said, "No way, dweeb."
TEEN: (emotional) I-fel-twapt.
INTERPRETER: I felt trapped.
TEEN: (more emotional) So-o-poob-by-ireperense-lperstry-riss-n-pur-dis-irenwing-tro-dem.
INTERPRETER: So to prove my independence, I pierced my lips and put this iron ring through them.
TEEN: (losing it) Naw-et-hurs-do-tauk.
INTERPRETER: Now it hurts to talk.
TEEN: Ad-by-rom-is-rakeen-be-wer-id-duh-ho-sumuh.
INTERPRETER: And mom is making me wear it the whole summer.
TEEN: Fogus!
INTERPRETER: Bogus!
PSA STYLE ANNOUNCER: Please, teenagers. Piercing body parts is no way to prove your independence. Buy a UTA Summer Youth Pass. It's a rippin' dog tag you wear around your neck. And a Summer Youth Pass gets you around without help from mom or your gomer brother.
TEEN: (under control again) Sukin-denah-troo-a-sraw-boes.
INTERPRETER: Sucking dinner through a straw blows.
ANNOUNCER: Kids seventeen and under can purchase one for twenty-five dollars, two or more for twenty each. Call BUS-INFO for details.
TEEN: (emotional again) Den-dere's-my-navel-wing.

GOLD ON GOLD

I think our business has attracted better and better creative people over the past decade. Writers and art directors who are in the advertising business by choice, not default. They like what they're doing for a living and that shows in the work. Combine that talent with a strong business economy and yes, this is a good era for advertising creativity.

LYLE WEDEMEYER
One Show Judge

GOLD AWARD
outdoor: single

client
CALIFORNIA FLUID MILK PROCESSORS

agency
GOODBY SILVERSTEIN & PARTNERS/
SAN FRANCISCO

We would like to be able to say that the "Snap, Krackle and Pop" Milk outdoor board was the result of great strategies and creative thinking, but the truth is that the idea came to us in the grocery store. In the cereal aisle. While we were buying lunch. Proof that it's good to get out of the office sometimes.

BLAKE DALEY
VALERIE ANG-POWELL

GOLD AWARD
newspaper over 600 lines
campaign

client
WATERSTONE'S
BOOKSELLERS

agency
BDDP.GGT/LONDON

Bloody amazing. When you think that most of us now have the means to access, literally within a matter of moments, information on virtually every subject–whether it's for work, education, or leisure–that we could possibly imagine. No, not the information superhighway. That zero gigabyte information picturesque-country-road that's been with us for centuries, otherwise known as a good bookshop. A Waterstone's bookshop, for instance.

The first thing Waterstone's told us when we talked about doing their brand campaign was that they don't sell books. This, we thought, could be a problem, given that they're a chain of bookshops. "Other bookshops just sell books," they said, "we do more than that. We love books."

So, to convey this affection, we wrote a load of headlines (we know, we know, words are yesterday, man–blah, blah, visual age–blah, blah), we wrote a load of headlines extolling the various virtues of books, using insights that might serve as a reminder to those who've forgotten about them, while displaying an empathy with those who haven't.

Given uncluttered, timeless and unequivocally relevant art direction, and thanks to an understanding and appreciative client, we had the first ads in the Waterstone's campaign.

Books. Waterstone's loves 'em. We love 'em. In fact, we're particularly fond of the 1998 One Show Annual.

NIGEL ROBERTS
PAUL BELFORD

It's funny watching middle-aged actors try to climb a chain fence just to get a part in a commercial. Sarge from "Chips" came in, but he wasn't right for the part. Plus Baker said we couldn't afford him. One day, we wanted to drive by OJ's house but everyone said we didn't have enough time. The hotel was nice. There was a fountain in the lobby. If you stood there for very long, you had to go pee. Also, we saw Ton Loc in the elevator.

JON SOTO
AL KELLY

We wanted to create a connection between Nike and skateboarders, and to help non-skateboarders understand what street skaters go through. Competing in a crowded market, the campaign had to "make kids shake their heads and go 'Yeah, I've been there.'"

Tennis was a natural because it's such a fancy pants sport.

one. a magazine, vol. II issue i

GOLD AWARD
consumer television
:30 single

client
NIKE
agency
GOODBY SILVERSTEIN
& PARTNERS/
SAN FRANCISCO

CD1 #11

SECURITY GUARD: Excuse me!
TENNIS PLAYER MAN 1: Ah, nuts!
SECURITY GUARD: Hold your horses there, McEnroe. Do you see the sign?
TENNIS PLAYER MAN 2: What sign?
SECURITY GUARD: I've seen you guys playing tennis here before.
TENNIS PLAYER MAN 1: Look we're not from around here.
SECURITY GUARD: I'm just trying to do my job, understand that. I'm trying to help you out here.
TENNIS PLAYER MAN 1: Run, Ashley, run!
SECURITY GUARD: Hey! Hey, hey, hey, hey, hey, hey. HEY! Off the fence! Couple o' monkeys up there.
SUPER: What if we treated all athletes the way we treat skateboarders?
SECURITY GUARD: Game over. The night's done. Jackasses.

GOLD AWARD
magazine: color
full page or spread
single

client
SIMS SNOWBOARDS

agency
HAMMERQUIST SAFFEL
& HALVERSON/SEATTLE

GOLD ON GOLD

Everyone has their own Tianamen Square. Whether it's a lone cat going up against a line of chihuahuas, or a single Twinkie standing before four fat kids, or a simple ad going up against a line of powerful One Show judges, or yes, even one man facing an ominous line of tanks. Yes, we all have our own Tianamen Squares. Ours just happens to be a lot less important than the real one. Thanks for this prestigious award.

IAN COHEN
GRANT HOLLAND
MATT PETERSON
MIKE PROCTOR

We wanted to stand out from the clutter of other ads featuring guys jumping off mountains.

Designed to look underground and subversive, the ad represented a shake up for the snowboarding industry, which traditionally sponsors established snowboarder teams to create their ads. It's a tough market to advertise to, and the aim was to have it not look like an ad.

one. a magazine, vol. II issue i

First, you must remember awards shows are not fair. They're a lot like life – the last time I checked, it's not fair either. We should remember that shows only reflect what went on last year, not what's happening now. They show what's been done, and the only real creative purpose of showing what's been done is to inspire us to take risks and fight battles for what hasn't been done yet. That's the purpose of shows.

BOB KUPERMAN
One Show Judge

GOLD AWARD
public service/
political newspaper or
magazine single

public service/
political newspaper or
magazine campaign

client
OUTWARD BOUND

agency
LOEFFLER KETCHUM
MOUNTJOY/CHARLOTTE

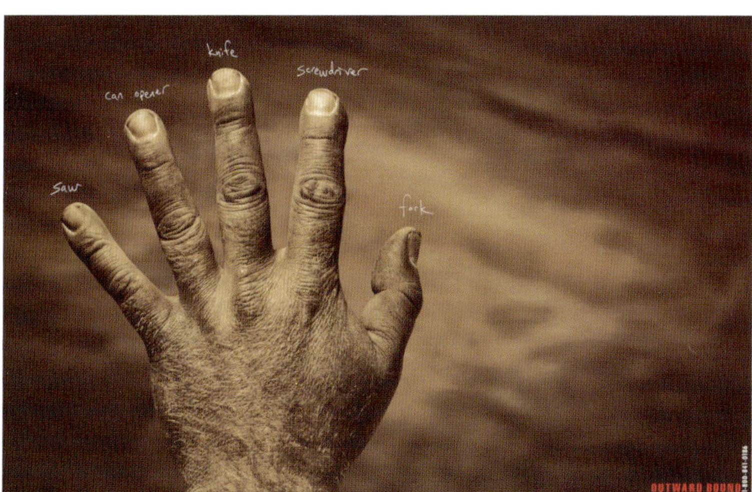

We were sitting around the woods one day when this concept just sort of crept up on us. It just goes to show, the best ideas are often the ones closest at hand.

Despite the fact that two writers worked on the campaign, this sentence contains more words than all three ads combined. Is this a great job or what?

DOUG PEDERSEN
CURTIS SMITH
MIKE DUCKWORTH

GOLD AWARD
collateral: point of purchase and in-store

client
SONY ELECTRONICS

agency
LOWE & PARTNERS/ SMS/NEW YORK

The brief said: "Reinforce Sony's image as an innovative and influential technology company with unparalleled vision and commitment to developing and providing proprietary, integrated technology in the emerging area of Technological Convergence."

Fortunately, the ads didn't come out saying that the same way.

DEAN HACOHEN
GARY GOLDSMITH

The thing to remember is that there will never be the perfect awards show. It's just a collection of people, who on that given day, have decided that a certain group of work was worthy of noting. A different group, on a different day, and you've got an entirely new show book.

JOHN VITRO
One Show Judge

GOLD AWARD
non-broadcast cinema
single

client
APPLE COMPUTER
agency
MOJO PARTNERS/
AUCKLAND

CD1 #28

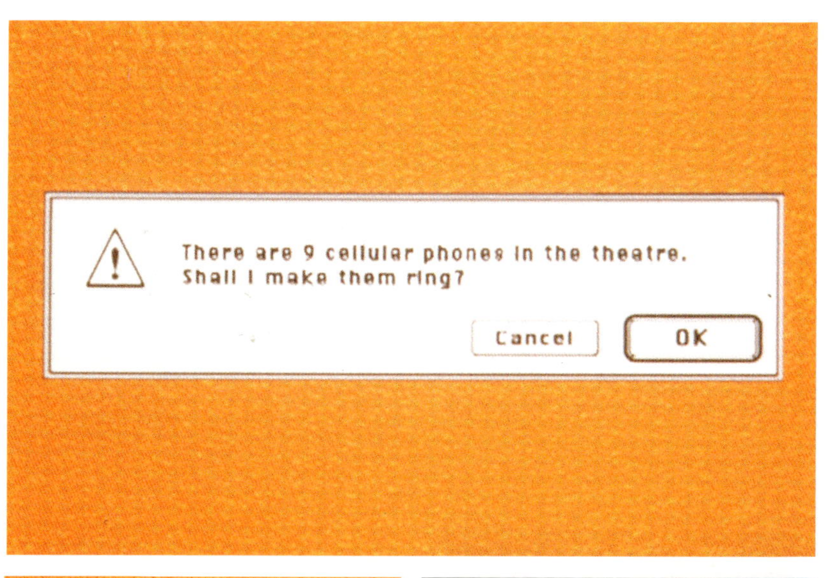

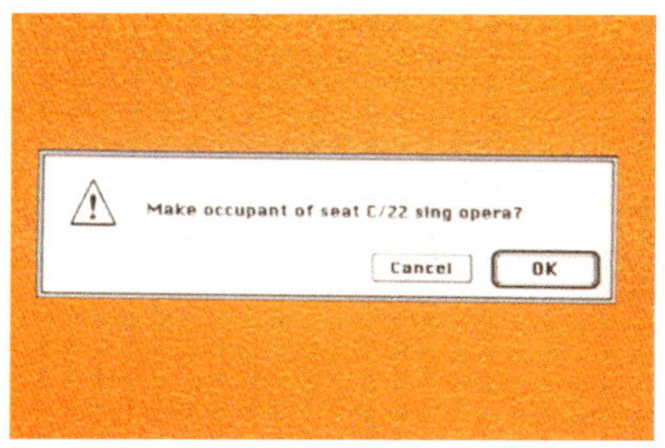

MULTIMEDIA DIALOGUE BOX: Play music? (OK/Cancel). OK selected.
SFX: Music track played.
DIALOGUE BOX: Left cinema speaker only? (OK/Cancel). OK selected.
SFX: Music and soundtrack is now played through left speaker only.
DIALOGUE BOX: Right cinema speaker only? (OK/Cancel). OK selected.
SFX: Music and soundtrack is now played through right speaker only.
DIALOGUE BOX: Stereo? (OK/Cancel). OK selected.
SFX: Music played in stereo again.
DIALOGUE BOX: Lights on? (OK/Cancel). OK selected. Lights go on.
DIALOGUE BOX: Lights off? (OK/Cancel). OK selected. Lights go off.
DIALOGUE BOX: Lights on? (OK/Cancel). OK selected. Lights go on.
DIALOGUE BOX: There are 9 cellular phones in the theater. Shall I make them ring? (OK/Cancel). OK selected.
SFX: 9 cellular phones ring.
DIALOGUE BOX: Stop phones ringing? (OK/Cancel). OK selected.
SFX: Phones all stop ringing at once.
DIALOGUE BOX: Make occupant of seat C-15 sing opera? (OK/Cancel). OK selected.
SFX: Person in seat gets up and sings opera at top of voice.
DIALOGUE BOX: He sounds terrible. Shall I make him leave? (OK/Cancel). OK selected.
DIALOGUE BOX: Shut down? (OK/Cancel). OK selected. The Apple Rocketbook shuts down.
SUPER: The Apple Rocketbook. So much power, anything is possible.

We thought we had a rock-solid idea. One that would work across all media and especially in cinema. So, we took a trip into the projectionist's room...

"So this is where it all happens guys."
'Cool...um what's this button do?'
'Nothing any more.'
'Oh, what about this one?'
'That's the fire alarm?'
'Can we use that?'
'Not unless there's a fire.'
'Right...well you see we're launching a new laptop by Apple and we want to demonstrate how much power it has by making things happen in the cinema.'
'Right.'
'Like opening and closing the curtain. Can we do that?'
'We don't have curtains anymore.'
'Okay...how about turning the lights on and off then?'
'Sure...but they take five minutes to go on and five to go off. They're on slow dimmer.'
'Right...um what else can you do up here then?'
'Project the movie.'
'Mmmm...that's handy...we'll just go away and have a think...thanks a lot...'

So we spoke to the cinema's electrician, begging him to rig up different light systems that we could manipulate. A case of beer would do it. We asked them how their speakers worked. We didn't understand, so we spoke to our sound technician who then spoke to theirs.

Then we decided we had to bring in other things to the cinema we could control – like nine plastic "realistic sounding" mobile phones and a chubby guy who couldn't sing but would for NZ$50 a session.

Actually, he deserves a lot of the credit. He had to sit through countless sessions of Jurassic Park II. A lot more goes to our fantastic and very flexible client. But most of all it goes to the rest of Mojo Partners, Auckland. Without their hard work and dedication, nothing at all would have been possible.

MIKE O'SULLIVAN
RICHARD MADDOCKS
MURRAY WATT

GOLD AWARD
magazine: color full page or spread campaign

client
BRODERBUND SOFTWARE

agency
SAATCHI & SAATCHI/ SAN FRANCISCO

The client expected several pieces of information to be incorporated into the advertising:

a) the name of the new computer game
b) the fact that it was a sequel to another game
c) a reminder of how popular the original was
d) assurance that the sequel was even better
e) a Web address
f) a call to action
g) the client's logo

In other words, shine a bright light on the product so that everyone can see exactly what it is. And granted, sometimes that's a good idea. But in this case, that would have been counter-productive. Our audience was gamers and gamers tend to like things wrapped in a mystery and hidden in the shadows. Therefore, the advertising couldn't spell everything out; it had to challenge our target in the same way the actual game would. So we made ads that weren't meant to be read, but solved.

STEVE SILVER
JOE KAYSER
TOM BAGOT

Designed to evoke the game itself, each ad contains Riven's Web site address etched somewhere into the scenery, as well as a sheet of paper lying on the ground. These ads are aimed at avid games fanatics and the paper is a salute to the earlier Myst.

one. a magazine, vol. II issue i

Awards shows are good for the industry. They keep us treating advertising like an art, instead of just another business. That being said, awards shows aren't perfect – even the good ones. This is a highly subjective business. A show is only as good as its judges.

MIKE SHINE
One Show Judge

GOLD AWARD
public service/
political television: single

client
COMPANION ANIMAL PLACEMENT

agency
SUBURBAN ADVERTISING/ JERSEY CITY

CD1 #1

MUSIC: Born Free
SUPER: That's the great thing about pets. They really don't care. Adopt today. Companion Animal Placement.

We were shocked by the number of dogs and cats killed in shelters every day just because the people who wanted them decided they didn't anymore. So we spoke to the ASPCA about an assignment. They said thank you, but they were happy to be using delightful cartoon animals in their ads. (And who could improve on that?) We then called Wendy Neu, director of Companion Animal Placement, one of the smaller adoption groups in New York City. Wendy had two overflowing shelters and almost no money to keep the animals alive. We came up with an idea, she liked it, and she even thanked us for it. If more clients were as passionate and focused as Wendy there'd be a lot more award-winning work that worked for the client, too. Thank you, Wendy, and everybody who donated their time and talents to this project: Steve Miller, Rick LeMoine, Tony Cantali, Jackie Kelman, Mary Gormely, Sarah Downes and Gregg DeSilvio. And big thanks to Snuffy for running around the beach with that guy (albeit after being coaxed out of his trailer with a 12-pound flank steak).

ERIC ARONIN
DAVE LADEN
JOHN WAGNER

GOLD AWARD
outdoor: campaign

client
APPLE COMPUTER

agency
TBWA CHIAT/DAY/
VENICE

GOLD ON GOLD

Apple is a company that makes incredible tools. People consider them to be far more than just a computer company. An Apple is not a machine you sit at just to crank out spreadsheets or e-mail (although it does that well). An Apple is the machine you use to create. It is used to make art, to make films, to make music, to make designs, to make news, to make Web sites, to make interactive games...to make history.

When we talked to people both who own computers and who don't have Macs or who have PCs – the response was the same...There are computers that just get the job done and then...well, there are Apples. And Apple computers are different.

However, the Apple and the Macintosh brands have not been safeguarded properly in recent years. The industry and the market have certainly changed, but the deep human truths that steer people to true values and to what they believe in do not change. The love of exploration and the innovation that people have associated with Apple from the beginning is still very much there.

This is why we developed this tribute to the true creative heroes of our world and why it was important to us to get this campaign out visually on the street where people live. This project, which was created under a very tight time frame, was a coming together of many talented people who researched, edited, designed and produced this work in collaboration with those we are paying tribute to, their estates, and their photographers. In honor of those who have changed the world and taken part, Apple Computer has provided their tools to creative geniuses of the future and to organizations that dare to make a difference.

LEE CLOW
JESSICA SCHULMAN

A lot of people ask us what a bunch of dead guys have to do with computers.

Tsch...what a dumb question.

CRAIG TANIMOTO
ERIC GRUNBAUM

GOLD AWARD
college competition

college
VCU ADCENTER/
RICHMOND

Assignment: Pastamatic - automatic pasta machine campaign

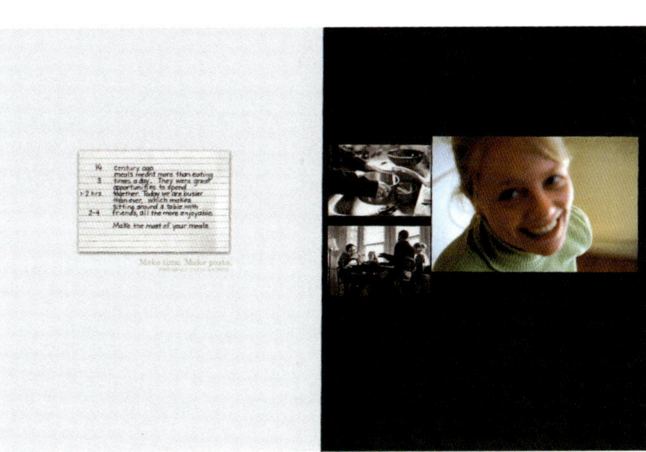

We received the 1981 gold pencil - winning Pastamatic ad, "Nobody makes pasta, fasta."

We went home. Matt called and said, "I've got it – maybe we can better the original concept by giving it legs." He came over. We worked through the night to come up with three new ads. "Are you ready, for fresh spaghetti?" "You'll like the Pastamatic, so it won't end up in your attic." "Pasta that's so good, you'll clean your plate."

(The third ad is always the hardest.)

We showed them to our creative director, Jelly Helm. He frowned. A week later we realized, people aren't buying pastamakers because they like fresh pasta. They're buying them because they like the idea of spending time in the kitchen with friends and family. We developed a way to communicate this idea in print. Matt photographed people making and enjoying pasta. I turned our sentiments into recipes. We finessed the layouts. Jelly smiled.

KEVIN PROUDFOOT
MATT STEIN

GOLD AWARD
consumer television
over :30 single

consumer television
varying lengths campaign

client
NIKE

agency
WIEDEN & KENNEDY/
PORTLAND

CD1 #4 & #22

We all know this campaign would've been turd-esque without Jan Hooks. But the other big reason it turned out well, the less obvious reason, was the chemistry on the set.

Jesse Peretz, the director, is a very mellow, easy-going guy with a very unintimidating presence. The athletes really liked him and really trusted him.

Jan Hooks was very collaborative and very easy to work with, which is surprising with someone of her stature.

And finally, the athletes. Athletes, as you can imagine, can be whiney, egotistical, and disinterested. On this job, we had five of the biggest names in sports, but there were absolutely no ego problems whatsoever. Perhaps they were all intimidated by each other's presence. Or by Larry Frey's presence. Who knows. But they took direction, gave us a million takes, and didn't demand any weird food for lunch. They also showed up having memorized their scripts, and were actually quizzing each other between shots. The point is, the chemistry on the set was great – everyone got along and had a great time – and we think it shows.

KILPATRICK ANDERSON
JAMES LEMAITRE

MODERATOR: People make fun of you because you're fast, because you wear Zoom Air. Well, let's turn the tables, let's pretend that I'm slow. I want you to insult me. Come on, Michael?
MICHAEL JOHNSON: You Turtle.
MODERATOR: Uh...Oh! Ouch! (laughing) Gary?
GARY PAYTON: Slow Poke.
MODERATOR: Good, only you can help you people...Okay, Al, I'm slow.
AL UNSER, JR.: Ketchup Bottle.
MODERATOR: Very good. Come on. Let out the aggression.
MICHAEL JOHNSON: Mr. Slow Pants.
MODERATOR: Okay, that's great!
GAIL DEVERS: Hey, Molasses!
MODERATOR: That kind of hit BOINNNNGGG, right between the eyes. Isn't this fun? Michael, come on, I can take it!
MICHAEL JOHNSON: Mrs. Butterworth.
MODERATOR: Mrs. Butterworth! She's slow! (laughing).
GARY PAYTON: Jerk.
MODERATOR: Okay, you said that with conviction, but I can take it 'cause I'm a professional.
SUPER: Thin, light, responsive Zoom Air.

MODERATOR: Gail, I believe it was your week to write something.
GAIL DEVERS: A faraway land by Gail Devers. Once upon a time there was a faraway land. A land where everyone was equal. Where people, fast and slow, could join hands and sing in harmony. Where you were judged by the size of your heart, not the size of your lead. Where people looked past the Zoom Air in your shoes and saw the real you. The end.
MODERATOR: Words can be powerful. Michael, hold my hand.
SUPER: Thin, light, responsive Zoom Air.

MODERATOR: You all wear Zoom Air. You're all aware that it's thin, light and responsive. So how do you feel about having to wear shoes that make you even faster? Gary? Conflicting emotions?
GARY PAYTON: I keep telling myself I'm doing it for the team. They need me to be explosive. But sometimes that's not enough. The hardest part is putting them on. When I'm lacing them up, I try to think about happy things. Like ice cream. Or puppies.
CHEF KOJI: Or shrimp.
MODERATOR: Gary, you are one sweet guy. Did everyone hear the puppy part?
SUPER: Thin, light, responsive Zoom Air.

One of the actors, the guy who played the sushi chef, ad-libbed some really bizarre, really funny "insults," when asked to think of some nicknames for slow people. And although they didn't make it to the final cut, a few of them are worth noting.

Among them "wounded bird" and "lava...at the end."

"Lava...at the end." Think about it. Lava gets really slow at the end of its trip down the side of a mountain, when it starts to cool off.

That's really funny. And then when you start to think about it as an actual nickname, it gets even funnier: "Hey, lava, at the end!" Or, "What's up, lava at the end?"

KILPATRICK ANDERSON
JAMES LEMAITRE

GOLD AWARD
consumer television
over :30 campaign

consumer television
under $50,000 budget
single

client
SEATTLE
SUPERSONICS

agency
WONGDOODY/SEATTLE

CD1 #25 & #8

If only they'd done this well against the Lakers.

DEAN SALING
FRANK CLARK

SUPER: The Sonics are coming to your home.
GARY: How y'all doin'?
RESIDENTS: Fine!
GARY: Huh? Oh, okay.
WOMAN 1: I always thought you were awfully thin.
WOMAN 2: Put your thread in back.
GARY: Put the thread in back? Like that?
WOMAN 3: Nooo...
GARY: Y-you own it. No...nobody own it. You wanna buy it? Okay, that's $400. You can have it now.
WOMAN 4: She's kinda tight with her money.
SUPER: See them in your home.
GARY: Ohhh...You been practicin'! (laughs).
SUPER: 56 games on free TV.
MAN: Go Sonics!

SUPER: The Sonics are coming to your home.
NATE: I heard there was a Tupperware party going on here!
TUPPERWARE LADY: There is a Tupperware party!
NATE: Am I a little late? My name is Nate McMillan and my favorite piece of Tupperware is the Cake Taker. I love making cakes.
TUPPERWARE LADY: And you push and you'll hear a burp. Are you ready? And the thing about the Modular Mate containers is that...
TUPPERWARE LADY: Yes?
NATE: Can you wash these in the dishwasher?
TUPPERWARE LADY: Yes, you can. Thank you for asking.
NATE: Oh, great!
TUPPERWARE LADY: And what's really great about the Remarkabowl is that the outside of it is rubberized. And it feels like a basketball that's been used on the cement.
NATE: Mmm...That's pretty good!
WOMAN: And you play quarterback, right?
NATE: (surprised) I play q...what?
SUPER: See them in your home.
NATE: I appreciate you having me. I really did enjoy myself. I did. Do you have a box or something for me?
SUPER: 56 games on free TV.
TUPPERWARE LADY: Go Sonics!

SUPER: The Sonics are coming to your home.
SAM: Just knock on the door?
CREW GUY: Just knock on the door.
MOM: Oh my goodness!
SAM: Wassup!
MOM: Nice to meet you!
SAM: You too.
DAD: Say hi to Big Smooth!
JORDAN: You wanna see my Chicago Bulls jersey?
SAM: Yeah. This is...this is what he has. We gonna wash this. We gonna wash this in here, okay?
JORDAN: No!
SAM: You the man!
JORDAN: Yeah–gimme the ball!
SAM: C'mon, be the man!
SAM: Oh, they ran a play on you! Where you at, man?
JORDAN: (giggles)
SAM: Okay, a little low-five, then!
JORDAN: Um, Sam? Did you bring your pajamas?
SAM: Hmm?
JORDAN: Did you bring your pajamas? I wanna be on TV!
SAM: Yeah...whatever.
SUPER: See them in your home.
MOM: Okay, time to go to bed! Sam, stop that! In the bed, now!
SUPER: 56 games on free TV.
JORDAN: Go Sonics!

The answers to the questions we've been asked most since we did this campaign:

1) Yes, the spots are finished.
2) No, they're not actors.
3) Frank's dining room table.
4) A jock strap and a sailor cap.
5) No, they didn't know the players were coming.
6) Rebecca Romijn and a bathtub full of lime Jello.
7) No, we never dreamed they'd be this successful.
8) Sporty Spice.
9) No, we have absolutely no idea what to do next season.
10) Yes, you can shoot on video and win a gold pencil.

DEAN SALING
FRANK CLARK

PRINT MERIT

MERIT AWARD
newspaper over 600 lines
single

art director
MARCELLO SERPA
writer
EUGENIO MOHALLEM
photgrapher
APPLE ARCHIVE
client
APPLE COMPUTER
BRAZIL
agency
ALMAP/BBDO/
SÃO PAULO

Why are the ads for IBM created on a Macintosh?

Na hora de fazer anúncios para mostrar o quanto seus computadores são bons, a concorrência prefere usar os nossos: o Power Macintosh é o computador mais usado em publicidade no mundo inteiro. A esmagadora maioria dos anúncios que você vê numa revista é feita num Power Macintosh. Talvez porque o Macintosh seja, na prática, tudo o que a propaganda dos outros computadores afirma: mais simples, mais rápido, mais versátil e mais compatível com outras plataformas. O único que pode dar a uma agência de publicidade a agilidade que ela precisa para satisfazer clientes muito exigentes. Como, por exemplo, uma IBM.

Apple

PRINT MERIT

MERIT AWARD
newspaper over 600 lines
single

art directors
RINGO WONG
RON CHEUNG
writer
STEVEN LEE
illustrator
SNAPSHOT DIGITAL ART
client
JAGUAR HONG KONG
agency
BATES/HONG KONG

MERIT AWARD
newspaper over 600 lines
single

art director
PAUL BELFORD
writer
NIGEL ROBERTS
photographer
LAURIE HASKELL
client
WATERSTONE'S
BOOKSELLERS
agency
BDDP.GGT/LONDON

PRINT MERIT

MERIT AWARD
newspaper over 600 lines
single

art director
PAUL BELFORD
writer
NIGEL ROBERTS
photographers
JAMES NACHTWEY
LAURIE HASKELL

client
WATERSTONE'S
BOOKSELLERS
agency
BDDP.GGT/LONDON

MERIT AWARD
newspaper over 600 lines
single

art director
PAUL BELFORD
writer
NIGEL ROBERTS
photographers
LAURIE HASKELL
JOEL-PETER WITKIN
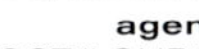
client

WATERSTONE'S
BOOKSELLERS
agency
BDDP.GGT/LONDON

MERIT AWARD
newspaper over 600 lines
single

art director
JEREMY CRAIGEN
writer
JEREMY CRAIGEN
client
ANHEUSER-BUSCH
agency
BMP DDB/LONDON

MERIT AWARD
newspaper over 600 lines
single

art director
DAVE DYE
writer
SEAN DOYLE
photographer
GEOF KERN
client
SONY
agency
BMP DDB/LONDON

MERIT AWARD
newspaper over 600 lines
single

art director
DAVE DYE
writer
SEAN DOYLE
photographer
GEOF KERN
client
SONY
agency
BMP DDB/LONDON

PRINT MERIT

MERIT AWARD
newspaper over 600 lines
single

art director
JOANNA WENLEY
writer
JEREMY CRAIGEN
illustrator
PAUL SLATER
client
VOLKSWAGEN
GROUP UK
agency
BMP DDB/LONDON

MERIT AWARD
newspaper over 600 lines
single

art director
PAUL SHARP
writer
PAUL TURNER
photographer
OXFORD SCIENTIFIC
FILMS
client
HONDA
agency
CDP/LONDON

MERIT AWARD
newspaper over 600 lines
single

art director
WAYNE BEST
writers
JEFF BITSACK
JOSH MILLER
ADAM CHASNOW
illustrator
STEVEN GARCIA
client
LITTLE CAESARS
agency
CLIFF FREEMAN &
PARTNERS/NEW YORK

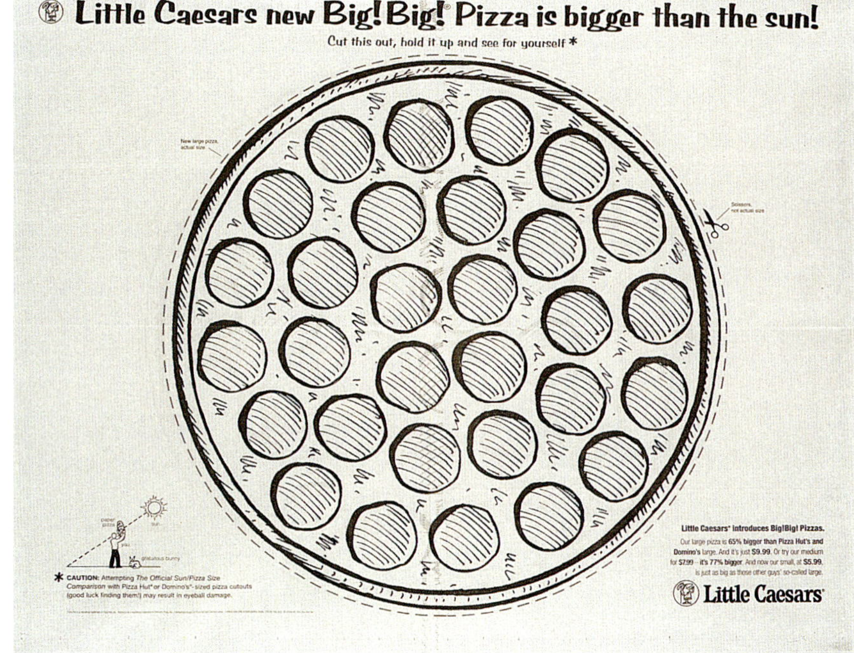

MERIT AWARD
newspaper over 600 lines
single

art director
BRIAN STEWART
writer
MARK WALDRON
photographer
VIC HUBER
client
CHRYSLER
agency
DELANEY FLETCHER
BOZELL/LONDON

MERIT AWARD
newspaper over 600 lines
single

art director
RONNIE BROWN
writer
PETER KEW
photographer
CHRIS SIMPSON
client
CHRYSLER
agency
DELANEY FLETCHER
BOZELL/LONDON

PRINT MERIT

MERIT AWARD
newspaper over 600 lines
single

art directors
JOHN DOYLE
MARY AVERY

writer
KARA GOODRICH

photographer
GEOFF STEIN

client
SHREVE CRUMP & LOW

agency
DOYLE, INC./WESTON

The holidays are over. It's months until your birthday. Think. Think.

You want it. There. That's reason enough to purchase yourself something from the Dilaro jewelry collection. And what woman wouldn't want something this collection has to offer? There are huggie earrings sprinkled liberally with diamonds. A Roman drop pendant suitable for an emperor's wife. Matte 18k gold finish rings with Rhodolite garnets, sapphires and diamonds. These are stackable rings which complement the stackable gemstone bracelets. (And, no, two does not constitute a stack.)

Designer John Apel, the master craftsman of Dilaro, has once again utilized precious metals and stones to artfully express the relationship between art and nature. Let the gold come in waves and let the stones create small rock piles in your jewelry box. Better still, his concept translates to jewelry that is appropriate for almost any occasion and surprisingly affordable. And, in Massachusetts, this amazing collection is exclusive to Shreve, Crump & Low. South Dakota's Statehood Day? National Tuba Day? Grover Cleveland's Birthday? (Actual or observed?) Never mind. Justification really is such a nag. Instead just select a special piece from the Dilaro Collection and then mark the day with bright red ink on your calendar. And, next year you can celebrate the occasion in the customary way: by purchasing another.

SHREVE, CRUMP & LOW

Two floors. And who knows how many stories.

MERIT AWARD
newspaper over 600 lines
single

art directors
JOHN DOYLE
MICHELLE CARACCIA

writer
KARA GOODRICH

photographer
GEOFF STEIN

clients
SHREVE CRUMP & LOW

agency
DOYLE, INC./WESTON

Decidedly not the week to renounce all worldly goods.

Oh, no, not now, not this week, not ever. How impregnable would the human heart need to be to resist the beauty and charm of a piece from the Damiani Collection? Far more unbreachable than your own.

It is marvelous, is it not? The sparkle of myriad diamonds conjoined within 18k white gold ringlets of 18k white gold balls. Ultimately destined to encircle your wrist and heart, not necessarily in that order. Then there are the earrings. It would be a shame to break up a perfectly matched set. Which leads us naturally to the bold and singular ring. It is a vexing but glorious predicament.

Casa Damiani has been the source of the finest precious gem jewelry for over 40 years. Craftsmen, trained under the tutelage of Damiano Grassi himself, carry on the Italian tradition of goldsmithing harking back to the crowded Pontevecchio. Housed in a Palace in Milan (how appropriate) are masterworks in progress that will do no less than advance the art of jewelrymaking. They have the International awards to prove it. Yet, more importantly, Damiani has a following of zealous devotees who share one goal: Increasing their own personal prized collections. That can be done. Exclusively at Shreve, Crump & Low in New England. Eschew romance novels. Give up Rocky Road ice cream. Even forgo the temptation of sun worship. Just stop yourself short of disavowing your passion for wearing beautiful jewelry. At least for this week.

SHREVE, CRUMP & LOW

Two floors. And who knows how many stories.

MERIT AWARD
newspaper over 600 lines
single

art director
CAROL HENDERSON
writer
TOM ROSEN
photographer
MICHAEL RAUSCH
client
BMW OF NORTH AMERICA
agency
FALLON MCELLIGOTT/
MINNEAPOLIS

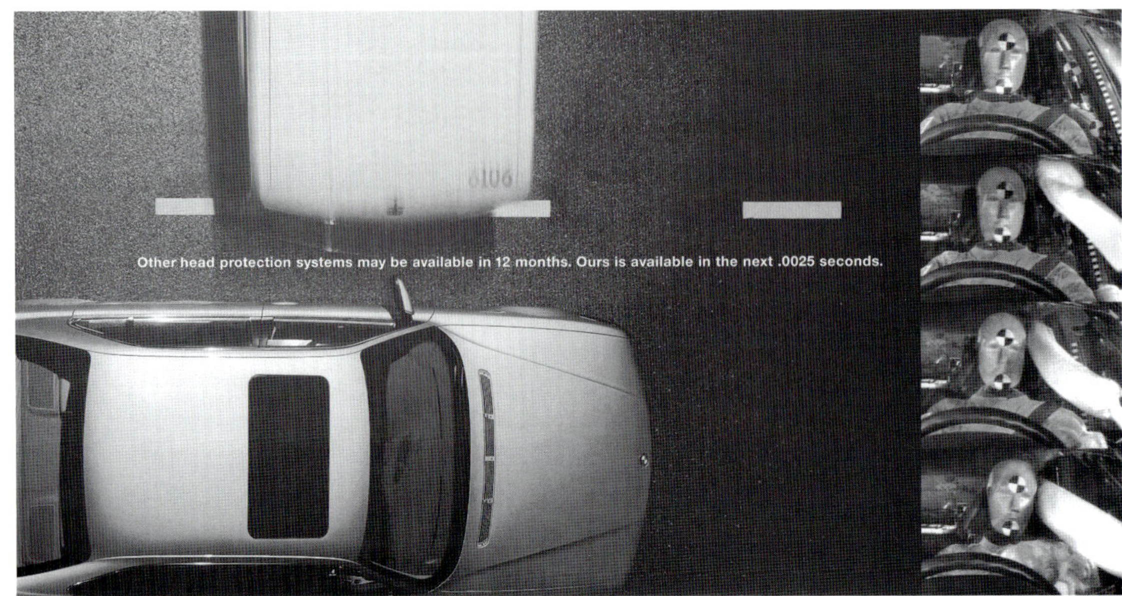

When it comes to your safety, timing is everything. Precisely why our 7 Series now comes equipped with the ITS head protection system. This is the only system that helps protect the head of the driver during side-impact collisions. Which is critical when you realize that 70% of side-impact collisions cause head injuries. It's part of our total safety philosophy that includes front and side-impact airbags, crush tubes and a rigid safety cage. BMW drivers are smart. And we intend to keep them that way.

The Ultimate Driving Machine®

MERIT AWARD
newspaper over 600 lines
single

art director
MIKKO TIMONEN
writer
FILIP NILSSON
photographer
HÅKAN LUDWIGSSON
client
VOLVO PB SVERIGE/
VOLVO V40
agency
FORSMAN &
BODENFORS/
GOTHENBURG

VOLVO

MERIT AWARD
newspaper over 600 lines
single

art director
MIKKO TIMONEN
writer
FILIP NILSSON
client
VOLVO PB SVERIGE/
VOLVO C70
agency
FORSMAN &
BODENFORS/
GOTHENBURG

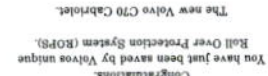

VOLVO

MERIT AWARD
newspaper over 600 lines
single

art director
STEVE TOM
writer
BRIAN HAYES
photographer
CORBIS-BETTMAN
client
THE BOSTON GLOBE
agency
INGALLS ADVERTISING/
BOSTON

DR. KING LEADS CIVIL RIGHTS DEMONSTRATORS, 5,000 STRONG, OUT OF CAMP ON THE SELMA-TO-MONTGOMERY MARCH.

DOCTORS

PRESCRIBE WALKING TO

TREAT MANY ILLNESSES.

DR. KING USED IT

TO CURE RACISM.

There are many benefits to walking. One use, as Dr. Martin Luther King Jr. proved, is as an instrument of social protest. Inspired by Mohandas Gandhi's principle of passive resistance, Dr. King embraced the notion of nonviolent direct action. His march on Washington, involving 250,000 marchers (60,000 whites), was the largest civil rights demonstration in history. And his five day march from Selma to Montgomery brought civil rights into every household in America. This kind of direct action, in Dr. King's words, "creates the kind of tension in society that will help men rise from the dark depths of prejudice and racism to the majestic heights of understanding and brotherhood." Today we remember his contribution to making this world a better place to live.

The Boston Globe

PRINT MERIT

MERIT AWARD
newspaper over 600 lines
single

art director
JIM O'BRIEN
writer
MARTIN DAVIDSON
client
THE BOSTON GLOBE
agency
INGALLS ADVERTISING/
BOSTON

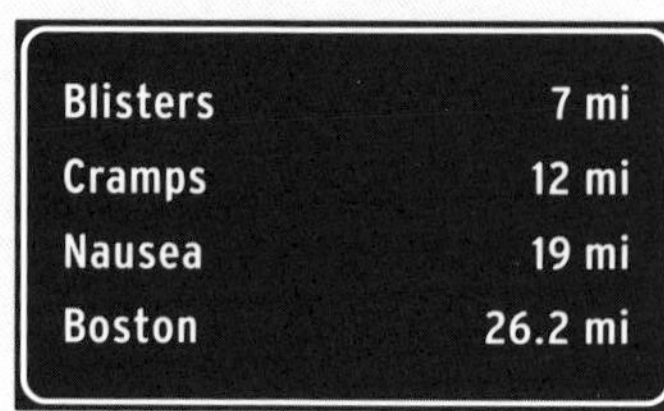

The Boston Marathon. For over 100 years, The Globe has brought you the stories behind the stamina of the country's most famous footrace. Look for interviews. Analysis. And special sections. It's the most exhaustive coverage of the race you can get without having to run it yourself.

THE 101ST BOSTON MARATHON

MERIT AWARD
newspaper over 600 lines
single

art director
PETER NICHOLSON
writer
SCOTT WILD
client
ADIDAS AMERICA
agency
LEAGAS DELANEY/
SAN FRANCISCO

MERIT AWARD
newspaper over 600 lines
single

art director
YOONG SEOW FONG

writers
ADRIAN MILLER
SIMON BEAUMONT

illustrator
UNTOLD IMAGES

photographer
BARNEY STUDIO

client
LAND ROVER/MALAYSIA

agency
LEO BURNETT/
KUALA LUMPUR

OBITUARIES

THE FILM

Worked with the world's greatest photographers: Cartier Bresson, Doisneau, Penn.

THE NEGATIVES

The negatives (born February 26, 1835) have ceased to exist, due to Olympus now allowing pictures to be stored on computer disc.

Negatives: very fragile, requiring careful handling.

THE DARKROOM

The enlarger: just one of the components of a well equipped darkroom.

The life of the darkroom (born March 2, 1835) has been cut short with prints that come direct from the Olympus digital camera.

THE 1 HOUR PROCESSING SERVICE

The 1 Hour processing service (born June 3, 1981) has passed away with the arrival of the 3 second processing service, courtesy of Olympus digital cameras.

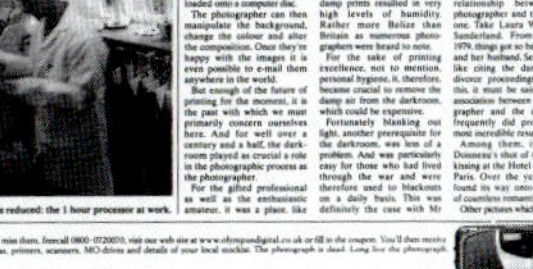

The wait for pictures reduced: the 1 hour processor at work.

OLYMPUS DIGITAL SYSTEMS

MERIT AWARD
newspaper over 600 lines
single

art director
GARY MARSHALL

writer
PAUL MARSHALL

photographer
ROBERT WALKER

client
OLYMPUS

agency
LOWE HOWARD-SPINK/
LONDON

MERIT AWARD
newspaper over 600 lines
single

art director
JIM CARROLL

writers
TOM MILLER
EDDIE VAN BLOEM

client
ESPNEWS

agency
LOWE & PARTNERS/
SMS/NEW YORK

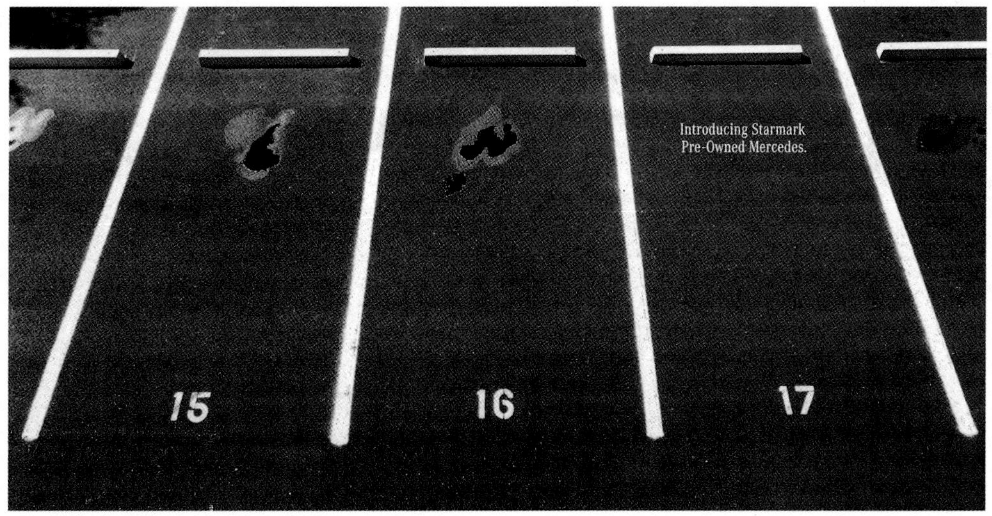

An oil leak here, some brake fluid over there, and—what's that funny, clicking sound? Ah, the joys of owning a used car. Unless, of course, it's a Starmark Pre-Owned Mercedes. With its rigorous inspections, road tests, and reconditioning. Its standard 12-month limited warranty, extendable up to 48 months/100,000 miles.* Even its 7-day/500-mile exchange privilege.** All of which help to provide you with a stress-free driving experience—not to mention a stain-free parking space. Visit your local Starmark certified Mercedes-Benz dealer or call 1-800-FOR-MERCEDES.

STARMARK
PRE-OWNED MERCEDES-BENZ

MERIT AWARD
newspaper over 600 lines
single

art director
CHRIS BRIGNOLA

writer
JOHN BROCKENBROUGH

client
MERCEDES-BENZ OF NORTH AMERICA

agency
LOWE & PARTNERS/SMS/NEW YORK

PRINT MERIT

MERIT AWARD
newspaper over 600 lines
single

art director
GRACE LERNER

writer
JAY SHARFSTEIN

photographer
BRIAN KOSOFF

client
PERDUE FARMS

agency
LOWE & PARTNERS/SMS/NEW YORK

The government has a name for chickens that don't live up to Perdue standards.

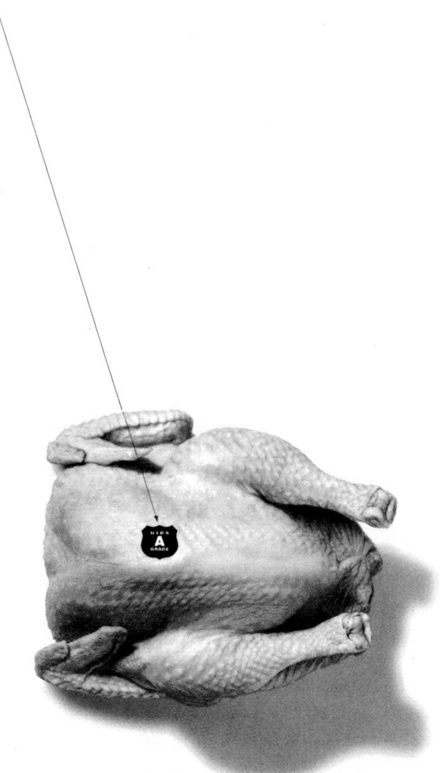

The U.S. government requires 43 quality inspections before a chicken can be called Grade A. Not bad. But not good enough for Perdue. We subject our chickens to 65 tough quality inspections – 22 more than the government says we have to. Why do we take all this extra time and effort to put our birds through such rigorous inspections? Because we know that they'll pass them.

MERIT AWARD
newspaper over 600 lines
single

art director
DAVE COOK

writer
DEACON WEBSTER

photographers
JEFF GLANZ
MATTHEW HUBER

client
NEW YORK
RESTAURANT GROUP

agency
MAD DOGS &
ENGLISHMEN/
NEW YORK

It ain't Hooters.

MERIT AWARD
newspaper over 600 lines
single

art director
TOM KIM

writer
JIM SCHMIDT

photographer
ALLAN SHORTALL

client
ILLINOIS POWER

agency
MCCONNAUGHY STEIN
SCHMIDT BROWN/
CHICAGO

{ILLINOIS POWER • COMMUNITY INVOLVEMENT}

Thanks, you know, to our, uh, you know, literacy programs, hopefully, you know, fewer kids will, um, you know, talk like this.

At Illinois Power, we realize there's nothing more important than making sure the kids of today are prepared to be the adults of tomorrow. That's why we make an extra effort to support education in the communities we serve through our Teacher Grant Program. Partnering with teachers, as well as parents and students, our efforts have touched on everything from reading and science to ethnic diversity and after-school athletics. The way we see it, the more confident today's students are in their academic skills, the better off everyone will be. You know? For more information, visit us at www.illinova.com.

ILLINOIS POWER
An Illinova Company

{WE'RE HERE FOR YOU}

PRINT MERIT

MERIT AWARD
newspaper over 600 lines
single

art director
MIKE FERRER

writer
TIM SPROUL

photographer
MARK HOOPER

client
PORTLAND BREWING
COMPANY

agency
MOFFATT/ROSENTHAL/
PORTLAND

MERIT AWARD
newspaper over 600 lines
single

art director
MIKE FERRER

writer
TIM SPROUL

photographer
MARK HOOPER

client
PORTLAND BREWING
COMPANY

agency
MOFFATT/ROSENTHAL/
PORTLAND

MERIT AWARD
newspaper over 600 lines
single

art director
JOOST HULSBOSCH

writer
MARK VARDER

client
REEBOK

agency
SONNENBERG MURPHY
LEO BURNETT/
JOHANNESBURG

This is an unusually long headline for a print ad. With good reason though. By the time you've read from the first word to the last, including all these words you're trying to hurry past right now - you are, aren't you? - anyway, as we were saying, by the time you get to the last word, you'll have an idea of just how much time Elana Meyer carved off a world record - a world record - not just 0,2 seconds or 2,2 seconds - when she competed in a half marathon in Tokyo on Sunday, running in a pair of Reeboks.

Most people will take just over 20 seconds to read the headline above. Last Sunday Elana Meyer returned to international athletics in Tokyo by slicing an incredible 22 seconds off the woman's world half-marathon record. She covered 21,1 kilometres in 67 minutes 36 seconds. But then she is Elana Meyer. And she was running in the best shoes on earth.

www.reebok.com

MERIT AWARD
newspaper over 600 lines
single

art directors
LEE CLOW
JESSICA SCHULMAN

writers
ROB SILTANEN
STEVE JOBS
KEN SEGALL

photographers
MAGNUM PHOTO
ARCHIVE PHOTOS
TIME LIFE
BETTMAN ARCHIVE
NASA
EDISON HISTORIC SITE

client
APPLE COMPUTER

agency
TBWA CHIAT/DAY/
VENICE

To the crazy ones.

Here's to the crazy ones.
The misfits.
The rebels.
The troublemakers.
The round pegs in the square holes.
The ones who see things differently.

They're not fond of rules.
And they have no respect for the status quo.

You can praise them, disagree with them, quote them,
disbelieve them, glorify them or vilify them.
About the only thing you can't do is ignore them.

Because they change things.
They invent. They imagine. They heal.
They explore. They create. They inspire.
They push the human race forward.

Maybe they have to be crazy.
How else can you stare at an empty canvas and see a work of art?
Or sit in silence and hear a song that's never been written?
Or gaze at a red planet and see a laboratory on wheels?

We make tools for these kinds of people.
While some see them as the crazy ones, we see genius.

Because the people who are crazy enough to think they can
change the world, are the ones who do.

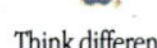

Think different.

PRINT MERIT

TOASTMASTERS: (011) 672 8817

MERIT AWARD
newspaper over 600 lines
single

art director
PORKY HEFER

writer
SUE ANDERSON

illustrators
PORKY HEFER
CANDICE WADDELL

client
TOASTMASTERS

agency
TBWA HUNT LASCARIS/
JOHANNESBURG

THE NEW GASTON AMBULATORY SURGERY CENTER. THE BEST PART IS WE'LL HAVE YOU IN AND OUT OF HERE BEFORE DINNER.

Outpatient surgery is the specialty of the day. It's more efficient. More convenient. And certainly more cost effective. Which is why Gaston Memorial has created a new area devoted solely to outpatient services. The Gaston Ambulatory Surgery Center. While it's connected to the main hospital, this new center has six large operating rooms of its own, eighteen private patient rooms and a separate pediatric unit. Patients usually arrive about an hour before treatment and leave a couple of hours after surgery. It's that easy. And it's all part of our mission to provide the people of the Gaston region with high-quality medical care that's still easily accessible. The same reason we've brought in 35 new surgeons over the past five years from some of the top medical schools in the country. And now our staff of over 70 surgeons perform more than 10,000 procedures on almost every part of the body, every year. Many of them before mealtime.

Gaston Health Care
WE'RE HERE FOR LIFE

MERIT AWARD
newspaper over 600 lines
single

art director
JENNIFER APPLEBY

writer
TOM COCKE

photographer
MIKE CARROLL

client
GASTON HEALTH CARE

agency
WRAY WARD LASETER/
CHARLOTTE

MERIT AWARD
newspaper over 600 lines
campaign

art director
DAVE DYE

writer
SEAN DOYLE

photographer
GEOF KERN

client
SONY

agency
BMP DDB/LONDON

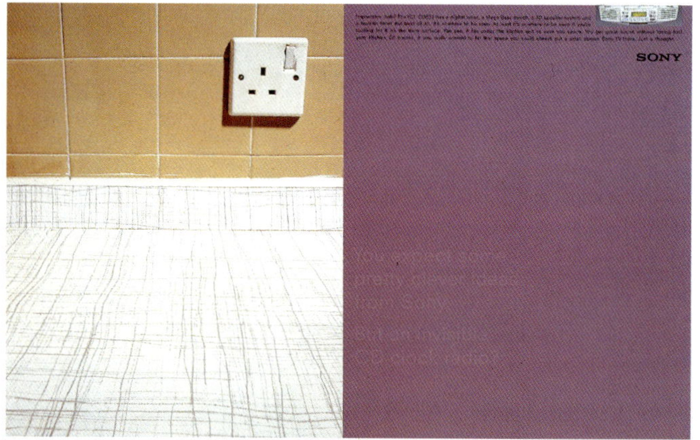

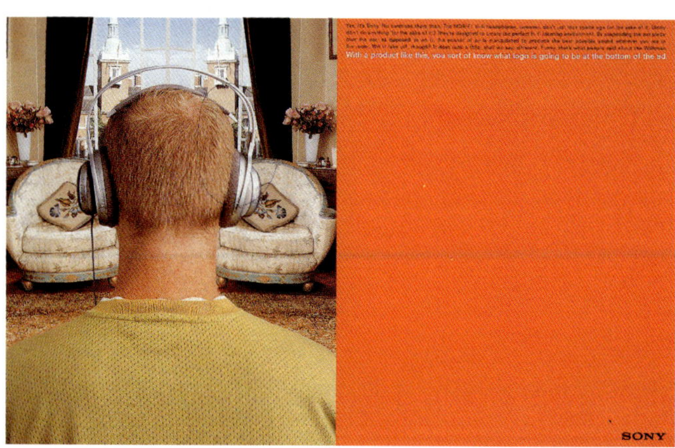

MERIT AWARD
newspaper over 600 lines
campaign

art directors
MARK ROSENTHAL
TONYA RINEHART

writers
DAVE REYBURN
SCOTT BOSWELL
ALEX MURRAY

illustrator
JIM SHERIDAN

client
KENTUCKY STATE FAIR

agency
CREATIVE ALLIANCE/
LOUISVILLE

PRINT MERIT

MERIT AWARD
newspaper over 600 lines
campaign

art director
TONY CALCAO

writer
SCOTT LINNEN

photographer
PHILIP-JON

client
SHIMANO AMERICAN CORPORATION

agency
CRISPIN PORTER & BOGUSKY/MIAMI

MERIT AWARD
newspaper over 600 lines
campaign

art directors
NICOLAS VONTOBEL
EDI ANDRIST
writer
CLAUDE CATSKY
client
TA MEDIA AG
agency
MCCANN-ERICKSON/
ZURICH

MERIT AWARD
newspaper over 600 lines
campaign

art directors
VIKAS GAITONDE
KANAD BANERJEE

writer
ALOK NANDA

illustrator
PRASHANT KANYALKAR

client
MAURITIUS TOURISM
INFORMATION SERVICE

agency
TRIKAYA GREY
ADVERTISING
INDIA/MUMBAI

The laziest man in the world contest.

Enter this contest, and you could win two free tickets to Mauritius, and a stay for three nights at the 5-star Maritim Hotel.

See, most contest ads with 'offers' like this tuck in a complicated set of rules, deep into paragraph 12.

Not us.

We know you're too lazy to go out and buy three plastic spoons or some such rubbish to make you eligible to enter.

There are no purchases necessary. No complicated entry forms to fill out.

All we seek is your enthusiasm. Or better still, the lack of it. Our objective is to identify the laziest specimen of the human species and steer him towards his natural habitat: Mauritius.

WHAT TO DO. (OR NOT TO.)

You'll have to lift a pen in your right hand. Unless you're left-handed. If this is too tiring, get someone else to lift the pen.

Then we could begin by asking you difficult questions. Like 'Why do you want to go to Mauritius?'

This tiny island off the coast of Africa has been around for four million years. And yet, has one tourist per mile of beach to show for it.

Hardly inspiring, right?

There are no hordes of camera-clicking tourists.

What are they going to click anyway? Palm trees? Crystal blue waters? White sand? Oh, come on.

In fact, not much activity has taken place since the Dutch first landed on the island in 1638. Vast tracts of tropical jungle lie preserved in time.

This leads us to the next question we could possibly ask you: 'What does one do in Mauritius?'

The Mauritians, with enough time on their hands, have figured out the meaning of life. It's a philosophy that can be summed up in two words: pina colada. (Preferably made from Green Island rum.)

This is best served with a white hammock or deck chair, and a dash of setting sun.

Not all Mauritians abide by this culture, though. Like all nations, we have our wayward lot.

A few uncouth characters are known to take advantage of this idyllic setting.

And indulge in frenzied watersports like sailing, yachting, snorkelling and deep-sea diving. Or dancing the sega on the beach with wild abandon.

Now you know there *are* things to do in Mauritius.

But this contest is for the laziest man. Is this a devious trap? Are you being set-up?

Or more importantly, when faced with such brain-taxing questions, do you think of food?

FOOD.

One of the lesser known facts about Mauritius is that it is home to five different cuisines.

The lazy person will immediately jump (er, sorry) to the conclusion that there is no need to visit China, England, France, Africa, or the southern coast of India for a gourmet tour.

In fact, Mauritians have added some rather exotic home-grown delights to the menu. Like heart of palm, smoked blue marlin and octopus chutney.

The best part is, the lazy man need never cook for himself. There are enough restaurants and small cafés along the seafront.

HOW TO GET THERE.

If you've made it this far, you are obviously a Type A personality, full of zeal, vigour and perseverance. Tch, tch. Shame. These qualities could disqualify you immediately. Proceed from here with caution.

1) Did you actually read this advertisement? (Tick one.)
☐ Yes. ☐ No. ☐ Wake me up when this is over.
2) Who first inhabited Mauritius?
☐ The Dutch ☐ Does it matter?
3) Name four watersport activities you would absolutely not indulge in: ______, ______, ______, ______
4) Your wife wants to go shopping for fine wine, cheese and crystal. What excuse will you give to continue lying on the beach? ______
5) Write in not more than 15, no make that 2 words, why you want to go to Mauritius: ______
Name ______
Address ______

Send your entries to Mauritius Tourism Information Service, Block 2-D, 3rd floor, Phoenix Estate, 462, Tulsi Pipe Road, Mumbai 400 013. Or fax us at: 022-4939355. The last date for receiving entries is 25th October 1997, but why hurry?

MAURITIUS
99% fun. 1% land.

So you don't want a free holiday to Mauritius. How about a lousy T-shirt?

This is our third advertisement, and it's just struck us.

We're looking for the laziest man in the world.

And what are we offering?

A free *trip* to Mauritius.

Do you know what that means?

Asking a bunch of lazy bums to get off the chair and toddle off to a distant land.

The very idea!

So we've decided to make amends to those of you who we may have inadvertently offended.

We've looked at other promotions that advertising agencies foist upon unsuspecting clients, which in turn are palmed off to customers.

Exhibit 'A'

Like offers of a free bar of soap, or a sachet of shampoo. We even seriously considered an unbreakable plastic jar.

And finally settled for a T-shirt. (Exhibit 'A'.)

We're giving away 50 of these as runner-up prizes. Each one says: "I entered the laziest man in the world contest and all I got was this lousy T-shirt."

Our people think it's a wildly brilliant marketing coup. Witty, clever, amusing, and above all, dirt cheap.

So now the lazy contestant can wear one, sit at home, close his eyes (not a difficult thing to do) and think of Mauritius.

WHAT TO IMAGINE.

Since you're slothful and lazy, with a complete lack of imagination, we'll help you along.

You could imagine, for instance, savouring a four-course meal of heart of palm, fillet of shark, crisp fried baby octopus and smoked blue marlin.

Followed by a steaming cup of Chamarel coffee and one of our award-winning beers.

You could imagine winning vast sums of money at one of our casinos. And spending it just as fast on French crystal, jade and jewellery.

You could imagine sailing in a crystal-blue lagoon surrounded by a coastline that's remained untouched since the Dutch first landed in 1638.

You could imagine sipping Green Island rum while listening to a blues band at one of the cafés that dot the seafront at Grand Baie.

Or you could imagine coming face-to-face with some rare species that can be found on this tropical island: people.

PEOPLE.

Yes, there are such creatures in Mauritius.

What we lack in quantity, we make up for in quality.

On a clear day, the visitor can spot Brigitte Bardot, Jeanne Moreau, Ursula Andress or Gerard Depardieu.

Steffi Graff and Boris Becker can be seen doing time out.

The island is a favourite with the royals given its lazy, er, regal pace. King Carl Gustav of Sweden, Princess Caroline and Princess Stephanie can be spotted.

All, dare we say, sporting T-shirts.

WHAT WILL IT BE?

Fill in the form below. If you can demonstrate with utmost fidelity, your appreciation of the Laws of Inertia, you could win two free tickets to Mauritius and a stay for three nights at the 5-star Maritim Hotel.

But if you're *really* lucky, you could end up wearing one of our T-shirts. You don't even have to step out of the house. We'll mail it to you.

1) Did you actually read this advertisement? (Tick one.)
☐ Yes. ☐ No. ☐ Wake me up when this is over.
2) Who first inhabited Mauritius?
☐ The Dutch ☐ Does it matter?
3) Name four watersport activities you would absolutely not indulge in: ______, ______, ______, ______
4) Your wife wants to go shopping for fine wine, cheese and crystal. What excuse will you give to continue lying on the beach? ______
5) Write in not more than 15, no make that 2 words, why you want to go to Mauritius: ______
Name ______
Address ______

Send your entries to Mauritius Tourism Information Service, Block 2-D, 3rd floor, Phoenix Estate, 462, Tulsi Pipe Road, Mumbai 400 013. Or fax us at: 022-4939355. The last date for receiving entries is 25th October 1997, but why hurry?

MAURITIUS
99% fun. 1% land.

Are you the laziest man in the world? Get someone to read this and find out.

Before you begin reading, let us warn you, this advertisement contains 623 words.

It would be wise to enlist the help of someone more enthusiastic than yourself.

It'll also help if you're lying comfortably in a hammock by the sea. With a glass of gloriously chilled beer.

The sound of swaying palms wouldn't do much harm either.

And would a lobster in white wine sauce, with just a sliver of smoked blue marlin be too much to ask?

You could get all of this in Mauritius. But since you're not there yet, you will unfortunately, have to read.

The objective of this advertisement is to seek out the laziest human being on this planet, and transport him with minimum bodily discomfort to the isle of Mauritius.

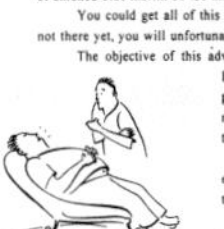

"I won the contest, but I was too lazy to go to Mauritius."

All you have to do is enter the contest by filling in the form at the end of this ad.

If you can display that sterling quality that so few men of today possess - sloth - you could find yourself with two free tickets and a stay for three nights at the 5-star Maritim Hotel.

YOUR TEST BEGINS HERE.

There is much to see and do in Mauritius.

You could, for instance, take a jeep safari through the forest at Domaine Les Pailles to see wild boar and deer.

You could visit the Vanille Crocodile Nature Park, or see rare species of birds at the Casela Bird Park.

You could descend a volcano crater at Trou aux Cerfs and live to tell the tale.

You could go on a shark hunt expedition, or a stag hunt at Domaine du Chasseur.

You could trek through the Black River Gorges past spectacular waterfalls that have remained untouched since the Dutch first landed in 1638.

You could go snorkelling, deep-sea diving, yatching or wind surfing.

You *could*.

But will you?

Ah ha, come now. Confess.

There comes a time in every man's life when he has to make that firm, decisive move.

We trust you'll leave that to the wife.

Should she insist on dragging you along, we have a remedy.

SHOPPING.

There are many places in Mauritius where you can get rid of your wife.

If you are a food lover, you could send her packing with a long list. We have over 300 varieties of cheese, and some classic French and South African wines to choose from.

Having consumed large quantities of these, chances are you would need a new wardrobe. Send her packing once again for some of the world's finest knitwear.

Surely, after all the effort she has taken on your behalf, she deserves a few gifts for herself. Dear me, send her off yet again for silk scarves, jade, French crystal and jewellery.

DO YOU HAVE IT IN YOU?

"Whenever I feel the urge to exercise coming on, I lie down till it passes over." We're not certain Mark Twain wrote that. Or dictated it to his secretary from the confines of his bed.

Clever man, that Mark. He would most certainly have won this contest had he been around.

1) Did you actually read this advertisement? (Tick one.)
☐ Yes. ☐ No. ☐ Wake me up when this is over.
2) Who first inhabited Mauritius?
☐ The Dutch ☐ Does it matter?
3) Name four watersport activities you would absolutely not indulge in: ______, ______, ______, ______
4) Your wife wants to go shopping for fine wine, cheese and crystal. What excuse will you give to continue lying on the beach? ______
5) Write in not more than 15, no make that 2 words, why you want to go to Mauritius: ______
Name ______
Address ______

Send your entries to Mauritius Tourism Information Service, Block 2-D, 3rd floor, Phoenix Estate, 462, Tulsi Pipe Road, Mumbai 400 013. Or fax us at: 022-4939355. The last date for receiving entries is 25th October 1997, but why hurry?

MAURITIUS
99% fun. 1% land.

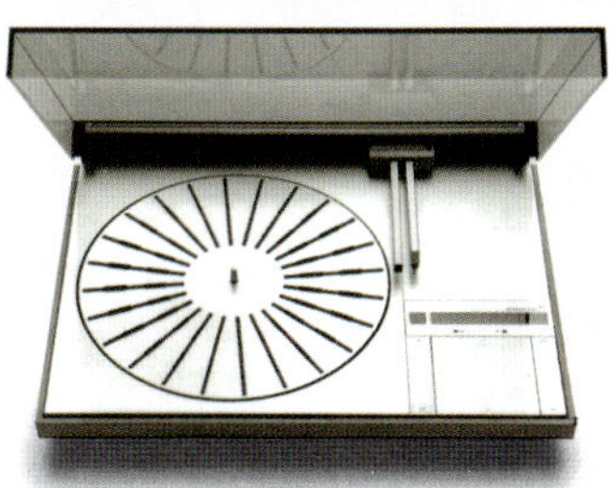

222

222. Bang and Olufsen. Turntable. 1972. "Beogram 4000". Steel, aluminum and rosewood. 3¾ x 18⅞ x 14¾" (9.5 x 48 x 37.5 cm). Gift of Bang and Olufsen A/S.

223

223. Park Hyatt Hotel. Grilled Norwegian Salmon. Flown in daily. Iced, not frozen. Hand-trimmed. 9 oz. filet. Brushed with garlic and herb oil. Grilled to an indisputable medium rare. Drizzled with an intense Zinfandel reduction. Melts in mouth. Served on a bed of crispy, potato hay with a side of wild prairie mushrooms and a medley of root vegetables that aren't merely for presentation. Original creation of world-renowned Master Chef, Brian McBride. Part of the culinary collection available exclusively at the Park Hyatt. Locations: Los Angeles, Philadelphia, San Francisco, Washington D.C. and Chicago (1998). Buenos Aires, Canberra, Johannesburg, London, Madrid, Sydney and Tokyo. (Reservations: 1 800 233 1234) The Park Hyatt. Classic. Modern. Luxury.

224. Le Corbusier (Charles-Edouard Jeanneret), Pierre Jeanneret, and Charlotte Perriand. Chaise Lounge. 1928. Adjustable chrome cradle, matte black base and black leather. 22¼ x 63 x 28¾" (56.5 x 160 x 73 cm). Manufactured by Cassina Italy, under license from the Le Corbusier Foundation.

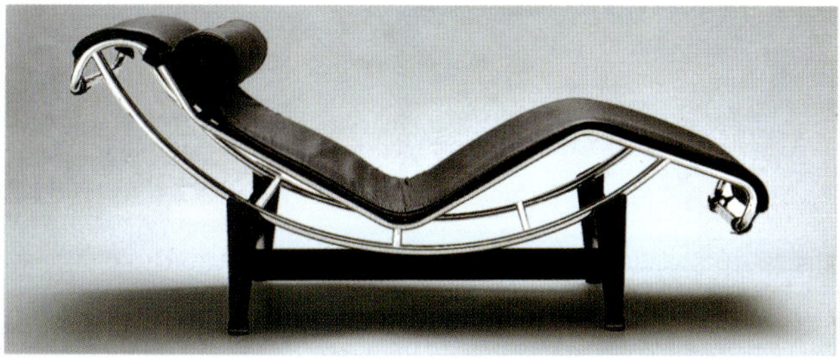

224

Architecture and Design

MERIT AWARD
newspaper 600 lines or less: single

art director
LISA HOWARD

writer
LARRY LIPSON

photographers
HANS GISSINGER
TIM TURNER

client
HYATT HOTELS & RESORTS

agency
CRAMER-KRASSELT/CHICAGO

MERIT AWARD
newspaper 600 lines
or less: single

art director
TIM FOLEY
writer
MARTY DONOHUE
client
PROVIDENCE BICYCLE
agencies
HILL HOLLIDAY CONNORS
COSMOPULOS/BOSTON

MERIT AWARD
newspaper 600 lines
or less: single

art director
TIM FOLEY
writer
MARTY DONOHUE
client
PROVIDENCE BICYCLE
agency
HILL HOLLIDAY CONNORS
COSMOPULOS/BOSTON

TOUR *de* FRANCE ?
ROUTE *de* PAPER ?

We've got every kind of bike imaginable. Come check them out. 725 Branch Avenue.

MERIT AWARD
newspaper 600 lines or less: single

art director
MICHAEL COHEN

writer
CURTIS SMITH

photographer
PAT STAUB

client
MOON PIE

agency
LOEFFLER KETCHUM MOUNTJOY/CHARLOTTE

MERIT AWARD
newspaper 600 lines or less: single

art director
TOM GIANFAGNA

writer
AMY BORKOWSKY

client
CLUB MED

agency
LOWE & PARTNERS/SMS/NEW YORK

8 ST THE NEW YORK TIMES **WEDDINGS** SUNDAY, NOVEMBER 23, 1997

Alexis Brinkley, Jeremiah Collins

Dawn Zappetti, Patrick Sullivan

Lisa Toyama, Peter Brzechffa

Miss Snow-Johnson, Mr. Moynihan

Stacey Orbuch, Stephen Blumberg

Veronica Lynn, Robert Chasanoff

Jeffay Chang, Elaine Cheng

Renée Healy And Eric Fill

Dyan Finguerra, Seth Du Charme

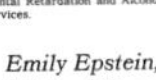

Martha Schall, Morris Czaczkes

Emily Epstein, Michael Vines

Sara Eisner, Michael Richter

Kathleen Mellon, Rahamim Ron

Amy Norman, Barry Surman

Lori Fiverson, Joseph Tahl

Sheila Moore, Michael Potter

It could be the best trip you ever take. Next to your honeymoon. Call your travel agent or 1·800·CLUB MED

PRINT MERIT

MERIT AWARD
newspaper 600 lines
or less: single

art director
JOHN BOONE

writer
DAVID OAKLEY

photographers
RICK DUBLIN
KERRY PETERSON

client
WRANGLER COMPANY

agency
THE MARTIN AGENCY/
CHARLOTTE

MERIT AWARD
newspaper 600 lines
or less: single

art director
JOHN BOONE

writer
DAVID OAKLEY

photographers
JOE LAMPI
KERRY PETERSON

client
WRANGLER COMPANY

agency
THE MARTIN AGENCY/
CHARLOTTE

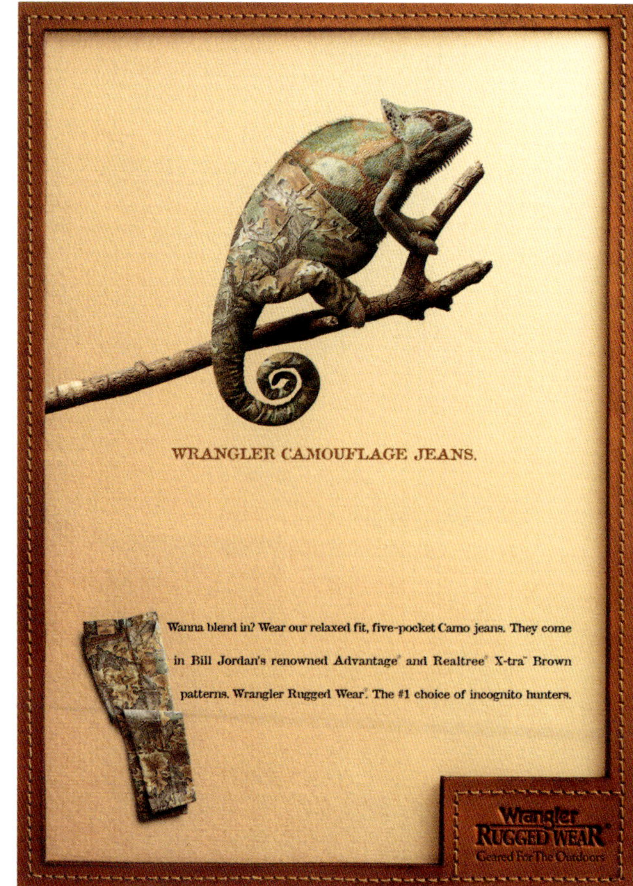

PRINT MERIT

MERIT AWARD
newspaper 600 lines
or less: single

art director
MICHAEL ANCEVIC
writer
STEPHEN MIETELSKI
illustrator
STOCK
client
THE BIG 4
agency
MULLEN ADVERTISING/
WENHAM

MERIT AWARD
newspaper 600 lines
or less: single

art director
NANCY VONK
writers
JANET KESTIN
NANCY VONK
illustrator
ELSIE FEHR
client
TIMEX CANADA
agency
OGILVY & MATHER
CANADA/TORONTO

MERIT AWARD
newspaper 600 lines
or less: single

art director
DOUG MICKSCHL
writer
TROY LONGIE
photographer
STUART BLOCK
client
REYNOLD GUITAR
LESSONS
agency
PERISCOPE/
MINNEAPOLIS

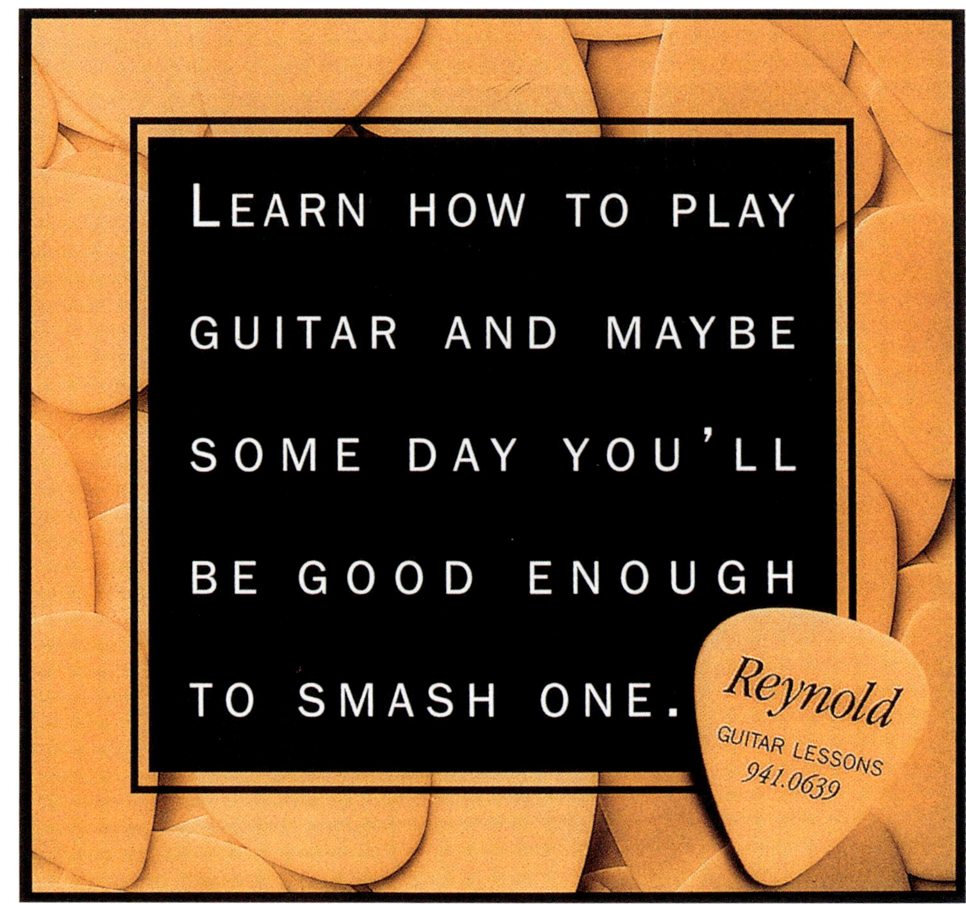

MERIT AWARD
newspaper 600 lines
or less: single

art director
DOUG MICKSCHL
writer
TROY LONGIE
photographer
STUART BLOCK
client
REYNOLD GUITAR
LESSONS
agency
PERISCOPE/
MINNEAPOLIS

ONLY ONE PAGE FOR WEATHER?
WHAT KIND OF NEWSPAPER IS THIS?

MERIT AWARD
newspaper 600 lines or less: single

art director
CHRIS GRAVES

writer
ERIK MOE

client
WEATHER CHANNEL

agency
TBWA CHIAT/DAY/VENICE

MERIT AWARD
newspaper 600 lines or less: campaign

art director
HARVEY MARCO

writer
ERIC SORENSEN

client
JACOB'S WELL

agency
FALLON MCELLIGOTT/MINNEAPOLIS

MERIT AWARD
newspaper 600 lines
or less: campaign

art director
TOM GIANFAGNA

writer
AMY BORKOWSKY

client
CLUB MED

agency
LOWE & PARTNERS/
SMS/NEW YORK

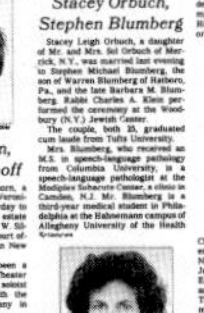

CLUB MED

SINGLES VILLAGES.

ENJOY THEM

WHILE YOU CAN.

It could be the best trip you ever take. Next to your honeymoon.
Call your travel agent or **1-800-CLUB MED**

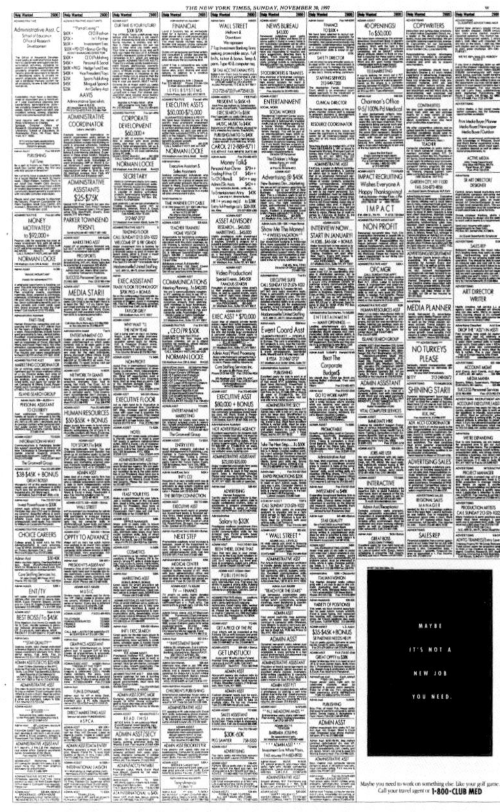

MAYBE

IT'S NOT A

NEW JOB

YOU NEED.

Maybe you need to work on something else. Like your golf game.
Call your travel agent or **1-800-CLUB MED**

WANT TO BE

ENTERTAINED?

WATCH

OTHER PEOPLE LEARN

HOW TO WATER SKI.

Or come learn a new sport yourself. (Our instructors won't laugh.)
Call your travel agent or **1-800-CLUB MED**

PRINT MERIT

MERIT AWARD
newspaper 600 lines
or less: campaign

art director
JOHN BOONE

writer
DAVID OAKLEY

photographers
JOE LAMPI
KERRY PETERSON
RICK DUBLIN

client
WRANGLER COMPANY

agency
THE MARTIN AGENCY/
CHARLOTTE

PRINT MERIT

MERIT AWARD
newspaper 600 lines or less: campaign

art director
TED ROYER

writer
ROWAN CHANEN

illustrators
TED ROYER
POK CHENG HAI

client
RAFFLES INTERNATIONAL

agency
SAATCHI & SAATCHI/ SINGAPORE

Grand Hotel d'Angkor, Kingdom of Cambodia

On our walls are pictures of 12th century Cambodia. They're called windows.

Though the mystery of the surrounding temples has always been open to debate, the question of where to stay has not. Since 1929, a visit to Grand Hotel d'Angkor has been synonymous with a visit to the Kingdom of Cambodia. Now restored along with the celebrated Hotel Le Royal in Phnom Penh, the treasure of an ancient civilisation is just a hotel room away.

HOTEL LE ROYAL
GRAND HOTEL D'ANGKOR

For reservations fax (855) 23-368-88, e-mail raffles.grand.royal@cm17.com or write to 68 Monivong Boulevard, Phnom Penh, Kingdom of Cambodia. A member of Small Luxury Hotels of the World.

Angkor Wat, Kingdom of Cambodia

On a clear day you can see for 800 years.

Amongst temples to the gods, a shrine to mortals. Since 1929, Grand Hotel d'Angkor has been as much a legend as the celebrated ruins that surround it. No adventurer worth his elephant and porter would have stayed anywhere else in the Kingdom of Cambodia. Now restored along with Hotel Le Royal in Phnom Penh, the treasure of an ancient civilisation is just a hotel room away.

HOTEL LE ROYAL
GRAND HOTEL D'ANGKOR

For reservations fax (855) 23-368-118, e-mail raffles.grand.royal@cm17.com or write to 68 Monivong Boulevard, Phnom Penh, Kingdom of Cambodia. A member of Small Luxury Hotels of the World.

Hotel Le Royal, Cambodia

The perfect time for cocktails? Between 1922 and 1928.

Guests will be forgiven for wondering what year it is. For old Phnom Penh is alive and well and living at Hotel Le Royal. The preferred address of writers and adventurers fond of absorbing a drink as well as the culture of the Kingdom of Cambodia. Jointly restored with Grand Hotel d'Angkor in Siem Reap, the splendour of an ancient civilisation is now just a hotel room away.

HOTEL LE ROYAL
GRAND HOTEL D'ANGKOR

Hotel Le Royal, 68 Monivong Boulevard, Phnom Penh, Kingdom of Cambodia. Fax (855) 23-368-118 or e-mail raffles.grand.royal@cm17.com. A member of Small Luxury Hotels of the World.

PERSONALLY, WE HOPE "SHINE" WINS BEST PICTURE.

THE WEATHER CHANNEL®

www.weather.com

NO RERUNS. EVER.

www.weather.com

IF HELL FREEZES OVER, YOU'LL HEAR IT HERE FIRST.

www.weather.com

MERIT AWARD
newspaper 600 lines or less: campaign

art director
DOUG MUKAI

writers
SUSAN NICHOLAS-GRAVES
RICH SIEGAL

client
WEATHER CHANNEL

agency
TBWA CHIAT/DAY/VENICE

MERIT AWARD
magazine b/w full page or spread: single

art director
ERIC TILFORD

writer
TODD TILFORD

client
DR. MARTENS

agency
PYRO/DALLAS

MERIT AWARD
magazine b/w full page
or spread: single

art director
MARK MARTIN
writer
CHRIS RICKABY
photographer
ROBERT WALKER
client
HOUSE OF HARDY
agency
ROBSON BROWN/
LONDON

MERIT AWARD
magazine b/w full page
or spread: single

art director
MARK MARTIN
writer
CHRIS RICKABY
photographer
ALEX TELFER
client
HOUSE OF HARDY
agency
ROBSON BROWN/
LONDON

The only parts of this magazine that were not made by a Power Macintosh.

Toda esta revista foi diagramada num Power Macintosh: a capa, as matérias, os anúncios - até os anúncios de outros computadores são criados num Mac. O Power Macintosh é o computador mais usado em Editoração, Publicidade, Design, Internet Authoring e Multimídia em todo o mundo. E não é para menos: ele é mais rápido, mais fácil, compatível com outras plataformas e cheio de recursos multimídia e Internet. Se você trabalha com computação gráfica, não há meio termo: ou você tem um Power Macintosh - ou você tem um problema.

MERIT AWARD
magazine b/w full page or spread: single

art director
MARCELLO SERPA

writer
EUGENIO MOHALLEM

photographer
APPLE ARCHIVE

client
APPLE COMPUTER BRAZIL

agency
ALMAP/BBDO/ SAO PAOLO

From impressionism to expressionism in 7,6 seconds.

Na história da arte, o impressionismo está separado do expressionismo por um curtíssimo espaço de tempo. Numa estrada também. Você só precisa de uma bela paisagem e do Novo Golf VR6, o Volkswagen mais potente de todos os tempos.

Motor 2.8 alemão com 6 cilindros posicionados em V e digital Multipoint Injection, equipado com 174 cavalos, capaz de levar o ponteiro do velocímetro de zero aos 100 km/h em apenas 7,6 segundos e 224 km/h de velocidade final. Com apenas 0,30 de coeficiente de penetração aerodinâmica, um dos menores da

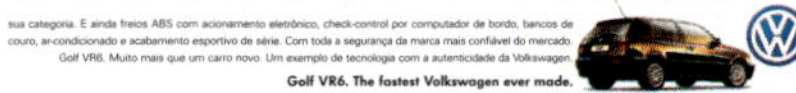

MERIT AWARD
magazine b/w full page or spread: single

art director
JULIO ANDERY

writer
RICARDO CHESTER

photographers
TONY STONE
IMAGE BANK
VOLKSWAGEN ARCHIVE

client
VOLKSWAGEN BRAZIL

agency
ALMAP/BBDO/ SAO PAULO

PRINT MERIT

MERIT AWARD
magazine b/w full page or spread: single

art director
CHRIS ROBB

writers
KATHY HEPINSTALL
HAROLD EINSTEIN

photographer
GEOF KERN

client
LA CELLULAR

agency
BBDO WEST/ LOS ANGELES

MERIT AWARD
magazine color full page
or spread: single

art director
STEVE STONE
writer
BOB KERSTETTER
photographer
KIRK AMYX
client
PETE'S WICKED ALE
agency
BLACK ROCKET/
SAN FRANCISCO

Is it okay for a beer to be more interesting than you?

Here's a little test. Think about how you'd describe yourself in an ad. Not one of those personals ads. No one cares if you're a "Sagittarius" or that you "look forward to long, moonlit walks on the beach with your 'soulmate.'"

We're talking about an actual full page ad about yourself. Would it show you as an astronaut? A celebrated jazz musician? A world class fencing champion?

Most of us are just trying to get through this thing (life) with a minimum amount of hassle and strife. And the truth is, most of us totally wimp out when it comes to being even remotely "interesting."

"Wicked Ale"

"Dennis"

- Great body
- Roasted barley aroma
- Dark ruby color
- Complex flavors
- Dry hopped
- American original
- Available on tap
- Fun at parties
- At peace with self
- Not as bitter as Dennis
- Likes funk music
- No real 'problems'
- Always there

- Likes basketball
- Reads a little
- Sometimes funny
-
-
-
-
-
-
-
-
-
-

Don't get us wrong. We know some of you are absolutely brilliant. (We get letters from doctors and lawyers and computer programmers, saying that you love our beer, and jeez, thanks.)

But what about the big picture? What's stopping us? Where is it written that we can't sign up for race car lessons tomorrow. Or enroll in a stunt man school.

Maybe you're a fireman, but you'd rather be a blimp pilot. Maybe you're a pastry chef and you'd rather be teaching scuba diving in Belize. Heck, maybe you'd rather make beer for a living. So? What's stopping you? Break out the phone book. Make some calls. Change the channel.

Look at Pete. He goes from driving a cab, to working at a big high tech company. Just like you're "supposed" to do. Everything was hunky dory. Yet at some point, he said, "You know what? I think I'm gonna make the best beer I've ever tasted." And he did. He could have easily stopped after making Pete's Wicked Ale. You know, win a bunch of awards, settle back into a nice, comfy lounge chair. But he decides to keep pushing it. Make a bunch of truly unique, full-flavored beers. Pete didn't "know" he was going to be happy making beer. Just like you may not "know" you'd be happy being an opera singer (okay, that's a bad example - sorry).

The point is, human beings are wonderful things. Just when you think you've figured 'em out, they surprise you. They go climb a big frozen mountain in a wheelchair. Or start an organic vegetable stand. Yeah, your friends may think you've lost your marbles, but so what? Let them talk.

Pete didn't make Wicked Ale for the "masses." He made it for "himself" (okay, himself *and* a few of his weird friends).

So think of these words as a call to arms. Sure, this is an ad for beer. And we'd be lying if we said we didn't dream of you savoring a couple of frosty pints of Pete's Wicked Ale while plotting your course.

But the most important thing? Don't - give - in. We need people out there kicking mediocrity in its shiny, little butt.

Are there rewards? Think about it. When was the last time someone whispered in your ear, "Hey, you know something? You're the most interesting person I've ever met." (Wow.)

PETE'S Wicked BREWS

MERIT AWARD
magazine color full page
or spread: single

art director
JEREMY CRAIGEN
writer
JEREMY CRAIGEN
client
ANHEUSER-BUSCH
agency
BMP DDB/LONDON

CUSTER'S LAST STAND

GUNFIGHT AT THE O.K. CORRAL

STATUE OF LIBERTY UNVEILED

NEW YORK SUBWAY OPENS

FORD BUILDS MODEL T

WORLD WAR I ENDS

PROHIBITION

BONNIE AND CLYDE KILLED

MOUNT RUSHMORE COMPLETED

CUBAN MISSILE CRISIS

FIRST MOON LANDING

CLINTON RE-ELECTED

PRINT MERIT

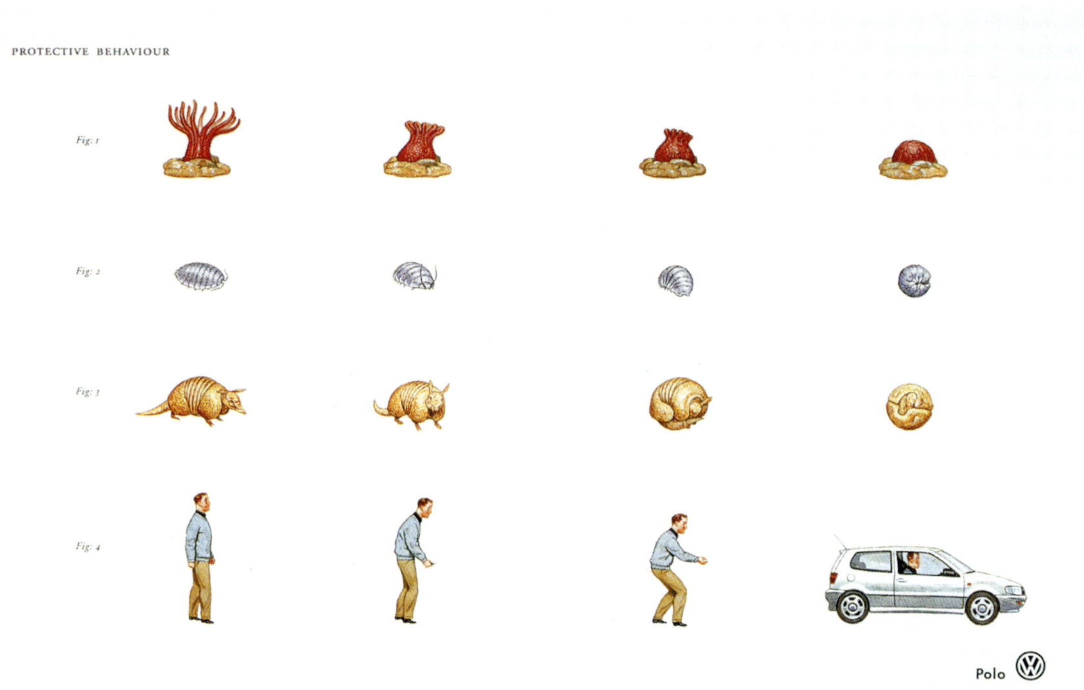

PROTECTIVE BEHAVIOUR

Fig: 1

Fig: 2

Fig: 3

Fig: 4

Polo

MERIT AWARD
magazine color full page
or spread: single

art director
JOANNA WENLEY

writer
JEREMY CRAIGEN

illustrator
PAUL SLATER

client
VOLKWAGEN
GROUP UK

agency
BMP DDB/LONDON

PRINT MERIT

HE PICKS UP A SNOWBOARD, HE WINS A

GOLD MEDAL.

HE TRIES MOUNTAIN BIKING, HE WINS A

GOLD MEDAL.

DO NOT INTRODUCE THIS MAN TO YOUR

GIRLFRIEND.

ESPN's Winter X Games. One man, two gold medals. One in the Boarder X, and one in the Snow Mountain Biking Dual Downhill. Ladies and gentlemen, we proudly introduce Shaun Palmer. Just not to our girlfriends. *LEARN MORE AT WWW.SPECIALIZED.COM*

MERIT AWARD
magazine color full page
or spread: single

art director
MELANIE
MENKEMELLER

writer
MATT ASHWORTH

photographer
STOCK

client
SPECIALIZED BICYCLES

agency
BUTLER SHINE &
STERN/SAUSALITO

MERIT AWARD
magazine color full page
or spread: single

art director
BRIAN KROENING

writer
GLEN WACHOWIAK

photographers
ROBERT HOLLAND
UNIPHOTO
BRAD PALM

client
POLARIS WATERCRAFT

agency
CARMICHAEL LYNCH/
MINNEAPOLIS

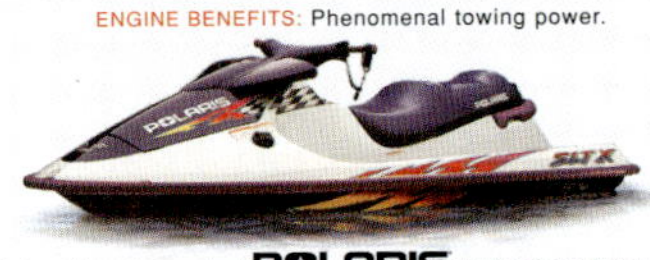

PRINT MERIT

MERIT AWARD
magazine color full page
or spread: single

art director
JOHN DAMES

writer
WADE PASCHALL

photographer
JOHN HUET

client
ZEBCO/QUANTUM

agency
CORE/ST. LOUIS

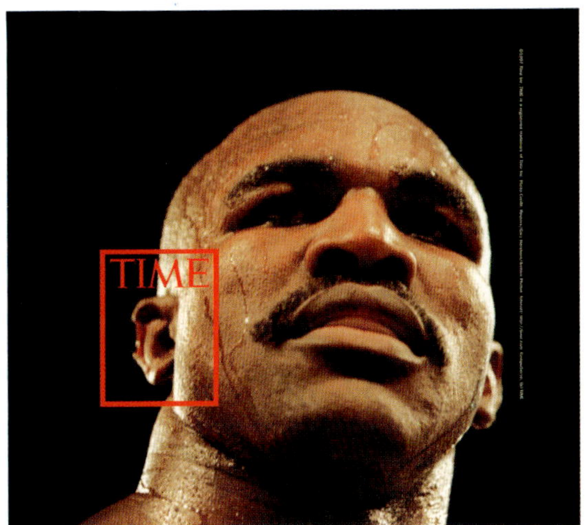

What kind of bandage can

boxing possibly put on this?

The world's most interesting magazine.

A weekly reminder that the

world is a pretty amazing place.

The world's most interesting magazine.

MERIT AWARD
magazine color full page
or spread: single

art director
BOB BARRIE

writer
DEAN BUCKHORN

photographer
GARY HERSHORN

client
TIME MAGAZINE

agency
FALLON MCELLIGOTT/
MINNEAPOLIS

MERIT AWARD
magazine color full page
or spread: single

art director
BOB BARRIE

writer
DEAN BUCKHORN

photographer
ROBERT ALLISON

client
TIME MAGAZINE

agency
FALLON MCELLIGOTT/
MINNEAPOLIS

PRINT MERIT

At what point do science

and morality collide?

At what point do science

and morality collide?

The world's most interesting magazine. **The world's most interesting magazine.**

MERIT AWARD
magazine color full page
or spread: single

art director
BOB BARRIE

writer
DEAN BUCKHORN

photographer
ARCHIVE PHOTO

client
TIME MAGAZINE

agency
FALLON MCELLIGOTT/
MINNEAPOLIS

MERIT AWARD
magazine color full page
or spread: single

art directors
JEREMY POSTAER
PAUL VENABLES

writers
PAUL VENABLES
JEREMY POSTAER

photographer
CLINT CLEMENS

client
PORSCHE

agency
GOODBY SILVERSTEIN
& PARTNERS/
SAN FRANCISCO

My other car is...um...I forget.

Presenting the Boxster. Top back. Power down. Reality blurred. When firmly planted in the cockpit of a six-cylinder 200-horsepower, mid-engine Porsche roadster, the memory of the utilitarian vehicle parked in the garage is the first to go. Starting at $39,980. Contact us at 1-800-Porsche or http://www.porsche.com and readily agree: Porsche. There is no substitute.™

MERIT AWARD
magazine color full page
or spread: single

art director
PATRICK SUTHERLAND

writer
ARI MERKIN

photographer
VIC HUBER

client
LAND ROVER NORTH
AMERICA

agency
GRACE & ROTHSCHILD/
NEW YORK

Coincidentally, the African baobab tree also seats seven.

LAND ROVER

THAT'S where the similarities end. BECAUSE for those seeking refuge along the barbarous plains of the Serengeti, a Land Rover Discovery can offer a great deal more than the appropriate seating arrangements. IT offers alpine windows and elevated stadium seats, which make it possible to spot carnivorous intruders long before their lunch hour. AND with the assistance of permanent four-wheel drive, coil spring suspension, and a 4.0-liter V8 engine, the Discovery can help seven panic-stricken passengers evade the perils of any such environment. THAT is, provided they haven't ventured outside the sheltering parameters of its reinforced steel inner body cage. WHEN you consider all this and a price tag starting at just $32,000*, there's only one thing that can keep you from driving away in a Discovery. AND he can't stay there forever. SO why not visit our Web site at http://www.LandRover.com? OR simply call 1-800-FINE 4WD to experience a Discovery at your nearest Land Rover retailer. IT'S certainly preferable to going out on a limb.

DISCOVERY

Always use your seatbelts. SRS/airbags alone do not provide sufficient protection.

MERIT AWARD
magazine color full page
or spread: single

art director
DAVID CARTER

writer
KIRT GENTRY

photographer
NADAV KANDER

client
SATURN

agency
HAL RINEY &
PARTNERS/
SAN FRANCISCO

PRINT MERIT

MERIT AWARD
magazine color full page
or spread: single

art director
DAVID CARTER

writer
KIRT GENTRY

photographer
NADAV KANDER

client
SATURN

agency
HAL RINEY
& PARTNERS/
SAN FRANCISCO

PRINT MERIT

MERIT AWARD
magazine color full page
or spread: single

art director
JIM MOUNTJOY

writer
ED JONES

photographer
STEVE MURRAY

client
NORTH CAROLINA
TRAVEL & TOURISM

agency
LOEFFLER KETCHUM
MOUNTJOY/CHARLOTTE

MERIT AWARD
magazine color full page
or spread: single

art director
JIM MOUNTJOY

writer
ED JONES

photographers
JACK MOBES
STEVE MURRAY

client
NORTH CAROLINA
TRAVEL & TOURISM

agency
LOEFFLER KETCHUM
MOUNTJOY/CHARLOTTE

MERIT AWARD
magazine color full page
or spread: single

art director
GARY ANDERSON

writer
TONY MILLER

client
SMIRNOFF

agency
LOWE HOWARD-SPINK/
LONDON

MORRIS RECRUITMENT

ITALIAN SPEAKING SECRETARY £16K neg
Are you career minded and looking for a challenge? This is the high profile one to one role offering full involvement. A true PA role, where you will be expected to give your input to ideas. Full banking benefits including bonus and immediate health care. REF: 2501/JM

RECEPTIONIST/TYPIST £14k + bens
A front line receptionist is desired to work for a busy and lively financial services company. Your duties will inclu[...]lients, answering the switchboard, and arranging meetings. Key[...]ssential. REF: 2502/JM

PARTNERS SECRETARY £18k pa
Working for one Partner and a team of his [...]ed to be team spirited. You will have fast, accurate typing skills, wil[...] your initiative, and will have worked at management level [...]ssional organisation. Head office based in Charing Cross REF: 2503/JM

SECRETARY REQUIRED £15k +bens
Easy going PA is required for the executive lecher of large West End firm of accountants. Shorthand & W4W (50 wpm) is unnecessary. Must be well organised have excellent telephone manner and generous cleavage. Position available for 6 months maternity cover. REF: 2504/JM

MANAGEMENT POSITION £45k neg
The ideal candidate should be an Oxbridge chinless wonder. They will have leadership skills and will have attended public school. Ineptitude helpful, but it is far more important to have a father on the board of directors. REF: 2505/JM

SALES EXEC £20k
We're interested in ambitious scheming schmoozers who thrive on tension in dynamic, thrusting, and two-faced working enviro[...] The ideal candidate will have experience of toadying to all levels of management plus superior communication and backstabbing skills. [...] and details of your salary. References will be blatantly falsified. REF: 2506JM

GIRL FRIDAY 16K neg
We are a young, dynamic and pretentious PR company [...] including media. You are a bubbly, enthusiastic and clueless PA. You w[...] typing skills, possess a complete range of novelty gonks for computer [...] with clients, and should have a fluency in inane baby talk. REF: 2507/JM

SECRETARY £14k
A fabulous new opportunity [...] reading *Hello!* magazine [...] duties will include preparing reports, and playing Solitaire on your [...] Powerpoint

MERIT AWARD
magazine color full page
or spread: single

art director
GARY ANDERSON

writer
TONY MILLER

client
SMIRNOFF

agency
LOWE HOWARD-SPINK/
LONDON

close to tube, fitted carp[...] glazing, washing machine, sate[...]ry, gch & bills included. Tel 017[...]4.

• **Luxury 1st flr** studio coop for rent. Would suit a prof single dwarf. £95 per week. View over water works. Phone 01771 55863.

• **We are looking** for a devotee to join house shared by cult members. Would suit a cheerful and gullible person. Will have to share all earthly possessions. Tel 01771 42198 b4 The Day of Reckoning or all day Sunday.

BEDSITS, HOVELS STUDIOS & HUTCHES

Luxury properties available. 01771 49822

• **Nice room** in condemned [...]

PRINT MERIT

MERIT AWARD
magazine color full page
or spread: single

art director
GARY GOLDSMITH
writer
DEAN HACOHEN
photographer
STOCK
client
SONY ELECTRONICS
agency
LOWE & PARTNERS/
SMS/NEW YORK

MERIT AWARD
magazine color full page
or spread: single

art director
GARY GOLDSMITH
writer
DEAN HACOHEN
photographer
STOCK
client
SONY ELECTRONICS
agency
LOWE & PARTNERS/
SMS/NEW YORK

MERIT AWARD
magazine color full page
or spread: single

art director
GARY GOLDSMITH
writer
DEAN HACOHEN
photographer
STOCK
client
SONY ELECTRONICS
agency
LOWE & PARTNERS/
SMS/NEW YORK

MERIT AWARD
magazine color full page
or spread: single

art director
GARY GOLDSMITH
writer
DEAN HACOHEN
photographer
STOCK
client
SONY ELECTRONICS
agency
LOWE & PARTNERS/
SMS/NEW YORK

MERIT AWARD
magazine color full page
or spread: single

art director
GARY GOLDSMITH
writer
DEAN HACOHEN
photographer
STOCK
client
SONY ELECTRONICS
agency
LOWE & PARTNERS/
SMS/NEW YORK

MERIT AWARD
magazine color full page
or spread: single

art director
TOM GIANFAGNA
writer
EDDIE VAN BLOEM
client
SONY ELECTRONICS
agency
LOWE & PARTNERS/
SMS/NEW YORK

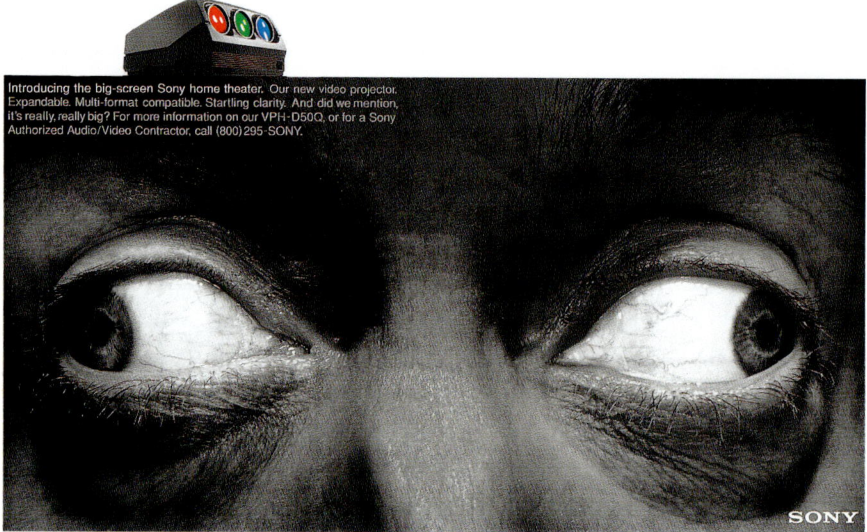

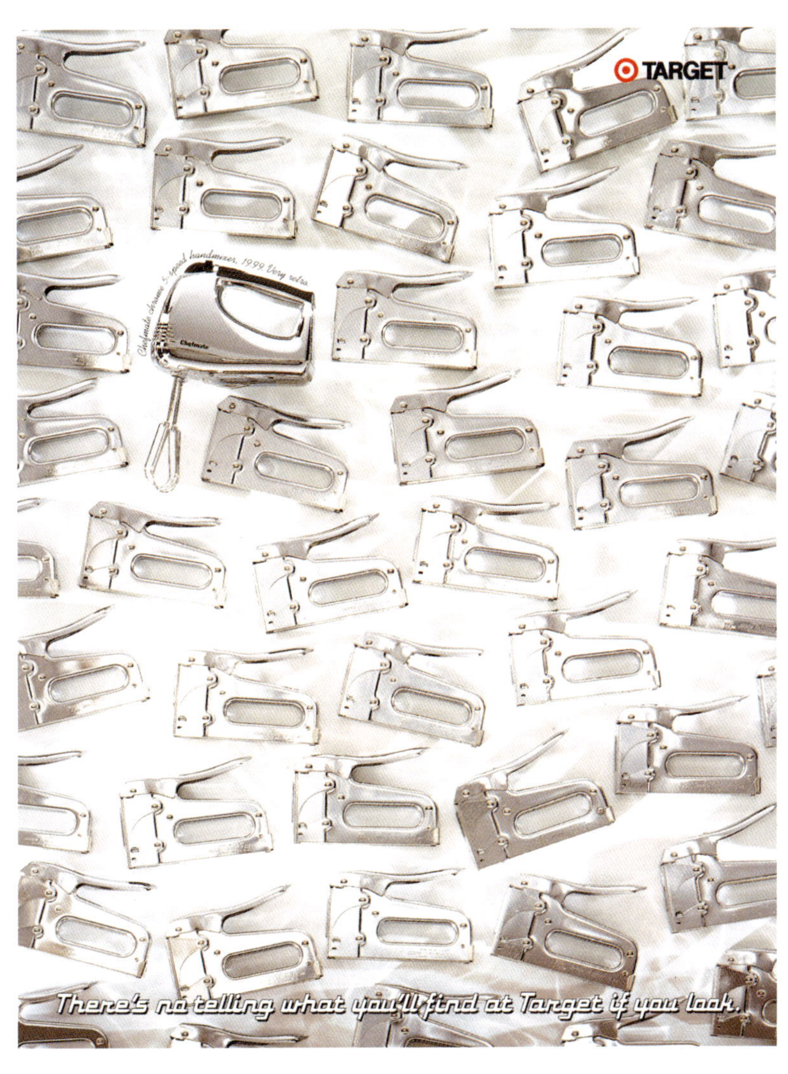

MERIT AWARD
magazine color full page
or spread: single

art director
DOUG TRAPP

writer
CHRISTOPHER WILSON

photographer
CHUCK SMITH

client
TARGET

agency
MARTIN/WILLIAMS
ADVERTISING/
MINNEAPOLIS

MERIT AWARD
magazine color full page
or spread: single

art director
MIKE FERRER

writer
TIM SPROUL

illustrators
GEORGE CHANEY
JEFF FOSTER
ERIC WHITE

photographers
MARK EBSEN
STOCK

client
WIZARDS OF THE
COAST

agency
MOFFATT/ROSENTHAL/
PORTLAND

MERIT AWARD
magazine color full page
or spread: single

art director
MIKE FERRER
writer
TIM SPROUL
illustrator
HUNGRY DOG STUDIO
& MISC
photographers
MARK EBSEN
TOM MILLESON
STOCK
client
WIZARDS OF THE
COAST
agency
MOFFATT/ROSENTHAL/
PORTLAND

PRINT MERIT

MERIT AWARD
magazine color full page
or spread: single

art director
PEPE MARAIS
writer
CRAIG CRAWFORD
photographer
STEVE GOLDBERG
client
NISSAN
agency
NET#WORK/
JOHANNESBURG

Introducing the highly sought after Maxima QX.

Incredible?

Well, stop to consider that its 3 litre 24 valve engine reaches 100 km/h in just 7,68 seconds, has a top speed of 230 km/h and is also 96% recyclable, fuel-efficient and environmentally friendly.

That its Multi-Link Beam Suspension is designed to keep it firmly on the road and you firmly in your seat.

That its posture perfect seats are designed to devastate the hopes of every chiropractor.

That, thanks to its streamlined suspension configuration and engine, the Maxima accommodates 5 adults. Comfortably.

That its safety features include dual airbags, ABS brakes, strengthened door bars and seatbelt pre-tensioners.

And that a keyless entry system makes it as secure as it's safe.

Perhaps that is why there are some people who simply cannot wait to lay their hands on it.

You can with a Nissan.

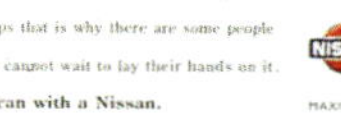

MERIT AWARD
magazine color full page
or spread: single

art director
JIM RONSON
writer
SUZANNE POPE
photographer
PHILIP ROSTRON
client
MIDAS CANADA
agency
OGILVY & MATHER
CANADA/TORONTO

MERIT AWARD
magazine color full page
or spread: single

art director
JOE KAYSER

writers
STEVE SILVER
TOM BAGOT

illustrator
JEFF ALEXANDER

photographers
HUNTER FREEMAN
BOB MIZONO

client
BRODERBUND
SOFTWARE

agency
SAATCHI & SAATCHI/
SAN FRANCISCO

MERIT AWARD
magazine color full page
or spread: single

art director
JOE KAYSER

writers
STEVE SILVER
TOM BAGOT

photographers
HUNTER FREEMAN
BOB SACHA

client
BRODERBUND
SOFTWARE

agency
SAATCHI & SAATCHI/
SAN FRANCISCO

MERIT AWARD
magazine color full page or spread: single

art director
JESSICA SCHULMAN
writers
CRAIG TANIMOTO
ERIC GRUNBAUM
photographer
ARCHIVE PHOTOS
client
APPLE COMPUTER
agency
TBWA CHIAT/DAY/VENICE

MERIT AWARD
magazine color full page or spread: single

art directors
SUSAN ALINSANGAN
KEN YOUNGLIEB
writers
CRAIG TANIMOTO
ERIC GRUNBAUM
photographer
CORBIS
client
APPLE COMPUTER
agency
TBWA CHIAT/DAY/VENICE

MERIT AWARD
magazine color full page or spread: single

art directors
JESSICA SCHULMAN
JENNIFER GOLUB
writers
CRAIG TANIMOTO
ERIC GRUNBAUM
photographer
ARCHIVE PHOTOS
client
APPLE COMPUTER
agency
TBWA CHIAT/DAY/VENICE

PRINT MERIT

MERIT AWARD
magazine color full page
or spread: single

art directors
JESSICA SCHULMAN
MARGARET MIDGETT
writers
CRAIG TANIMOTO
ERIC GRUNBAUM
photographer
ARNOLD NEWMAN
client
APPLE COMPUTER
agency
TBWA CHIAT/DAY/
VENICE

MERIT AWARD
magazine color full page
or spread: single

art directors
SUSAN ALINSANGAN
JESSICA SCHULMAN
writers
CRAIG TANIMOTO
ERIC GRUNBAUM
photographer
SHOOTING STAR
client
APPLE COMPUTER
agency
TBWA CHIAT/DAY/
VENICE

Here's to the crazy ones.
The misfits.
The rebels.
The troublemakers.
The round pegs in the square holes.

The ones who see things differently.

They're not fond of rules.
And they have no respect for the status quo.

You can praise them, disagree with them, quote them,
disbelieve them, glorify or vilify them.
About the only thing you can't do is ignore them.

Because they change things.

They invent. They imagine. They heal.
They explore. They create. They inspire.
They push the human race forward.

Maybe they have to be crazy.
How else can you stare at an empty canvas and
see a work of art? Or sit in silence and hear a song
that's never been written? Or gaze at a red planet and see
a laboratory on wheels?

We make tools for these kinds of people.
While some see them as the crazy ones,
we see genius.

Because the people who are crazy enough to think
they can change the world, are the ones who do.

Think different.

MERIT AWARD
magazine color full page
or spread: single

art directors
LEE CLOW
JESSICA SCHULMAN
writers
ROB SILTANEN
STEVE JOBS
KEN SEGALL
photographers
MAGNUM PHOTO
TIME LIFE
BETTMAN ARCHIVE
NASA
CORBIS
SHOOTING STAR
ARCHIVE PHOTOS
client
APPLE COMPUTER
agency
TBWA CHIAT/DAY/
VENICE

MERIT AWARD
magazine color full page
or spread: single

art directors
REED COLLINS
RICHARD BULLOCK

writers
RICHARD BULLOCK
REED COLLINS

photographer
MICHAEL LEWIS

client
BMW SOUTH AFRICA

agency
TBWA HUNT LASCARIS/
JOHANNESBURG

MERIT AWARD
magazine color full page or spread: single

art director
MARIKE VENTER

writer
LEIGH LOMBARD

illustrator
MARIKE VENTER

client
WONDERBRA

agency
TBWA HUNT LASCARIS/
JOHANNESBURG

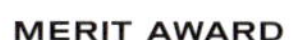

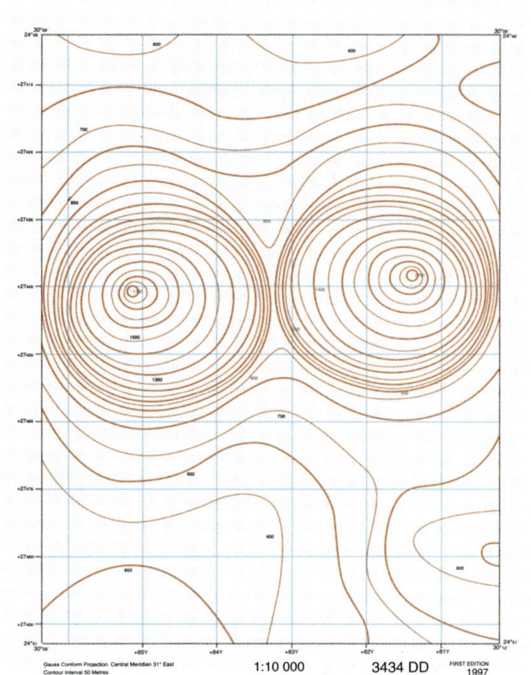

MERIT AWARD
magazine color full page or spread: single

art directors
GUY MOORE
ANDY AMADEO

writers
TONY MALCOLM
MICK MAHONEY

illustrator
DAVID HISCOCK

photographer
DAVID HISCOCK

client
NIKE UK

agency
TBWA SIMONS PALMER/LONDON

MERIT AWARD
magazine color full page or spread: single

art director
KELLY BECK

writer
JOHN ROBERTSON

photographer
BRETT COLVIN

client
ODYSSEY GOLF

agency
VITROROBERTSON/
SAN DIEGO

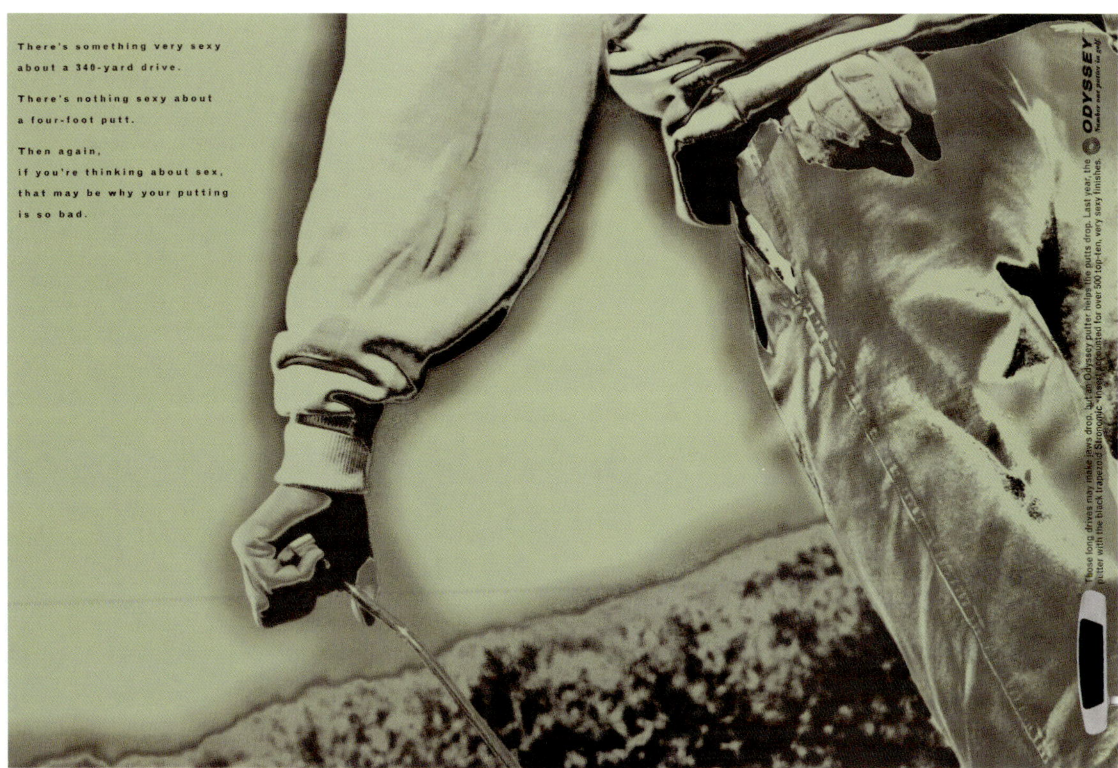

PRINT MERIT

MERIT AWARD
magazine color full page
or spread: single

art director
KELLY BECK
writer
JOHN ROBERTSON
photographer
BRETT COLVIN
client
ODYSSEY GOLF
agency
VITROROBERTSON/
SAN DIEGO

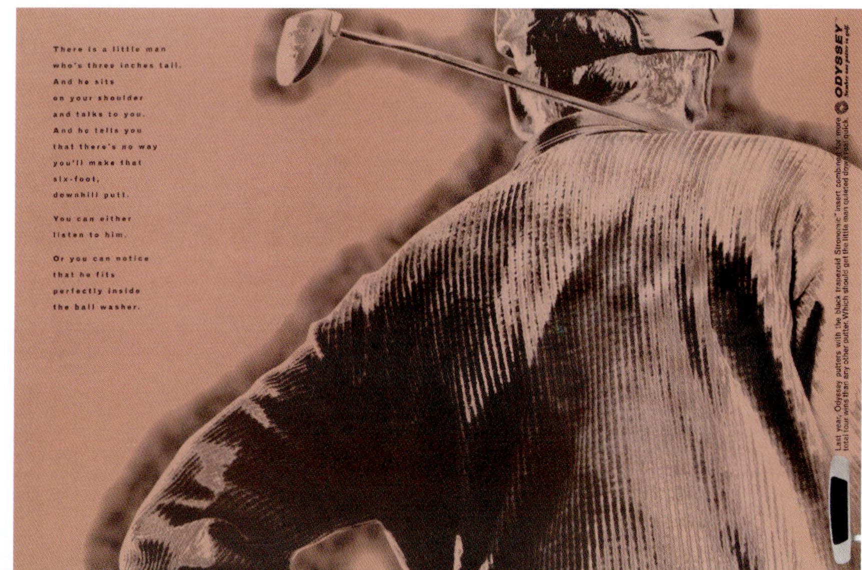

MERIT AWARD
magazine color full page
or spread: single

art director
KELLY BECK
writer
JOHN ROBERTSON
photographer
BRETT COLVIN
client
ODYSSEY GOLF
agency
VITROROBERTSON/
SAN DIEGO

PRINT MERIT

MERIT AWARD
magazine color full page
or spread: single

art director
KELLY BECK
writer
BRIAN GOLD
photographer
BRETT COLVIN
client
ODYSSEY GOLF
agency
VITROROBERTSON/
SAN DIEGO

MERIT AWARD
magazine color full page or spread: single

art director
KELLY BECK
writer
BRIAN GOLD
photographer
BRETT COLVIN
client
ODYSSEY GOLF
agency
VITROROBERTSON/
SAN DIEGO

MERIT AWARD
magazine color full page or spread: single

art director
KELLY BECK
writer
BRIAN GOLD
photographer
BRETT COLVIN
client
ODYSSEY GOLF
agency
VITROROBERTSON/
SAN DIEGO

MERIT AWARD
magazine color full page or spread: single

art director
KELLY BECK
writer
BRIAN GOLD
photographer
BRETT COLVIN
client
ODYSSEY GOLF
agency
VITROROBERTSON/
SAN DIEGO

MERIT AWARD
magazine color full page
or spread: single

art director
KELLY BECK
writer
BRIAN GOLD
photographer
BRETT COLVIN
client
ODYSSEY GOLF
agency
VITROROBERTSON/
SAN DIEGO

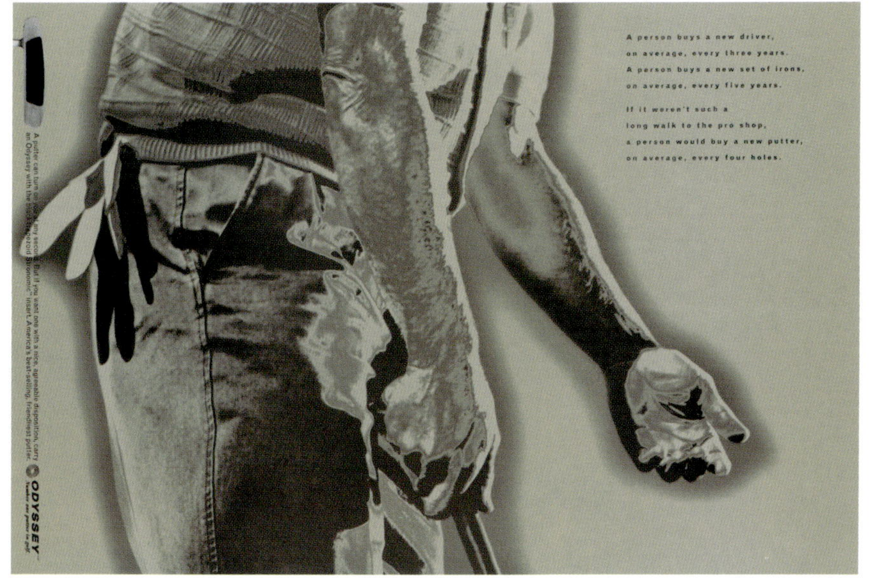

MERIT AWARD
magazine color full page
or spread: single

art director
KELLY BECK
writer
JOHN ROBERTSON
photographer
BRETT COLVIN
client
ODYSSEY GOLF
agency
VITROROBERTSON/
SAN DIEGO

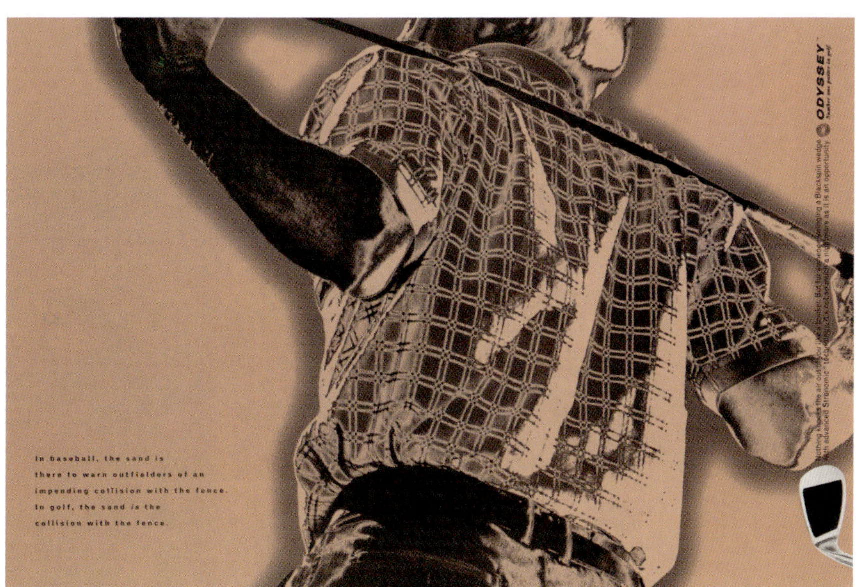

MERIT AWARD
magazine color full page
or spread: single

art director
KELLY BECK
writer
BRIAN GOLD
photographer
BRETT COLVIN
client
ODYSSEY GOLF
agency
VITROROBERTSON/
SAN DIEGO

PRINT MERIT

MERIT AWARD
magazine color full page
or spread: single

art director
JOHN VITRO

writer
JOHN ROBERTSON

photographer
CHRIS WIMPEY

client
TAYLOR GUITARS

agency
VITROROBERTSON/
SAN DIEGO

A couple of years ago, Elie Garfinkel started looking in the want ads and scouring all the music stores.

He was looking for a good, used Taylor.

He says he knew "he would probably have better luck winning the lottery," but he kept looking. He believed in fate.

Then, after a year of searching, he decided to end his frustration. He took the plunge and bought a brand new Taylor 510 model.

About three weeks later, out of habit, he was glancing through the classified ads. The word "Taylor," in boldface type, caught his eye.

It was an older model, in perfect condition.

At about the same time, his thirteen-year-old son announced he was getting tired of his electric guitar, and was ready for an acoustic.

Elie Garfinkel believes in fate. He just knows that sometimes it's a few weeks behind schedule.

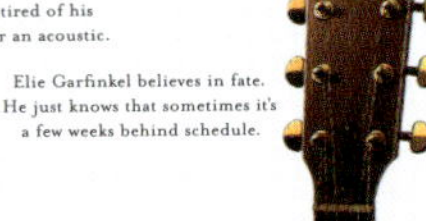

MERIT AWARD
magazine color full page
or spread: single

art director
JOHN VITRO

writer
JOHN ROBERTSON

photographer
CHRIS WIMPEY

client
TAYLOR GUITARS

agency
VITROROBERTSON/
SAN DIEGO

Bud Lawson decided to take up the guitar as a hobby.

And considering that Bud was 70 at the time, he wanted to make it as easy as possible on himself.

So, in Bud's words, he decided to "start at the top."

"After a thorough search, I found the Taylor 910 Dreadnought was the guitar for me," wrote Bud in a letter.

Bud says that since it'll be a while before he sounds like Chet Atkins, at least he has something beautiful to look at in the meantime.

We hope you like it, Bud.

We've always thought it's easier to play guitar if you start with a guitar that's easy to play.

And if you start early. Say, before you're eighty.

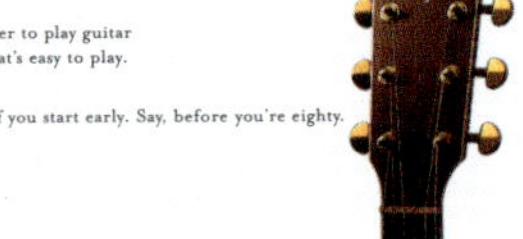

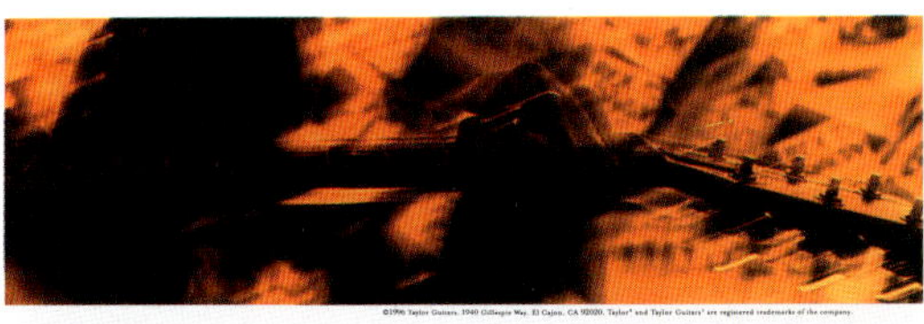

John Blaesi visited about 15 different guitar shops
before he found a Taylor six-string model.

He knew it was the guitar for him.

The only problem was, then he picked up a
Taylor twelve-string model and, in his words,
"could not put it down."

That's when John's wife stepped in.

She said, half-jokingly, that she wasn't going
to let him buy another guitar for several years,
so he'd better buy them both if he wanted to.

Now John's only dilemma is that he has
to practice twice as much.

John, if you're reading this,
we'd like to offer a suggestion.

In-between all that practicing,
take your wife out to a very nice dinner
every now and then.

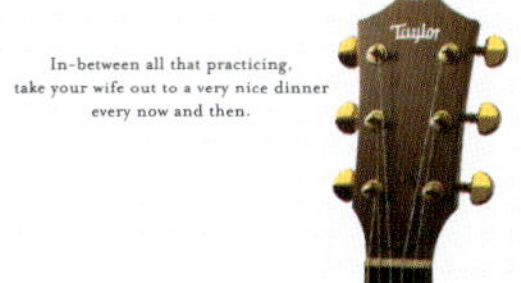

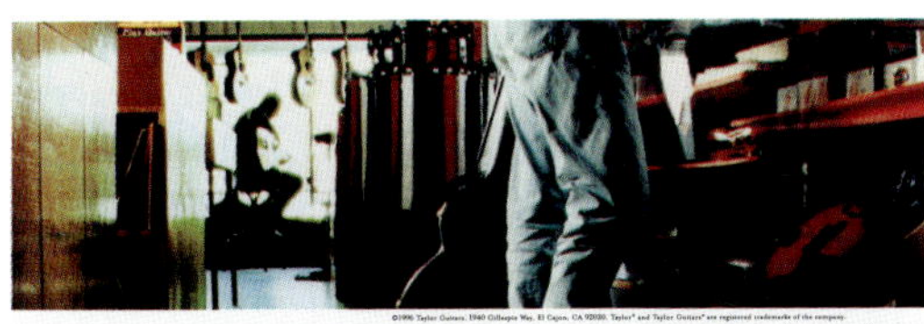

Keith Parmentier walked into a music store in Michigan.
He needed some new strings for his guitar.

Several hours later, he walked out with
a brand new Taylor.

In Falls Church, Virginia, Donald Waldron went into
a music store, looking to buy some new strings.

And when he left, he was carrying a brand new Taylor.

And a while back, Joshua Mills went into a store in
San Rafael, California, "just for some strings."

You probably think you know how this story ends.
But no, Joshua did not leave with a new Taylor.

He's got it on layaway, though.

MERIT AWARD
magazine color full page
or spread: single

art director
JOHN VITRO

writer
JOHN ROBERTSON

photographer
CHRIS WIMPEY

client
TAYLOR GUITARS

agency
VITROROBERTSON/
SAN DIEGO

MERIT AWARD
magazine color full page
or spread: single

art director
JOHN VITRO

writer
JOHN ROBERTSON

photographer
CHRIS WIMPEY

client
TAYLOR GUITARS

agency
VITROROBERTSON/
SAN DIEGO

Jak Marshall had been, in his words,
"yearning after" a certain used guitar for 2½ years.

He had saved his money for "months and months
and months," and one day, he was happily standing
in a music store actually buying it.

That's when he wandered over to a corner of
the acoustic room and, while the salesperson was
writing up his order, he picked up a Taylor.

It didn't take long.
By the time the salesperson was counting out his change,
Jak had learned something important about himself.

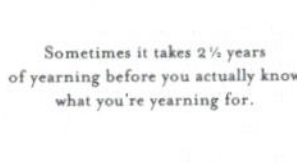

Sometimes it takes 2½ years
of yearning before you actually know
what you're yearning for.

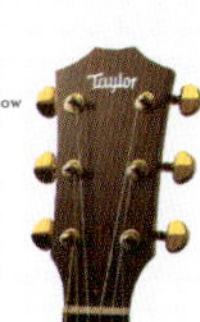

MERIT AWARD
magazine color full page
or spread: single

art director
JOHN VITRO

writer
JOHN ROBERTSON

photographer
CHRIS WIMPEY

client
TAYLOR GUITARS

agency
VITROROBERTSON/
SAN DIEGO

PRINT MERIT

MERIT AWARD
magazine color full page or spread: single

art director
LINDA KNIGHT

writer
MIKE MCCOMMON

photographer
KURT MARCUS

client
NIKE

agency
WIEDEN & KENNEDY/
PORTLAND

MERIT AWARD
magazine b/w full page or spread: campaign

art directors
HAJIME ANDO
LUCHO ORTEGA

writers
STEPHANIE CRIPPEN
DEAN WEI

illustrator
LUCHO ORTEGA

photographer
STOCK

client
RITCHEY DESIGN

agency
BUTLER SHINE & STERN/SAUSALITO

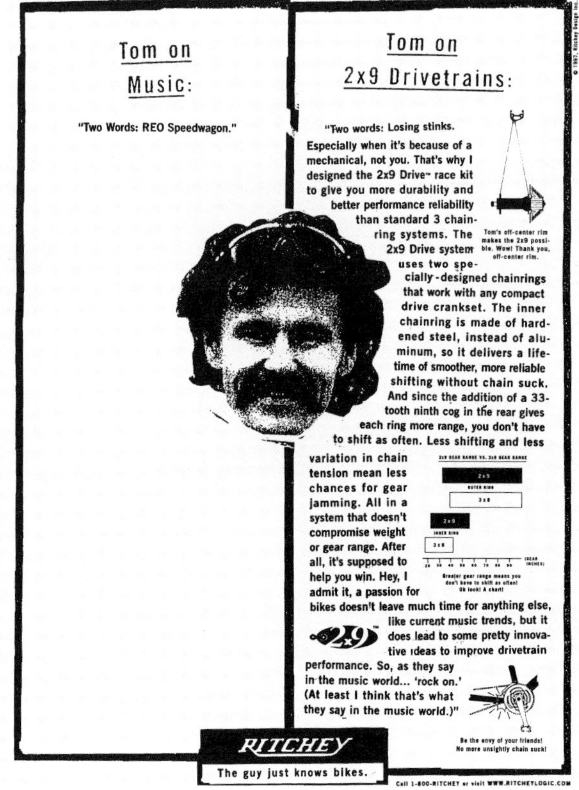

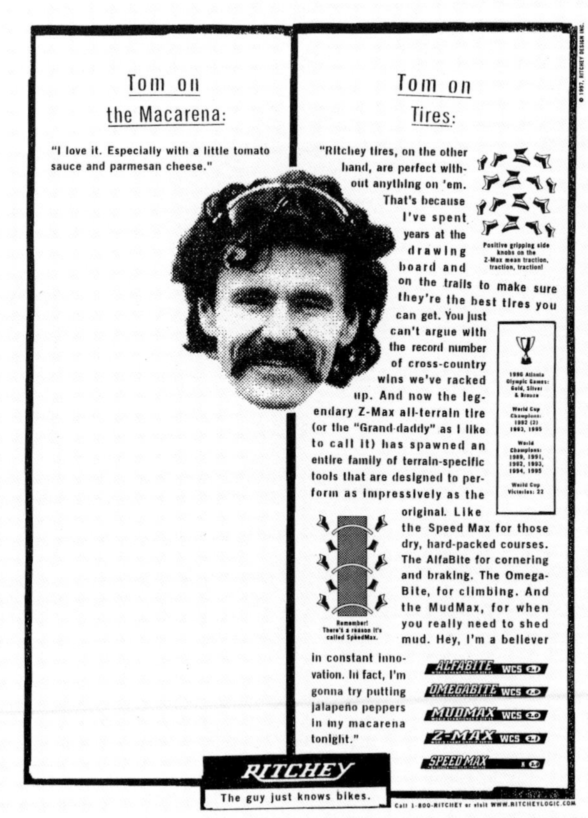

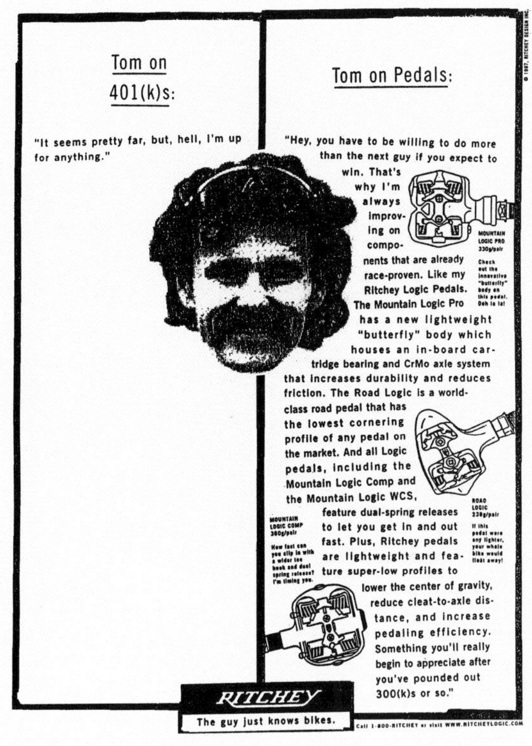
Tom on 401(k)s:
"It seems pretty far, but, hell, I'm up for anything."
Tom on Pedals:
"Hey, you have to be willing to do more than the next guy if you expect to win. That's why I'm always improving on components that are already race-proven. Like my Ritchey Logic Pedals. The Mountain Logic Pro has a new lightweight "butterfly" body which houses an in-board cartridge bearing and CrMo axle system that increases durability and reduces friction. The Road Logic is a world-class road pedal that has the lowest cornering profile of any pedal on the market. And all Logic pedals, including the Mountain Logic Comp and the Mountain Logic WCS, feature dual-spring releases to let you get in and out fast. Plus, Ritchey pedals are lightweight and feature super-low profiles to lower the center of gravity, reduce cleat-to-axle distance, and increase pedaling efficiency. Something you'll really begin to appreciate after you've pounded out 300(k)s or so."
MOUNTAIN LOGIC PRO 330g/pair
Check out the innovative "butterfly" body on this pedal. Ooh la la!
ROAD LOGIC 238g/pair
If this pedal were any lighter, your whole bike would float away!
MOUNTAIN LOGIC COMP 380g/pair
How fast can you clip in with a wider toe hook and dual spring release? I'm timing you.
RITCHEY
The guy just knows bikes.
Call 1-800-RITCHEY or visit WWW.RITCHEYLOGIC.COM

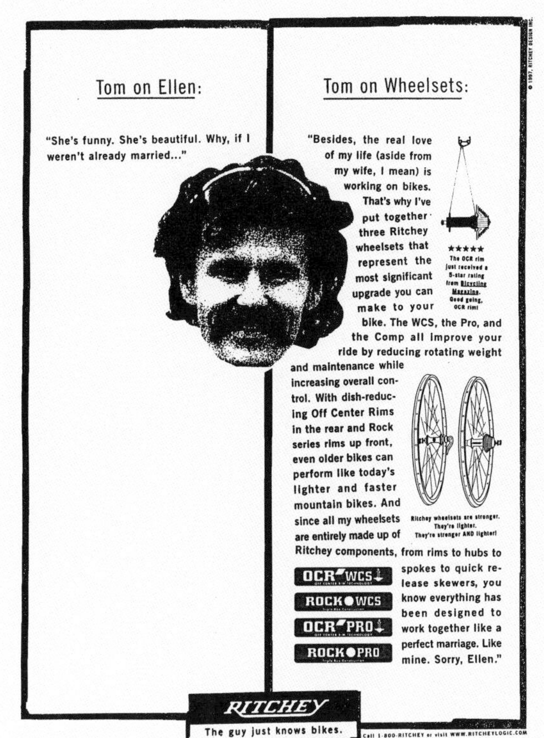
Tom on Ellen:
"She's funny. She's beautiful. Why, if I weren't already married..."
Tom on Wheelsets:
"Besides, the real love of my life (aside from my wife, I mean) is working on bikes. That's why I've put together three Ritchey wheelsets that represent the most significant upgrade you can make to your bike. The WCS, the Pro, and the Comp all improve your ride by reducing rotating weight and maintenance while increasing overall control. With dish-reducing Off Center Rims in the rear and Rock series rims up front, even older bikes can perform like today's lighter and faster mountain bikes. And since all my wheelsets are entirely made up of Ritchey components, from rims to hubs to spokes to quick release skewers, you know everything has been designed to work together like a perfect marriage. Like mine. Sorry, Ellen."
★★★★★
The OCR rim just received a 5-star rating from Bicycling Magazine. Good going, OCR rim!
Ritchey wheelsets are stronger. They're lighter. They're stronger AND lighter!
OCR WCS
ROCK WCS
OCR PRO
ROCK PRO
RITCHEY
The guy just knows bikes.
Call 1-800-RITCHEY or visit WWW.RITCHEYLOGIC.COM

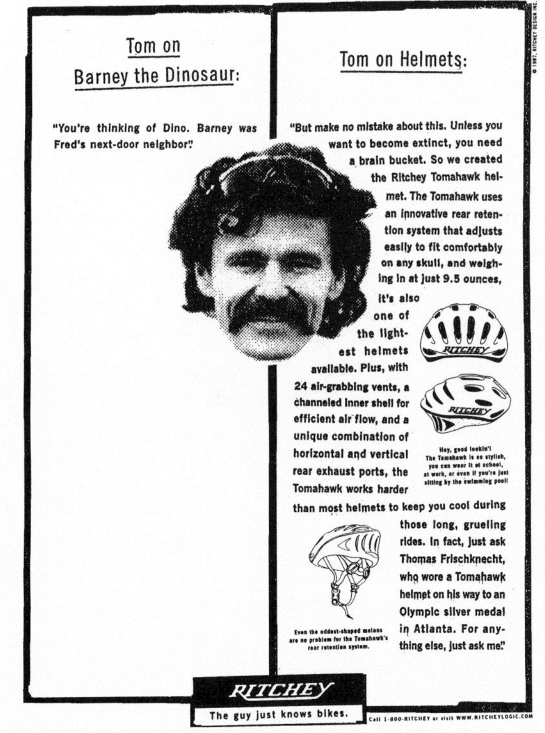
Tom on Barney the Dinosaur:
"You're thinking of Dino. Barney was Fred's next-door neighbor."
Tom on Helmets:
"But make no mistake about this. Unless you want to become extinct, you need a brain bucket. So we created the Ritchey Tomahawk helmet. The Tomahawk uses an innovative rear retention system that adjusts easily to fit comfortably on any skull, and weighing in at just 9.5 ounces, it's also one of the lightest helmets available. Plus, with 24 air-grabbing vents, a channeled inner shell for efficient air flow, and a unique combination of horizontal and vertical rear exhaust ports, the Tomahawk works harder than most helmets to keep you cool during those long, grueling rides. In fact, just ask Thomas Frischknecht, who wore a Tomahawk helmet on his way to an Olympic silver medal in Atlanta. For anything else, just ask me."
Hey, good lookin'! The Tomahawk is so stylish, you can wear it at school, at work, or even if you're just sitting by the swimming pool!
Even the oddest-shaped melons are no problem for the Tomahawk's rear retention system.
RITCHEY
The guy just knows bikes.
Call 1-800-RITCHEY or visit WWW.RITCHEYLOGIC.COM

PRINT MERIT

MERIT AWARD
magazine b/w full page
or spread: campaign

art director
CLAUDIA JÄH
writer
CARLOS OBERS
photographer
MATTHIAS ZIEGLER
client
STRELLSON
agency
RG WIESMEIER/
MUNICH

Stoffe, Schnitte und Muster
sind Stammesabzeichen, an denen
sich die Häuptlinge erkennen.

strellson
menswear

Ein Mann von Geist kann
sich sehr präzise ausdrücken.
Auch, wenn er schweigt.

strellson
menswear

PRINT MERIT

MERIT AWARD
magazine color full page
or spread: campaign

art director
PAUL BELFORD

writer
NIGEL ROBERTS

photographers
LAURIE HASKELL
JAMES NACHTWEY
GLEN ERLER
JOEL-PETER WITKIN

client
WATERSTONE'S
BOOKSELLERS

agency
BDDP.GGT/LONDON

YOU CAN
TAKE
A
BOOK
ANYWHERE
&
VICE-VERSA
W
WATERSTONE'S
READ ON

NOTHING COULD ever BE MORE
OFFENSIVE
in a BOOK THAN CENSORSHIP
OFF
-EN-
SIVE
W
WATERSTONE'S
READ ON

MERIT AWARD
magazine color full page or spread: campaign

art director
BOB BARRIE

writer
DEAN BUCKHORN

photographers
ROBERT ALLISON
DIANA WALKER
GARY HERSHORN

client
TIME MAGAZINE

agency
FALLON MCELLIGOTT/MINNEAPOLIS

A weekly reminder that the world is a pretty amazing place.

The world's most interesting magazine.

War. Politics. Business.

Sometimes all in the same article.

The world's most interesting magazine.

At what point do science and morality collide?

At what point do science and morality collide?

The world's most interesting magazine.

The world's most interesting magazine.

We cover the scenes behind the scenes behind the scenes.

The world's most interesting magazine.

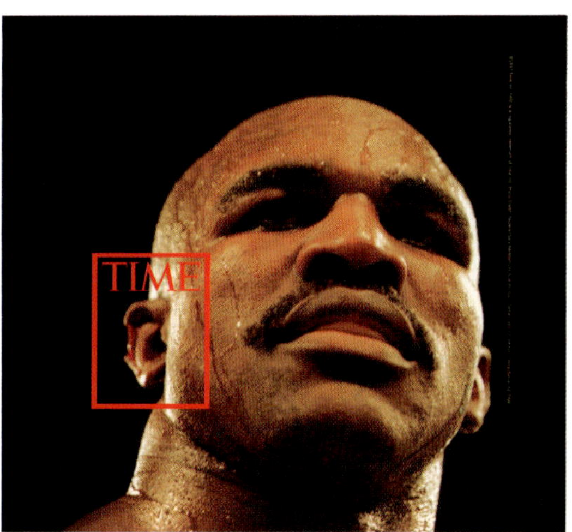

What kind of bandage can boxing possibly put on this?

The world's most interesting magazine.

MERIT AWARD
magazine color full page
or spread: campaign

art directors
JON SOTO
PAUL HIRSCH

writers
AL KELLY
JOSH DENBERG

photographers
HEIMO
BILL THOMAS

client
NIKE

agency
GOODBY SILVERSTEIN
& PARTNERS/
SAN FRANCISCO

PRINT MERIT

PRINT MERIT

MERIT AWARD
magazine color full page
or spread: campaign

art director
DAVID CARTER

writer
KIRT GENTRY

photographer
NADAV KANDER

client
SATURN

agency
HAL RINEY &
PARTNERS/
SAN FRANCISCO

very reasonable. Contact PO Box 1372 for details.

SKIING EXERCISE MACHINE for sale. In perfect working order. Hardly used (still in box). Contact Billy on 01771 125 102 any time after 5.30pm.

Lonely Hearts

27, TALL, PROFESSION **MALE,** genuine, seeks easy going le, for that special romance. I en SMIRNOFF alking, reading, theatre, the arts, pubs films, and eating out. Box 1728.

YOUNG ATHLETIC MALE, 89, 6ft tall svelte and n/s, is seeking nurse 28-38. Contact Box 1730.

MAN 38, gsoh, recently bankrupt. I'm seeking mature lady with angina. Must possess vitality, and lots of capital. Box 1731 for details.

POLISH LADY 32, seeks passport for lasting relationship. Naivety a SMIR d essential. Box 1735.

BUBBLY VIVACIOUS, psychopath, 4 slim, seeks husband number 16 for fun. Box 1738.

MALE 42, lives in mum's house seeking a sensitive dominatrix to tie the knot. Box 1739.

close to tube, fitted carp glazing, washing machine, sate ry, gch & bills included. Tel 017 4.

● **Luxury 1st flr** studio coop for rent. Would suit a prof single dwarf. £95 per week. View over water works. Phone 01771 55863.

● **We are looking** for a devotee to join house shared by cult members. Would suit a cheerful and gullible person. Will have to share all earthly possessions. Tel 01771 42198 b4 The Day of Reckoning or all day Sunday.

BEDSITS, HOVELS, STUDIOS & HUTCHES

Luxury properties available. 01771 49822

● Nice room in condemned se

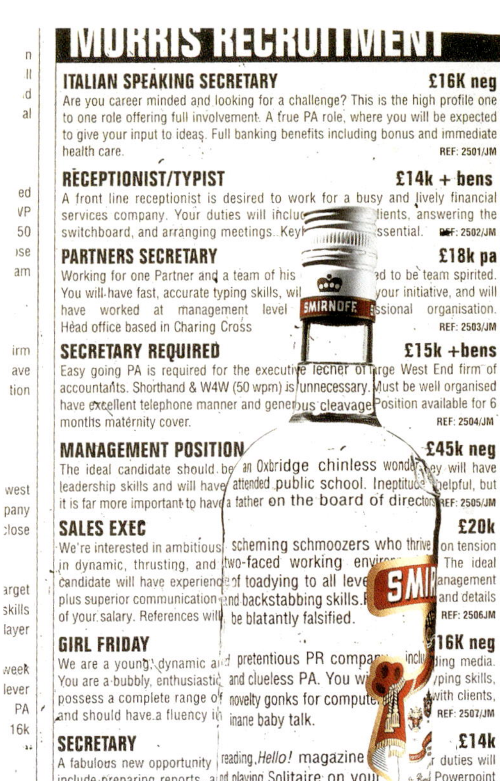

MORRIS RECRUITMENT

ITALIAN SPEAKING SECRETARY **£16K neg**
Are you career minded and looking for a challenge? This is the high profile one to one role offering full involvement. A true PA role, where you will be expected to give your input to ideas. Full banking benefits including bonus and immediate health care. REF: 2501/JM

RECEPTIONIST/TYPIST **£14k + bens**
A front line receptionist is desired to work for a busy and lively financial services company. Your duties will inclu lients, answering the switchboard, and arranging meetings. Key ssential. REF: 2502/JM

PARTNERS SECRETARY **£18k pa**
Working for one Partner and a team of his ed to be team spirited. You will have fast, accurate typing skills, wi your initiative, and will have worked at management level ssional organisation. Head office based in Charing Cross REF: 2503/JM

SECRETARY REQUIRED **£15k +bens**
Easy going PA is required for the executive lecher of large West End firm of accountants. Shorthand & W4W (50 wpm) is unnecessary. Must be well organised have excellent telephone manner and generous cleavage. Position available for 6 months maternity cover. REF: 2504/JM

MANAGEMENT POSITION **£45k neg**
The ideal candidate should be an Oxbridge chinless wonder. They will have leadership skills and will have attended public school. Ineptitude helpful, but it is far more important to have a father on the board of directors. REF: 2505/JM

SALES EXEC **£20k**
We're interested in ambitious scheming schmoozers who thrive on tension in dynamic, thrusting, and two-faced working envir The ideal candidate will have experience of toadying to all leve anagement plus superior communication and backstabbing skills. and details of your salary. References will be blatantly falsified. REF: 2506JM

GIRL FRIDAY **16K neg**
We are a young dynamic and pretentious PR compa incl ing media. You are a bubbly, enthusiastic and clueless PA. You w ping skills, possess a complete range of novelty gonks for compute with clients, and should have a fluency in inane baby talk. REF: 2507/JM

SECRETARY **£14k**
A fabulous new opportunity reading *Hello!* magazine duties will include preparing reports, and playing Solitaire on your Powerpoint

MERIT AWARD
magazine color full page or spread: campaign

art director
GARY ANDERSON

writer
TONY MILLER

client
SMIRNOFF

agency
LOWE HOWARD-SPINK/
LONDON

MERIT AWARD
magazine color full page or spread: campaign

art director
GARY GOLDSMITH

writer
DEAN HACOHEN

photographer
STOCK

client
SONY ELECTRONICS

agency
LOWE & PARTNERS/ SMS/NEW YORK

PRINT MERIT

MERIT AWARD
magazine color full page
or spread: campaign

art director
MICHAEL IPP

writers
DOMINIQUE LE CLEZIO
PAIGE NICK

photographer
JAN VERBOOM

client
LEVI STRAUSS & CO

agency
TBWA HUNT LASCARIS/
CAPETOWN

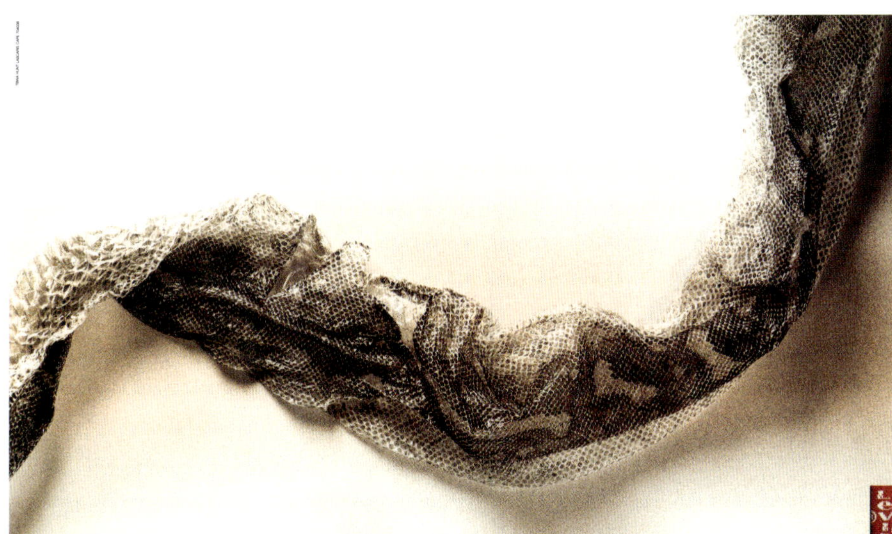

MERIT AWARD
magazine color full page or spread: campaign

art director
KELLY BECK

writer
BRIAN GOLD

photographer
BRETT COLVIN

client
ODYSSEY GOLF

agency
VITROROBERTSON/
SAN DIEGO

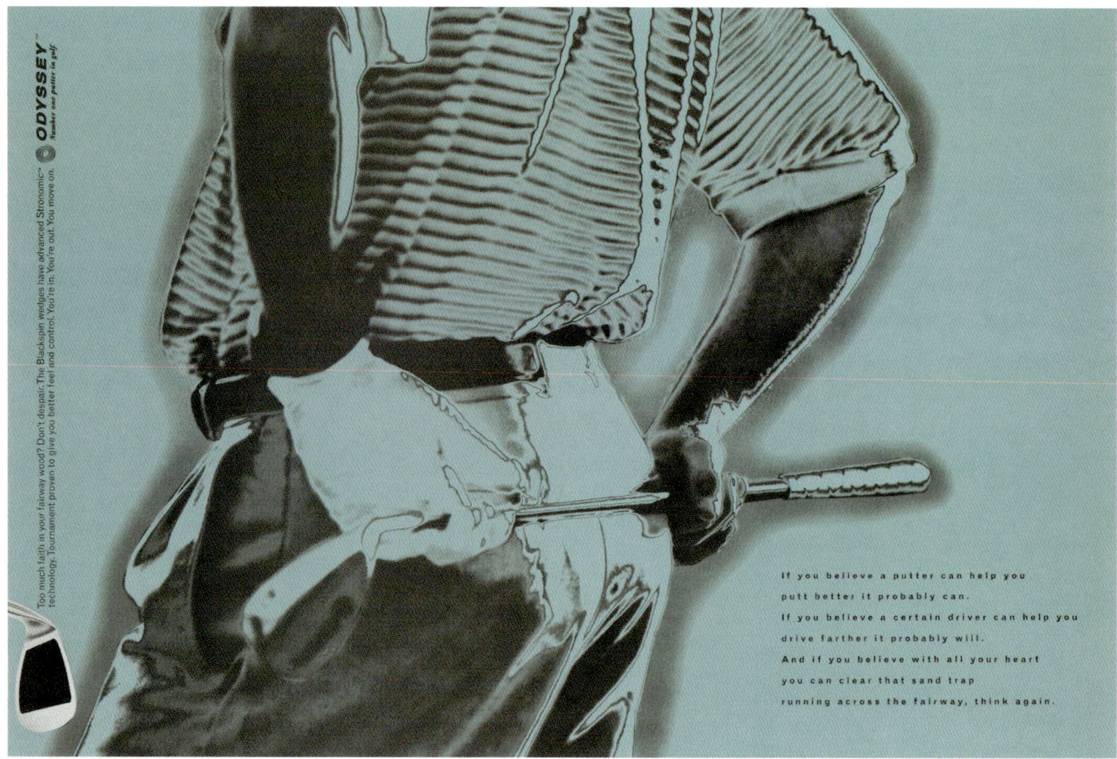

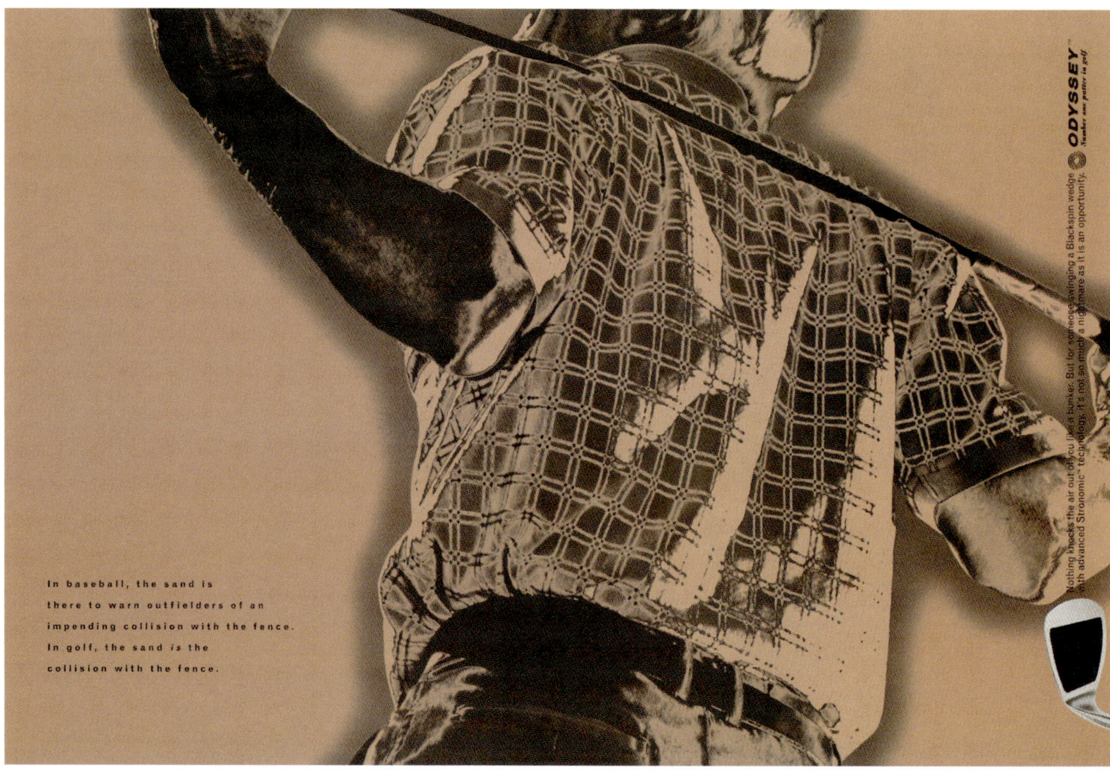

PRINT MERIT

The term "clubhead" is misleading.
It indicates there's some sort of
brain present.
You can't talk sense into your clubhead. But you can switch to one of Odyssey's Blackspin wedges with our advanced Stronomic™ technology. It can't think, but it can read your mind.
ODYSSEY
Number one putter in golf

It's okay to let your mind wander.
Just don't be surprised if your ball
tags along to keep it company.
Odyssey's Blackspin wedges have our soft, sensitive insert technology for better feel and control.
But if you happen to be thinking about what you want for lunch it really doesn't matter, does it?
ODYSSEY

PRINT MERIT

MERIT AWARD
magazine color full page
or spread: campaign

art director
JOHN VITRO

writer
JOHN ROBERTSON

photographer
CHRIS WIMPEY

client
TAYLOR GUITARS

agency
VITROROBERTSON/
SAN DIEGO

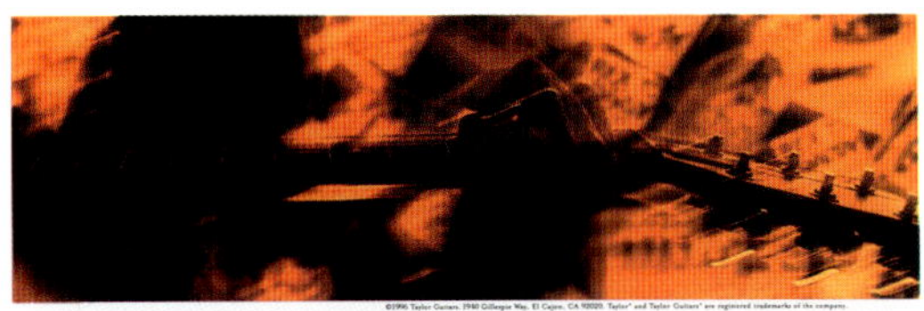

John Blaesi visited about 15 different guitar shops
before he found a Taylor six-string model.

He knew it was the guitar for him.

The only problem was, then he picked up a
Taylor twelve-string model and, in his words,
"could not put it down."

That's when John's wife stepped in.

She said, half-jokingly, that she wasn't going
to let him buy another guitar for several years,
so he'd better buy them both if he wanted to.

Now John's only dilemma is that he has
to practice twice as much.

John, if you're reading this,
we'd like to offer a suggestion.

In-between all that practicing,
take your wife out to a very nice dinner
every now and then.

©1996 Taylor Guitars. 1940 Gillespie Way, El Cajon, CA 92020. Taylor® and Taylor Guitars® are registered trademarks of the company.

Keith Parmentier walked into a music store in Michigan.
He needed some new strings for his guitar.

Several hours later, he walked out with
a brand new Taylor.

In Falls Church, Virginia, Donald Waldron went into
a music store, looking to buy some new strings.

And when he left, he was carrying a brand new Taylor.

And a while back, Joshua Mills went into a store in
San Rafael, California, "just for some strings."

You probably think you know how this story ends.
But no, Joshua did not leave with a new Taylor.

He's got it on layaway, though.

©1996 Taylor Guitars. 1940 Gillespie Way, El Cajon, CA 92020. Taylor® and Taylor Guitars® are registered trademarks of the company.

Jak Marshall had been, in his words,
"yearning after" a certain used guitar for 2 ½ years.

He had saved his money for "months and months
and months," and one day, he was happily standing
in a music store actually buying it.

That's when he wandered over to a corner of
the acoustic room and, while the salesperson was
writing up his order, he picked up a Taylor.

It didn't take long.
By the time the salesperson was counting out his change,
Jak had learned something important about himself.

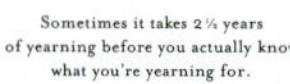

Sometimes it takes 2 ½ years
of yearning before you actually know
what you're yearning for.

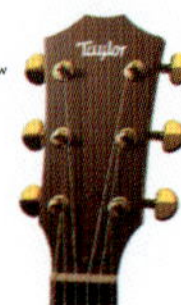

PRINT MERIT

MERIT AWARD
magazine color full page or spread: campaign

art director
JOHN VITRO

writer
JOHN ROBERTSON

photographers
CHRIS WIMPEY
STOCK

client
TAYLOR GUITARS

agency
VITROROBERTSON/
SAN DIEGO

A couple of years ago, Elie Garfinkel started looking in the want ads and scouring all the music stores.

He was looking for a good, used Taylor.

He says he knew "he would probably have better luck winning the lottery," but he kept looking. He believed in fate.

Then, after a year of searching, he decided to end his frustration. He took the plunge and bought a brand new Taylor 510 model.

About three weeks later, out of habit, he was glancing through the classified ads. The word "Taylor," in boldface type, caught his eye.

It was an older model, in perfect condition.

At about the same time, his thirteen-year-old son announced he was getting tired of his electric guitar, and was ready for an acoustic.

Elie Garfinkel believes in fate
He just knows that sometimes i
a few weeks behind schedule.

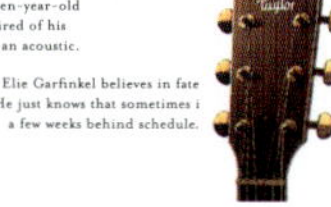

Ross Powell and his wife were driving back from a vacation in the mountains.

Ross saw a sign for a guitar shop, pulled over and said, "I'll be right out."

He went inside and fell in love with a Taylor.

In Ross' words, he "talked about that guitar all the way home."

Which was 195 miles.

Finally, after talking about it all the next week, he drove back to the same store to buy it. Which was almost 400 miles round trip.

If you ever get a chance to pull over and try a Taylor, we hope you will.

It'll give you something to chat about for the next three or four hundred mil

Bud Lawson decided to take up the guitar as a hobby.

And considering that Bud was 70 at the time, he wanted to make it as easy as possible on himself.

So, in Bud's words, he decided to "start at the top."

"After a thorough search, I found the Taylor 910 Dreadnought was the guitar for me," wrote Bud in a letter.

Bud says that since it'll be a while before he sounds like Chet Atkins, at least he has something beautiful to look at in the meantime.

We hope you like it, Bud.

We've always thought it's easier to play guitar if you start with a guitar that's easy to play.

And if you start early. Say, before you're eighty

MERIT AWARD
magazine color full page or spread: campaign

art director
LINDA KNIGHT

writer
MIKE MCCOMMON

illustrator
PATTY FORK

client
NIKE

agency
WIEDEN & KENNEDY/ PORTLAND

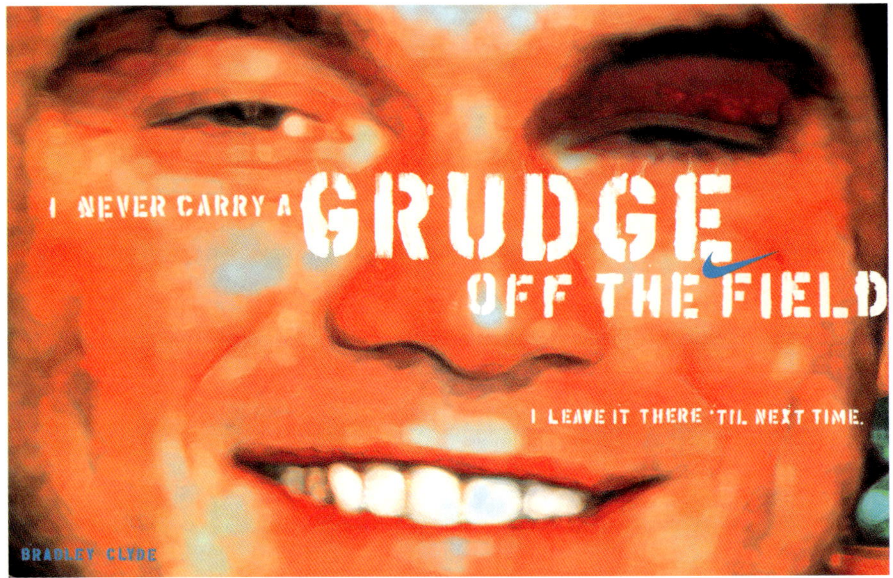

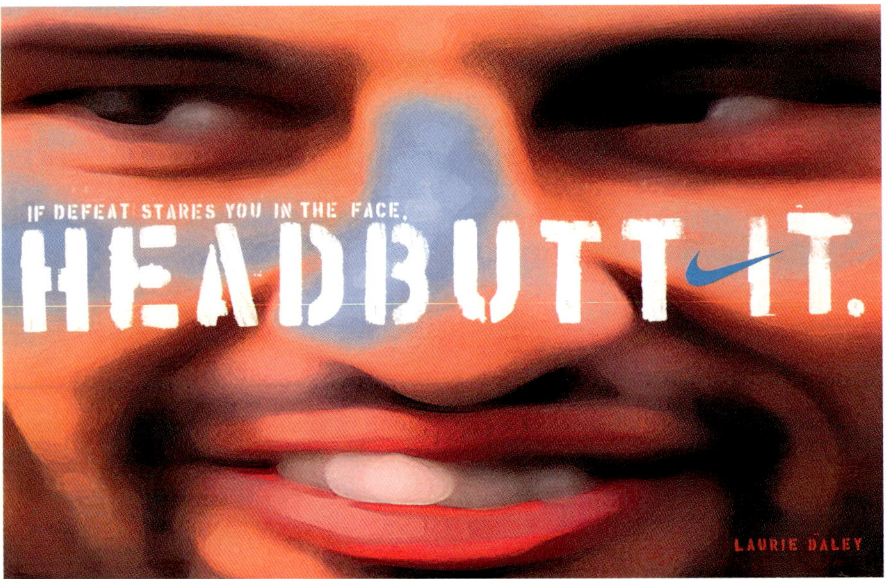

MERIT AWARD
magazine b/w or color
less than a page: single

art director
DAVID SZABO

writer
DAVID SZABO

photographer
CHARLES LIDDALL

client
EXCELSIOR

agency
BATES/HONG KONG

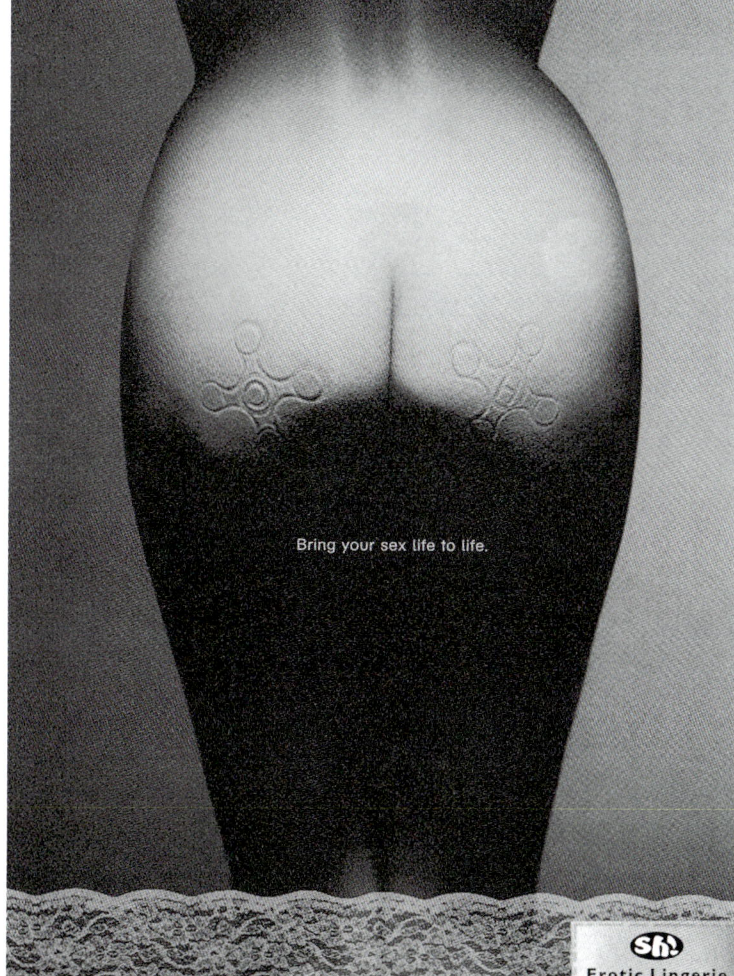

MERIT AWARD
magazine b/w or color
less than a page: single

art directors
PAUL ALDERMAN
PETE OGDEN

writer
PAUL ALDERMAN

photographer
TONY MAY

client
SH! EROTIC LINGERIE EMPORIUM

agency
BATES DORLAND/ LONDON

MERIT AWARD
magazine b/w or color
less than a page: single

art director
PATRICK PLUTCHOW

writer
RYAN EBNER

photographer
HEIMO

client
SPECIALIZED BICYCLES

agency
BUTLER SHINE &
STERN/SAUSALITO

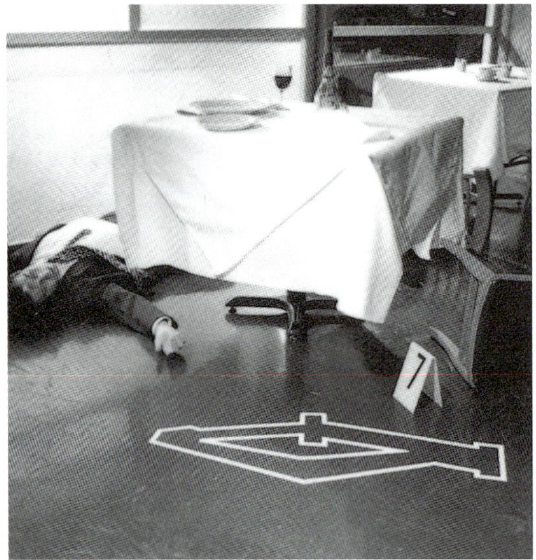

PRINT MERIT

MERIT AWARD
magazine b/w or color
less than a page: single

art director
JEFF TERWILLIGER
writer
JIM NELSON
photographer
HUNTER FREEMAN
client
HARLEY-DAVIDSON
agency
CARMICHAEL LYNCH/
MINNEAPOLIS

MERIT AWARD
magazine b/w or color
less than a page: single

art director
JEFF TERWILLIGER
writer
JIM NELSON
photographer
HUNTER FREEMAN
client
HARLEY-DAVIDSON
agency
CARMICHAEL LYNCH/
MINNEAPOLIS

MERIT AWARD
magazine b/w or color
less than a page: single

art director
GLENN GRAY
writer
TOM CAMP
photographer
JERRY STEBBINS
client
NORMARK RAPALA
agency
CARMICHAEL LYNCH/
MINNEAPOLIS

The only drawback on charter boats is it leaves little time for drinking beer.

MERIT AWARD
magazine b/w or color
less than a page: single

art director
ANDY AZULA
writer
DAVE PULLAR
photographer
ROBERT MCDONALD
client
NIKON SCHOOL
agency
FALLON MCELLIGOTT/
MINNEAPOLIS

We can all feel a tad overwhelmed now and then, and photographers are certainly no exception. Which is exactly why we recommend taking our 8-hour class, where you'll learn everything from basic composition to advanced exposure techniques. You also get the 157-page Nikon School Handbook and a lunch, all for $99. Call us at (516) 547-8666 for more information.

MERIT AWARD
magazine b/w or color
less than a page: single

art director
ELLEN STEINBERG
writer
TOM ROSEN
photographer
SHAWN MICHIENZI
client
KNOB CREEK
agency
FALLON MCELLIGOTT/
MINNEAPOLIS

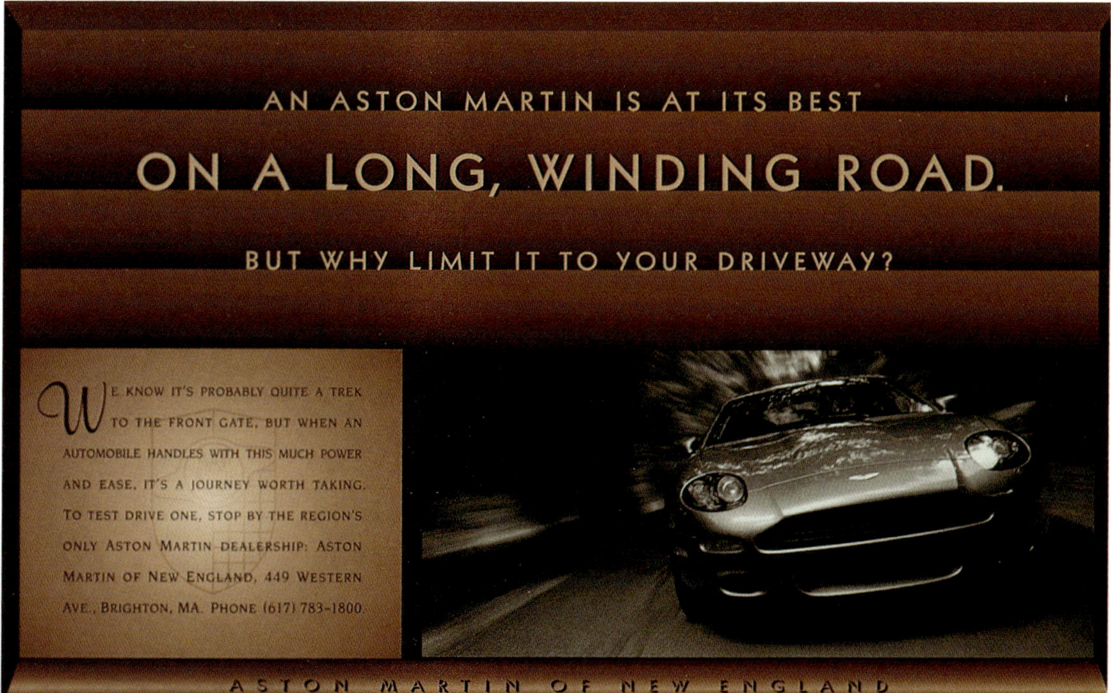

MERIT AWARD
magazine b/w or color
less than a page: single

art director
SEAN FARRELL
writer
CHRIS DECARLO
photographer
JIM FLYNN
client
ASTON MARTIN
agency
INGALLS ADVERTISING/
BOSTON

MERIT AWARD
magazine b/w or color
less than a page: single

art director
ERIC TILFORD

writer
TODD TILFORD

client
DR. MARTENS

agency
PYRO/DALLAS

MERIT AWARD
magazine b/w or color
less than a page: single

art director
JOE KAYSER

writers
STEVE SILVER
ANDY SOHN

illustrator
DONALD GRAHAM

client
BRODERBUND
SOFTWARE

agency
SAATCHI & SAATCHI/
SAN FRANCISCO

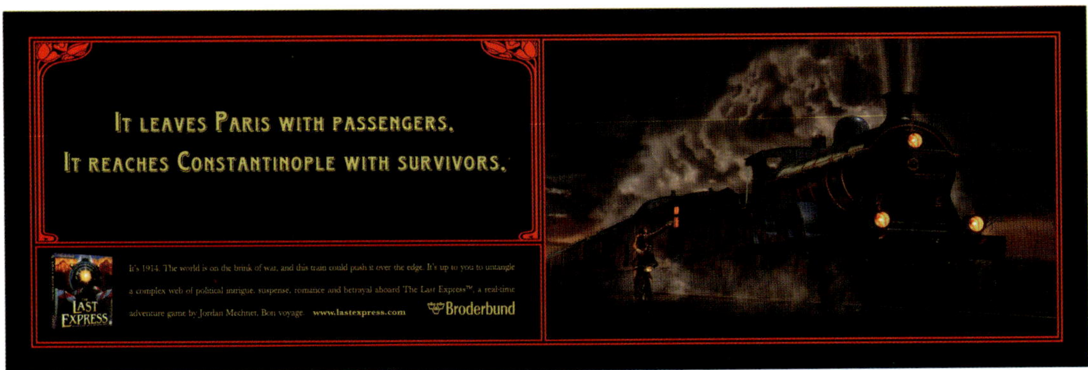

PRINT MERIT

On a clear day
you can see for 800 years.

Amongst temples to the gods, a shrine to mortals. Since 1929, Grand Hotel d'Angkor has been as much a legend as the celebrated ruins that surround it. No adventurer worth his elephant and porter would have stayed anywhere else in the Kingdom of Cambodia. Now restored along with Hotel Le Royal in Phnom Penh, the treasure of an ancient civilisation is just a hotel room away.

Hotel Le Royal
Grand Hotel d'Angkor

For reservations fax (855) 23-368-118, e-mail raffles.grand.royal@cm17.com or write to 68 Monivong Boulevard, Phnom Penh, Kingdom of Cambodia. A member of Small Luxury Hotels of the World.

MERIT AWARD
magazine b/w or color
less than a page: single

art director
TED ROYER

writer
ROWAN CHANEN

illustrators
TED ROYER
POK CHENG HAI

photgrapher
STOCK

client
RAFFLES
INTERNATIONAL

agency
SAATCHI & SAATCHI/
SINGAPORE

MERIT AWARD
magazine b/w or color
less than a page
campaign

art director
ROBB BURNHAM
writer
STEVE CASEY
photographer
JERRY STEBBINS
client
NORMARK BLUE FOX
agency
CARMICHAEL LYNCH/
MINNEAPOLIS

PRINT MERIT

ULTIMATE LOW-LIGHT REFLECTION.
THE NEW SILVER PLATED MINNOW SPIN.
A stunning new example of Blue Fox innovation. Genuine silver plating adhered to balsa. A premium finish that reflects every available particle of light combined with the wounded-minnow action only balsa can achieve. The renowned silver Vibrax® blade flashes and pulsates to make this lure "the total package."

USA 20

Kenny –
SMELL THIS POSTCARD.
Bill

POSTCARD

Remember...
BLUE FOX
Fish Smart!!!

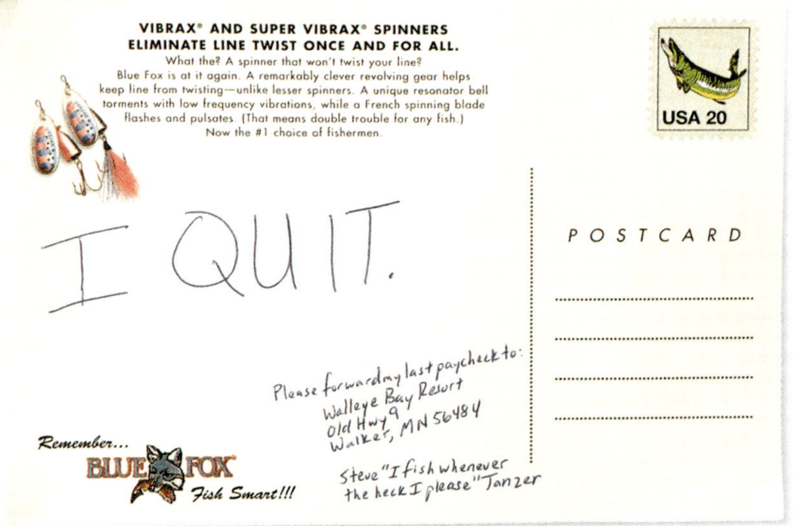

MERIT AWARD
magazine b/w or color
less than a page
campaign

art director
ELLEN STEINBERG

writer
TOM ROSEN

photographer
SHAWN MICHIENZI

client
KNOB CREEK

agency
FALLON MCELLIGOTT/
MINNEAPOLIS

MERIT AWARD
magazine b/w or color
less than a page
campaign

art director
ANDY AZULA

writer
DAVE PULLAR

photographers
JOE SWEET
ROBERT MCDONALD
JOHN CONRAD FINK

client
NIKON SCHOOL

agency
FALLON MCELLIGOTT/
MINNEAPOLIS

Good photographers don't let anything stand in the way of a great picture. Which you'll learn at our 8-hour class, covering everything from basic composition to advanced exposure techniques. You also get the 157-page Nikon School Handbook and a lunch, all for $99. Call us at (516) 547-8666 to learn the date and time a class will be offered in your city.

We can all feel a tad overwhelmed now and then, and photographers are certainly no exception. Which is exactly why we recommend taking our 8-hour class, where you'll learn everything from basic composition to advanced exposure techniques. You also get the 157-page Nikon School Handbook and a lunch, all for $99. Call us at (516) 547-8666 for more information.

A good photographer wouldn't be caught dead using the wrong film. So be sure to attend our 8-hour class, where you'll learn everything from basic composition to advanced exposure techniques. You'll also get the 157-page Nikon School Handbook and a lunch, all for $99. Call us at (516) 547-8666 to learn the date and time a class will be offered in your city.

Protects against foot-in-mouth disease.

The Economist

MERIT AWARD
outdoor: single

art director
GARY MARTIN

writer
TIM RILEY

typographer
JOE HOZA

client
THE ECONOMIST

agency
ABBOTT MEAD VICKERS.BBDO/ LONDON

In opinion polls, 100% of Economist readers had one.

MERIT AWARD
outdoor: single

art directors
MIKE DURBAN

writer
TONY STRONG

typographer
JOE HOZA

client
THE ECONOMIST

agency
ABBOTT MEAD VICKERS.BBDO/ LONDON

MERIT AWARD
outdoor: single

art directors
MARCELLO SERPA
JULIO ANDERY

writer
MARCELLO SERPA

photographer
MAURICIO NAHAS

client
VOLKSWAGEN BRAZIL

agency
ALMAP/BBDO/ SAO PAULO

MERIT AWARD
outdoor: single

art director
MELANIE MENKEMELLER
writer
RYAN EBNER
photographer
STOCK
client
SCOTTISH AND NEWCASTLE IMPORTERS
agency
BUTLER SHINE & STERN/SAUSALITO

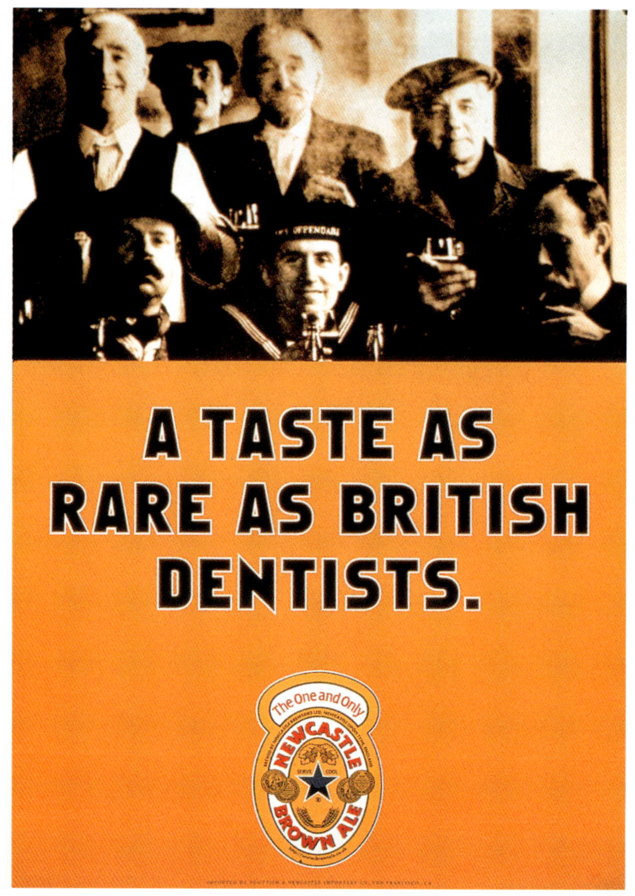

MERIT AWARD
outdoor: single

art director
MELANIE MENKEMELLER
writer
RYAN EBNER
photographer
STOCK
client
SCOTTISH AND NEWCASTLE IMPORTERS
agency
BUTLER SHINE & STERN/SAUSALITO

PRINT MERIT

MERIT AWARD
outdoor: single

art director
WAYNE BEST
writer
IAN REICHENTHAL
photographer
CRAIG CUTLER
client
SAUZA
COMMEMORATIVO
agency
CLIFF FREEMAN
& PARTNERS/
NEW YORK

PRINT MERIT

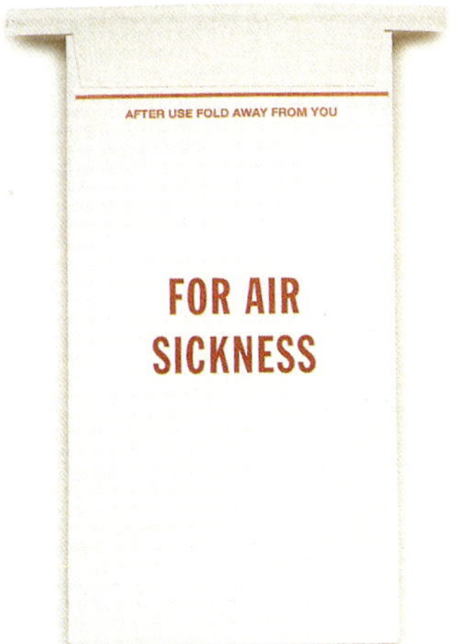

MERIT AWARD
outdoor: single

art director
DAVID KELSO
writer
JANA PECK
photographer
TERRY COLLIER
client
NIKE CANADA
agency
COSSETTE
COMMUNICATIONS-
MARKETING/TORONTO

MERIT AWARD
outdoor: single

art director
VALERIE ANG-POWELL
writer
BLAKE DALEY
photographer
HUNTER FREEMAN
client
CALIFORNIA FLUID MILK PROCESSORS
agency
GOODBY SILVERSTEIN & PARTNERS/ SAN FRANCISCO

MERIT AWARD
outdoor: single

art director
VALERIE ANG-POWELL
writer
LORI NYGAARD
photographer
HOLLY STEWART
client
CALIFORNIA FLUID MILK PROCESSORS
agency
GOODBY SILVERSTEIN & PARTNERS/ SAN FRANCISCO

MERIT AWARD
outdoor: single

art director
VALERIE ANG-POWELL
writer
BLAKE DALEY
photographer
HUNTER FREEMAN
client
CALIFORNIA FLUID MILK PROCESSORS
agency
GOODBY SILVERSTEIN & PARTNERS/ SAN FRANCISCO

MERIT AWARD
outdoor: single

art director
PETER NICHOLSON

writer
SCOTT WILD

photographer
LARS TOPELMANN

client
ADIDAS AMERICA

agency
LEAGAS DELANEY/
SAN FRANCISCO

MERIT AWARD
outdoor: single

art directors
ALEX HACKWORTH
MARK FAULKNER
writers
DAVE CLAUS
STEFFAN POSTAER
photographer
TONY D'ORIO
client
CALLARD & BOWSER-SUCHARD/ALTOIDS
agency
LEO BURNETT COMPANY/CHICAGO

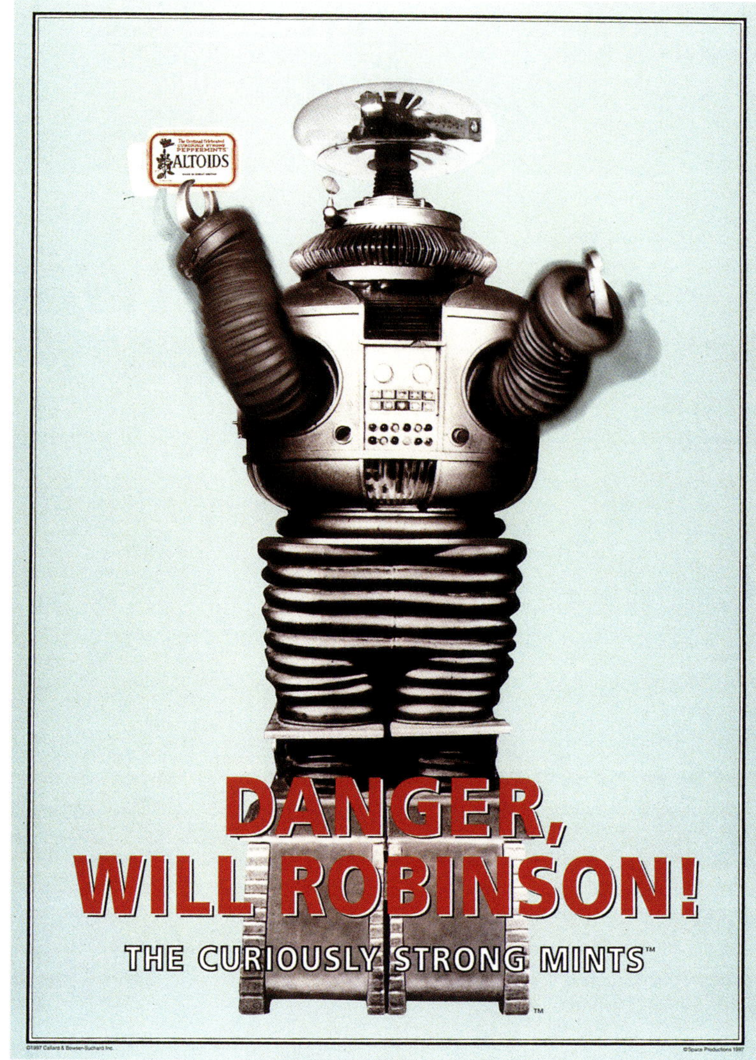

PRINT MERIT

MERIT AWARD
outdoor: single

art directors
MARK FAULKNER
NOEL HAAN
writer
STEFFAN POSTAER
client
CALLARD & BROWSER-SUCHARD/ALTOIDS
agency
LEO BURNETT COMPANY/CHICAGO

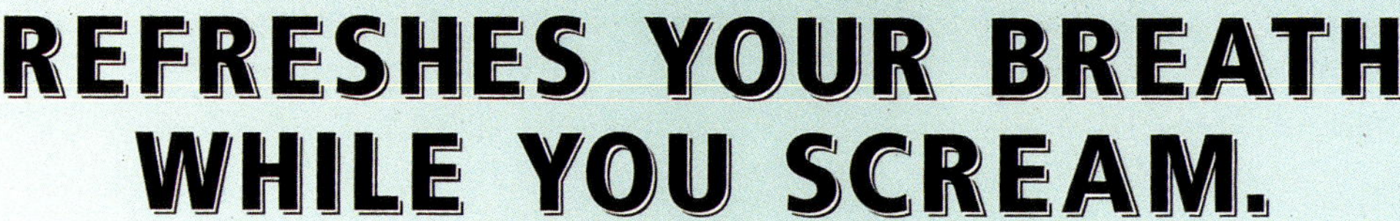

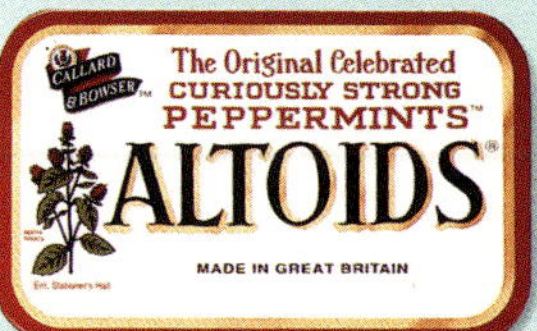

THE CURIOUSLY STRONG MINTS™

©1996 Callard & Bowser-Suchard Inc.

MERIT AWARD
outdoor: single

art director
GARY ANDERSON

writer
TONY MILLER

client
SMIRNOFF

agency
LOWE HOWARD-SPINK/
LONDON

PRINT MERIT

MERIT AWARD
outdoor: single

art director
PEPE MARAIS

writer
CRAIG CRAWFORD

client
VIRGIN ATLANTIC

agency
NET#WORK/
JOHANNESBURG

PRINT MERIT

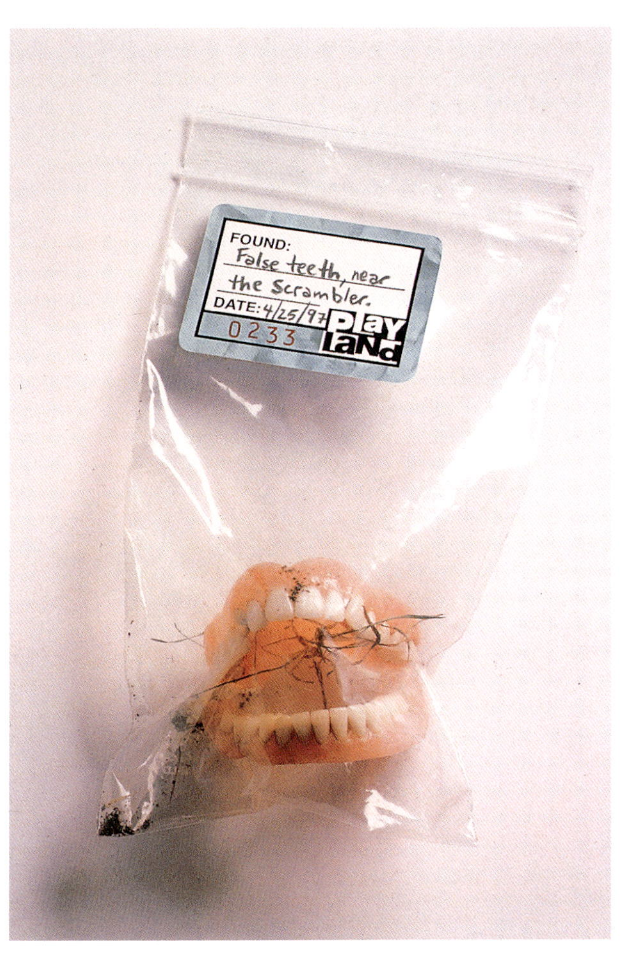

MERIT AWARD
outdoor: single

art director
IAN GRAIS

writer
ALAN RUSSELL

photographer
HANS SIPMA

client
PLAYLAND

agency
PALMER JARVIS DDB/
VANCOUVER

MERIT AWARD
outdoor: single

art director
IAN GRAIS

writer
ALAN RUSSELL

photographer
HANS SIPMA

client
PLAYLAND

agency
PALMER JARVIS DDB/
VANCOUVER

MERIT AWARD
outdoor: single

art director
JOHN SHIRLEY
writer
RICH SIEGEL
client
ABC TELEVISION
agency
TBWA CHIAT/DAY/
VENICE

MERIT AWARD
outdoor: single

art directors
LEE CLOW
JESSICA SCHULMAN
writers
CRAIG TANIMOTO
ERIC GRUNBAUM
photographer
MAGNUM PHOTO
client
APPLE COMPUTER
agency
TBWA CHIAT/DAY/
VENICE

MERIT AWARD
outdoor: single

art director
JESSICA SCHULMAN
writers
CRAIG TANIMOTO
ERIC GRUNBAUM
photographer
BETTMAN ARCHIVE
client
APPLE COMPUTER
agency
TBWA CHIAT/DAY/
VENICE

MERIT AWARD
outdoor: single

art director
JESSICA SCHULMAN
writers
CRAIG TANIMOTO
ERIC GRUNBAUM
photographer
MAGNUM PHOTO
client
APPLE COMPUTER
agency
TBWA CHIAT/DAY/
VENICE

MERIT AWARD
outdoor: single

art directors
SUSAN ALINSANGAN
KEN YOUNGLIEB
JESSICA SCHULMAN

writers
CRAIG TANIMOTO
ERIC GRUNBAUM

photographer
NASA

client
APPLE COMPUTER

agency
TBWA CHIAT/DAY/
VENICE

MERIT AWARD
outdoor: single

art director
MARGARET MIDGETT

writers
CRAIG TANIMOTO
ERIC GRUNBAUM

photographer
CORBIS BETTMAN

client
APPLE COMPUTER

agency
TBWA CHIAT/DAY/
VENICE

MERIT AWARD
outdoor: campaign

art directors
ANDY ARGHYROU
MIKE DURBAN
PAUL BRIGINSHAW
MIKE HARRIS

writers
DAVID NEWTON
TONY STRONG
MALCOLM DUFFY
GIDEON TODES

photographer
SARA MORRIS

typographer
JOE HOZA

client
THE ECONOMIST

agency
ABBOTT MEAD
VICKERS.BBDO/
LONDON

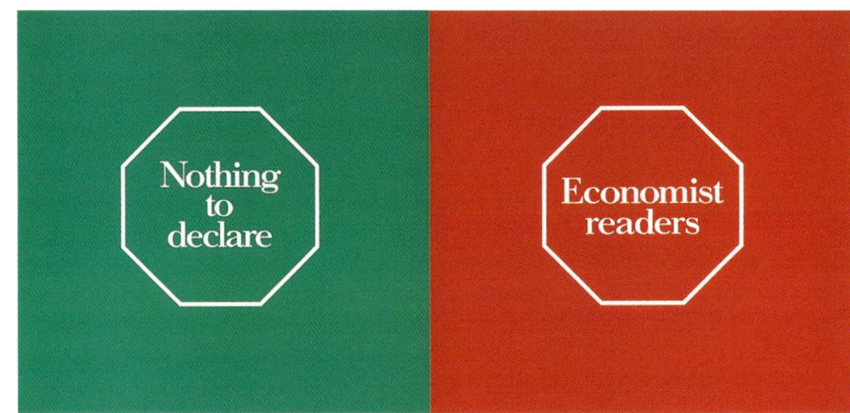

PRINT MERIT

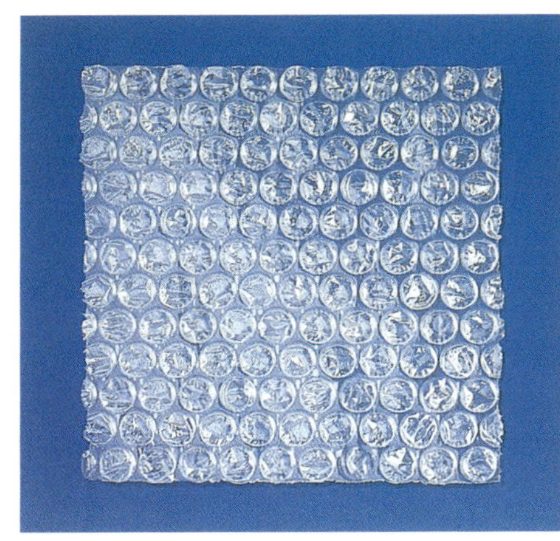

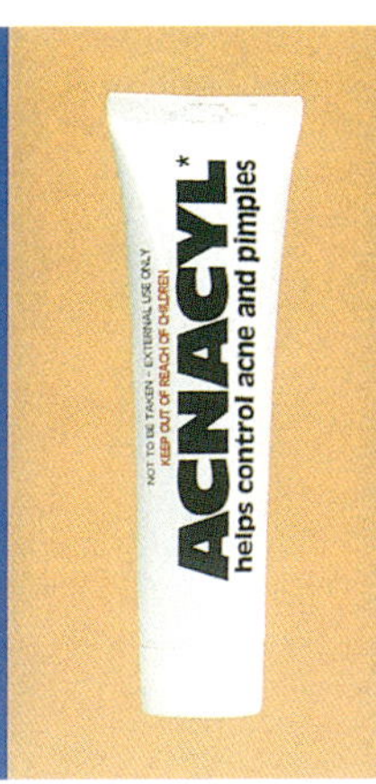

MERIT AWARD
outdoor: campaign

art director
PAUL BENNELL

writer
JAY FURBY

photographer
JOHN CLANG

client
PARKE DAVIS

agency
BATEY ADS/
SINGAPORE

MERIT AWARD
outdoor: campaign

art directors
ROGER CAMP
SALLY OVERHEU

writer
MICHELLE ROUFA

illustrator
STEVEN GARCIA

client
THE COCA-COLA COMPANY/
CHERRY COKE

agency
CLIFF FREEMAN & PARTNERS/
NEW YORK

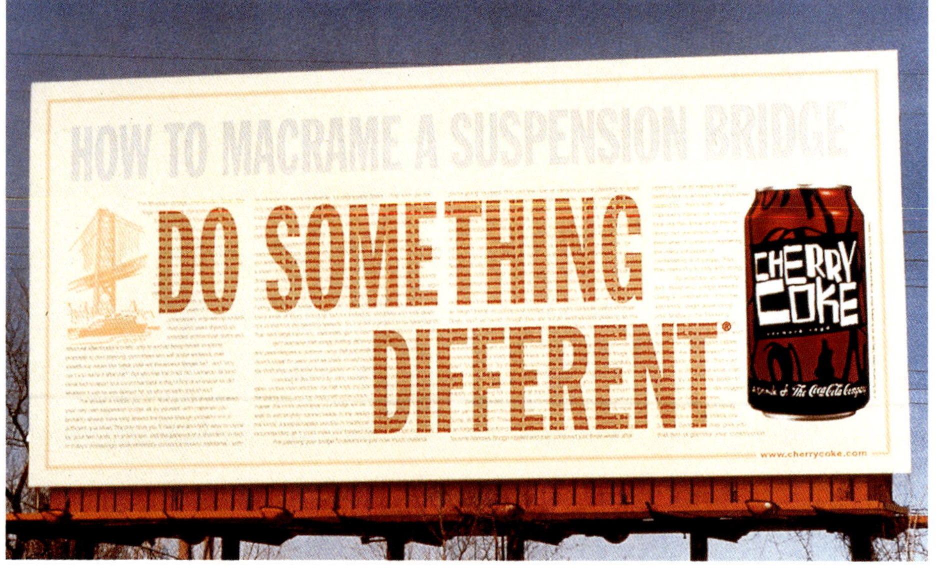

PRINT MERIT

HOW TO WRESTLE A KODIAK BEAR
(GRECO-ROMAN STYLE)

HOW TO WRESTLE A KODIAK BEAR
(GRECO-ROMAN STYLE)
DO SOMETHING
DIFFERENT

HOW TO CONFUSE A RODEO CLOWN
ELLER

HOW TO WRESTLE A KODIAK BEAR
(GRECO-ROMAN STYLE)
DO SOMETHING
DIFFERENT
CHERRY
COKE

HOW TO CONFUSE A RODEO CLOWN
DO SOMETHING
DIFFERENT
ELLER

HOW TO CONFUSE A RODEO CLOWN
DO SOMETHING
DIFFERENT
CHERRY
COKE
ELLER

MERIT AWARD
outdoor: campaign

art director
VALERIE ANG-POWELL

writer
BLAKE DALEY

illustrator
JEAN PERRAMON

photographers
HUNTER FREEMAN
JOHN E. BARRETT

client
CALIFORNIA FLUID MILK PROCESSORS

agency
GOODBY SILVERSTEIN & PARTNERS/
SAN FRANCISCO

PRINT MERIT

MERIT AWARD
outdoor: campaign

art director
PETER NICHOLSON

writer
SCOTT WILD

photographer
LARS TOPELMANN

client
ADIDAS AMERICA

agency
LEAGAS DELANEY/
SAN FRANCISCO

MERIT AWARD
outdoor: campaign

art director
GAIL YACULA

writer
DAN ZIMERMAN

photographer
MICHAEL MAHOVLICH

client
PROCTER & GAMBLE

agency
LEO BURNETT COMPANY/TORONTO

PRINT MERIT

MERIT AWARD
outdoor: campaign

art director
JOHN SHIRLEY

writer
RICH SIEGEL

client
ABC TELEVISION

agency
TBWA CHIAT/DAY/
VENICE

MERIT AWARD
outdoor: campaign

art director
SCOTT CARLSON
writer
SHALOM AUSLANDER
photographer
SCOTT CARLSON
client
MAXIM MAGAZINE
agency
TBWA CHIAT/DAY/
NEW YORK

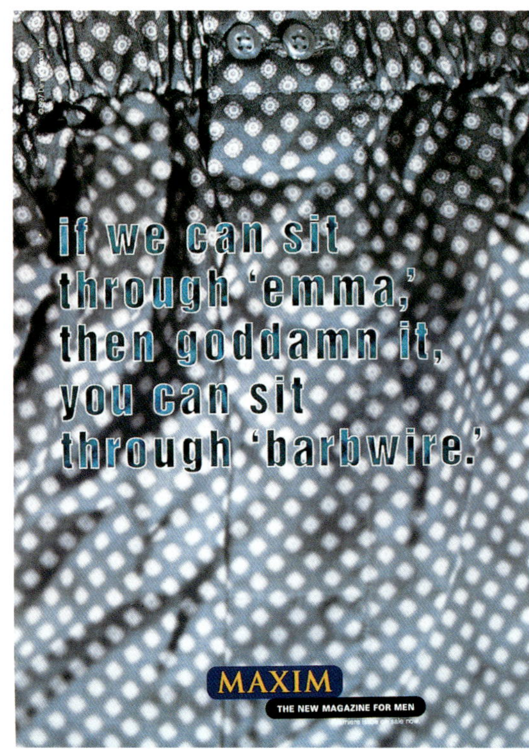

PRINT MERIT

MERIT AWARD
outdoor: campaign

art director
LINDA KNIGHT

writer
ANDY MCKEON

illustrator
DAVID HUGHES

client
NIKE

agency
WIEDEN & KENNEDY/
PORTLAND

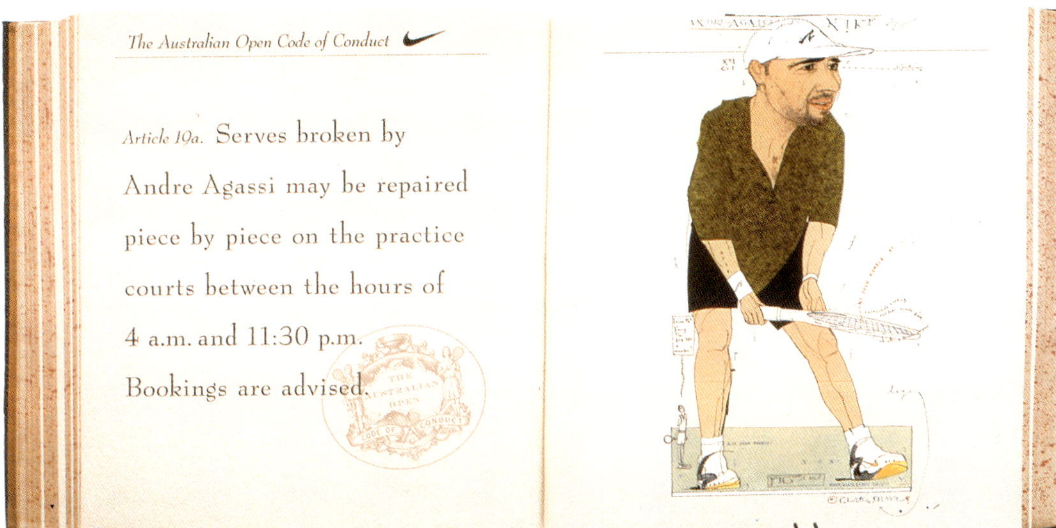

PRINT MERIT

MERIT AWARD
outdoor: campaign

art director
JOE SHANDS

writer
MICHAEL FOLINO

illustrators
MARK BENNETT
ART PASTUSAK

client
NIKE

agency
WIEDEN & KENNEDY/
PORTLAND

EVEN CORNERBACKS MISS YOU.

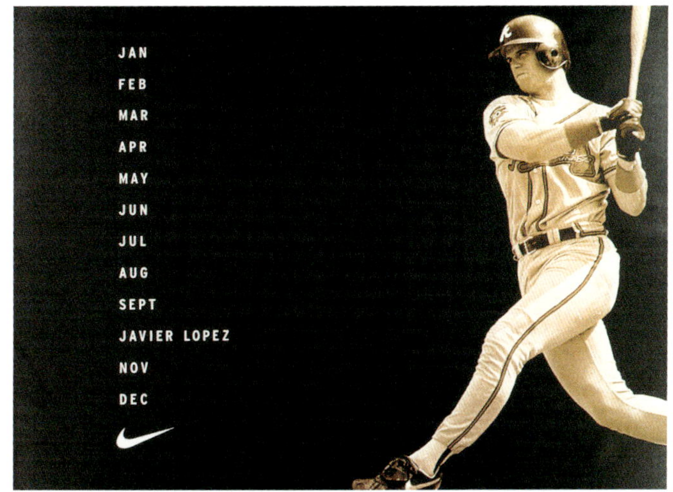
JAN
FEB
MAR
APR
MAY
JUN
JUL
AUG
SEPT
JAVIER LOPEZ
NOV
DEC

1682
1932
1997
PHILADELPHIA FOUNDED
CHEESE STEAK INVENTED
DAWN STALEY RETURNS HOME

PRINT MERIT

MERIT AWARD
trade b/w full page
or spread: single

art director
VINNY MATASSA
writer
GLEN WACHOWIAK
photographer
PEGGY DAY
client
MACK TRUCKS
agency
CARMICHAEL LYNCH/
MINNEAPOLIS

ON THE ROAD FOR YEARS TO COME.

Time flies with a Mack® E7 E-Tech™ engine. The company that invented the 12-liter presents our most fuel efficient engine ever. It'll be looking good long after everything else on the road starts to show its age.

MERIT AWARD
trade b/w full page
or spread: single

art director
STEVE MITCHELL
writer
DOUG ADKINS
client
DUBLIN PRODUCTIONS
agency
HUNT ADKINS/
MINNEAPOLIS

DID YOU EVER NOTICE HOW DUCKS HAVE FEATHERS BUT WINNEBAGOS DON'T? *or* OBSERVATIONAL HUMOR.

Ever notice that trains run on tracks but cars run on gas? Why do they call them wristwatches when it isn't your wrist that's doing the watching? And why do garbage men pick up garbage but snowmen don't pick up snow? Clearly, we live in an upside-down insane-asylum of a world, a veritable vortex of insanity in which sense and reason are but mere leaves tossed in the wind. (We also considered comparing sense and reason to mackerel tossed in a duffel bag; however, we had this nagging suspicion that that had been used by Shakespeare at one time.)

The Dublin Laugh Probe, seen here just before plummeting to earth and destroying Switzerland.

At the Dublin Giant Foodstuffs Laboratories, our scientists create giant foods to eat and laugh at, although usually not in that order. Rick's favorite oversized food is giant spaghetti, despite recently discovering that its primary ingredients are fuzzy bunny rabbits, wide-eyed abandoned puppies and koala bears.

SHEEP DUNG: OBSERVATIONAL MOTHER LODE

Such delightful syndicated observational sitcoms as "Real-Life Animal Maulings" and "America's Funniest Farm Accidents" didn't just happen overnight. It was only after enduring centuries of arduously slow progression marked by many-a-decade with nary a humorous discovery, that we have arrived at our current state of observational brilliance. The first observational humorists had only a rudimentary grasp of the art, as evidenced by these inscriptions on an Aztecan tomb: "Did you ever notice rocks? Did you ever notice ears? Did you ever notice dirt? Did you ever notice sheep dung?" Within 1000 years, however, observationalists had begun to notice absurdities that involved more than just one object, such as "Did you ever notice that rocks aren't ears?" and "Why is dirt called 'dirt' and not 'sheep dung'?" The renaissance of observational humor had begun. Today, however, as we reach the zenith of the form, we are able to look back at this long history of observational humor and remark, "Ever notice that our ancestors were morons?"

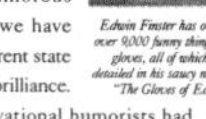

Edwin Finster has observed over 9,000 funny things about gloves, all of which are detailed in his saucy new book "The Gloves of Eden."

YOU ARE BEING OBSERVED RIGHT NOW— LAUGH, DAMN YOU!

Big Brother has nothing on the Dublin Nerve Center of Observational Hilarity. With dozens of satellites circling the earth, cameras mounted in every tree and bathroom soap dispenser, and Jerry Pope looking into people's bedroom windows, we have every inch of the Earth under constant observation (except for seven square inches in Mahajanga which are quite unfunny and therefore not worth the expense). No trace of humor escapes our watchful gaze; if it's funny, our observational lawyers see to it that we own it. To hear Jerry Pope's observation of the day, and to receive a hilarious picture that Jerry took of you last night while you were sound asleep, call 612-332-8864 (Mpls.) or 213-960-3322 (L.A.).

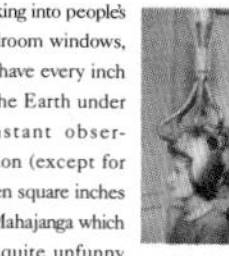

We find that having warm tapioca pumped into a tight-fitting helmet increases your observational powers tenfold.

MERIT AWARD
trade b/w full page
or spread: single

art director
STEVE MITCHELL
writer
DOUG ADKINS
client
DUBLIN PRODUCTIONS
agency
HUNT ADKINS/
MINNEAPOLIS

I JUST TELEPORTED IN FROM CHICAGO AND BOY ARE MY MOLECULES OSCILLATING *or* HUMOR OF THE FUTURE.

The evolution of humankind is now moving forward at such an alarming rate that within 4-6 weeks we will all have evolved into giant brains suspended in jars of ectoplasmic fluid. This will pose some unique problems for comedians. Pratfalls will invariably result in broken jars, leaving brains to flop about helplessly on sidewalks. Brain ventriloquists will forever have to deal with hecklers yelling, "Hey, I can see your speech neurons firing." On the other hand, replacing a person's brain fluid with tapioca while they're sleeping, and lines such as, "Is that a malignant brain tumor or are you just happy to see me?" are humoric opportunities we can only dream about today.

Dublin micro-skyscrapers, the size of electrons, will house thousands of shrunken employees.

For years it was thought that Jerry Pope was stealing his humor. This photo seems to implicate Jerry as he receives a knock-knock joke from galaxy G-58. But later in court, Jerry would stun the jury by demonstrating that the Zuboniumritron could not be operated by his tiny, doll-like hands.

A HUMORTRON IN EVERY HOME

After years of conducting complex scientific experiments and reading lots of supermarket tabloids, we have compiled the following predictions for the future: 2015: Comedian cloning will be all the rage. On any given night there will be as many as 10,000 Buddy Hacketts performing at separate dinner theaters, each every bit as hilarious as the next. Imagine all the neon signs on the Las Vegas strip announcing, "Yes, we have a Buddy Hackett!" 2023: Humorless rich people will pay handsomely to have the humorous parts of poor people's brains grafted onto their own. 2040: A laugh epidemic will wipe out one-third of the world's population when laughter suddenly becomes contagious. People with the disease will laugh incessantly while blood shoots from the tops of their heads in a huge geyser. This will be nature's way of telling us, "It's all fun and games until your head erupts in a bloody geyser." 2102: Nipsey Russell will be thawed from his cryogenic chamber and then flown to Neptune where his unique brand of rhyming humor will make him a demi-god among the Neptunians. 3999: We will evolve into pure energy; fart jokes will make a big comeback. 4697: Ducks will take over the Earth and immediately outlaw all human humor while forcing us to dance on hot plates in their horrific duck nightclubs.

The development of the Earmographer will prevent the embarrassment of losing your ears during time travel.

"LOST IN SPACE" –EERILY PROPHETIC

Soon after you finish reading this you will be approached by two mysterious figures (unremarkable save for their silver spandex jumpsuits) — members of the elite Dublin Time-Traveling Conquistadors. They will ask you a series of questions about this piece and then go back in time[1] to make any necessary changes to it according to your feedback, repeating this process until it has achieved perfection. By the way, this is the 45,674th time you have read this. Now is the moment in the time-loop where you call us at 612-332-8864 (Minneapolis), 213-960-3322 (Los Angeles) or Ω≠¥-ΔπΩ - ø∞∑π (Pluto) and beg us to release you from this time imprisonment (in response, we invariably laugh demonically while imitating your pathetic pleas).

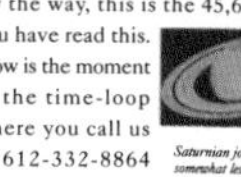

Saturnian jokes will become somewhat less popular after they vaporize the Earth.

1 A brain-wrenching conundrum: If your future self were to travel into the past and encounter your present self, and you told your future self a joke that he obviously already knew, would your future self give you a courtesy laugh? And if you then killed your future self with a crowbar, stole the time machine, traveled into the future and heckled your future self during his comedy club routine, thus prompting your future self to kill you with a Crowbar-3000, would this be funny or would the traveling-into-the-future-to-heckle-your-future-self-and-then-have-your-skull-crushed-by-your-own-hand routine have been done to death?

MERIT AWARD
trade b/w full page
or spread: single

art director
JEAN ROBAIRE

writer
SALLY HOGSHEAD

client
MICHAEL RUPPERT

agency
MARTIN CREATIVE LA/
LOS ANGELES

CONSUMER MAGAZINE
COLOR FULL PAGE OR
SPREAD: CAMPAIGN

263
ART DIRECTOR:

WRITER:

PHOTOGRAPHER:
Michael Ruppert, LA
CLIENT:

AGENCY:

263

MERIT AWARD
trade b/w full page
or spread: single

art director
JEAN ROBAIRE

writer
SALLY HOGSHEAD

client
MICHAEL RUPPERT

agency
MARTIN CREATIVE LA/
LOS ANGELES

1

Consumer Magazine Ads

1

art director
writer
Michael Ruppert, LA photographer
creative director
agency
client

PRINT MERIT

MERIT AWARD
trade b/w full page
or spread: single

art director
IAN GRAIS

writer
JIM HUNTER

client
AREA 51

agency
PALMER JARVIS DDB/
VANCOUVER

Why nobody reads long, boring newspaper ads.

Travel back with us to an era when you could open a newspaper such as this and read it in its entirety while enjoying a leisurely waffle, bacon, sausage and four-egg breakfast. Aside from it being a time that pre-dated cholesterol studies, it was also a time when detailed information could be absorbed at a relaxing pace.

Today, we have no such luck.

More than 50 percent of Canadians are too busy to even eat breakfast. And every second of the day, there are thousands of television, radio, Internet, newspaper, magazine, blimp, and washroom-stall messages vying for your undivided attention.

Time is precious, so the chances of you reading this long, boring, convoluted newspaper ad in its entirety are quite slim.* We feel that you'd probably have a better chance of getting struck by lightning than finishing this lengthy message.

Of course, there is an alternative to plodding through this ad. It's called the Internet – and it's a lot more fun than staring at a bunch of boring words on a newspaper page, that's for sure.

The Net lets you communicate with your customers like no other medium can.

It's vibrant. It's intimate. It's engaging. It's really quite cool. And we're not just saying all this because we're in the business of providing Internet solutions for a living.

Well, actually, we are. But before we say any more, please allow us to introduce ourselves. We're Area 51 Interactive. And we design Web sites for corporate clients. Unfortunately, we can't effectively demonstrate our Web design prowess on these pages, so we decided our only alternative was to try and explain the process by cramming a bunch of information into this ad.

As a public service to you, our cherished reader, we'd like to tell you that there is a better way to learn how we can help your company than to continue reading. And we highly urge you to consider it. You've suffered enough visual cruelty already. Nobody reads ads like these. So why punish yourself. Please, we beg you, run to your nearest computer and type in our Web address – www.area51interactive.com.

Then you can learn about what our company does, and see the effectiveness of a Web page first-hand. Just wait till you get a glimpse of the colours. The sounds. The vivid graphics. The sheer entertainment. It's all there just waiting for you.

So in closing, please enjoy our Web site, then let's get together and talk about your Web site needs. Give Dave Schulz a call when you're done at 604-608-4451. Or e-mail us at longboringad@area51interactive.com. We look forward to hearing from you. Thanks for your time. Happy surfing.

What, you're still here? We were certain that you were going to leave. We thought you'd rather stick pins in your eyes before you read any further. Hmm. Maybe you're in your dentist's office and need some mundane reading material to go with the elevator music that's playing in the background. Or maybe your computer's in the shop.

Hey, no problem. You have time to kill. And we have space to fill. So just sit back and enjoy our verbosity.

You know, we liked you from the moment you set eyes on our copy. You seem like a very nice person. And a very wise person. The kind of person who knows that the Internet's explosive growth is too impressive for your business to ignore.

But friend, we'd be beset with guilt if we didn't share this little piece of advice our grandfather told us just last week: "If you're getting on the Net simply to have a token presence, then www.don'tbother.com."

There's a lot of truth to granddad's cyber wisdom. Directing people to your site is one thing, but the moment of truth comes when they arrive at your home page, and begin sniffing around with the tenacity of a truffle-smelling pig.

Surfers-o-the-Web like to give a site about eight entire seconds to gain their interest. And if it doesn't rock their world, they click once for bub, once for bye, and it's off to see what your competition is up to.

A Web site shows off your business to the world. But if you're letting three guys in a basement dictate your global image, all we can say is "yikes."

An ill-designed site that is off strategy and frustrating for consumers to use could actually erode your overall branding efforts. And as any dirt farmer will tell you, erosion just isn't a fun thing.

Plenty of Web design companies out there, including ours, offer extraordinary graphic effects. Hey, don't get us wrong. We love to see gynormous four-eyed, fire-breathing dragons spit multi-coloured corporate logos out of their mouths as much as the next person. But if there's no apparent reason for such a creation, then what's the point?

Good programming is an essential component of any successful Web site. And fortunately, our programmers are some of the best in the business.

But we believe that a Web site is first and foremost a marketing driven entity. And we believe that what sets us apart from other Web design companies is our ability to combine technical expertise with exceptional marketing savvy. We also believe we've just set a record for sharing beliefs in a single paragraph.

Are you getting tired yet, cherished reader? Because we sure are. So before we go any further on this arduous journey that we both seem destined to finish, let's take a break.

Intermissions have been a part of the theatre scene for centuries. Some say they were added to help alleviate boredom. So without any further adieu, let's mercifully drop the curtain on this ad and take a spontaneous intermission right now.

Please feel free to have a quick stretch, or make yourself a cup of coffee. We're going to make some ice cream soup. It's delicious. Hey, why don't you try some, too? Here's the recipe. We'll meet you back here in five minutes.

ICE CREAM SOUP

3 cups of vanilla ice cream
2 graham wafers
1 chocolate bar

Mix and mash ingredients in a large bowl. When the concoction starts to look soup-like, dig in.

We seem to be developing a bit of a reader/writer rapport here, which is nice. It's our philosophy that building a rapport is important with all our Web site clients.

That's why one of the first things we do when we sit down together is to ask a simple, yet critical question that judging by many Web sites, often gets overlooked: What do you want your Web site to do for your business?

(a) Enhance your image?
(b) Generate sales leads?
(c) Provide product information?
(d) Sell products online?
(e) Create a dialogue with consumers?
(f) Provide the latest sports scores?
(g) Promote your secret fascination with fire ants?
(h) a and c, but not d?
(i) e and f, but not g?
(j) b, e and g?
(k) c, d, and maybe a?
(l) None of the above?
(m) All of the above, except the part about fire ants?
(n) Just give scores from sports that fire ants play?
(o) Disregard n, because as far as you know, fire ants don't participate in organized sports?

We could go on, but as you can plainly see, there are an infinite number of things a Web site can do for your business. The secret is to work together to determine the scope of your site well before it's up and running.

Can we be honest? If there's one weakness we have, it's that our psychic powers just aren't up to snuff. Try as we may, we can't predict the future. Or even bend nails with our mind, for that matter. And we have no plans to start a psychic buddies network anytime soon.

Instead, we rely on plenty of good old-fashioned research to play an integral part in our strategic planning process. We think it's crucial to not only get to know you and your company, but to also determine what your competitors are doing on the Web. And to understand the end-user as well.

Once we agree on the direction, it's time for our creative people to begin brainstorming. This is one of the most interesting parts of the process. There's frenzied doodling. Hurried arm gestures. Flying chairs. Spontaneous puppet shows. Lots of cold pizza. And one time, there was even a Danish hymn sung in honour of a chipmunk.

The birthing process for ideas is unique, to say the least. But through it all, our people never lose sight of the marketing and technical criteria.

Next, it's time to unroll the blueprints and start building and decorating. There's a lot of technical programming stuff that happens during this phase, but no actual hammering or sawing or door-wreath weaving takes place. It's probably why we don't get many visits from Bob Vila or Martha Stewart.

When the site is finished, it's launch time. It's not like the launching of a boat though, where a bottle of champagne is broken against the bow. Contrary to semi-popular belief, most computers can't float. So sadly, they don't have bows. What we do instead is spritz a mouse with a few drops of tequila, and that seems to do the trick.

Now you were probably praying that at this point, we'd mercifully end this ad. We wanted to, but there's still more to say. Because once we build the site, our work isn't finished.

It just begins, really, since post-construction management is crucial to ensuring a Web site's success. If your customers are sending you e-mail that needs answering, or are placing orders on your site, this important information needs to be coordinated. We also track customer behavior on the site and provide you with a critical analysis of what's taking place.

On-going security is another important consideration. We create sites that are secure from hackers, viruses, and unwanted manipulation. And we monitor each site to ensure its safety.

We also make sure your information is put into a safe, reliable server environment that provides optimum performance for your Web site. McGruff the Crime Dog would be proud of us, because we do our best to put the bite on computer crime. Mike Tyson may also be proud of us, simply because we bit something.

Blah, blah. (Just checking to see if you're still with us.)

Another thing we take care of is site promotion. We'll handle all your online and offline advertising and public relations needs by working with your marketing people, or by accessing our contacts with some of Canada's most experienced communicators. We know how to drive quality traffic to your site.

Okay, so hopefully by about now, you're getting more than a bit suspicious. You're probably saying to yourself "Self, these people sure have a gift for the gab, but are they legit, or really just blowing smoke up one of my most crucial of orifices."

Well, although the World Wide Web was introduced so recently that it still has that new-car smell, we've already developed a successful track record in the field of Web page design.

We've created sites for clients ranging from the financial industry to the grocery industry to the tourism sector.

It's hard to describe each site in great detail, but two that have gotten tons of positive results are for Richmond Savings, available for viewing at www.humungous.com, and for Pacific Press, available for viewing at www.vancouversun.com or www.vancouverprovince.com.

Do you believe in miracles? You should, because this ad is coming to an end. We did everything in our power to dissuade you from reaching this point, but you persevered, and here you are. Congratulations, you truly are one in a million.

Why don't you give Dave a call at 604-608-4451? Or send us an e-mail at longboringad@area51interactive.com? Or check out our site at www.area51interactive.com? We'd love to build an effective Web site for you. After all, we've succeeded in getting you to read this ad, so just think of the success we could achieve providing Internet solutions for your company.

The end. (We promise.)

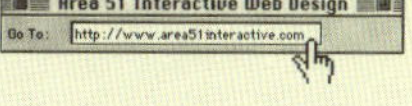

*We should warn you that when we say this ad is long, we're talking more than 2,000 words long. When we say it's boring, three of the proofreaders fell asleep while checking it. And when we say it's convoluted, there's a recipe for ice cream soup.

MERIT AWARD
trade color full page or spread: single

art director
MIKE HANNETT
writer
DAVE BUCHANAN
illustrator
LARA HARWOOD
client
VOLKSWAGEN GROUP UK
agency
BMP DDB/LONDON

In Wolfsburg any underground pipe that carries anything more harmful than water is enclosed in another pipe. The space between the two pipe walls is filled with a pressurised non-toxic, non-combustible gas. Any change in pressure is immediately detected by monitors at the factory and the leak is initially contained by the outer pipe before being rectified permanently. At Volkswagen, even the pipes are safety conscious.

MERIT AWARD
trade color full page or spread: single

art director
MIKE HANNETT
writer
DAVE BUCHANAN
illustrator
CHRIS CORR
client
VOLKSWAGEN GROUP UK
agency
BMP DDB/LONDON

There is no smoke without fire

and in Wolfsburg you won't find too many fires.

Heating for hundreds of homes is provided by the surplus energy generated by the local Volkswagen factory.

In Wolfsburg fuel efficiency is up, emissions are down

Just what you'd expect from Volkswagen.

MERIT AWARD
trade color full page
or spread: single

art director
MIKE HANNETT
writer
DAVE BUCHANAN
illustrator
PAUL POWIS
client
VOLKSWAGEN
GROUP UK
agency
BMP DDB/LONDON

MERIT AWARD
trade color full page
or spread: single

art director
MIKE HANNETT
writer
DAVE BUCHANAN
illustrator
MEILO SO
client
VOLKSWAGEN
GROUP UK
agency
BMP DDB/LONDON

PRINT MERIT

MERIT AWARD
trade color full page
or spread: single

art director
MIKE HANNETT
writer
DAVE BUCHANAN
illustrator
JOHN PAUL EARLY
client
VOLKSWAGEN
GROUP UK
agency
BMP DDB/LONDON

MERIT AWARD
trade color full page
or spread: single

art director
VINNY MATASSA

writer
GLEN WACHOWIAK

photographer
PEGGY DAY

client
MACK TRUCKS

agency
CARMICHAEL LYNCH/
MINNEAPOLIS

MERIT AWARD
trade color full page
or spread: single

art director
JEFF TERWILLIGER

writer
DEREK PLETCH

client
HARLEY-DAVIDSON

agency
CARMICHAEL LYNCH/
MINNEAPOLIS

PRINT MERIT

MERIT AWARD
trade color full page or spread: single

art director
JOHN DAMES

writers
WADE PASCHALL

photographer
MICHAEL EASTMAN

client
MONSANTO PROTIVA

agency
CORE/ST. LOUIS

MERIT AWARD
trade color full page or spread: single

art director
JOHN DAMES

writer
TODD MITCHELL

photographer
MICHAEL EASTMAN

client
MONSANTO PROTIVA

agency
CORE/ST. LOUIS

MERIT AWARD
trade color full page
or spread: single

art director
JOHN DAMES

writers
WADE PASCHALL
TODD MITCHELL

photographer
MICHAEL EASTMAN

client
MONSANTO PROTIVA

agency
CORE/ST. LOUIS

PRINT MERIT

MERIT AWARD
trade color full page
or spread: single

art director
MARK ARNOLD

writer
WADE PASCHALL

photographer
JAMES SCHWARTZ

client
SOUND EMPORIUM

agency
CORE/ST. LOUIS

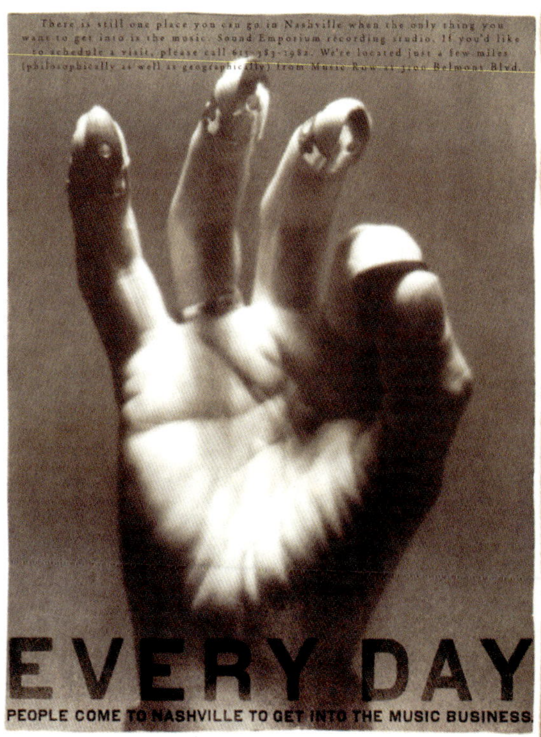

Announcing InTIME, the newsmagazine for teenagers. Every bit as engaging and informative as its parent magazine, InTIME speaks directly to students on the important issues of the day. Published biweekly during the school year with a rate base of 200,000, it promises to be an ideal vehicle for youth marketers. For more information, please call Jack Haire, Publisher, at 212-522-4160 at the offices of TIME. The world's most interesting magazine.

MERIT AWARD
trade color full page or spread: single

art director
JOEL CLEMENT

writer
LUKE SULLIVAN

client
TIME MAGAZINE

agency
FALLON MCELLIGOTT/
MINNEAPOLIS

Could anything be more inspiring than a life devoted to closing this gap?

The world's most interesting magazine.

MERIT AWARD
trade color full page or spread: single

art director
BOB BARRIE

writer
DEAN BUCKHORN

photographer
JP LAFFONT

client
TIME MAGAZINE

agency
FALLON MCELLIGOTT/
MINNEAPOLIS

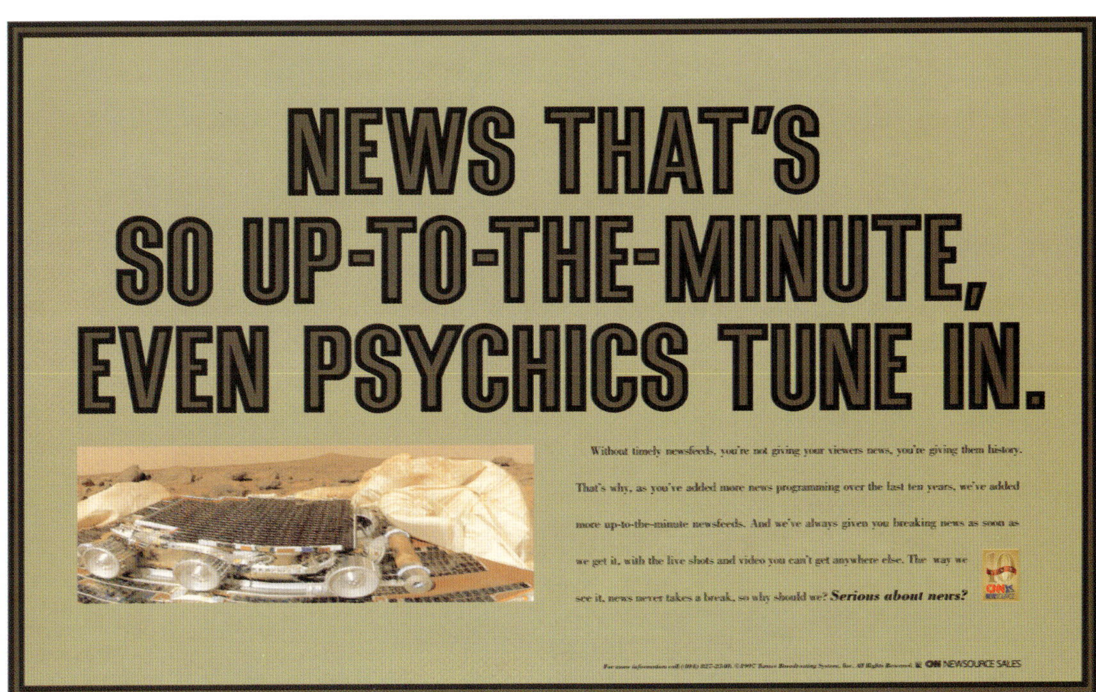

MERIT AWARD
trade color full page or spread: single

art director
DAMON WILLIAMS

writers
CATHY CARLISI
JOHN SPALDING

client
CNN NEWSOURCE

agency
FLETCHER MARTIN
ASSOCIATES/ATLANTA

MERIT AWARD
trade color full page
or spread: single

art director
STEVE MITCHELL

writer
DOUG ADKINS

client
DUBLIN PRODUCTIONS

agency
HUNT ADKINS/
MINNEAPOLIS

MERIT AWARD
trade color full page
or spread: single

art director
STEVE TOM

writer
DERRICK OGILVIE

photographer
HORNICK-RIVLIN

client
THE BOSTON GLOBE

agency
INGALLS ADVERTISING/
BOSTON

MERIT AWARD
trade color full page
or spread: single

art director
KEVIN RAGLAND
writer
ANDRIA KUSHAN
client
IBID
STOCK PHOTOGRAPHY
agency
KETCHUM ADVERTISING/
PITTSBURG

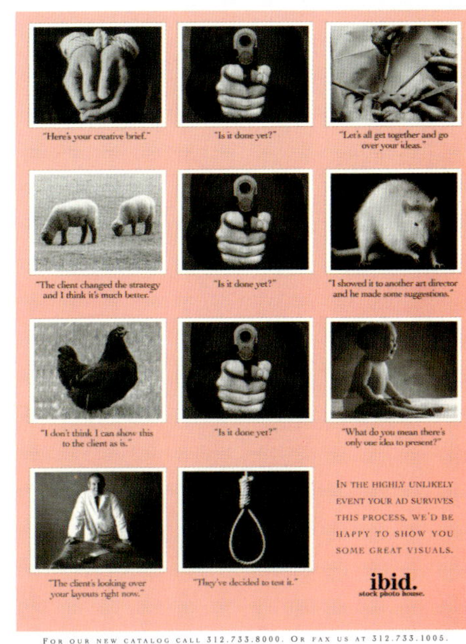

MERIT AWARD
trade color full page
or spread: single

art director
KEVIN RAGLAND
writer
ANDRIA KUSHAN
client
IBID
STOCK PHOTOGRAPHY
agency
KETCHUM ADVERTISING/
PITTSBURGH

MERIT AWARD
trade color full page
or spread: single

art director
KEVIN RAGLAND
writer
ANDRIA KUSHAN
client
IBID
STOCK PHOTOGRAPHY
agency
KETCHUM ADVERTISING/
PITTSBURGH

MERIT AWARD
trade color full page
or spread: single

art director
DAVE BEVERLEY
writer
ROB BURLEIGH
photographer
TIM SIMMONS
client
ADIDAS
agency
THE LEAGAS DELANEY
PARTNERSHIP/LONDON

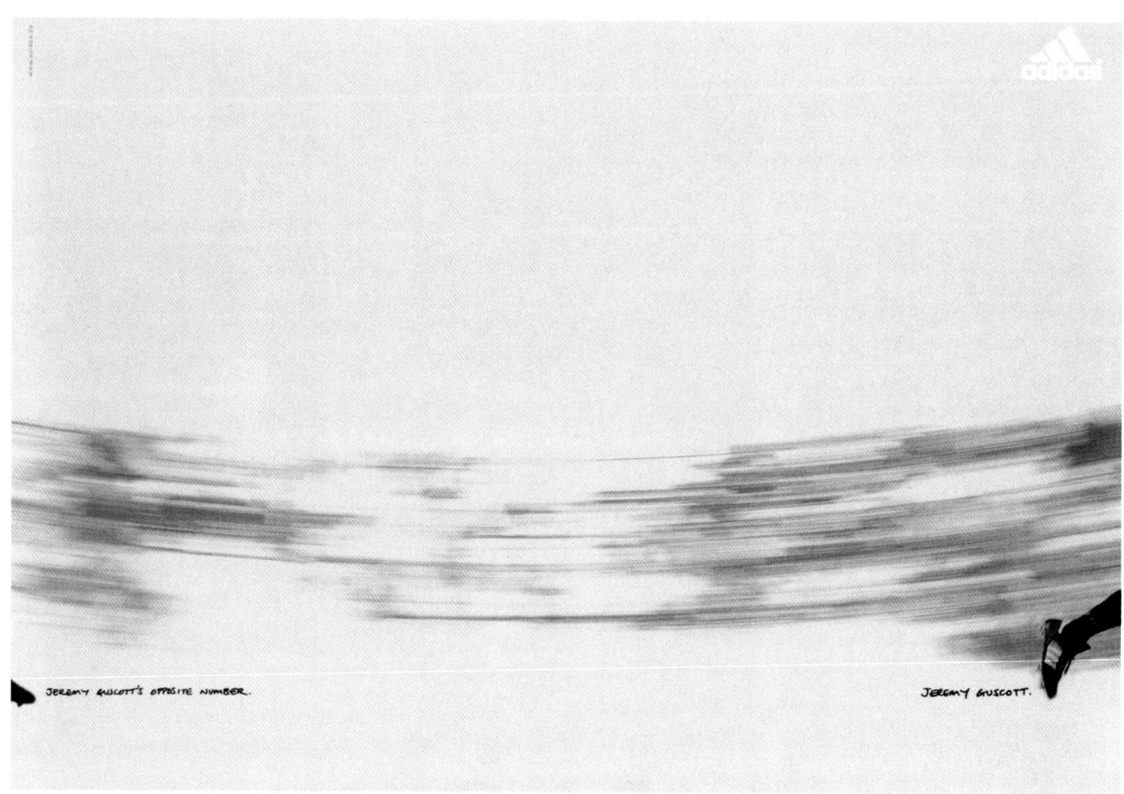

MERIT AWARD
trade color full page or
spread: single

art director
DAVE BEVERLEY
writer
ROB BURLEIGH
photographer
TIM SIMMONS
client
ADIDAS
agency
THE LEAGAS DELANEY
PARTNERSHIP/LONDON

For further information on the new 911 please call Porsche on 0345 911 911.

Not even Charles Darwin
would have believed you could have
come this far in 34 years.

MERIT AWARD
trade color full page
or spread: single

art director
DAVE BEVERLEY

writer
ROB BURLEIGH

client
PORSCHE

agency
THE LEAGAS DELANEY
PARTNERSHIP/LONDON

For further information on the new 911 please call Porsche on 0345 911 911.

There should be tougher laws
against advertising this
manipulative and persuasive.

MERIT AWARD
trade color full page
or spread: single

art director
DAVE BEVERLEY

writer
ROB BURLEIGH

client
PORSCHE

agency
THE LEAGAS DELANEY
PARTNERSHIP/LONDON

MERIT AWARD
trade color full page
or spread: single

art director
DING YEW MOONG

writer
CURT DETWEILER

photographers
SHOOTING GALLERY
WISHING WELL

client
ASSOCIATION OF
ACCREDITED
ADVERTISING
AGENTS SINGAPORE

agency
LEO BURNETT/
SINGAPORE

MERIT AWARD
trade color full page
or spread: single

art director
RALPH WATSON

writer
KARA GOODRICH

photographers
LARS TOPELMANN

client
POLAROID

agency
LEONARD/MONAHAN/
FOXBOROUGH

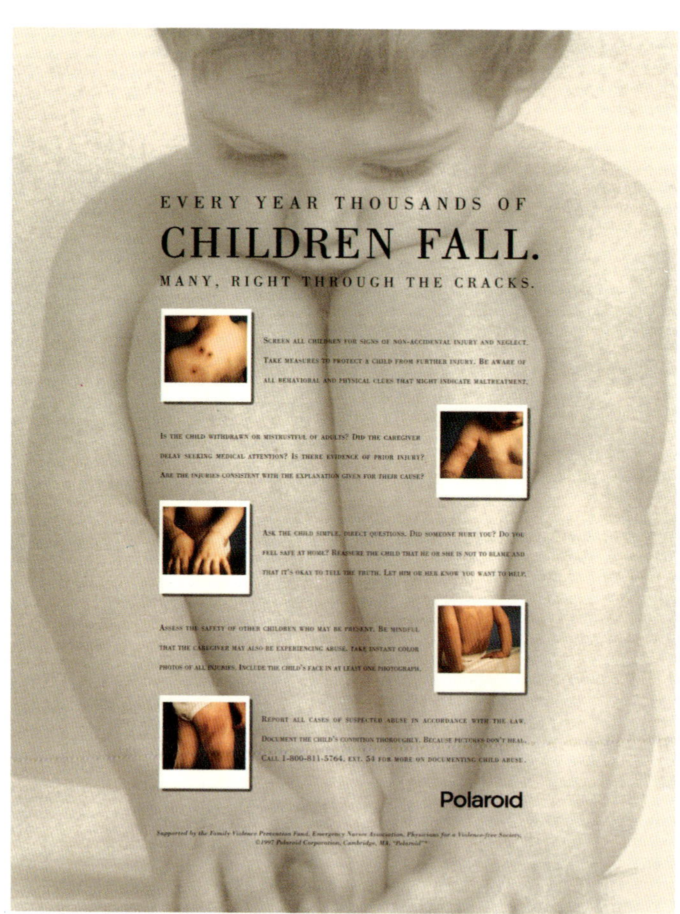

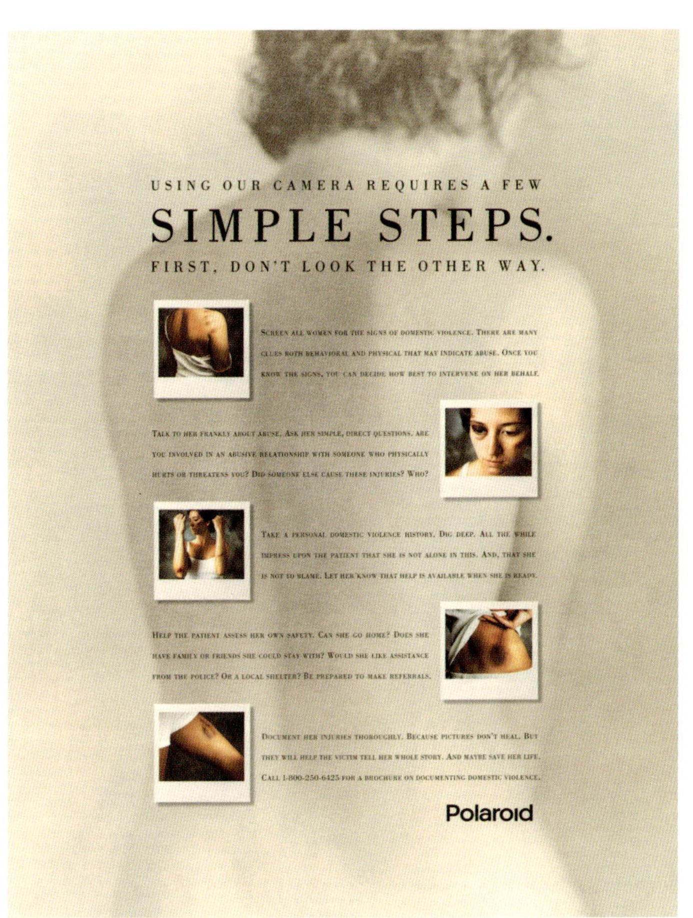

MERIT AWARD
trade color full page
or spread: single

art directors
HAL CURTIS
ALYSSA D'ARIENZO

writer
KARA GOODRICH

photographers
MICHELE CLEMENT

client
POLAROID

agency
LEONARD/MONAHAN/
FOXBOROUGH

THERE'S ONLY ONE PROBLEM WITH SHOOTING IN THOSE FAMOUS BIG CITIES. SOMEBODY MIGHT SHOOT BACK.

Fade up. Gritty urban location. You'd swear by the look that you're somewhere in Brooklyn. Southside Chicago. L.A. But the feel is entirely different. People are friendly. Cooperative. Even government officials. No traffic nightmares. No sea of red tape to wade through. You're having a blast on the shoot. You're getting really good craft service. When you yell "Cut" nobody knifes you. It's the way things should be. You're able to concentrate on your art instead of a lot of moronic distractions. Get your acceptance speech ready. The end.

North Carolina Film Commission

MERIT AWARD
trade color full page
or spread: single

art director
JIM MOUNTJOY

writer
ED JONES

client
NORTH CAROLINA FILM
COMMISSION

agency
LOEFFLER KETCHUM
MOUNTJOY/CHARLOTTE

MERIT AWARD
trade color full page
or spread: single

art director
JIM MOUNTJOY
writer
ED JONES
illustrator
DAVID WILGUS
photographer
HARRY DEZITTER
client
MANNINGTON FLOORS
agency
LOEFFLER KETCHUM
MOUNTJOY/CHARLOTTE

PRINT MERIT

MERIT AWARD
trade color full page
or spread: single

art directors
BARNEY GOLDBERG
HAL TENCH
writer
ANNIE MARIE FLOYD
photographer
CHRIS WIMPEY
client
FMC CORPORATION
agency
THE MARTIN AGENCY/
RICHMOND

MERIT AWARD
trade color full page
or spread: single

art director
SHYAM MADIRAJU

writer
SALLY HOGSHEAD

photographer
PETE MCARTHUR

client
JOHNS + GORMAN

agency
MARTIN CREATIVE LA/
LOS ANGELES

MERIT AWARD
trade color full page
or spread: single

art director
SHYAM MADIRAJU

writer
PETER BLIKSLAGER

illustrators
GRAHAM JACOBS

client
ART CENTER COLLEGE
OF DESIGN

agency
MARTIN CREATIVE LA/
LOS ANGELES

MERIT AWARD
trade color
full page or spread: single

art director
RANDY HUGHES

writer
TOM KELLY

photographers
JOE PACZKOWSKI
RIPSAW PHOTOGRAPHY

client
FLYSHACKER

agency
MARTIN/WILLIAMS
ADVERTISING/
MINNEAPOLIS

PRINT MERIT

MERIT AWARD
trade color
full page or spread: single

art director
JON MONTGOMERY

writer
JOHN FRANCIS

photographer
ANDY ANDERSON

client
3M SCIENTIFIC
ANGLERS

agency
MARTIN/WILLIAMS
ADVERTISING/
MINNEAPOLIS

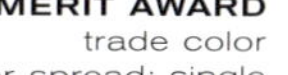

MERIT AWARD
trade color
full page or spread: single

art director
MARK MIZGALA

writer
JAMES LEE

illustrator
KARACTERS

client
PACIFIC PRESS

agency
PALMER JARVIS
DDB/VANCOUVER

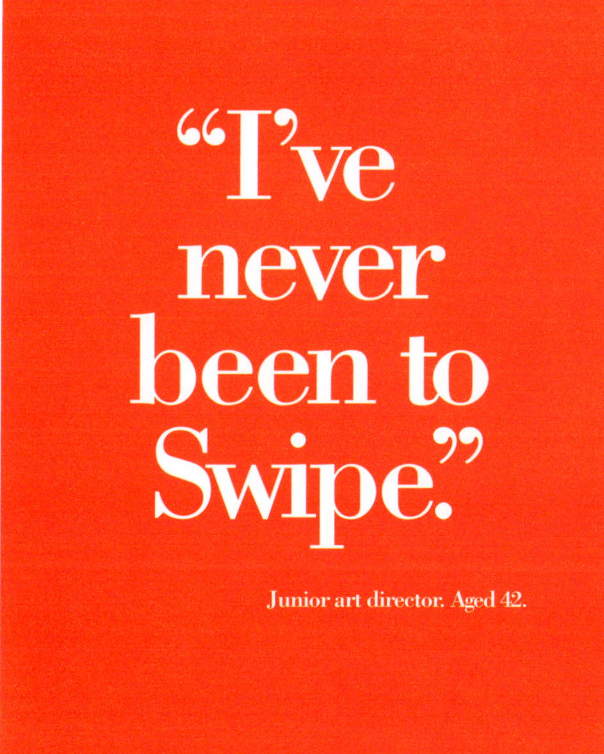

MERIT AWARD
trade color
full page or spread: single

art director
GARY HOLME

writers
AUBREY SINGER
BRETT CHANNER

client
SWIPE BOOKSTORE

agency
TBWA CHIAT/DAY/
TORONTO

MERIT AWARD
trade color
full page or spread: single

art director
LISA GARGANO
writer
KENNY LEE
photographers
BOB D'AMICO
ANDREW ECCLES
GREG GORMAN
GREGORY HEIZLER
SAM JONES
GEORGE LANG
BLAKE LITTLE
BOB SEBREE
client
ABC TELEVISION
agency
TBWA CHIAT/DAY/
VENICE

Television's equivalent of that new car smell.

INTRODUCING OUR NEW FALL SHOWS.

C-16
Cracker
Nothing Sacred
Timecop
Total Security
abc

PRINT MERIT

MERIT AWARD
trade color
full page or spread: single

art director
LISA GARGANO
writer
KENNY LEE
photographers
BOB D'AMICO
ANDREW ECCLES
GREG GORMAN
GREGORY HEIZLER
SAM JONES
GEORGE LANG
BLAKE LITTLE
BOB SEBREE
client
ABC TELEVISION
agency
TBWA CHIAT/DAY/
VENICE

Here's what the Amish will be missing out on.

MERIT AWARD
trade color
full page or spread: single

art director
DEB HAGAN
writer
MICKEY TAYLOR
client
SONY COMPUTER
ENTERTAINMENT
agency
TBWA CHIAT/DAY/
VENICE

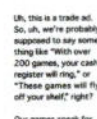

MERIT AWARD
trade color
full page or spread: single

art directors
GUY MOORE
SEAN THOMPSON

writer
TONY MALCOLM

illustrator
TIVY DAVIES

client
NIKE UK

agency
TBWA SIMONS PALMER/LONDON

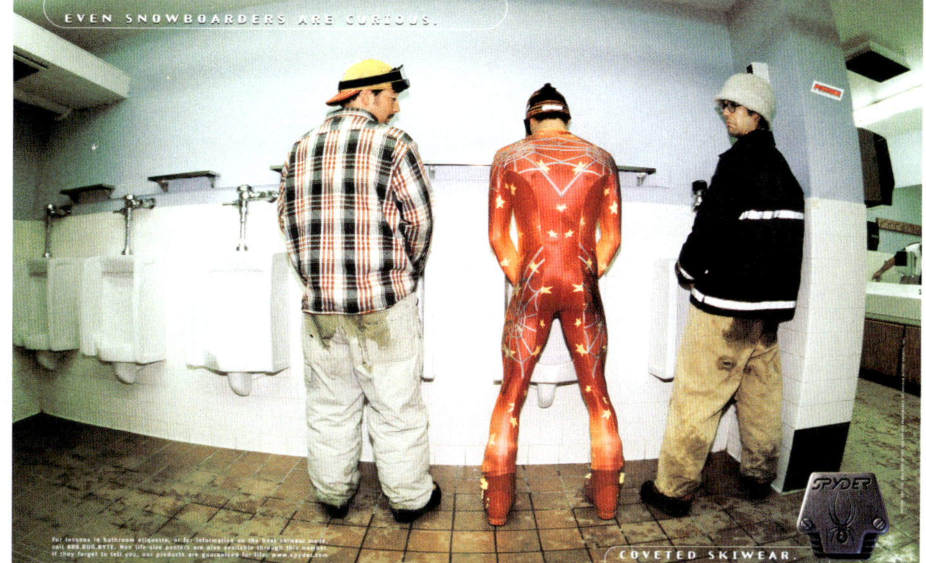

MERIT AWARD
trade color
full page or spread: single

art director
MATT LEAVITT

writer
JONATHAN SCHOENBERG

photographer
BROOKS FREEHILL

client
SPYDER SKIWEAR

agency
TDA ADVERTISING AND DESIGN/LONGMONT

MERIT AWARD
trade b/w or color
less than a page: single

art directors
PAUL NORWOOD
JAMES CLUNIE
writer
MIKE CONNELL
client
COHN GODLEY NORWOOD
agency
COHN GODLEY NORWOOD/BOSTON

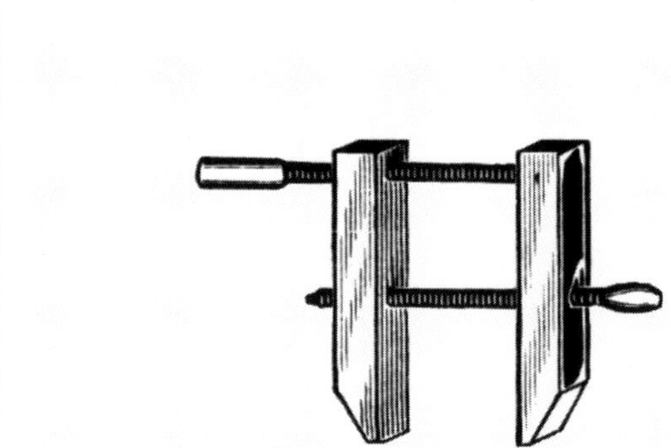

Become our new Production Manager and get this free hat.

Sure, things can get a bit stressful here. But we're a busy, growing, young agency. What do you expect? That's why we need an experienced Production Manager who can deal with tight deadlines and semi-annoying creative and account people. Please fax your resume to Debrah Garro at 617-426-1126.

COHN GODLEY NORWOOD

MERIT AWARD
trade b/w or color
less than a page: single

art directors
DEREK KIRKMAN
MIKE PROCTOR
writer
IAN COHEN
photographer
DON MASON
client
ALEXANDER MOORFORD & WOO
agency
KPC/SEATTLE

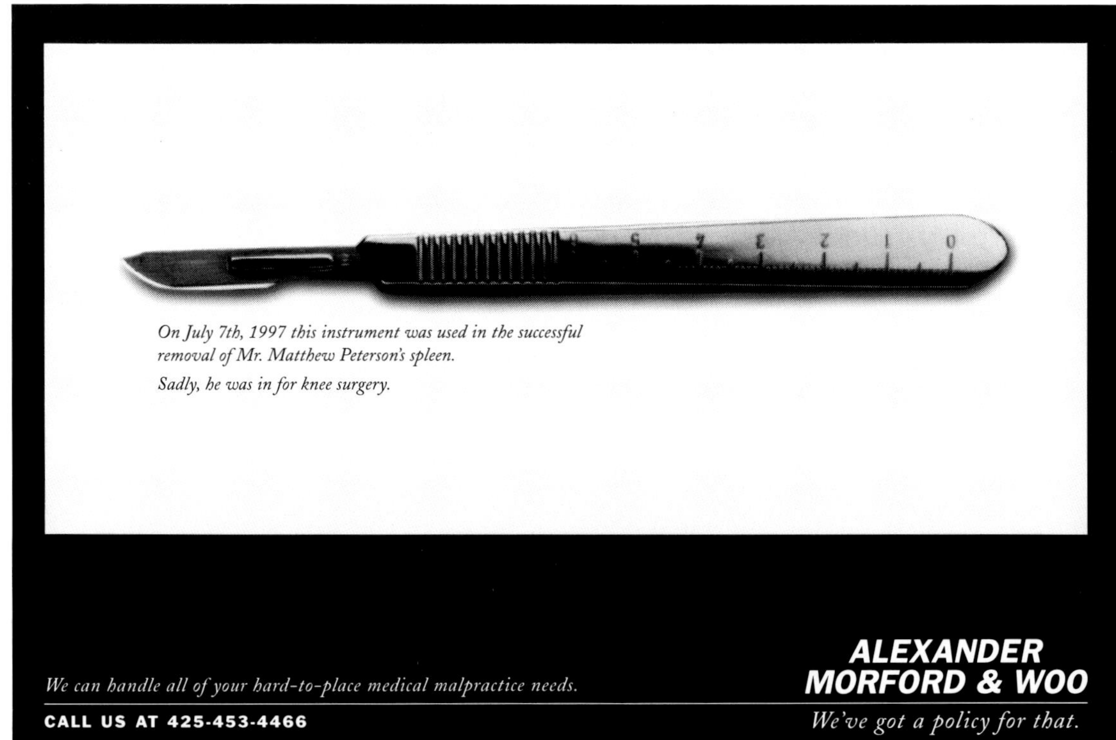

PRINT MERIT

MERIT AWARD
trade b/w or color
less than a page: single

art directors
MANNY DEL ROSARIO
JUN CARANGAN

writer
DAVID GUERRERO

client
OGILVY & MATHER PHILIPPINES

agency
OGILVY & MATHER PHILIPPINES/ MAKATI CITY

AN ADVERTISEMENT FOR ADVERTISING EXECUTIVES FROM AN ADVERTISING AGENCY THAT LOVES ADVERTISING.

STILL INTERESTED?

Good. After all, we're not just any advertising agency. We're Ogilvy & Mather. And if you're the kind of person we're interested in, you'll probably know what that means.

It means believing, for instance, that the customer is not always right. That's right. *Not* always right.

Think about it. Would you really have faith in a Doctor whose motto was: The Patient Knows Best? Or trust a Lawyer who asked your opinion on the wording of a contract? What if a bank manager called *you* for advice: 'We can't decide if interest rates are going up or down. Any ideas?'

These scenarios may seem odd. Bizzare. Unthinkable even. But it is exactly the way most advertising agencies deal with their clients.

Never mind that agencies are composed of people who spend their entire working lives listening to consumers' innermost feelings about canned fruit, credit cards and condoms. Though not necessarily all at once.

Or that they contain people who talk lengthily on subjects like target audience rating points, the leveraging of brand equity and the emotional impact of a sans serif typeface. Often in the same sentence.

Because most agencies believe it's in their clients' best interests to tell them exactly what they want to hear. That the world will change to suit their sales forecasts if everyone just wishes hard enough. That 'nothing else works because we've never tried it.'

It's attitudes like these that lead to mistakes. Big, expensive mistakes. Cleverly disguised as safe conservative choices.

"Let's do an ad just like the one our competitor came out with" (Yes, that way everyone will think *they* did it.) "We just want something like we did last year" (It didn't work then but at least we have an excuse.) "I don't like it but if we air it over and over and over and over again people will start to get it." (Uh-uh, uh-uh, uh-uh, uh-uh.)

If you work in advertising you may recognize these situations. And if you're really honest, you might recognize yourself. But you've probably thought you couldn't do anything about it. Because it will be just the same anywhere else. Or worse. And you'll fall behind in the queue for the corner office. Which may be the only job satisfaction you've got to look forward to.

Which brings us, at long last, to our point. Or rather points. Because, like Rockefeller, we believe this business is built on three unshakable principles: Great Ads, Great Ads and Great Ads.

OK, Good. No problem. That's settled then. Yep. We can almost hear the entire advertising industry nodding its pony-tailed head in unison. So, by the way, just asking, what are Great Ads? Ah.

Our opinion? Great ads are ads which you're proud of. Ads you point out to friends, enemies and acquaintances. Ads you tell your mom about. Ads you hope your ex-boss, ex-girlfriend, first husband or former English teacher who gave you such bad grades is reading. (Or should that be 'are' reading.)

Oh, and by the way, great ads are also ones that get up to 19 times more awareness than regular, ordinary, boring ones that cost just as much to produce, air and have long meetings about. Which means they're also up to 19 times more effective. Which means your client is going to be up to 19 times happier. Which means you're going to get paid 19 times more...hang on a minute, this is going too far.

As you'll have gathered we're an agency that believes in great ads. With people willing to stay up all night writing them, re-writing them and then deciding it's better with just a visual.

What we really need now are the people who can help make more of them happen. The type that create opportunities. Think unconventionally. Devise strategies so brilliant the ads practically write themselves. And who win the trust and respect of clients by being as passionate about our business as they are about theirs.

In other words, the very best Account Executives and Account Directors. And, most of all, the finest Group Account Director in the business. The titles aren't as important as the passion to create excellent work. And naturally, the rewards will be as exceptional as the people we're looking for.

(But if it's just the money you're interested in we'd rather you try medicine, law, banking or, indeed, one of our competitors.)

To get things moving call Tina Coscolluela, during office hours, on 892 3795. Alternatively, send a brief letter and a couple of your favourite ads to her private fax line: 892 4983. Or you could even send a message via e-mail to: tina.coscolluela@ogilvy.com.

In return, we'll be happy to send you a book of our own recent advertisements. And, who knows, the chance to create some great ads of your own.

PRINT MERIT

MERIT AWARD
trade b/w or color
less than a page: single

art director
JAN TRUDEL

writer
MARC STOIBER

client
PALMER JARVIS DDB

agency
PALMER JARVIS DDB/VANCOUVER

Proudly turning young artists into capitalist tools for 28 years.

Palmer Jarvis Advertising

MERIT AWARD
trade b/w or color
any size: campaign

art director
MIKE HANNETT

writer
DAVE BUCHANAN

illustrators
CHRIS CORR
JOHN PAUL EARLY
MELIO SO
LARA HARWOOD
PAUL POWIS

client
VOLKSWAGEN
GROUP UK

agency
BMP DDB/LONDON

There is no smoke without fire

and in Wolfsburg you won't find too many fires.

Heating for hundreds of homes is provided by the surplus energy generated by the local Volkswagen factory.

In Wolfsburg fuel efficiency is up, emissions are down

Just what you'd expect from Volkswagen.

You don't have to be long, short or portly to work here but it helps. It helps our designers. They keep a record of any employee blessed with extraordinary dimensions so, when they design a Volkswagen, they make sure it's fit to fit all kinds of people.

PRINT MERIT

At Volkswagen, 80% of all water used in car production is recycled. However, before it can be deemed clean enough to be used again, the water will undergo as many as 13 different treatments.
As part of the process the water passes through a pond where bass and carp swim. The pond is always free from toxins and pollutants. But not from fishermen. Sorry fish.

While oil companies continue to search for new oilfields, we've found a new oil.
Since May 1996 every Volkswagen diesel engine has had the capability to run on a derivative of rape-seed oil called Bio-diesel.
And already, pumps dispensing our new fuel are sprouting up all over Germany.

Volkswagen's new oilfield.

In Wolfsburg any underground pipe that carries anything more harmful than water is enclosed in another pipe. The space between the two pipe walls is filled with a pressurised non-toxic, non-combustible gas. Any change in pressure is immediately detected by monitors at the factory and the leak is initially contained by the outer pipe before being rectified permanently. At Volkswagen, even the pipes are safety conscious.

PRINT MERIT

MERIT AWARD
trade b/w or color
any size: campaign

art director
VANESSA PEARSON
writer
LAWRENCE SEFTEL
photographer
STOCK
client
AAA SCHOOL
OF ADVERTISING
agency
THE JUPITER
DRAWING ROOM/
JOHANNESBURG

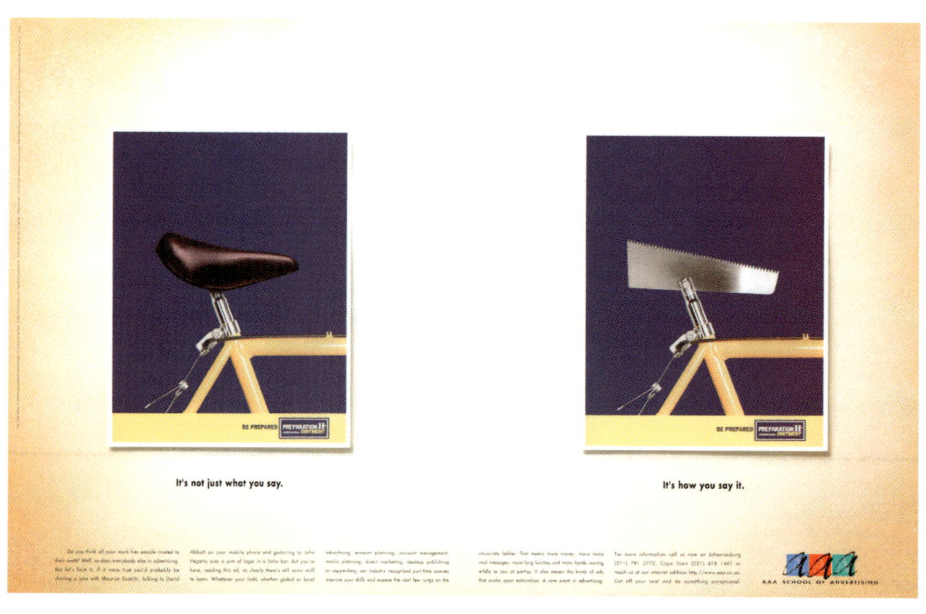

PRINT MERIT

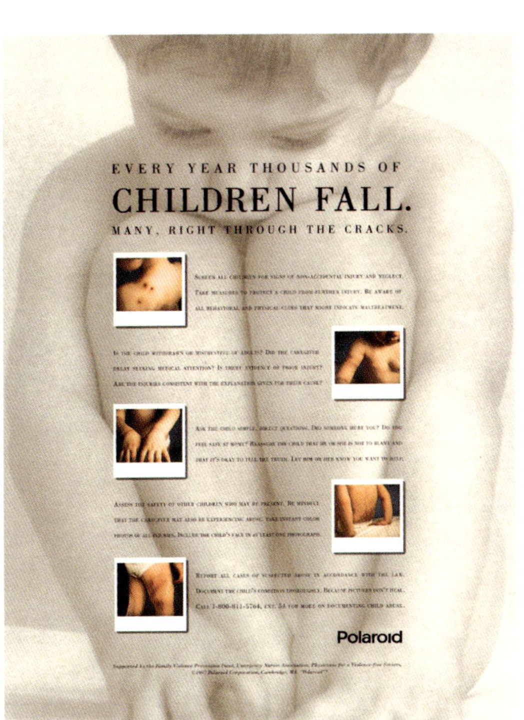

MERIT AWARD
trade b/w or color
any size: campaign

art directors
HAL CURTIS
RALPH WATSON
ALYSSA D'ARIENZO

writer
KARA GOODRICH

photographers
MICHELE CLEMENT
LARS TOPELMANN

client
POLAROID

agency
LEONARD/MONAHAN/
FOXBOROUGH

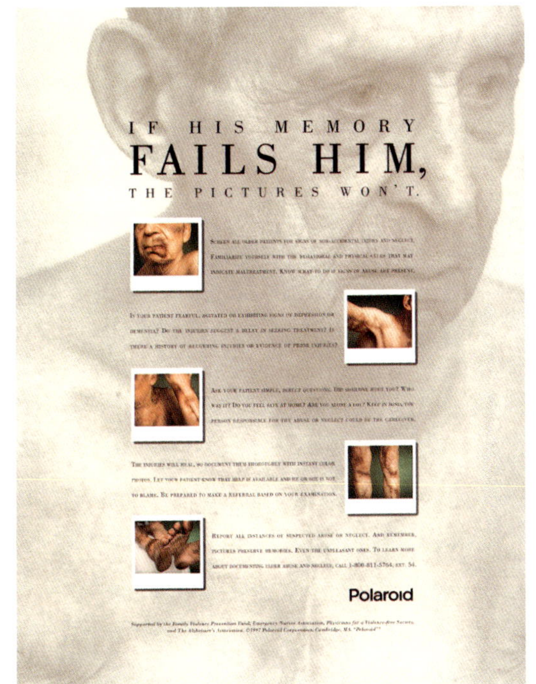

MERIT AWARD
trade b/w or color
any size: campaign

art director
JEAN ROBAIRE

writer
SALLY HOGSHEAD

client
MICHAEL RUPPERT

agency
MARTIN CREATIVE LA/
LOS ANGELES

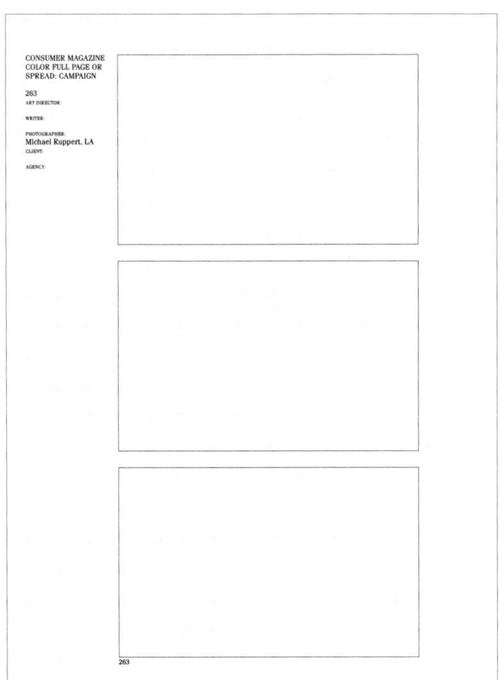

CONSUMER MAGAZINE
COLOR FULL PAGE OR
SPREAD: CAMPAIGN

263
ART DIRECTOR:

WRITER:

PHOTOGRAPHER:
Michael Ruppert, LA
CLIENT:

AGENCY:

263

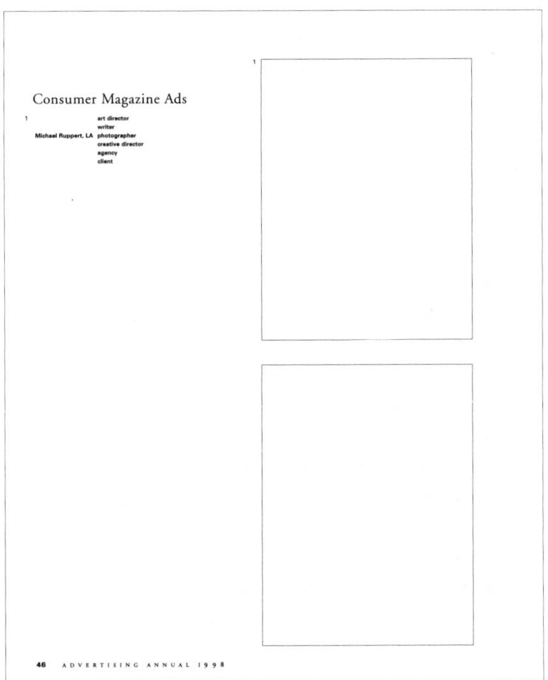

Consumer Magazine Ads

1 art director
writer
Michael Ruppert, LA photographer
creative director
agency
client

1

46 ADVERTISING ANNUAL 1998

Miscellaneous

Michael Ruppert, LA

29 5.9735

MERIT AWARD
trade b/w or color
any size: campaign

art director
JON MONTGOMERY

writer
JOHN FRANCIS

photographer
ANDY ANDERSON

client
3M SCIENTIFIC ANGLERS

agency
MARTIN/WILLIAMS ADVERTISING/ MINNEAPOLIS

MERIT AWARD
trade b/w or color
any size: campaign

art director
CHRIS HARRISON

writer
IAN MACKELLAR

illustrator
ERIK JOHNSON

photographer
PHILIP ROSTRON

client
CANADIAN BUSINESS

agency
ROCHE MACAULAY & PARTNERS ADVERTISING/TORONTO

THE STEP BY STEP GUIDE TO BEING RICH AND POWERFUL

Lesson Twenty-One

ORCHESTRATING YOUR *first* HOSTILE TAKEOVER

WITH A LITTLE PLANNING, and the right materials, in no time at all, you can overrun an unsuspecting corporation and claim it as your own.

YOU'LL NEED

Ask your average wealthy and successful business person what troubles them the most, and they'd probably all give you the same answer. They just don't know how to take over a large corporation. Well, at long last, help is here. Just follow these simple steps.

STEP ONE

Okay, the first thing you're going to have to do is find a suitable target. (A Word of Caution: Before attempting any of these steps, it is essential that you have all the recommended items in the "You'll Need" box. Failure to do so could result in embarrassment among your peers or possible jail time.)

For acquisition purposes, insurance companies are a good bet. For that matter, so are small manufacturing companies or electronics corporations. And if you're feeling particularly energetic, there's always software companies. Have someone in mind? Good. Let's go to Step Two.

STEP TWO

STEP THREE

STEP FOUR

WHAT to READ

CANADIAN BUSINESS MAGAZINE. NOW TWICE MONTHLY.

Canadian Business
This Way UP

THE STEP BY STEP GUIDE TO BEING RICH AND POWERFUL

Lesson Seventeen

BUYING YOUR VERY *own* CORPORATE JET

WITH A LITTLE BIT OF RESEARCH and a certified cheque for 35 million dollars, in no time at all you too can join the exciting world of corporate air travel.

YOU'LL NEED

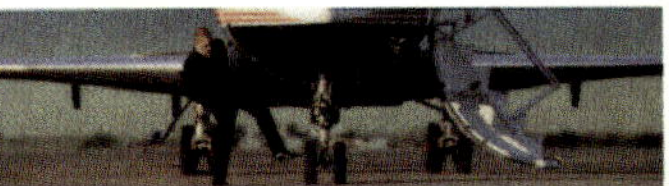

STEP ONE

STEP TWO

STEP THREE

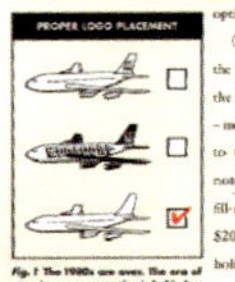

STEP FOUR

STEP FIVE

WHAT to READ

CANADIAN BUSINESS MAGAZINE. NOW TWICE MONTHLY.

Canadian Business
This Way UP

THE STEP BY STEP GUIDE TO BEING RICH AND POWERFUL

Lesson Thirty-Two

BUYING YOUR *own* ISLAND

YOU'LL NEED

STEP ONE

WITH THE RIGHT ISLAND BROKER, a sea plane, and a pre-approved mortgage for several million dollars, you too can have your very own piece of the world.

STEP TWO

STEP THREE

STEP FOUR

STEP FIVE

WHAT to READ

CANADIAN BUSINESS MAGAZINE. NOW TWICE MONTHLY.

Canadian Business
This Way UP

PRINT MERIT

MERIT AWARD
collateral: brochures

art directors
BILL CAHAN
BOB DINETZ

writer
JOHN MANNION

illustrators
MARK TODD
RICCARDO VECCHIO
JASON HOLLEY
BOB DINETZ

photographers
TONY STROMBERG
AMY GUIP

client
CADENCE DESIGN SYSTEMS

agency
CAHAN & ASSOCIATES/
SAN FRANCISCO

MERIT AWARD
collateral: brochures

art directors
BILL CAHAN
KEVIN ROBERSON

writers
MARC BERNSTEIN
ALICIA CIMBORA

illustrator
KEVIN ROBERSON

photographers
KEITH BARDIN
JOHN KOLESA
TONY STROMBERG

client
COR THERAPEUTICS

agency
CAHAN & ASSOCIATES/
SAN FRANCISCO

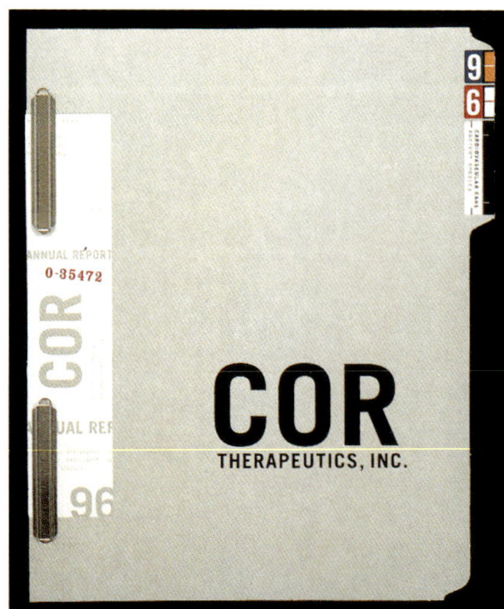

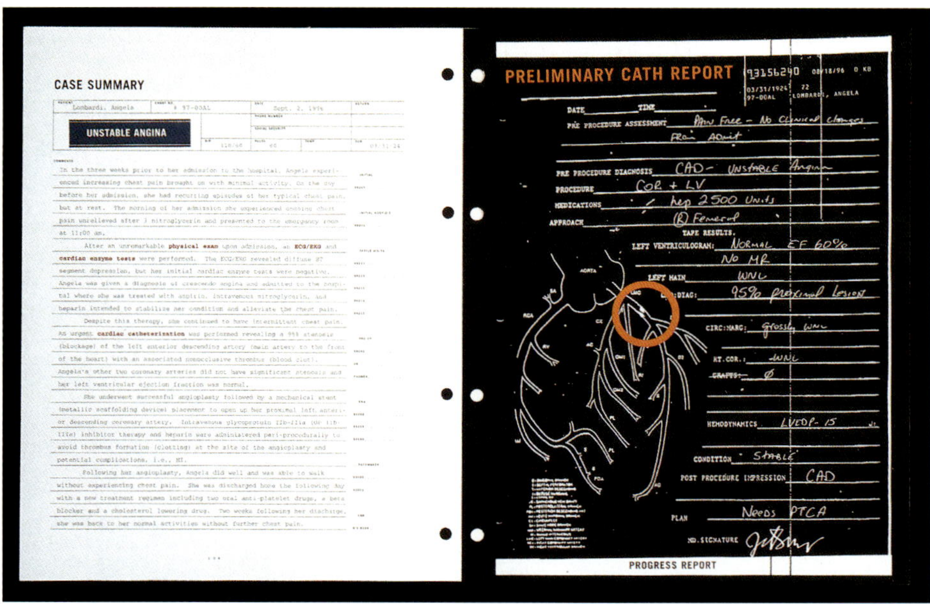

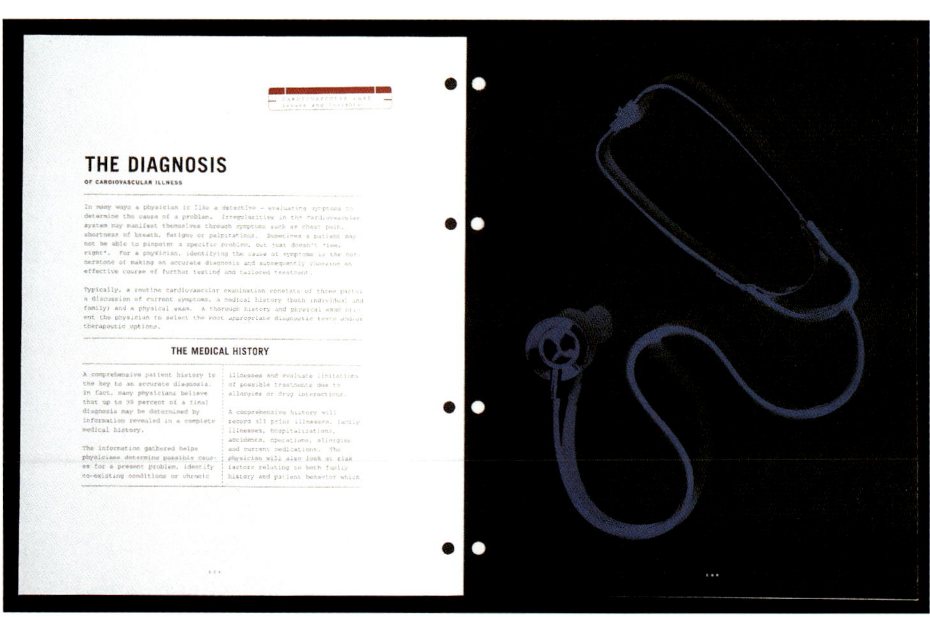

MERIT AWARD
collateral: brochures

art director
SHARON AZULA

writer
MICHAEL ATKINSON

illustrators
BERNARD MAISNER
JACK MALLOY
PETER SIU
KEN JACOBSEN

designers
SHARON AZULA
HEATHER COOLEY

photographer
RAYMOND MEEKS

client
MILLENIUM IMPORT CO

agency
CLARITY COVERDALE
FURY/MINNEAPOLIS

MERIT AWARD
collateral: brochures

art directors
HILARY WOLFE
PETER LOCKE

writer
PAUL VENABLES

photographer
HEIMO

client
SOUTHWESTERN BELL

agency
GOODBY SILVERSTEIN
& PARTNERS/
SAN FRANCISCO

PRINT MERIT

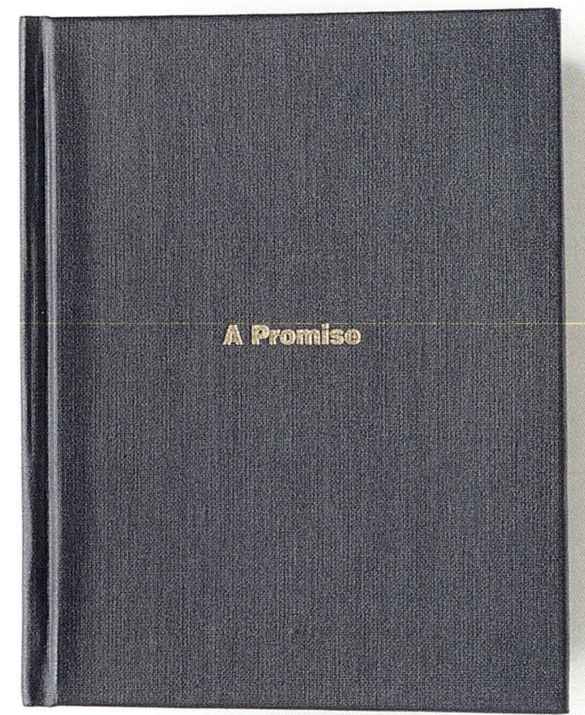

MERIT AWARD
collateral: brochures

art directors
PAUL CURTIN
ROB PRICE
KEITH ANDERSEN

illustrator
KEITH ANDERSEN

photographer
WILLIAM ABRAMOWICZ

client
WILLIAMS-SONOMA

agency
GOODBY SILVERSTEIN
& PARTNERS/
SAN FRANCISCO

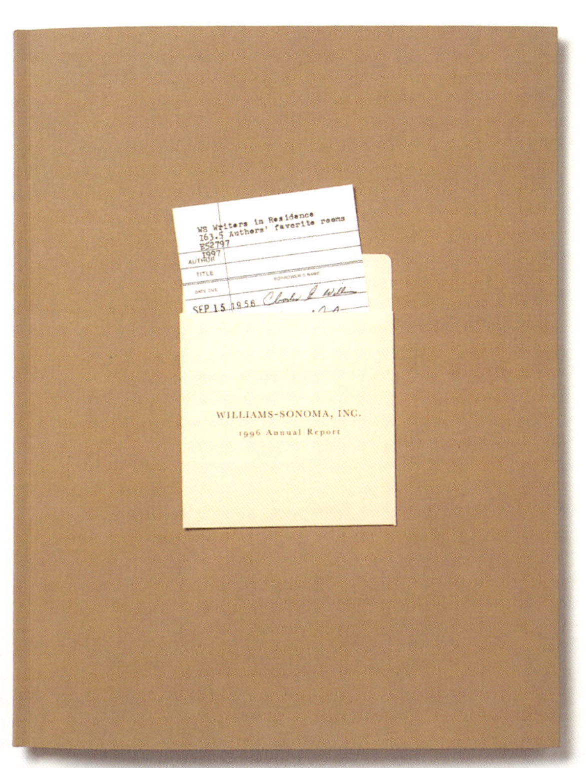

PRINT MERIT

MERIT AWARD
collateral: brochures

art director
SLATOFF AND COHEN PARTNERS

writer
ROBERT LEIGHTON

illustrators
CHIP WASS
EDWIN FATHERINGHAM

designers
TAMAR COHEN
DAVID SLATOFF

client
NICK AT NITE

agency
NICKELODEON/
MTV NETWORKS/
NEW YORK

MERIT AWARD
collateral: brochures

art director
AXEL THOMSEN

writer
ALEXANDER SCHILL

photographers
JULIA DROOP
STOCK

client
DAILMER-BENZ

agency
SPRINGER & JACOBY
WERBUNG GMBH/
HAMBURG

Alle
Menschen
sind nicht
gleich.

Mercedes-Benz
Die Zukunft des Automobils.

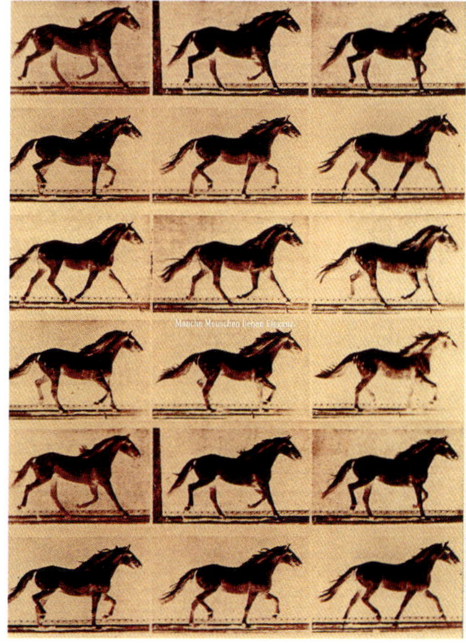

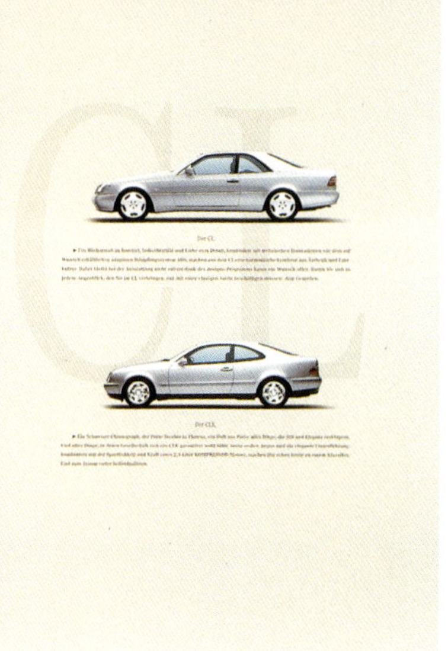

PRINT MERIT

MERIT AWARD
collateral: brochures

art director
JO ANN BOUTIN

writers
KENNY LEE
GRADY HINSCHE

illustrators
GREG CAPULLO
LAURA LEVINE
KIRK CALDWELL

photographers
MEREDITH PARMALEE
PETE MCARTHUR

client
SONY COMPUTER
ENTERTAINMENT

agency
TBWA CHIAT/DAY/
VENICE

MERIT AWARD
collateral: sales kits

art director
JOANINA PASTOLL

illustrator
PETER SIMPSON

client
MERCEDES-BENZ
SOUTH AFRICA

agency
CROSS COLOURS/
JOHANNESBURG

MERIT AWARD
collateral: sales kits

art directors
STEVE SANDSTROM
STEVE SMITH

writer
STEVE SANDOZ

client
TAZO

agency
SANDSTROM DESIGN/
PORTLAND

MERIT AWARD
collateral direct mail
single

art director
WADE KONIAKOWSKY

writer
OLIVER ALBRECHT

illustrators
GLENN FRANCIS
DAVE BLANK
AMY BUTZEN

client
THE ADVERTISING
CLUB OF SAN DIEGO

agency
BIG BANG IDEA
ENGINEERING/
CARLSBAD

MERIT AWARD
collateral: direct mail
single

art director
STEVE MAPP
writer
GREG COLLINS
photographers
SHARPSHOOTERS
client
WHY NOT COCO
agency
COMMAND-Z/
HERMOSA BEACH

MERIT AWARD
collateral: direct mail
singlee

art director
STEVE MAPP
writer
GREG COLLINS
photographer
IMAGE BANK
client
WHY NOT COCO
agency
COMMAND-Z/
HERMOSA BEACH

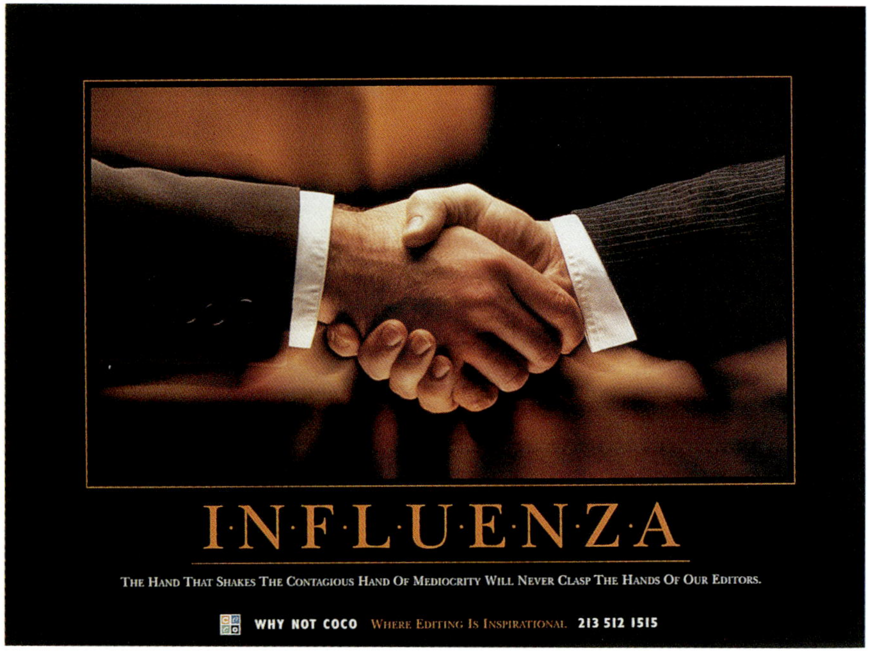

PRINT MERIT

MERIT AWARD
collateral: direct mail
single

art director
MARTY JEWETT
writer
RANKIN MAPOTHER
client
MAKER'S MARK
agency
DOE ANDERSON/
LOUISVILLE

MERIT AWARD
collateral: direct mail
single

art director
TOM LICHTENHELD
writer
TOM ROSEN
client
BMW OF NORTH
AMERICA
agency
FALLON MCELLIGOTT/
MINNEAPOLIS

PRINT MERIT

MERIT AWARD
collateral: direct mail
single

art director
GUY SHELMERDINE
writer
STEVE O'BRIEN
illustrator
STEVE O'BRIEN
photographer
CRAIG SARUWATARI
client
ESPNEWS
agency
GROUND ZERO/
SANTA MONICA

PRINT MERIT

MERIT AWARD
collateral: direct mail
single

art director
TREY FORTNER
writer
SCOTT DAHL
photographer
STEVE MCHUGH
client
THE SHOW '97
agency
PERISCOPE/
MINNEAPOLIS

MERIT AWARD
collateral: direct mail
single

art director
JENNY ROLLINGS

writer
CAREY MOORE

illustrator
JENNY ROLLINGS

client
WHISTLER'S MUSIC

agency
SHOES 4 INDUSTRY/
LOUISVILLE

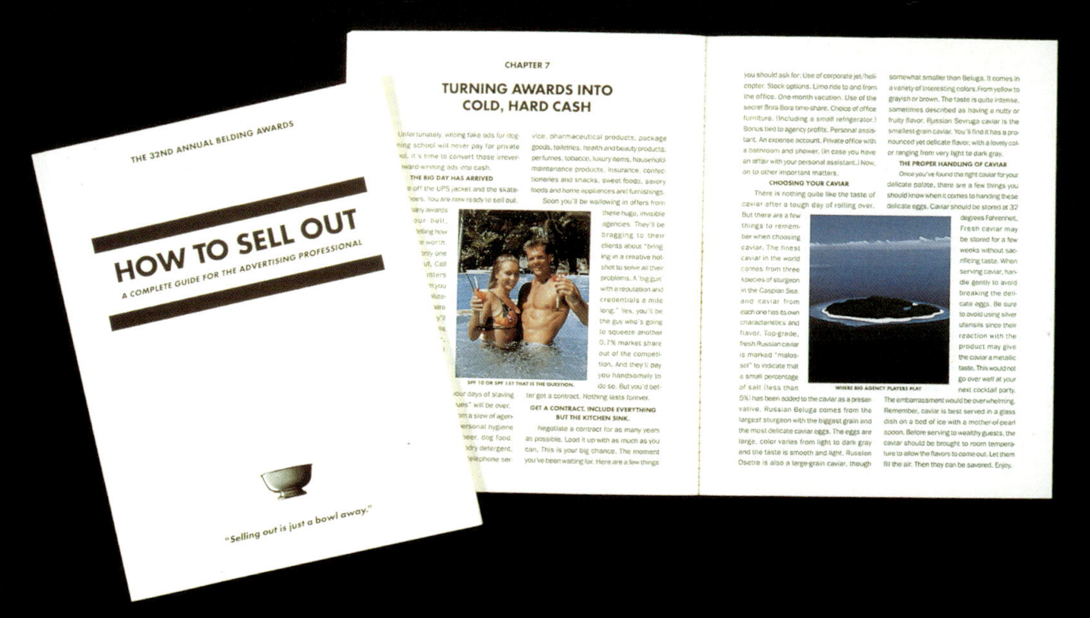

MERIT AWARD
collateral: direct mail
single

art director
SCOTT MACGREGOR

writer
MICHAEL MCKAY

photographer
SMITH/NELSON

client
THE ADVERTISING
CLUB OF LOS ANGELES

agency
TBWA CHIAT/DAY/
VENICE

MERIT AWARD
collateral: direct mail
single

art director
MATT LEAVITT
writer
JONATHAN
SCHOENBERG
photographer
BROOKS FREEHILL
client
SPYDER SKIWEAR
agency
TDA ADVERTISING
AND DESIGN/
LONGMONT

MERIT AWARD
collateral: direct mail
single

art director
DAVID FULLER
writer
CLIFF WATSON
illustrator
JOHN ROBINETTE
client
THOMAS & BETTS
agency
THOMPSON &
COMPANY/MEMPHIS

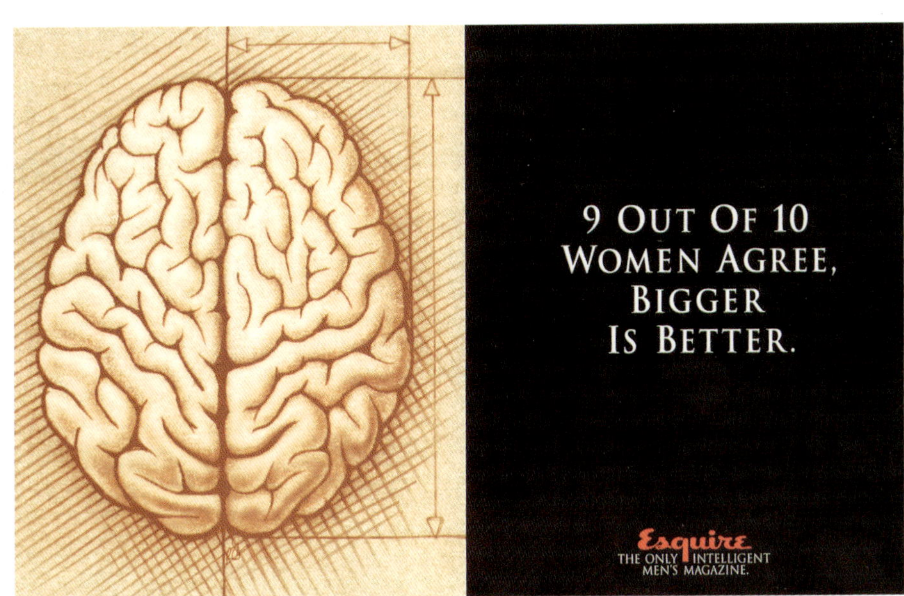

MERIT AWARD
collateral: direct mail campaign

art directors
VINNY TULLEY
ROB CARDUCCI
AARON EISEMAN
ABI ARON SPENCER

writers
ABI ARON SPENCER
AARON EISEMAN
ROB CARDUCCI
VINNY TULLEY
SAL DEVITO

illustrator
RICHARD LAROCCO

photographers
STEVE HELLERSTEIN
JEFFREY APOIAN

client
ESQUIRE MAGAZINE

agency
DEVITO/VERDI/
NEW YORK

MERIT AWARD
collateral: direct mail campaign

art director
BOB BARRIE

writer
LUKE SULLIVAN

illustrators
NEIL SHIGLEY
JOHN DOYLE CARROLL

client
BASSET-WALKER

agency
FALLON MCELLIGOTT/
MINNEAPOLIS

PRINT MERIT

MERIT AWARD
collateral: direct mail campaign

art director
MIKE FETROW

writer
MIKE GIBBS

photographer
MIKE KRIETER

client
FLOWERS OF EDINA

agency
FALLON MCELLIGOTT/
MINNEAPOLIS

Flowers of Edina 7025 Amundson Ave. Edina, 944-5770

Flowers of Edina 7025 Amundson Ave. Edina, 944-5770

Flowers of Edina 7025 Amundson Ave. Edina, 944-5770

MERIT AWARD
collateral: direct mail campaign

art director
DAVE DICKEY

writer
MARK WEGWERTH

client
WOODSON COFFEE COMPANY

agency
PERISCOPE/ MINNEAPOLIS

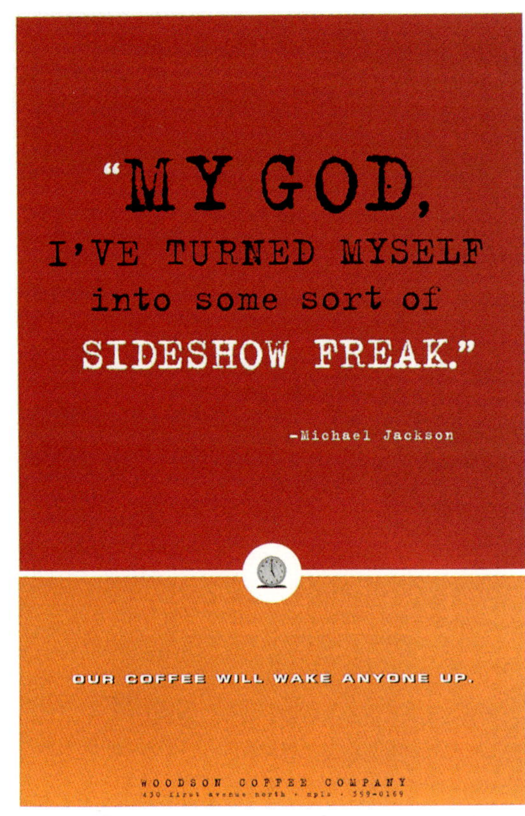

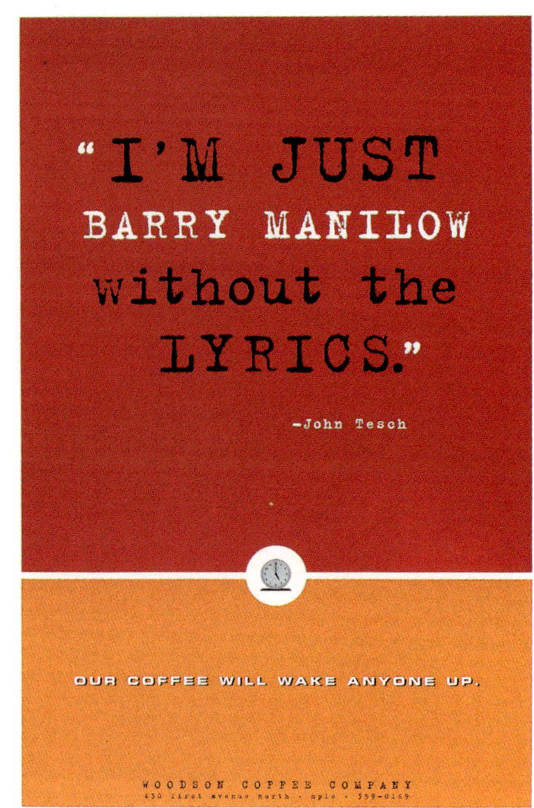

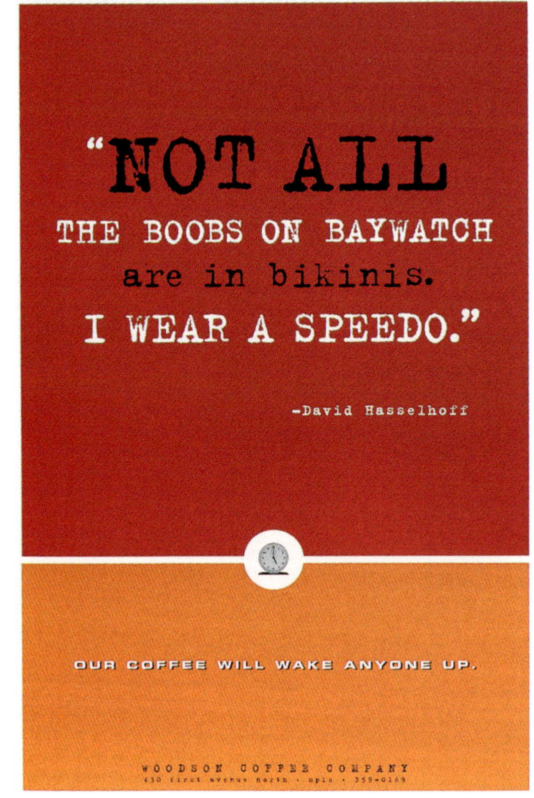

PRINT MERIT

MERIT AWARD
collateral: direct mail campaign

art director
DOUG EYRING

writer
BRAD WALK

illustrator
KEITH GRAVES

photographer
BARTH TILOTSON

client
KEITH GRAVES/ ILLUSTRATOR

agency
THE RICHARDS GROUP/ DALLAS

MERIT AWARD
collateral: point of purchase and in-store

art director
TODD RIDDLE

writer
STUART D'ROZARIO

photographer
JIM FLYNN

client
DEDHAM MEDICAL ASSOCIATION

agency
ARNOLD COMMUNICATIONS/ BOSTON

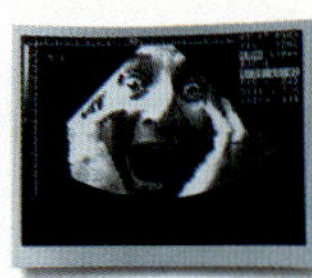

Great Expectations.

A month-by-month guide for the expectant father.

For all those to-be dads interested in learning a little bit about the realities of pregnancy and childbirth, here's a helpful guide on what to expect, what to do and most important, what not to do.

MONTH 1

There is no month one. By the time you've figured out what you've done, it's month two.

MONTH 2

Along with the wonderful news comes nausea. This is caused by the sudden realization that you are going to have to do all the cooking and cleaning for the next few months. This is the month when you learn how to operate the dishwasher and the washing machine.

MONTH 3

The reading begins. Be prepared to read pregnancy books for the next seven months. (It doesn't matter if you're a speed-reader who finishes a book while the rest of us are still trying to differentiate the author's name from the publisher's name, more books will keep appearing on your nightstand out of nowhere.)

So don't try and fight it. Go to the bookstore yourself and buy the biggest childbirth book you can find. This will a) get you huge brownie points, and b) provide ample cover at bedtime for copies of Rolling Stone.

MONTH 4

The to-be mother starts to feel better. And life slowly returns to normal. The first sign of her revival is an admonishment about the state of the kitchen. In the fourth month the socializing begins again. After several weeks of hibernation, the to-be mother is ready to party. But then the realization dawns. No alcohol, no coffee, no alcohol. In that order.

MONTH 5

Finally, the baby starts showing. This is a very delicate time for the to-be mother. She knows she's pregnant but the passerby on the street doesn't. And that doesn't make her happy. You need to support her in every possible way. But don't even think of telling her she's not looking fat. Because she wants to look fat. That's the irony. She just wants to look fat for the right reasons. There's a fine line. And you have to walk it.

MONTH 6

Here's one important fact to keep in mind. To-be parents are the biggest suckers in the world. The to-be mother, anxious to be the perfect mother, wants one of every product, in every product catalogue, in every store. The to-be father, carrying the guilt of generations of fathers for whom the big moment was the moment they got to light their cigars, doesn't dare argue.

Of course, on all the hundreds of shopping trips don't expect to actually buy anything. You can't buy anything at this point. That would be silly. "We're just looking. We'll come back and buy stuff once we've finished looking."

(There's one important thing to remember when buying things for the baby. Don't penny-pinch. In fact, be generous with your money. This will probably be the last time you'll have money to be generous with.)

MONTH 7

The shopping continues. In this month you can expect to make your first purchase. The crib. Examine the rail mechanism very closely. Don't ever buy a crib that squeaks or has potential to squeak. When you finally put the baby to sleep and in the crib, you have to raise the side of the crib. If it squeaks, so will the baby.

Month seven is also the month when the Lamaze classes begin. For the uninitiated, these are sessions where people get to compare their taste in pillowcases.

The main objective of these sessions is to make the 15 to 20 hours of labor a little less painful. Of course, to accomplish that you have to sit through approximately 15 to 20 hours of excruciatingly painful lectures. Go figure. It's all part of the preparation for being a good parent.

MONTH 8

The focus is now completely on the baby and the delivery. The day is drawing near and everything is becoming more and more real. It's a time for introspection. You look back on your own childhood, at the mistakes you think your parents made. Then you make resolutions.

Take some good advice, don't waste too much time on these resolutions. The first time you trip over a dinosaur in your living room and have a near-death experience, you'll break every one of them.

MONTH 9

There are two important things to remember in labor. Be calm. And don't ever, ever say "pain is a state of mind."

The summary of the Lamaze classes does turn out to be true: in labor, as in life, breathing helps. But brave is the man who, when his wife is writhing in agony, can look her in the eye and say, "Honey, don't forget to breathe."

For the father, perhaps the most significant part of labor is the mandatory slap across the face. It is this slap, administered by the mother just before delivery, which actually creates the bond of oneness between father, mother and child.

MONTH 10

Of all the descriptions of parenthood, perhaps the most beautiful and succinct is: 'Until you're a parent you live in a world of black and white. Then suddenly, there's a spectrum of color.' It's true. Particularly about half an hour after the baby's had a large meal.

OB/GYN
DEDHAM MEDICAL ASSOCIATES

This handy reference guide is brought to you by Dedham Medical Associates, 1 Lyons Street, Dedham, MA 02026. Tel: 617-329-1400.

MERIT AWARD
collateral: point of purchase and in-store

art director
PAUL BENNELL

writer
JAY FURBY

photographer
JOHN CLANG

client
PARKE DAVIS

agency
BATEY ADS/
SINGAPORE

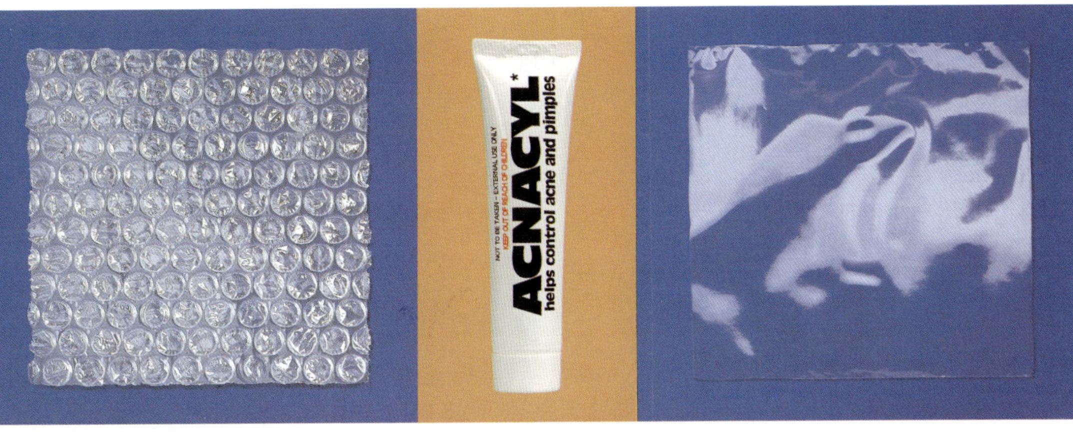

MERIT AWARD
collateral: point of purchase and in-store

art director
PAUL BENNELL

writer
JAY FURBY

photographer
JOHN CLANG

client
PARKE DAVIS

agency
BATEY ADS/
SINGAPORE

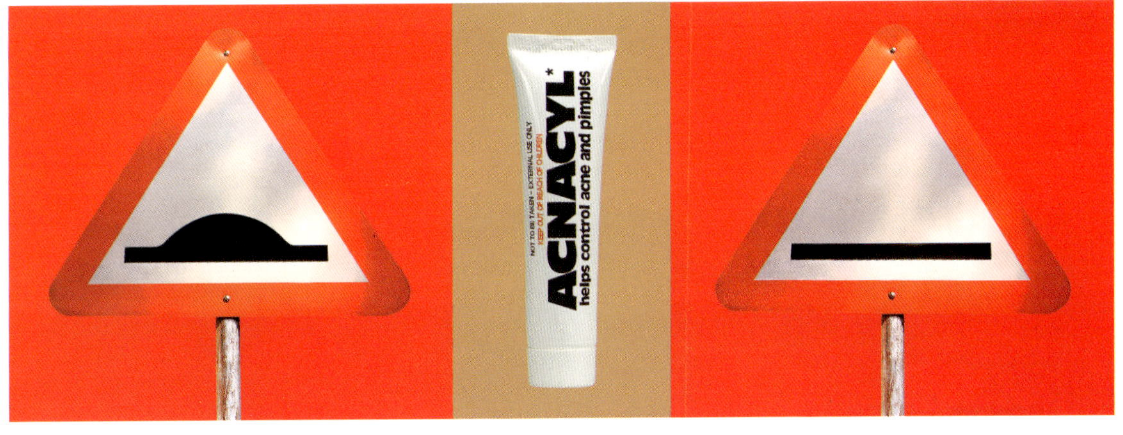

MERIT AWARD
collateral: point of purchase and in-store

art director
PAUL BENNELL

writer
JAY FURBY

photographer
JOHN CLANG

client
PARKE DAVIS

agency
BATEY ADS/
SINGAPORE

MERIT AWARD
collateral: point of purchase and in-store

art director
CHRIS ROBB

writers
KATHY HEPINSTALL
HAROLD EINSTEIN

photographer
GEOF KERN

client
LA CELLULAR

agency
BBDO WEST/
LOS ANGELES

MERIT AWARD
collateral: point of purchase and in-store

art director
CHRIS ROBB

writers
KATHY HEPINSTALL
HAROLD EINSTEIN

photographer
GEOF KERN

client
LA CELLULAR

agency
BBDO WEST/
LOS ANGELES

MERIT AWARD
collateral: point of purchase and in-store

art director
CHRIS ROBB

writers
KATHY HEPINSTALL
HAROLD EINSTEIN

photographer
GEOF KERN

client
LA CELLULAR

agency
BBDO WEST/
LOS ANGELES

MERIT AWARD
collateral: point of purchase and in-store

art director
CHRIS ROBB
writers
KATHY HEPINSTALL
HAROLD EINSTEIN
photographer
GEOF KERN
client
LA CELLULAR
agency
BBDO WEST/
LOS ANGELES

PRINT MERIT

MERIT AWARD
collateral: point of purchase and in-store

art directors
DAVE GARDINER
KIRSTEN WATTERS
writer
MIKE SHEEHAN
photographer
JIM FLYNN
client
MCCANN'S IRISH OATMEAL
agency
HILL HOLLIDAY CONNORS COSMOPULOS/BOSTON

MERIT AWARD
collateral: point of purchase and in-store

art director
STEVE MAPP

writer
SCOTT WILD

designer
DANE JOHNSON

photographers
DAN ESCOBAR
SIMON BRUTY

client
ADIDAS AMERICA

agency
LEAGAS DELANEY/
SAN FRANCISCO

MERIT AWARD
collateral: point of purchase and in-store

art director
GARY GOLDSMITH

writer
DEAN HACOHEN

client
SONY ELECTRONICS

agency
LOWE & PARTNERS/SMS/NEW YORK

MERIT AWARD
collateral: point of purchase and in-store

art director
GARY GOLDSMITH

writer
DEAN HACOHEN

photographer
STOCK

client
SONY ELECTRONICS

agency
LOWE & PARTNERS/SMS/NEW YORK

PRINT MERIT

MERIT AWARD
collateral: point of purchase and in-store

art director
GARY GOLDSMITH

writer
DEAN HACOHEN

photographer
STOCK

client
SONY ELECTRONICS

agency
LOWE & PARTNERS/ SMS/NEW YORK

MERIT AWARD
collateral: point of purchase and in-store

art director
GARY GOLDSMITH

writer
DEAN HACOHEN

photographer
STOCK

client
SONY ELECTRONICS

agency
LOWE & PARTNERS/ SMS/NEW YORK

MERIT AWARD
collateral: point of purchase and in-store

art director
MARY PATTON

writer
SCOTT JORGENSEN

client
VALENTINO'S PIZZA

agency
PETERSON MILLA HOOKS/MINNEAPOLIS

MERIT AWARD
collateral: point of purchase and in-store

art director
TERENCE REYNOLDS

writer
TODD TILFORD

photographer
RICHARD REENS

client
AM GENERAL CORPORATION

agency
PYRO/DALLAS

PRINT MERIT

THE WORLD IS FULL OF GENERIC,

MASS PRODUCED, HOMOGENIZED

PRODUCTS. DON'T BECOME ONE.

09281 03171

Dr. AirWair Martens

MERIT AWARD
collateral: point of purchase and in-store

art director
ERIC TILFORD

writer
TODD TILFORD

client
DR. MARTENS

agency
PYRO/DALLAS

MERIT AWARD
collateral: point of purchase and in-store

art director
ERIC TILFORD

writers
TODD TILFORD
CHAD REA

photographer
JAMES SCHWARTZ

client
DR. MARTENS

agency
PYRO DALLAS

MERIT AWARD
collateral: point of
purchase and in-store

art director
GUTO BUSSAB
writer
DESIREE BROWN
client
ROSE TAXIS
agency
SONNENBERG
MURPHY LEO
BURNETT/
JOHANNESBURG

PRINT MERIT

MERIT AWARD
collateral: point of purchase and in-store

art director
GUTO BUSSAB

writer
DESIREE BROWN

client
ROSE TAXIS

agency
SONNENBERG MURPHY LEO BURNETT/ JOHANNESBURG

PRINT MERIT

MERIT AWARD
collateral: self-promotion

art director
LES SOOS

writer
DAVID BONNER

client
BBDO CANADA

agency
BBDO CANADA/ TORONTO

Good-bye Apple. We're sorry to see you go. BBDO.

MERIT AWARD
collateral: self-promotion

art director
STEVE DRIGGS

writer
RILEY KANE

photographers
SHAWN MICHIENZI
RIPSAW

client
FALLON MCELLIGOTT

agency
FALLON MCELLIGOTT/
MINNEAPOLIS

MERIT AWARD
collateral: self-promotion

art director
KINKO'S

writer
ANNIE FINNEGAN

client
ANNIE FINNEGAN

agency
ANNIE FINNEGAN/
STONE MOUNTAIN

ANNIE FINNEGAN
4395 Briers Way
Stone Mountain, GA 30083
(404) 296-8544

Copywriter

PROFESSIONAL EXPERIENCE

- LOREM IPSUM DOLOR Sit amet, consecteteur adipisicing elit, sed do eius mod tempor incididunt ut labore et dolore magna aliqua.
- UT ENIM AD MINIM Veniam, quis nostrud exercitation ullamco laborisnisi ut aliquip ex ea commodo consequat.
- DUIS AUTE Irure dolor in reprehenderit in voluptate velit esse cil lum eu fugiat nulla pariatur. Excepteur sint occaecat cupidatat.

EDUCATIONAL BACKGROUND

- CULPA QUI OFFICIA Deserunt mollit anim id est laborum. Et harumd und, dereud facilis est dereud facilis est er expedit.
- NAM LIBER Te conscient to factor tum poen legum odioque civiud.

AFFILIATIONS/ ACTIVITIES

- TEMPORIBUD Autem quinusd voluptas, assumenda est aut tum rerum fugiat nulla, pariatur excepteur sint mollit.
- NECESSIT ATIB Saepe eveniet ut er repudiand sint et molestia recus. Dolore non eius mod tempor.

SUMMARY OF QUALIFICATIONS

- Nothing matters but the book.

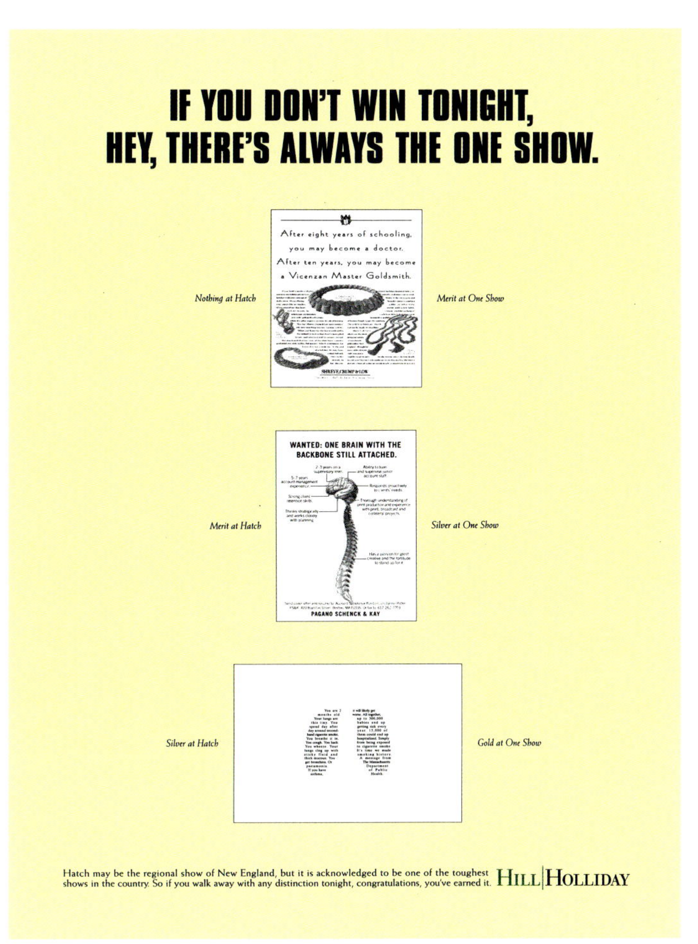

MERIT AWARD
collateral: self-promotion

art director
ASHLEY REESE

writer
PAUL SCHAUDER

client
HILL HOLLIDAY CONNORS COSMOPULOS

agency
HILL HOLLIDAY CONNORS COSMOPULOS/BOSTON

MERIT AWARD
collateral: self-promotion

art directors
MARC SOBIER
ANDREW KELLER

writers
DOUG LOWELL
TOM VAN NESS

illustrator
JANICE EMERSON

client
AKA ADVERTISING

agency
KARAKAS VANSICKLE OUELLETTE/PORTLAND

MERIT AWARD
collateral: self-promotion

art director
JON WYVILLE

writer
KEVIN LYNCH

photographer
STOCK

client
MCCONNAUGHY STEIN
SCHMIDT BROWN

agency
MCCONNAUGHY STEIN
SCHMIDT BROWN/
CHICAGO

MERIT AWARD
collateral: self-promotion

art directors
CABELL HARRIS
TOM GIBSON

writer
TOM GIBSON

illustrator
LUMPY MCCLANING

photographers
ABE SPEAR
KARL STEINBRENNER

client
WORK

agency
WORK/RICHMOND

MERIT AWARD
collateral: self-promotion

art directors
CABELL HARRIS
PAUL HOWALT

writers
JOE NAGY
TOM GIBSON

illustrators
PAUL HOWALT
TOM GIBSON
HOWARD BROWN
MIKE CALKINS

photographers
ABE SPEAR
KARL STEINBRENNER

client
WORK

agency
WORK/RICHMOND

MERIT AWARD
collateral: posters

art director
BRADLEY WOOD
writer
RYAN EBNER
photographers
LEON BEHAR
STOCK
client
SPECIALIZED BICYCLES
agency
BUTLER SHINE &
STERN/SAUSALITO

MERIT AWARD
collateral: posters

art director
BRADLEY WOOD
writer
RYAN EBNER
photographers
LEON BEHAR
STOCK
client
SPECIALIZED BICYCLES
agency
BUTLER SHINE &
STERN/SAUSALITO

MERIT AWARD
collateral: posters

art director
BRADLEY WOOD
writer
RYAN EBNER
photographers
LEON BEHAR
STOCK
client
SPECIALIZED BICYCLES
agency
BUTLER SHINE &
STERN/SAUSALITO

MERIT AWARD
collateral: posters

art director
TED JENKINS

writer
LARRY LIPSON

photographer
DICK REED

client
XXX CONDOMS

agency
CRAMER-KRASSELT/
CHICAGO

MERIT AWARD
collateral: posters

art director
MICHAEL COHEN

writer
DAVID OAKLEY

photographer
PAT STAUB

client
RICHARD MCCOY

agency
LOEFFLER KETCHUM
MOUNTJOY/CHARLOTTE

MERIT AWARD
collateral: posters

art directors
TOM SCHARPF
MICHAEL KIRKLAND

writer
MARCUS SAGAR

photographer
SHIN SUGINO

client
JAGUAR CANADA

agency
OGILVY & MATHER
CANADA/TORONTO

PRINT MERIT

MERIT AWARD
collateral: posters

art director
ANDREW CLARKE

writer
ANDREW CLARKE

illustrator
PROCOLOR

photographer
SHAUN PETTIGREW

client
BURGER KING

agency
SAATCHI & SAATCHI/
SINGAPORE

Fiery Fries.

MERIT AWARD
collateral: posters

art directors
SUSAN ALINSANGAN
KEN YOUNGLIEB

writers
CRAIG TANIMOTO
ERIC GRUNBAUM

photographer
CORBIS

client
APPLE COMPUTER

agency
TBWA CHIAT/DAY/
VENICE

PUBLIC SERVICE &
POLITICAL MERIT

MERIT AWARD
public service/political
newspaper or magazine
single

art directors
TROY KING
FRANK SCOTTI

writer
ELLEN CURTIS

photographer
CHRIS DAVIS

client
AMERICAN CANCER
SOCIETY

agency
BBDO SOUTH/ATLANTA

PUBLIC SERVICE MERIT

MERIT AWARD
public service/political
newspaper or magazine
single

art director
CHRISTOPHER COLE

writer
STEVE SAARI

photographers
MP WOLCOTT
LIBRARY OF CONGRESS
JOHN DIETER
JOHN ROCKWOOD

client
DELTA BLUES MUSEUM

agency
LAWLER BALLARD VAN
DURAND/BIRMINGHAM

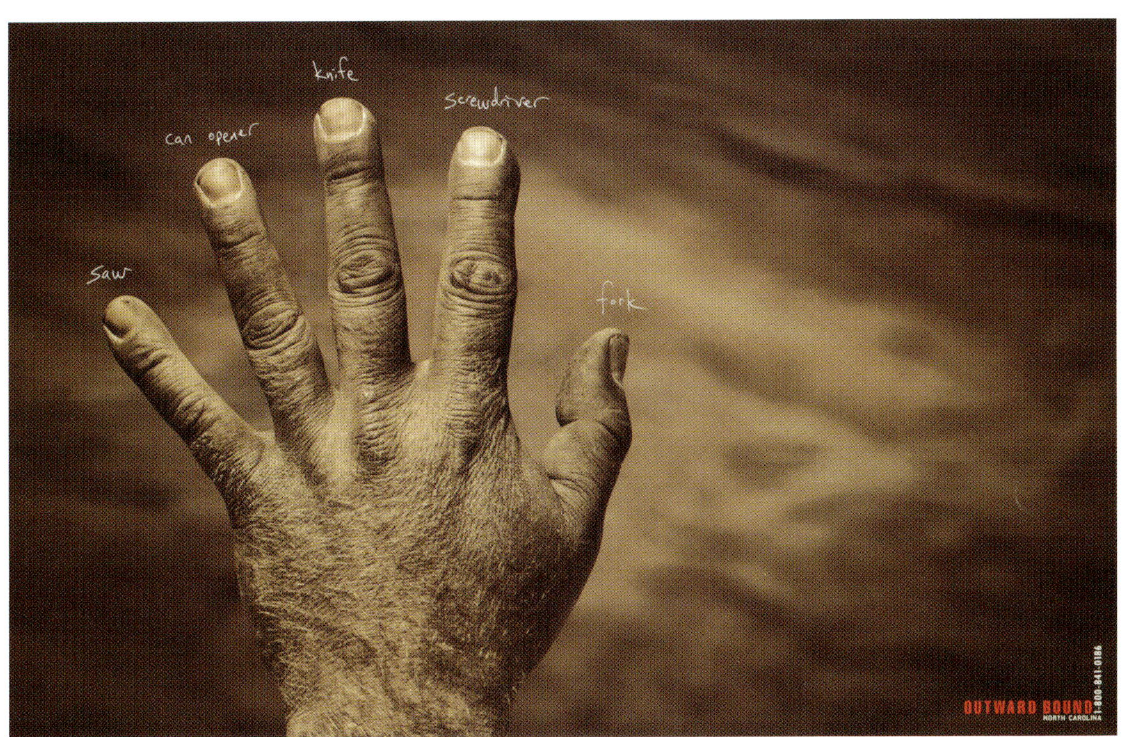

MERIT AWARD
public service/political
newspaper or magazine
single

art director
DOUG PEDERSEN
writers
CURTIS SMITH
MIKE DUCKWORTH
photographer
JIM ARNDT
client
OUTWARD BOUND
agency
LOEFFLER KETCHUM
MOUNTJOY/CHARLOTTE

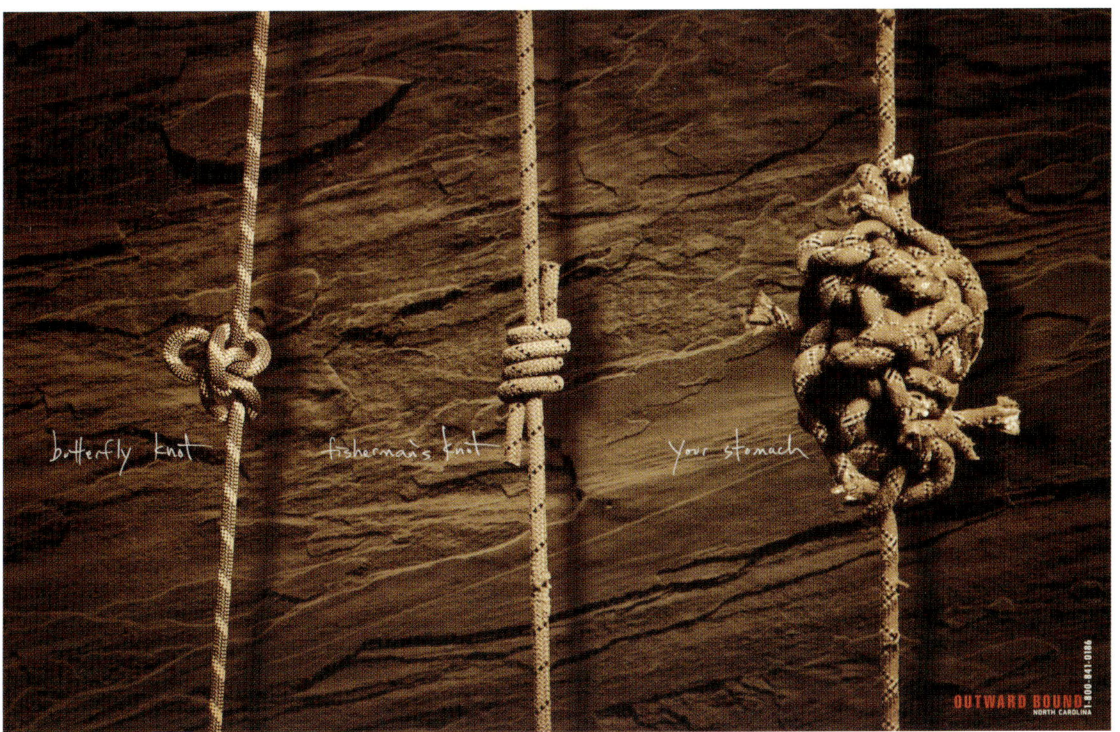

MERIT AWARD
public service/political
newspaper or magazine
single

art director
DOUG PEDERSEN
writers
CURTIS SMITH
MIKE DUCKWORTH
photographer
JIM ARNDT
client
OUTWARD BOUND
agency
LOEFFLER KETCHUM
MOUNTJOY/CHARLOTTE

MERIT AWARD
public service/political
newspaper or magazine
single

art director
CLIFF SORAH
writer
JOE ALEXANDER
photographer
AP/WORLD WIDE PHOTOS
client
JOHN F. KENNEDY
LIBRARY FOUNDATION
agency
THE MARTIN AGENCY/
RICHMOND

JUNE 3, 1961: RUSSIA SURRENDERS TO THE UNITED STATES.

The diplomatic power of Jacqueline Bouvier Kennedy: First Lady. Part of a new exhibit at **The John F. Kennedy Library & Museum.** Boston, Massachusetts.

MERIT AWARD
public service/political
newspaper or magazine
single

art director
CLIFF SORAH
writer
JOE ALEXANDER
photographers
LISA LARSEN
TIME LIFE
client
JOHN F. KENNEDY
LIBRARY FOUNDATION
agency
THE MARTIN AGENCY/
RICHMOND

JACQUELINE KENNEDY'S WEDDING. (THIS TIME YOU'RE INVITED.)

Jacqueline Bouvier Kennedy's wedding gown. On exhibit now through Labor Day. **The John F. Kennedy Library & Museum.** Boston, Massachusetts.

THE IRON CURTAIN NEVER CAME DOWN DURING JFK'S ADMINISTRATION.
HOWEVER, THE TACKY CURTAINS IN THE BLUE ROOM DID.

Mark Shaw Collection/Photo Researchers

Jacqueline Kennedy's historic restoration of the White House. Part of a new exhibit at **The John F. Kennedy Library & Museum.** Boston, Massachusetts.

MERIT AWARD
public service/political
newspaper or magazine
single

art director
CLIFF SORAH
writer
JOE ALEXANDER
photographers
MARK SHAW
PHOTO RESEARCHERS
client
JOHN F. KENNEDY
LIBRARY FOUNDATION
agency
THE MARTIN AGENCY/
RICHMOND

THERE HAS NEVER BEEN A MORE WELL-KNOWN WOMAN.
THERE HAS NEVER BEEN A LESS WELL-KNOWN WOMAN.

Photograph © 1997 Jacques Lowe

The many facets of Jacqueline Bouvier Kennedy: First Lady. Part of a new exhibit at **The John F. Kennedy Library & Museum.** Boston, Massachusetts.

MERIT AWARD
public service/political
newspaper or magazine
single

art director
CLIFF SORAH
writer
JOE ALEXANDER
photographer
JACQUES LOWE
client
JOHN F. KENNEDY
LIBRARY FOUNDATION
agency
THE MARTIN AGENCY/
RICHMOND

MERIT AWARD
public service/political
newspaper or magazine
single

art director
CHRISTOPHER GYORGY

writer
CHRIS JACOBS

photographer
THE NEGRO LEAGUES BASEBALL MUSEUM

client
THE NEGRO LEAGUES BASEBALL MUSEUM

agency
THE MARTIN AGENCY/ RICHMOND

WAS JOSH GIBSON THE BLACK BABE RUTH?

OR WAS BABE RUTH THE WHITE JOSH GIBSON?

For Josh Gibson, the comparisons to Babe Ruth all started in a championship series with the Lincoln Giants. First, Gibson blasted one over the center field fence at Forbes Field – roughly 475 feet. Next, he smashed one into the third tier of left field at Yankee Stadium – an estimated 500 feet. From then on, Josh Gibson would be known as the "black Babe Ruth."

Buck O'Neil had this to say about Josh Gibson, "I heard Ruth hit the ball. I'd never heard that sound before...And the next time I heard that sound, I'm in Washington, D.C., in the dressing room and I heard that sound of a bat hitting the ball – sounded just like when Ruth hit the ball. I rushed out, got on nothing but a jockstrap...we were playing the Homestead Grays and it was Josh Gibson hitting the ball."

"I don't break bats. I wear them out."
— Josh Gibson

Aside from the color of their skin, Babe Ruth and Josh Gibson even looked somewhat the same. At 6'2" and 220 lbs., Gibson could easily fill up every inch of the batter's box. But Gibson's frame was compact, not corpulent like Ruth's. All of his power came from his enormous arms and torso, rather than his legs. Instead of Ruth's wide swing that could send a ball rocketing over the moon, Gibson used a lightning quick snap of his wrists to send a line drive right over the top of the wall.

"He had the power of Ruth and the hitting ability of Ted Williams. That was Josh Gibson."
— Buck O'Neil

Gibson once hit a line drive so hard that when shortstop Willie Wells tried to catch it, the impact split his thumb and index finger apart.

In 1930, at only the age of 19, Gibson hit 65 home runs. The next year, he hit 72 home runs. There are even those who say his lifetime home run tally may have reached 1,000.

In fact, Josh Gibson supposedly crushed the longest home runs ever in Cincinnati's Crosley Field, Pittsburgh's Forbes Field, and even in "The House That Ruth Built," Yankee Stadium.

In the words of Walter Johnson, "There is a catcher that any big-league club would like to buy for $200,000. His name is Gibson...He can do everything. He hits the ball a mile. And he catches so easy he might as well be in a rocking chair....Too bad this Josh Gibson is a colored fellow."

The list of tall tales about Gibson was as long as one of his home runs. As legend has it, Gibson hit a ball in Pittsburgh that never came back to Earth. The next day, when he was playing in Philadelphia, a ball suddenly dropped out of the sky and right into an outfielder's glove. With that, the umpire pointed at Gibson and shouted, "You're out – yesterday, in Pittsburgh."

"The American All-Stars," 1945, on tour in Venezuela. Notice future Brooklyn Dodger, Jackie Robinson (far left, front row).

Josh Gibson, otherwise known as the "black Babe Ruth." Many believe his lifetime home run tally may have reached 1,000.

NEGRO LEAGUES MUSEUM OPENS

Every baseball fan knows the color line in organized baseball was broken in 1945 when Branch Rickey signed Jackie Robinson to the Brooklyn Dodgers. But what about the decades of black baseball that led up to this momentous event? What about the culture that produced players like Robinson?

The Negro Leagues Baseball Museum in Kansas City is dedicated to preserving and illuminating the history of black baseball in America. Our new 10,000 square-foot facility is filled with interactive exhibits, photographs, video presentations, and memorabilia from the 2,600 African-Americans who played in the Negro Leagues from 1884 to 1955.

For more information, please call (816) 221-1920. The Negro Leagues Baseball Museum, located at 18th Street and Vine, is open Tuesday through Saturday, 9:00 am to 6:00 pm, and Sunday, noon to 6:00 pm. You can also visit our new Web site at www.negroleaguesmuseum.com.

BUNTING? BASE STEALING? NIGHT GAMES? NEVER MIND THE RECORD BOOK. THESE GUYS REWROTE THE RULE BOOK.

If you've ever sat in a stadium at dusk with a hot dog in one hand, a beer in the other, and seven more innings to go, then you have one man to thank. J.L. Wilkinson, inventor of night baseball. He introduced night lights to the Negro Leagues six years before they ever made it to the white major leagues.

Surprised? Well, you shouldn't be. The Negro Leagues were responsible for many of the changes that helped shape modern-day baseball. Take, for instance, bunting and stealing. While they weren't invented in the Negro Leagues, they were, however, raised to an art form. With players like Cool Papa Bell, who could steal home from first, base stealing was a constant threat to pitchers. Pretty much the same way it is today.

You see, in the Negro Leagues they played by the so-called "Coonsberry" rules. As second baseman Newt Allen said, "That's just...any kind of play you think you can get by with." Simply put, blackball was slicker, faster, and a lot rougher than the major league style.

Center fielder Crush Holloway of the Baltimore Black Sox, for example, used to sharpen his spikes right in front of his opponents. In his words, "just to put a little something on your mind." Explaining to historian John Holway, Crush said, "Naw, I wouldn't hurt anybody or anything in the world. Unless it's necessary. Now you see, the only place you could score was home plate. All those other bases were just temporary. But if someone gets in your way there...when...you're trying to score! Yeah, better get out of the way – you're coming! Coming in there. That was baseball in those days..."

"We played by the 'Coonsberry' rules—any kind of play you think you could get by with."
— Newt Allen

Of course, no matter how rough the league was, the players always found a way to play through the injuries. They had no choice. As Riley Stewart explained, "You had to produce or they would send you home."

Buck Leonard was the third Negro League player to be inducted into the National Baseball Hall of Fame.

THEY WEREN'T BORN TOO EARLY. YOU WERE BORN TOO LATE.

Up until Jackie Robinson signed with the Brooklyn Dodgers, black ballplayers were completely shut out of the white major leagues. But that's no reason to feel sorry for them. If anything, feel sorry for yourself. After all, you're the one who missed out on seeing the immortal Satchel Paige and Josh Gibson go head-to-head. You missed Cool Papa Bell stealing home from first base. And, even worse, you missed "shadow ball." A warmup routine where the Indianapolis Clowns would hit, catch, and hurl an invisible ball around the field so fast and so convincingly that the fans couldn't believe it wasn't real.

If given the choice, sure, the Negro Leaguers would have preferred to play in the major leagues. They wanted the chance to prove without a doubt that they had some of the best players in the world. But don't think for a second they missed out.

In the words of Hall of Famer John "Buck" O'Neil, who played for the Kansas City Monarchs, "Baseball fulfilled me like music. I played most of my life and loved it. Waste no tears for me. I wasn't born too early. I was right on time."

Trappers would prefer that you didn't know the truth about snares. Because the fact is, snares are life-threatening to any animal that wanders by a trap line. Once caught, fear and pain drive the animal to struggle. This struggling causes the snare to tighten even more, cutting deeper into the animal's flesh. Dying can be drawn out for days, as Alaska is the only state that doesn't require trappers to check their traps routinely. Friends of Animals has waged campaigns to protect Alaska's wildlife for 27 years. Our hundreds of Alaskan members help support our efforts to abolish cruel, outdated practices that abuse animals. FoA spends over $150,000 a year in Alaska, gathering first-hand information in the field on wolves, bears and their interactions with other wildlife. If you agree cruel snaring and trapping practices should end, please help by joining Friends of Animals and returning the coupon below with your tax-deductible contribution.

I am opposed to cruel snaring and trapping practices. Please send me more information on how Friends of Animals is working to protect wildlife here and around the world. My tax-deductible donation, made payable to Friends of Animals c/o Priscilla Feral, President, is enclosed for: ______$10______$20______$50______$100______Other

Name ______________________ Address ______________________ State______ Zip______

FRIENDS OF ANIMALS (FoA) IS A NON-PROFIT MEMBERSHIP ORGANIZATION WHICH HAS BEEN PROTECTING ANIMALS FROM CRUELTY, ABUSE AND INSTITUTIONALIZED EXPLOITATION AROUND THE WORLD SINCE 1957.

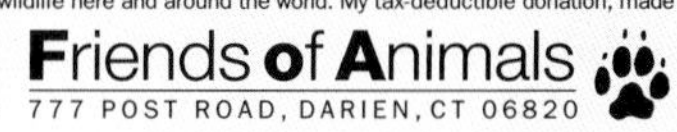

MERIT AWARD
public service/political
newspaper or magazine
single

art director
WADE DEVERS

writer
TED NELSON

photographer
GORDON HABER

client
FRIENDS OF ANIMALS

agency
PAGANO SCHENCK
& KAY/BOSTON

MERIT AWARD
public service/political
newspaper or magazine
single

art directors
JOHN MESSUM
COLIN JONES

writer
MIKE MCKENNA

typographer
ROGER KENNEDY

photographer
GRAHAM CORNTHWAITE

client
DEPARTMENT OF HEALTH/COI

agency
SAATCHI & SAATCHI/
LONDON

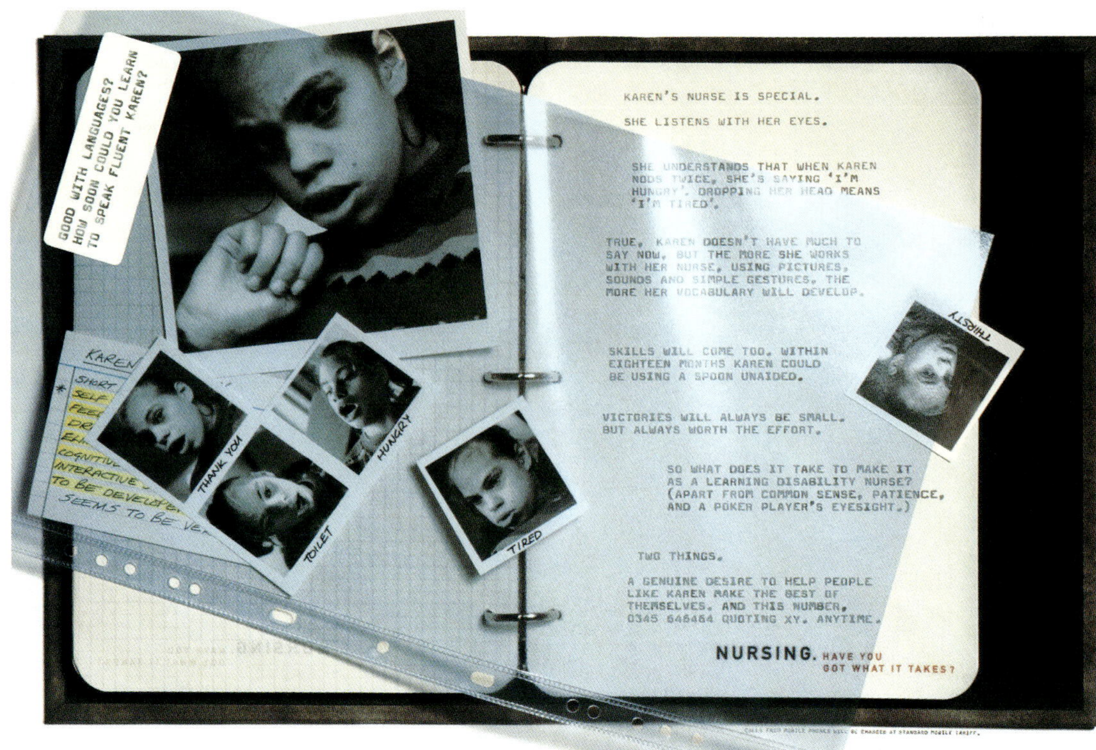

MERIT AWARD
public service/political
newspaper or magazine
single

art directors
JOHN MESSUM
COLIN JONES

writer
MIKE MCKENNA

typographer
ROGER KENNEDY

photographer
GRAHAM CORNTHWAITE

client
DEPARTMENT OF HEALTH/COI

agency
SAATCHI & SAATCHI/
LONDON

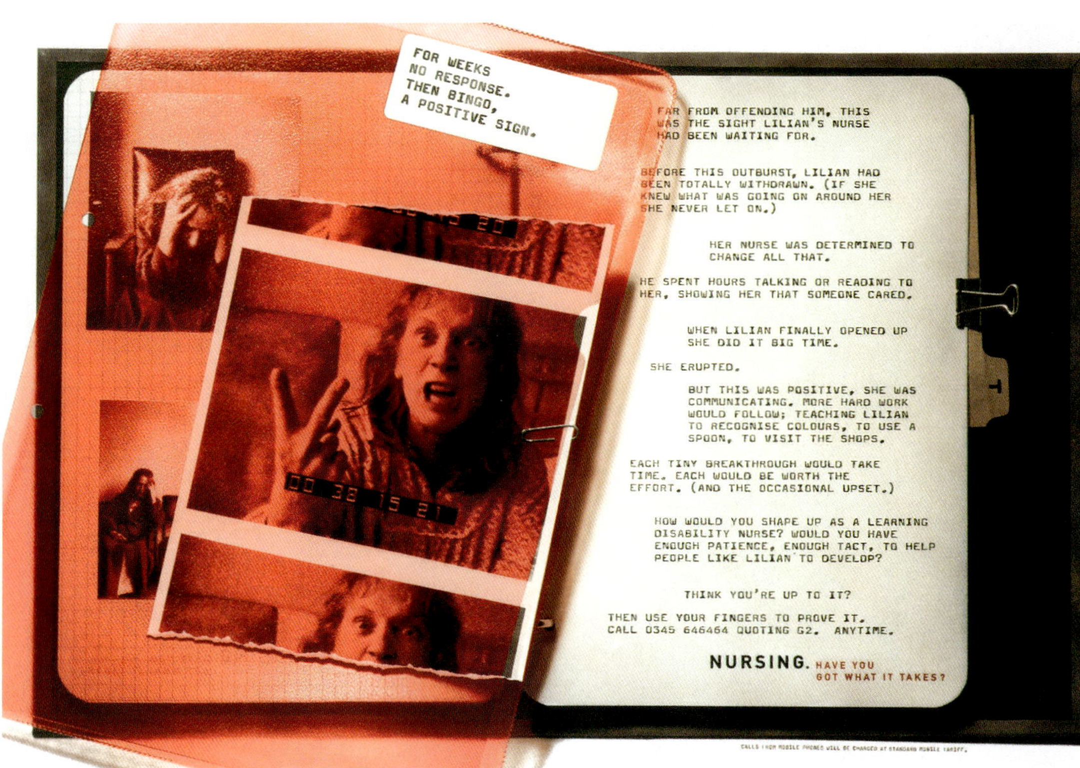

MERIT AWARD
public service/political
newspaper or magazine
single

art directors
JOHN MESSUM
COLIN JONES

writer
MIKE MCKENNA

typographer
ROGER KENNEDY

illustrator
GRAHAM CORNTHWAITE

client
DEPARTMENT OF HEALTH/COI

agency
SAATCHI & SAATCHI/ LONDON

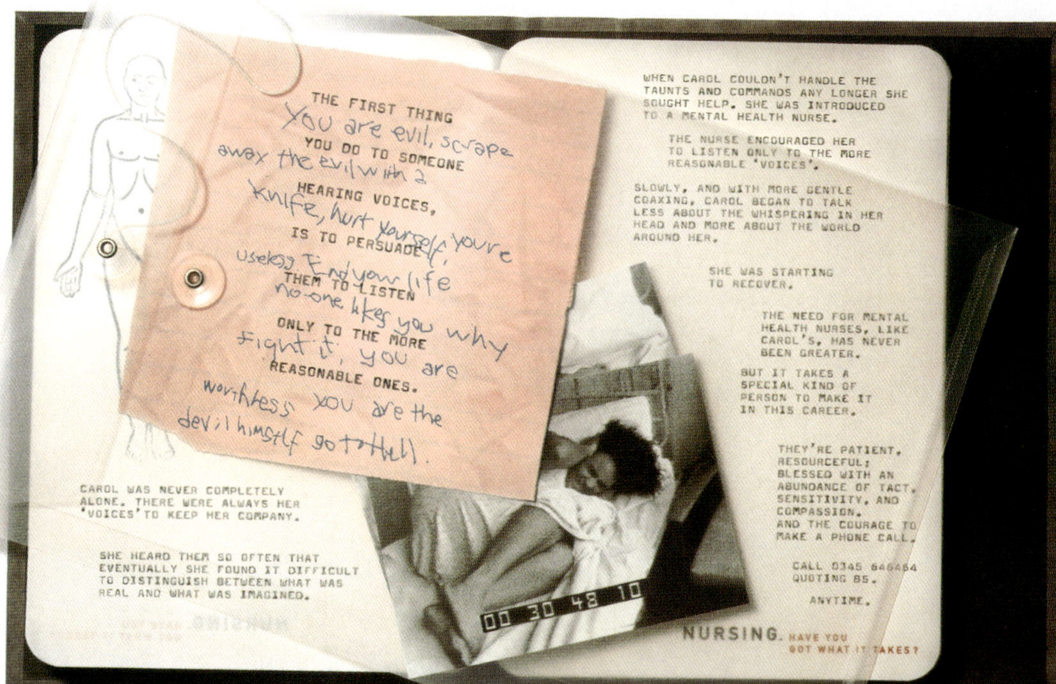

MERIT AWARD
public service/political
newspaper or magazine
single

art directors
JOHN MESSUM
COLIN JONES

writer
MIKE MCKENNA

typographer
ROGER KENNEDY

photographer
GRAHAM CORNTHWAITE

client
DEPARTMENT OF HEALTH/COI

agency
SAATCHI & SAATCHI/ LONDON

MERIT AWARD
public service/political
newspaper or magazine
single

art director
DAVID CABALLERO

writer
FÉLIX FDEZ DE CASTRO

photographer
RAMON SERRANO

client
DOCTORS WITHOUT BORDERS

agency
SCPF/BARCELONA

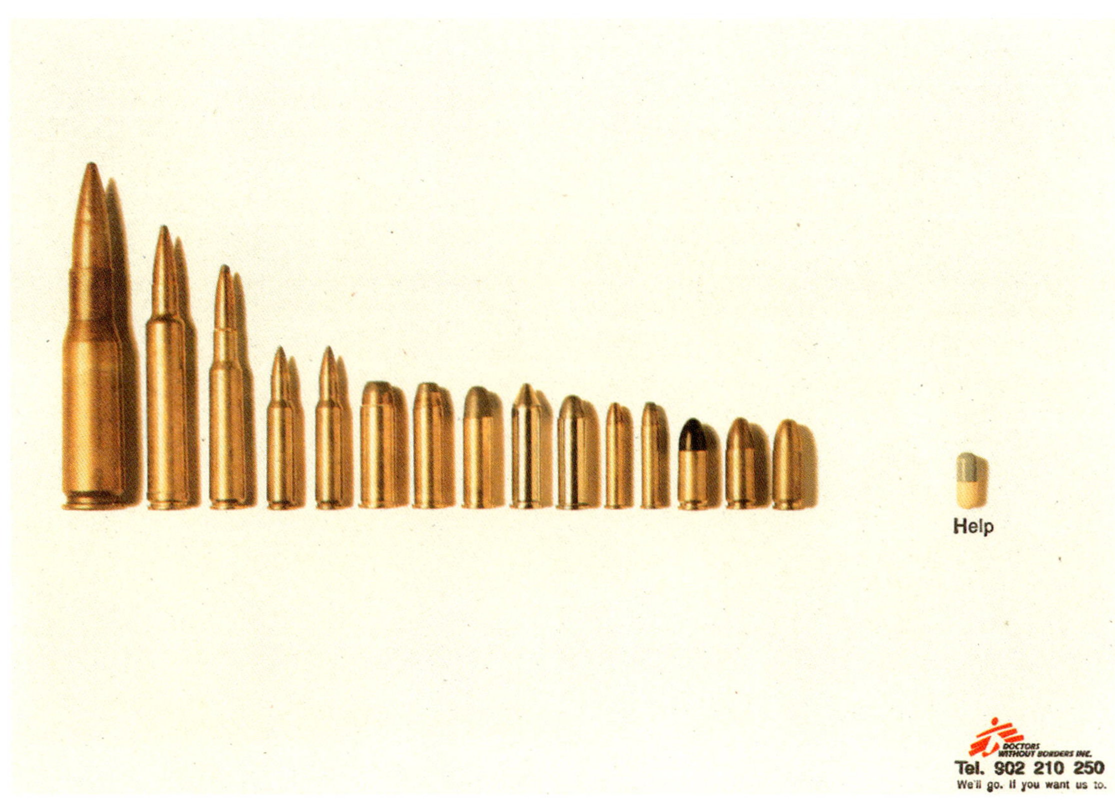

PUBLIC SERVICE MERIT

JUNE 3, 1961: RUSSIA SURRENDERS TO THE UNITED STATES.

The diplomatic power of Jacqueline Bouvier Kennedy: First Lady. Part of a new exhibit at ***The John F. Kennedy Library & Museum.*** *Boston, Massachusetts.*

THERE HAS NEVER BEEN A MORE WELL-KNOWN WOMAN.
THERE HAS NEVER BEEN A LESS WELL-KNOWN WOMAN.

Photograph © 1997 Jacques Lowe

The many facets of Jacqueline Bouvier Kennedy: First Lady. Part of a new exhibit at ***The John F. Kennedy Library & Museum.*** *Boston, Massachusetts.*

MERIT AWARD
public service/political newspaper or magazine campaign

art director
CLIFF SORAH

writer
JOE ALEXANDER

photographers
JACQUES LOWE
LISA LARSEN
TIME LIFE
AP/WORLD WIDE PHOTOS

client
JOHN F. KENNEDY LIBRARY FOUNDATION

agency
THE MARTIN AGENCY/ RICHMOND

JACQUELINE KENNEDY'S WEDDING.
(THIS TIME YOU'RE INVITED.)

Lisa Larsen, Life Magazine ©Time Inc.

Jacqueline Bouvier Kennedy's wedding gown. On exhibit now through Labor Day. ***The John F. Kennedy Library & Museum.*** *Boston, Massachusetts.*

MERIT AWARD
public service/political
newspaper or magazine
campaign

art director
JIM HENDERSON

writer
CHRISTOPHER WILSON

photographers
MARC NORBERG
BRADY WILLETTE

client
CATHOLIC CHARITIES

agency
MARTIN/WILLIAMS
ADVERTISING/
MINNEAPOLIS

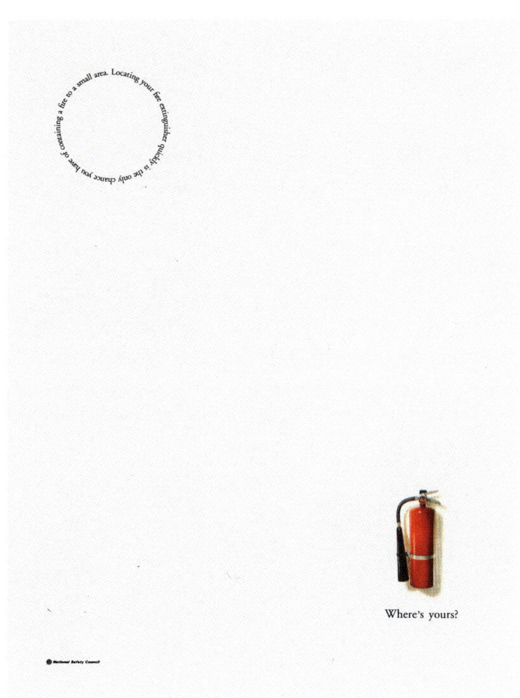

MERIT AWARD
public service/political
newspaper or magazine
campaign

art director
CAROL FOX

writer
MICHAEL CALIENES

photographer
CHRISTOPHER
HARDING

client
NATIONAL SAFETY
COUNCIL

agency
MULLEN ADVERTISING/
WENHAM

MERIT AWARD
public service/political
newspaper or magazine
campaign

art director
IAN GRAIS

writer
ALAN RUSSELL

photographer
HANS SIPMA

client
CRIMESTOPPERS

agency
PALMER JARVIS DDB/
VANCOUVER

MERIT AWARD
public service/political
outdoor and posters

art director
ART WEEKS
writer
ART WEEKS
photographer
MYRON BECK
client
CALIFORNIA DEPARTMENT
OF HEALTH SERVICES
agency
ASHER & PARTNERS/
LOS ANGELES

MERIT AWARD
public service/political
outdoor and posters

art director
LEE ST. JAMES
writers
KRYSTAL FALKNER
MARK ROBINSON
client
ATLANTA'S BLACK
PROFESSIONALS
agency
AUSTIN KELLEY
ADVERTISING/ATLANTA

MERIT AWARD
public service/political
outdoor and posters

art director
HEWARD JUE
writer
RYAN EBNER
photographer
HEWARD JUE
client
THE HEMLOCK SOCIETY
agency
BUTLER SHINE &
STERN/SAUSALITO

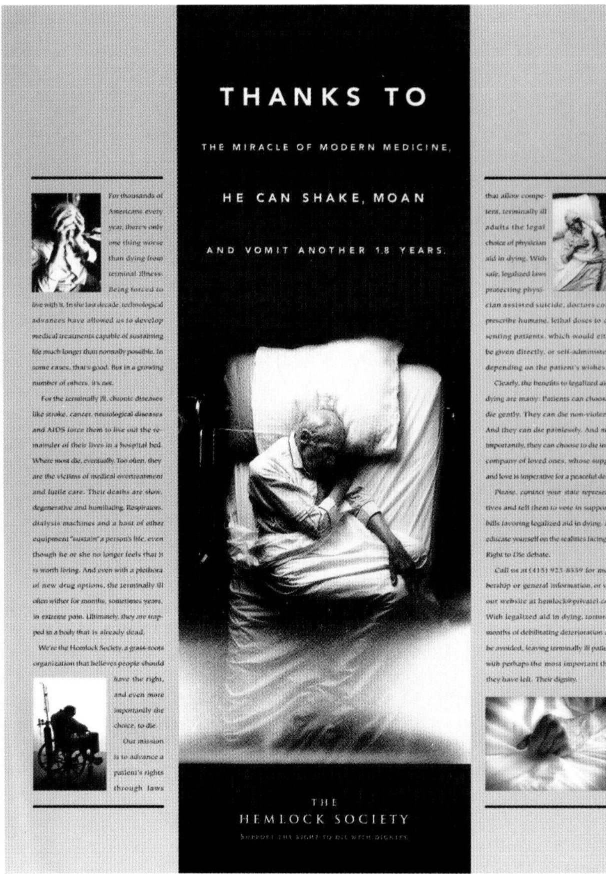

MERIT AWARD
public service/political
outdoor and posters

art director
HEWARD JUE
writer
RYAN EBNER
photographer
HEWARD JUE
client
THE HEMLOCK SOCIETY
agency
BUTLER SHINE &
STERN/SAUSALITO

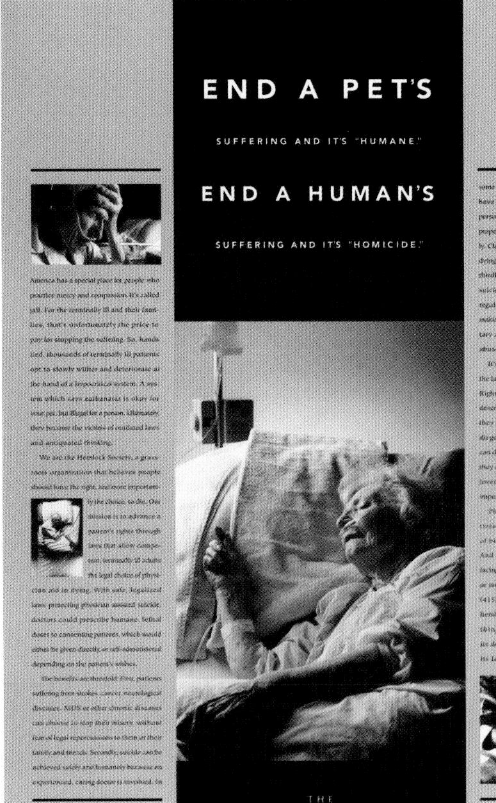

MERIT AWARD
public service/political
outdoor and posters

art director
CHRISTOPHER GYORGY
writer
CHRIS JACOBS
photographer
THE NEGRO LEAGUES BASEBALL MUSEUM
client
THE NEGRO LEAGUES BASEBALL MUSEUM
agency
THE MARTIN AGENCY/ RICHMOND

MERIT AWARD
public service/political
outdoor and posters

art director
CHRISTOPHER GYORGY
writer
CHRIS JACOBS
photographer
THE NEGRO LEAGUES BASEBALL MUSEUM
client
THE NEGRO LEAGUES BASEBALL MUSEUM
agency
THE MARTIN AGENCY/ RICHMOND

MERIT AWARD
public service/political
outdoor and posters

art director
CARLA MOONEY
writer
DYLAN LEE
client
MOTHERS AGAINST
DRUNK DRIVING
agency
PAGANO SCHENCK
& KAY/BOSTON

NO
GRAFFITI

Convicted persons may serve six months in jail. That's two months more than what a drunk driver served after smashing her car into 14-year-old Eric Zimmerman. Eric's head was pierced by a chain-link fence, which killed him.

Mothers Against Drunk Driving It's a serious crime. Let's treat it that way.

MERIT AWARD
public service/political
outdoor and posters

art director
CARLA MOONEY
writer
DYLAN LEE
client
MOTHERS AGAINST
DRUNK DRIVING
agency
PAGANO SCHENCK
& KAY/BOSTON

KEEP OFF
THE GRASS

Punishable by a fine of up to $99. That's $99 more than what a drunk driver paid after crashing into the car carrying 15-year-old Kerry Dunlop. The drunk driver got off scot-free. Kerry's neck broke and she died.

Mothers Against Drunk Driving It's a serious crime. Let's treat it that way.

SHOPLIFTERS WILL BE PROSECUTED

Guilty persons shall be imprisoned for up to one year. That would exceed the time served by the drunk driver who slammed into 26-year-olds Russ Gordon and Michael Albert. The drunk driver received eight months in jail with weekend furloughs. Russ and Michael received death.

Mothers Against Drunk Driving It's a serious crime. Let's treat it that way.

MERIT AWARD
public service/political
outdoor and posters

art director
CARLA MOONEY

writer
DYLAN LEE

client
MOTHERS AGAINST
DRUNK DRIVING

agency
PAGANO SCHENCK
& KAY/BOSTON

MERIT AWARD
public service/political
outdoor and posters

art director
IAN GRAIS

writer
ALAN RUSSELL

photographer
HANS SIPMA

client
CRIMESTOPPERS

agency
PALMER JARVIS DDB/
VANCOUVER

MERIT AWARD
public service/political
collateral: brochures
and direct mail

art directors
JEFFREY DECHAUSSE
VINNY WARREN
writers
VINNY WARREN
JEFFREY DECHAUSSE
photographer
MIKE RYAN
client
BOTTOMLESS CLOSET
agency
FIRE ESCAPE
ADVERTISING/BOSTON

MERIT AWARD
public service/political collateral: brochures and direct mail

art director
CHRIS WATSON

writer
KEN ERKE

photographer
DENNIS CHAULKIN

client
HUMANE SOCIETY

agency
HOLLAND ADVERTISING/ NEW YORK

MERIT AWARD
public service/political
collateral: brochures
and direct mail

art director
DOUG PEDERSEN
writers
CURTIS SMITH
MIKE DUCKWORTH
photographer
JIM ARNDT
client
OUTWARD BOUND
agency
LOEFFLER KETCHUM
MOUNTJOY/CHARLOTTE

MERIT AWARD
public service/political
collateral: brochures
and direct mail

art director
DOUG PEDERSEN
writers
CURTIS SMITH
MIKE DUCKWORTH
photographer
JIM ARNDT
client
OUTWARD BOUND
agency
LOEFFLER KETCHUM
MOUNTJOY/CHARLOTTE

WOMAN: This morning, some of you will wake up and kiss someone you don't really love. You will brush hair that is nine shades from your natural color. You will apply eyebrows and eyelashes and lips. You will slip clothes over breasts that have been lifted and a stomach that has been tucked. You will drive to a job you don't like in a car you do not own. You will smile at people you hate. You will eat a lunch you cannot afford paid for by a piece of plastic that is not really money. You will sit at a desk pretending to be busy. You will go home and serve a dinner that came in a frozen box. And before you go to bed, some of you will tell someone you don't really love what a wonderful day it has been.
ANNOUNCER: Starting May 15th, the Seattle International Film Festival presents 25 days filled with truth. Which is 25 more than you're probably used to. For tickets, call 325-6150.

MERIT AWARD
public service/political
radio: single

writer
NICOLE MICHELS
agency producer
NIKI POLYOCAN
production company
THE EARFORCE
client
SEATTLE
INTERNATIONAL FILM
FESTIVAL
agency
COLE & WEBER/
SEATTLE

CD2 #R7

MAN: You will become exactly like your parents no matter how hard you try otherwise. If you do something stupid, someone will be watching. The saying "If at first you don't succeed," does not apply to skydiving. Suicide is the only crime for which you can't be charged. When someone says, "Hi, how are you?" they don't really want to know. If you try to fall asleep on an airplane, a baby will start crying. Children never vomit in the toilet.
ANNOUNCER: Starting May 15th, the Seattle International Film Festival presents 25 days of truth. As if you need any more of that. For tickets, call 325-6150.
MAN: Hair lost from your head will eventually turn up in your nose.

MERIT AWARD
public service/political
radio: single

writer
NICOLE MICHELS
agency producer
NIKI POLYOCAN
production company
THE EARFORCE
client
SEATTLE
INTERNATIONAL
FILM FESTIVAL
agency
COLE & WEBER/
SEATTLE

CD2 #R8

MERIT AWARD
public service/political
television: single

art director
TRIS CASERIO

writers
KALEENY CANNON
RISA BERGER

agency producer
BRIDGET BLAKE WILSON

production company
PALOMAR PICTURES

director
NICK BRANDT

client
CALIFORNIA DEPARTMENT
OF HEALTH SERVICES

agency
ASHER & PARTNERS/
LOS ANGELES

CD2 #34

WOMAN: I had my first cigarette when I was 13. When I found out how bad it was I tried to quit...but I couldn't. They say nicotine isn't addictive...how could they say that?
SUPER: The Tobacco Industry denies that nicotine is addictive. California Department of Health Services.

MERIT AWARD
public service/political
television: single

art director
THOMAS HAYO

writer
RICHARD YELLAND

agency producer
LINDA RAFOSS

production company
CREATIVE FILM
MANAGEMENT

director
STANLEY TUCCI

client
NEW YORK CARES

agency
J. WALTER THOMPSON/
NEW YORK

CD2 #35

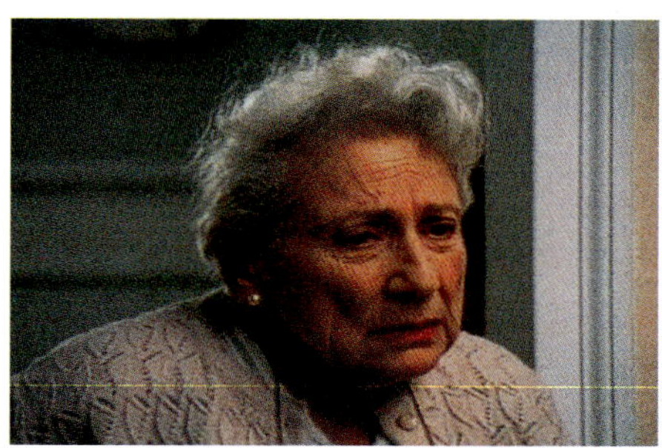

OLD WOMAN: Hello? (no answer). Hello? (no answer, phone continues to ring).
ANNOUNCER: If every New Yorker spent an hour of their time with the elderly, 100,000 wouldn't feel so alone.
SUPER: New York Cares. Don't you?

MERIT AWARD
public service/political
television: single

art directors
CURT DETWEILER
LINDA LOCKE

writer
CURT DETWEILER

agency producer
SHARON HOON

production company
YARRA FILMS
SINGAPORE

directors
RUSSEL WONG
GEOFF HUNT

client
SINGAPORE CANCER
SOCIETY

agency
LEO BURNETT/
SINGAPORE

CD2 #36

SFX: Music under throughout.
MAN: If only women... examined their breasts... as often... as men do...
SUPER: Consult your physician for advice on breast examination.
Singapore Breast Cancer.

MERIT AWARD
public service/political
television: single

art director
DARREN LIM

writer
DEACON WEBSTER

agency producer
SANDY BACHOM

production company
TONY KAYE FILMS

director
ROBERTO ESPINOSA

client
FRIENDS OF ANIMALS

agency
MAD DOGS &
ENGLISHMEN/
NEW YORK

CD2 #37

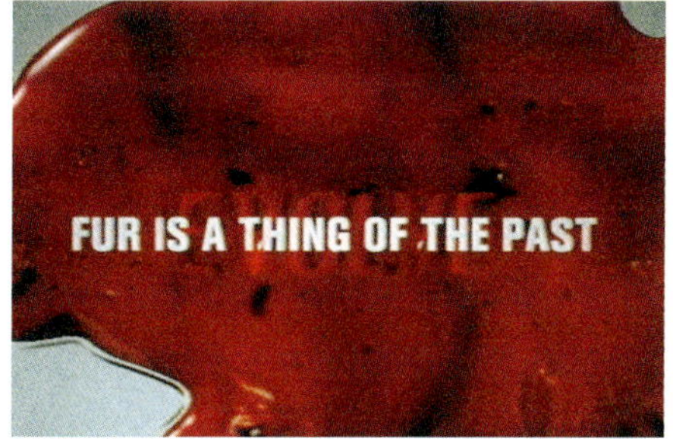

MUSIC: Sexy jazz throughout.
SUPER: Fur is a thing of the past. Evolve.

MERIT AWARD
public service/political television: campaign

art directors
DAVID ANGELO
JOHN FOLLIS

writers
DAVID ANGELO
JOHN FOLLIS

agency producer
HELEN POLISE

production company
TAPESTRY PRODUCTIONS

director
ANDRE MARCELL

client
CHILD HELP USA

agency
FOLLIS/NEW YORK

CD2 #38

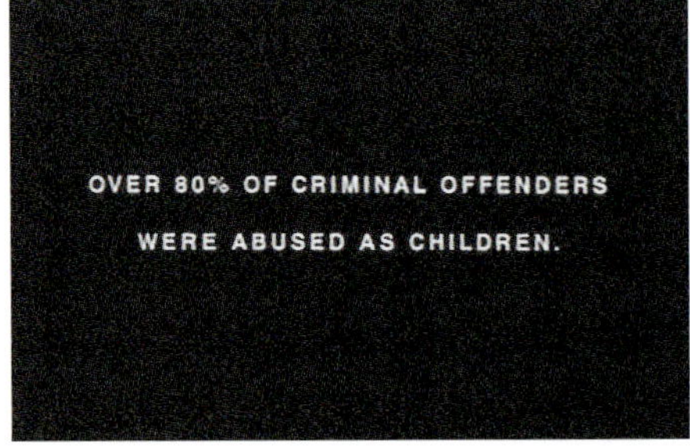

SUPER: Charles Dixon.
CHARLES: And he beat us up all the time. And it wasn't only the beating, it was...we'd have to...we'd have to strip naked. He couldn't just hit us, we'd have to be butt-naked.
SUPER: Charles is on trial for murder.
CHARLES: You know. So it was, like humiliating at the same time.
SUPER: Over 80 percent of criminal offenders were abused as children.
CHARLES: That went on till I ran away from home. No child should go through that. No child should go through that. They deserve better.
SUPER: Child abuse. It hurts all of us. 1-800-4-A-CHILD.

MERIT AWARD
public service/political
television: campaign

art director
PAUL KEISTER

writer
ANDY CARRIGAN

agency producer
SUE O'DONNELL

production company
PICTURE PARK

director
JOHN BECKMIER

client
ROGER WILLIAMS
PARK ZOO

agency
LEONARD/MONAHAN/
FOXBOROUGH

CD2 #39

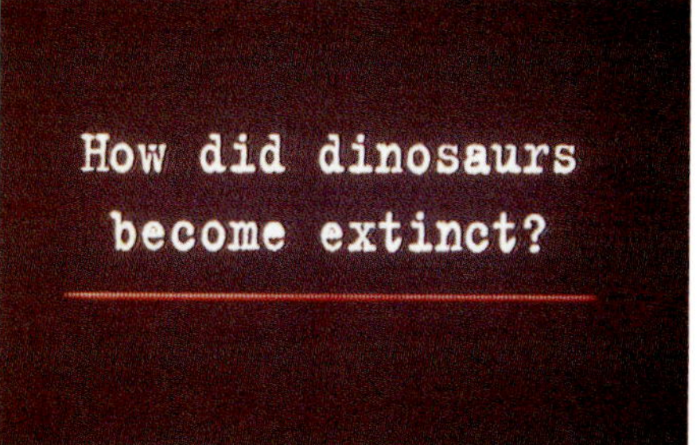

SFX: Ambient gas station noises.
SUPER: How did dinosaurs become extinct?
SFX: Huge explosion.
SUPER: Spend the day in a dinosaur's world at the Roger Williams Park Zoo.

RADIO

MERIT AWARD
consumer radio
single

writer
LUKE SULLIVAN
agency producer
KATHY JYDSTRUP
client
DUNWOODY
agency
FALLON MCELLIGOTT/
MINNEAPOLIS

CD2 #R9

ANNOUNCER: After graduation, as you sit in your parents' basement waiting for the phone to ring with job offers that will never come, you begin to hear them. The crickets.
SFX: Crickets.
ANNOUNCER: That lonely sound. The theme song of the disenfranchised. Sometimes you think you hear the phone ringing with a job offer.
SFX: Phone rings. More crickets.
ANNOUNCER: But, it's just them. The crickets. Soon you start to hear what they're really saying.
SFX: Loser. Loser.
ANNOUNCER: Now's probably not a good time to hear about the graduates of Dunwoody Institute.
SFX: Loser. (More crickets throughout)
ANNOUNCER: How there's an average of four job opportunities waiting for every Dunwoody graduate.
SFX: Loser.
ANNOUNCER: No, you're going to hold out. For a call that will never come...
SFX: Actual phone, ringing loud. Phone is picked up.
GUY: Hello??
SFX: Cricket, heard through phone speaker, "Loser." Cricket laughs.
ANNOUNCER: Call Dunwoody Institute and get training in one of sixteen interesting careers. Call 374-5800.

MERIT AWARD
consumer radio
single

writer
LINUS KARLSSON
agency producer
KIRSTEN TAKLO
production company
ABSOLUTE MUSIC
client
MILLER BREWING
COMPANY/MILLER LITE
agency
FALLON MCELLIGOTT/
MINNEAPOLIS

CD2 #R10

MUSIC: Miller Intro Music.
ANNOUNCER: Meet Dick. Dick is the creative superstar behind the advertising you are about to hear. We gave Dick a six-pack of Miller Lite and asked him to write a fun, entertaining and unexpected radio commercial. Dick figured it would be pretty cool to have an animal say Miller Lite. The only problem with this idea is that almost all animals are taken by other beer companies. The only animal Dick knew for sure wasn't taken was the mite. So Dick decided to hire a professional mite psychologist to train a mite to say Miller Lite. This is what happened.
MITE PSYCHOLOGIST: C'mon, c'mon...say Mi-ller Lite. Mi...mi...mi-ller...ller..ller. Lite.
MITE: Pssst!
MITE PSYCHOLOGIST: Mi-ller...
MITE: Pssst!
MITE PSYCHOLOGIST: Lite.
MITE: Pssst!
MITE PSYCHOLOGIST: Mi-ller Liiite.
MITE: Psttssiiissstttiisst!
MITE PSYCHOLOGIST: He said it! He said it! I am sure he said it! Can we listen to that part in slow motion again?
MITE IN SLOW MOTION: Mmmilllerrr Liiitttte!
ANNOUNCER: This has been a Miller Lite presentation by Dick. Thank you for your time.
SINGERS: Miller Time.
ANNOUNCER: Miller Brewing Company, Milwaukee, Wisconsin.

MUSIC: Miller Intro Music.
LADY ON THE PHONE: Thank you for dialing Miller Time. If you are drinking your Miller Lite from a can, press 1. From a bottle, press 2... If you are enjoying your Miller Lite with Mexican food, press 1. With burgers, press... If you are drinking your Miller Lite with friends, press 1. With friends you kind of know, but not really well, pre... Please stand by while your commercial is being prepared... Your call is important to us, please st... Here is your customized Miller Lite commercial.
MUSIC & SINGERS: Life is great when you're havin' a Miller Lite, poured cold out of a...
MONOTONE WOMAN'S VOICE:..can
SINGERS: Great all by itself, but even with a...
MONOTONE WOMAN'S VOICE:...burgers
SINGERS: All 'round you, sharing love and laughter are all your...
MONOTONE WOMAN'S VOICE:...some friends whose names escape you.
SINGERS: This moment, it's pure Miller Time.
WOMAN: Thank you for dialing Miller Lite.
SINGERS: Miller Time.
ANNOUNCER: Miller Brewing Company, Milwaukee, Wisconsin.

MERIT AWARD
consumer radio
single

writer
LUKE SULLIVAN
agency producer
KIRSTEN TAKLO
client
MILLER BREWING COMPANY/MILLER LITE
agency
FALLON MCELLIGOTT/ MINNEAPOLIS

CD2 #R11

MUSIC: Miller Intro Music
ANNOUNCER: Meet Dick. Dick is the creative superstar behind the advertising you are about to hear. We gave Dick a six-pack of Miller Lite and asked him to come up with a fun, entertaining and unexpected Miller Time donut. A donut is advertising slang for a radio commercial with a hole in it. You make a 60-second commercial like this one and then leave 20 seconds of silence somewhere in it and you've got–a donut! In that way, the local radio stations can put in local messages that suit you, the listener, better. This is Dick's idea for a Miller Time donut.
JINGLE: This is a Miller Lite donut. A donut is nothing but a radio commercial with a silent hole in it. But you never notice or hear the silent hole, because in that hole some local guys will put in a local message for you. Here it is.
SFX: 20 seconds of silence.
JINGLE: This has been a Miller Lite donut by Dick. Thank you for your time.
SINGERS: Miller Time.
ANNOUNCER: Miller Brewing Company, Milwaukee, Wisconsin.

MERIT AWARD
consumer radio
single

writer
LINUS KARLSSON
agency producer
KIRSTEN TAKLO
production company
ABSOLUTE MUSIC
client
MILLER BREWING COMPANY/MILLER LITE
agency
FALLON MCELLIGOTT/ MINNEAPOLIS

CD2 #R12

DJ: Well breakfast time once again, so another money saving tip from McDonald's. Let's go to line 3, good morning.
CALLER: Hi there, yeh, I've got a tip.
DJ: Great, what is it mate?
CALLER: Right, well these telecommunications companies should save money on multi-million pound satellite systems that cut out the speech delay on long distance calls.
DJ: Gosh, right, and so what are you saying?
CALLER: Yeh, well this delay problem is easily resolved without the cost.
DJ: How?
CALLER: Well all you do is start talking before the other person is finished.
DJ: Ah, I see, and that works for you?
CALLER: Yeh, yeh, I'm doing it now.
DJ: Ah, right.
CALLER: New Zealand.
DJ: So, where are you calling from? Hello...no we've lost him. That money saving tip was brought to you by McDonald's, where up until 10:30 every morning a Bacon and Egg McMuffin is still only 99p, at participating restaurants.
CALLER: (talking over the DJ's last sentence) It's worth the hassle.

MERIT AWARD
consumer radio
single

writer
JANE ATKINSON
MATT HAZELL
agency producer
YOLANDA IOANNIDES
production company
THE TAPE GALLERY
client
MCDONALD'S
agency
LEO BURNETT/ LONDON

CD2 #R13

MERIT AWARD
consumer radio
single

writer
CLAIRE HARRISON
agency producer
YOLANDI MES
production company
DIAL M
client
SEAGRAM SA
agency
NET#WORK/
JOHANNESBURG

CD2 #R14

ANNOUNCER: (Reciting in a very broad Scottish accent) The poem, "To a Mouse" by Robbie Burns.
Wee, sleekit, cow'rin tim'rous beastie,
I, what a panic's in thy breastie!
Thou need na start awa sae hasty,
Wi bickering brattle!
I wad be laith to rin an chase thee,
Wi murd'ring pattle!

I'm truly sorry man's dominion
Has broken nature's social union,
An' justifies that ill opinion
Which mak's thee startle
At me, thy poor earth-born companion,
An' fellow-mortal!

ANNOUNCER: If you're finding this Scotch too heavy for your palate, why not try something a little lighter. Something pale and clear with a bright, clean taste. Like Glen Grant.
Glen Grant single malt Scotch whisky: the clearly different Scotch whisky.

MERIT AWARD
consumer radio
single

writers
RICHARD BULLOCK
REED COLLINS
agency producer
ALISON THAME
production company
MEMPHIS STUDIOS
client
MOBILE TELEPHONE
NETWORK
agency
TBWA HUNT LASCARIS/
JOHANNESBURG

CD2 #R15

MALE VOICE: Yeah, Hello, Mega Records.
RUI: Mmm, great, I'm looking for a song. I saw it on MTV last night.
MALE VOICE: Yeah, okay, sure, what's the name of the band?
RUI: Um, I don't know the name...the name of the band. But I know how it goes.
MALE VOICE: Okay, shoot, tell me.
RUI: It goes naaa, naaa, dumph dumph (incoherent).
MALE VOICE: No, I don't recognize that one...No I don't know it, sorry.
RUI: Um, hold on, I remember now.
MALE VOICE: The name of the band?
RUI: No, no, I remember how it goes, it's kind of...The guitars sort of quiver a bit.
ANNOUNCER: Fortunately, MTN's Pulse Package gives you 120 free weekend minutes every month.
MALE VOICE: I gotta say I've got no idea...No, I don't know it.
RUI: Wait, the same band...They had quite a big hit a couple of months ago.
MALE VOICE: Is it?
RUI: Yeah, you gotta remember it–it goes naaa, naaa, dumph, dumph (fade off).

MERIT AWARD
07b consumer radio
campaign

writer
GREG HAHN
client
MILLER BREWING
COMPANY/MILLER LITE
agency
FALLON MCELLIGOTT/
MINNEAPOLIS

CD2 #R16

MUSIC: Dramatic, orchestral.
ANNOUNCER: Meet Dick, the creative superstar behind Miller Time advertising. We gave Dick a six-pack of Miller Lite and a pencil and asked him to come up with some entertaining ideas that beer-drinking people would like. Dick said "OK." Dick knows that beer-drinking men and women like beautiful people. And that having beautiful people in our commercials will make them like our beer, because that's the way advertising works. These are beautiful people.
BOY: Hi.
GIRL: Hi.
ANNOUNCER: This has been a Miller Time presentation by Dick. Thank you for your time. Miller Brewing Company, Milwaukee, Wisconsin.

WOMAN: (singing) I'm a woman and I'm angry.
I know three chords on the guitar.
That and Sprite are all you need.
To become a music star.

Sprite makes me intellectual.
Sprite shapes the way I think.
Sprite improves my self-esteem.
Just go and ask my shrink.

Sprite is more reliable
Than a man who can't commit.
Sprite gives me the strength to forgive
Guys who treated me like...dirt.

This song is just another ad jingle.
Every word is just a crock.
I'd sing about something more important
But I had writer's block.

All sprite does is quench your thirst.
Don't follow rock stars like sheep.
That's the only message of this song.
I guess I'm not that deep.

Image is nothing.
Thirst is everything.
Obey your thirst.
Sprite.

MERIT AWARD
consumer radio
campaign

writer
STEVE DOPPELT
agency producer
DAVID GERARD
production companies
BANG
FEARLESS MUSIC
UNDERGROUND MUSIC
client
THE COCA-COLA
COMPANY/SPRITE
agency
LOWE & PARTNERS/
SMS/NEW YORK

CD2 #R17

ANNOUNCER 1: How does it feel to drive a Mercedes Benz? Imagine yourself getting in.
SFX: Car door opens and closes.
ANNOUNCER 1: You start the car.
SFX: Car starts.
ANNOUNCER 1: Drive onto the the test track. Push the accelerator.
SFX: Car engine winding up.
ANNOUNCER 1: Hear the engine, still accelerating as you maneuver past other cars.
SFX: Other engines.
ANNOUNCER 1: Your heart as it begins to pound.
SFX: Heart pounding.
ANNOUNCER 1: The crowd as it rises to it's feet, screaming.
SFX: Huge crowd yelling.
ANNOUNCER 1: The checkered flag as you cross the line.
SFX: Flag waving.
ANNOUNCER 1: The announcer telling the crowd your name.
ANNOUNCER 2: And the winner is...
ANNOUNCER 1 and SFX: The photographers jockeying for position (cameras clicking), the champagne as it pops (champagne corks), the band as it plays in your honor (band), the endorsement money pouring in (cash register), the guest appearance on the sitcom (canned laughter), the fireworks spelling your name (fireworks), the call from the White House (telephone ringing), the hamburger named after you (sizzling), your memoirs being typed (typing), the parade in your hometown (marching band music), the morning cartoon based on your adventures (cartoons), the supermodels vying for your attention (women giggling).
ANNOUNCER: How does it feel to drive a Mercedes Benz?
SFX: All SFX reach crescendo and stop.
ANNOUNCER: It doesn't suck.

MERIT AWARD
consumer radio
campaign

writers
EDDIE VAN BLOEM
MIKE POLOVSKY
agency producers
KATHY WEISS
PEGGY MOORE
production company
MCHALE/BARONE
client
MERCEDES RETAIL
COMMUNICATION
PROGRAM
agency
LOWE & PARTNERS/
SMS/NEW YORK

CD2 #R18

TV MERIT

MERIT AWARD
consumer television
over :30 single

art director
DONNA WEINHEIM
writer
JEFF WATZMAN
agency producers
LISA GROSSMAN
RANI VAZ
production company
HOUSE OF USHER
director
KINKA USHER
client
HBO
agency
BBDO/NEW YORK

EXTERMINATOR: OK, let's see, you have your Germanic roach, your Yukka roach and your classic Water roach. Spitters. Let's see what we're dealing with here. Denny, get me the widow maker. Nighty-night.
SFX: Explosion
EXTERMINATOR: Oh, boy!
SFX: Roach thumbing his nose at us.
EXTERMINATOR: You have the most stubborn of all breeds. Denny, to the truck now! Trust me. I'm very good at what I do.
MUSIC: Jump in the Line.
ANNOUNCER: It's not TV. It's HBO.

MERIT AWARD
consumer television
over :30 single

art director
DON SCHNEIDER
writer
MICHAEL PATTI
agency producers
REGINA EBEL
BECKY FRIEDMAN
RANI VAZ
production company
PYTKA
director
JOE PYTKA
client
HBO
agency
BBDO/NEW YORK

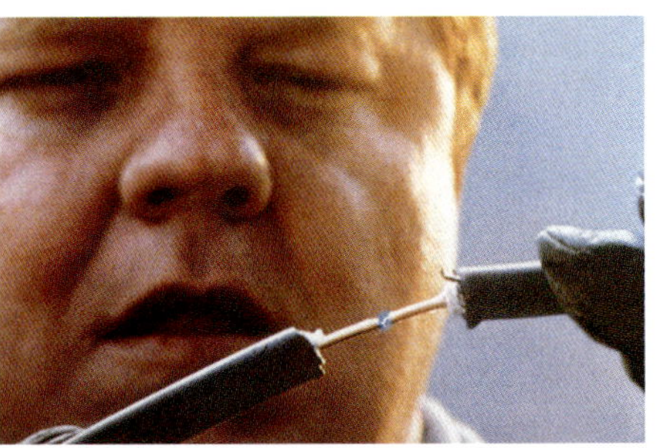

MAN: Oh!!!...Yee Hee!!
CROWD 1: Oh!!!...Yeah!!
CROWD 2: Oh!!!...Yeah!!!
CROWD 3: Oh!!!...Yeah!!!
CROWD 4: Oh!!!...Yeah!!
SFX: Static.
CROWD: Oh!!
SFX: Static.
CROWD: Yeah!!
CABLE GUY 1: Riley, you're one sick, sadistic puppy.
SFX: Static.
CROWD: Oh!!!
CABLE GUY 2: Heh-heh...
ANNOUNCER: It's not TV. It's HBO.

SUPER: Have you ever noticed how protected you feel when you make yourself small?
SUPER: VW Polo.

MERIT AWARD
consumer television
over :30 single

art director
JEREMY CRAIGEN
writer
JEREMY CRAIGEN
agency producer
HOWARD SPIVEY
production company
ACADEMY
director
JONATHAN GLAZER
client
VOLKSWAGEN
GROUP UK
agency
BMP DDB/LONDON

CD2 #40

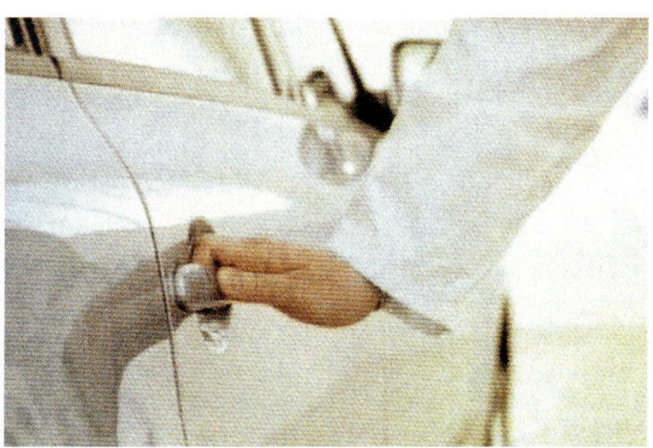

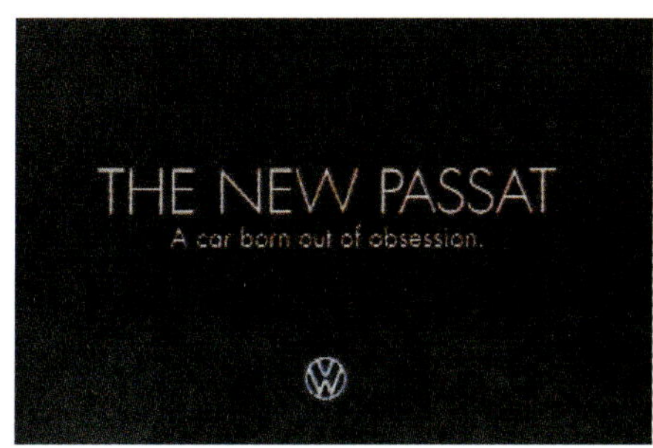

SUPER: The New Passat. A car born out of obsession. VW.

MERIT AWARD
consumer television: over
:30 single

art director
RICHARD FLINTHAM
writers
ANDY MCLEOD
NICK GILL
agency producer
HOWARD SPIVEY
production company
PRODUKTION
director
DOMINIC MURPHY
client
VOLKSWAGEN
GROUP UK
agency
BMP DDB/LONDON

MERIT AWARD
consumer television
over :30 single

art directors
WAIN CHOI
JEAN LAFRENIÉRE

writers
JANA PECK
JEAN LAFRENIÉRE

agency producer
SHEILA SONE

production company
AVION FILM
PRODUCTIONS

director
RAY DILLMAN

client
GENERAL MOTORS
OF CANADA

agency
COSSETTE
COMMUNICATION-
MARKETING/TORONTO

CD2 #41

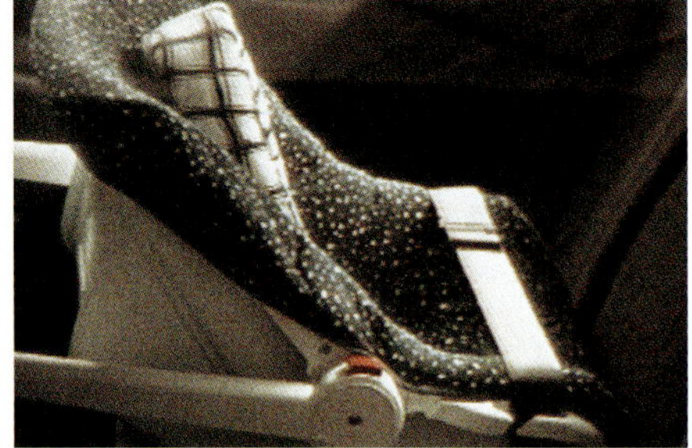

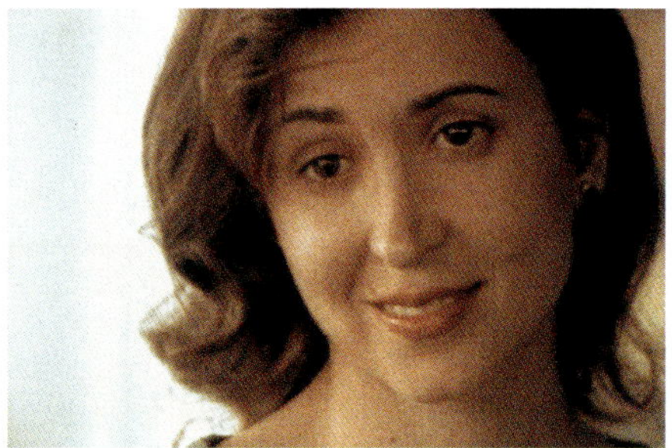

SANDI: Hi, Jim? It's Sandi Richards.
JIM: Oh, hey Sandi, we're just getting your car ready right now.
SANDI: Great. Um, do you guys really do a whole thing when someone picks up their Saturn?
JIM: (laughing) Well, yeah, it's sort of a big deal to us. Is that OK?
SANDI: Um, yeah...Listen, Jim, I was kind of wondering if you could do me a small favor.
SUPER: Saturn.

MERIT AWARD
consumer television
over :30 single

art director
PAUL MALMSTRÖM

writer
LINUS KARLSSON

agency producers
KRIS KNUTSON
RICHARD ULFUENGREN

production company
PARTIZAN

director
TRAKTOR

client
MILLER BREWING
COMPANY/MILLER LITE

agency
FALLON MCELLIGOTT/
MINNEAPOLIS

CD2 #42

ANNOUNCER: This is Dick.
SFX: Music throughout.
ANNOUNCER: Dick is the creative superstar and the man behind the advertising you're about to witness. We gave Dick a six-pack of Miller Lite and...a blank piece of paper and asked him...to create a Miller Time concept that beer-loving people would like. This is what he did:
MUSIC: Adios Amigo.
COWBOYS: (singing) Adios Amigo.
ANNOUNCER: This has been a Miller Time presentation by Dick. Thank you for your time.

WRESTLER 1: Good match there, buddy.
WRESTLER 2: Thanks, you too.
WRESTLERS: Ahhhhh!

MERIT AWARD
consumer television
over :30 single

art director
SCOTT MICHAEL DAVIS
writer
STEPHANIE CRIPPEN
agency producer
JULIE HAMPEL
production company
@RADICAL.MEDIA
director
TARSEM
client
MILLER BREWING COMPANY/MILLER LITE
agency
FALLON MCELLIGOTT/ MINNEAPOLIS

CD2 #43

CARD (reads): Ed, It's nice having a friend like you to share things with. Thanks, Joe.
SUPER: Hallmark. When you care enough to send the very best.

MERIT AWARD
consumer television
over :30 single

art director
BOB SHALLCROSS
writers
BOB SHALLCROSS
JIM FERGUSON
agency producer
BOB SHALLCROSS
production company
NEPTUNE PRODUCTIONS
director
BOB SHALLCROSS
client
HALLMARK CARDS
agency
LEO BURNETT COMPANY/CHICAGO

CD2 #44

MERIT AWARD
consumer television
over :30 single

art director
CHARLES INGE
writer
CHARLES INGE
agency producer
SARAH HALLATT
production company
PARTIZAN MIDI MINUIT
director
TRAKTOR
client
WHITBREAD BEER COMPANY
agency
LOWE HOWARD-SPINK/ LONDON

CD2 #45

ANNOUNCER: Labatt Ice is super-chilled to minus-four degrees during brewing to give it a clean, crisp taste. As it is unlike other beers some people are worried...This man brought a Labatt Ice, but he's afraid to drink it...In the warmth and amongst friends, he's OK. If you have no friends...ask a neighbor to keep you warm while you drink. If you don't have any neighbors...write a letter and address it to yourself. And when the postman comes...hug. If you're still worried or feeling cold, call this hotline. Labatt Ice. Technically the coolest beer in the world.

MERIT AWARD
consumer television
over :30 single

art directors
ANDY HIRSCH
RANDY SAITTA
writer
MARTY ORZIO
agency producer
RACHEL NOVAK
production companies
GERARD DE THAME FILMS
HSI PRODUCTIONS
director
GERARD DE THAME
client
MERCEDES-BENZ OF NORTH AMERICA
agency
LOWE & PARTNERS/ SMS/NEW YORK

CD2 #46

MUSIC: Marlene Dietrich's Falling in Love Again.
SUPER: Passion. Mercedes.

SUPER: Keep in touch.
Telecom New Zealand.

MERIT AWARD
consumer television
over :30 single

art director
GAVIN BRADLEY
writer
KIM THORP
agency producer
JULIET DREAVER
production companies
FLYING FISH NZ
director
GREGOR NICHOLAS
client
TELECOM NEW ZEALAND
agency
SAATCHI & SAATCHI/ WELLINGTON

CD2 #47

SUPER: This is Stefan.
SUPER: This is Ivan.
SUPER: They have never met before.
SUPER: Their countries are at war.
SUPER: Watch.
SUPER: What happened here?
SUPER: First.
SUPER: They talked.
SUPER: Keep in touch.
SUPER: Telecom New Zealand.

MERIT AWARD
consumer television
over :30 single

art director
GAVIN BRADLEY
writer
KIM THORP
agency producer
JULIET DREAVER
production company
FLYING FISH NZ
director
GREGOR NICHOLAS
client
TELECOM NEW ZEALAND
agency
SAATCHI & SAATCHI/ WELLINGTON

CD2 #48

MERIT AWARD
consumer television
over :30 single

art directors
LEE CLOW
YVONNE SMITH
JENNIFER GOLUB

writers
ROB SILTANEN
KEN SEGALL
STEVE JOBS
CRAIG TANIMOTO

agency producer
JENNIFER GOLUB

director
JENNIFER GOLUB

client
APPLE COMPUTER

agency
TBWA CHIAT/DAY/
VENICE

ANNOUNCER: Here's to the crazy ones. The misfits. The rebels. The troublemakers. The round pegs in the square holes. The ones who see things differently. They're not fond of rules. And they have no respect for the status quo. You can quote them, disagree with them, glorify or vilify them. About the only thing you can't do is ignore them. Because they change things. They push the human race forward. And while some may see them as the crazy ones, we see genius. Because the people who are crazy enough to think they can change the world, are the ones who do.
SUPER: Think different. Apple.

MERIT AWARD
consumer television
over :30 single

art director
CHRIS GRAVES

writer
ERIK MOE

agency producer
MICHELLE BURKE

production company
EPOCH FILMS

director
PHIL MORRISON

client
ENERGIZER

agency
TBWA CHIAT/DAY/
VENICE

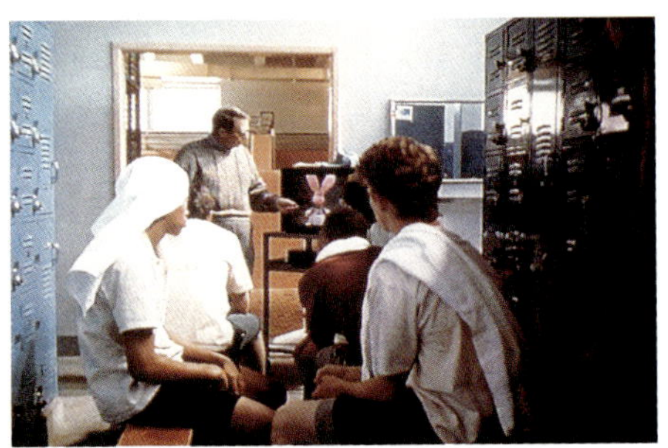

COACH BROWN: Had a real tough early season. They weren't able to finish the races, and...just nothing seemed to work.
MASCOT: We'll win next time. Don't worry about it.
COACH BROWN: Finally, I came up with this. You all know what this is. Each one of you guys has got a battery inside, just like he has, just like it.
RICK: We just think, um, think of the Bunny, and we keep going.
CHEERLEADER: That's cool.
RICK: Uh-huh.
COACH BROWN: I'm not a great coach. I'm no miracle worker, but yet something inside them has got to keep them going.
SUPER: 1997 Eveready Battery Company.

MERIT AWARD
consumer television
over :30 single

art director
CHRIS GRAVES
writer
ERIK MOE
agency producer
MICHELLE BURKE
production company
EPOCH FILMS
director
PHIL MORRISON
client
ENERGIZER
agency
TBWA CHIAT/DAY/
VENICE

COACH BROWN: I can't get out there and run that race for you. You've got to do it, Rick. You've got to do it there...Randy. (Pointing to Bunny.) This guy never complains. Does he make any excuses?
RICK: I had trouble breathing, and I started coughing.
COACH: Does he let any obstacles get in his way?
JOE: Some of the guys on the other team...they just started hitting me, then my foot started hurting.
COACH: Randy, what does he keep doing? He keeps...
RANDY: ...moving?
COACH: He keeps going and going, doesn't he? No hesitation. Be the Bunny, yeah, that's it.

SFX: Doorbell ringing.
MESSENGER: RW Kuperman?
MAN: Yeah...
MESSENGER: You've been served.
MAN: What? Half? She gets half? I'll give her half...On second thought, maybe we can work this out.
SUPER: Infiniti. Own one and you'll understand.

MERIT AWARD
consumer television
over :30 single

art director
SCOTT MACGREGOR
writer
MICHAEL MCKAY
agency producer
JENNIFER GOLUB
production company
PYTKA FILMS
director
JOE PYTKA
client
INFINITI
agency
TBWA CHIAT/DAY/
VENICE

CD2 #49

MERIT AWARD
consumer television
over :30 single

art director
SCOTT MACGREGOR
writer
MICHAEL MCKAY
agency producer
ELAINE HINTON
production company
SATELLITE FILMS
director
SPIKE JONZE
client
NISSAN
agency
TBWA CHIAT/DAY/
VENICE

CD2 #50

MR. K: Dogs love trucks.
SUPER: Nissan. Enjoy the ride.

MERIT AWARD
consumer television
over :30 single

art directors
DEB HAGAN
CHRIS GRAVES
writers
MICKEY TAYLOR
ERIK MOE
agency producer
CHERYL CHILDERS
production company
THE A&R GROUP
director
DAVID RAMSER
client
WEATHER CHANNEL
agency
TBWA CHIAT/DAY/
VENICE

CD2 #51

MAN: I'm soaked. My shoes are wet. My socks are wet. I hate the rain.
JERRY: Well, maybe the rain hates you!
PATRON 1: Yeah, you.
PATRON 2: Tell 'em, Jer.
MAN: Who me?
JERRY: Yeah, I'm talking to you. Maybe the rain hates you, huh? It irrigates the crops. Keeps things clean. Don't you forget it!
GUY: I think you just better leave. Alright?!
PATRONS: (Trying to calm Jerry.)
JERRY: (Trying to compose himself) I love the rain!
GUY: You picked the wrong bar on the wrong night, mister!
SUPER: The Weather Channel. Weather for you are not alone.

GUY: I'll make a plan. I promise I'll be there. No matter what it takes.
ANNOUNCER: Because different people have different needs, at MTN we offer you a choice of cellular packages. In fact, choice is such a big thing for us, we even giving you a choice of ending to our commercial.
SUPER: Option 1.
MUSIC: Something tells me I'm into something good...
SUPER: Option 2.
MUSIC: Some guys have all the luck.
SUPER: Option 3.
MUSIC: YMCA.
SUPER: MTN. It's your call.

TONY GWYNN: Thank you for letting me be the player I always wanted to be.
MATT WILLIAMS: For letting me compete against the very best.
KEN GRIFFEY, SR.: For letting fathers and sons realize their dreams.
KENNY LOFTON: For Reggie Jackson's three home runs.
HARRY CARAY: For Ernie Banks playing two.
ALEX RODRIGUEZ: For Roberto Clemente throwing to third.
VIN SCULLY: For Hank Aaron's seven hundred fifteenth.
WILLIE STARGELL: For my 21 years in the majors.
REGGIE JACKSON: For the chance to play in October.
ROD CAREW: For the joys of stealing home.
BUCK O'NEIL: For all of us that never got to play.
OZZIE SMITH: For enduring every taunt.
HANK AARON: And not lashing out in hate.
BARRY LARKIN: For standing up with dignity.
ERNIE BANKS: For standing up.
RICHIE ANDERSON: For opening our eyes.
FRANK ROBINSON: For empowering an entire race.
WILLIE STARGELL: Thanks, Jackie.
ERNIE BANKS: Thanks, Jackie.
REGGIE JACKSON: Thank you.
HANK AARON: Thank you.
KEN GRIFFEY, JR: Thank you, Jackie Robinson.
BUCK O'NEIL: Thank you.

MERIT AWARD
consumer television
over :30 single

art director
GREGG CAMERON
writer
ERIK VAN WYK
agency producer
HAZEL NEUHAUS
production company
PETER GIRD PRODUCTIONS
director
MICHAEL MIDDLETON
client
MOBILE TELEPHONE NETWORK
agency
TBWA HUNT LASCARIS/ JOHANNESBURG

CD2 #52

MERIT AWARD
consumer television
over :30 single

art director
HAL CURTIS
writer
MIKE FOLINO
agency producer
DONNA LAMAR
production company
PALOMAR PICTURES
director
NEIL ABRAMSON
client
NIKE
agency
WIEDEN & KENNEDY/ PORTLAND

CD2 #53

MERIT AWARD
consumer television
over :30 single

art director
FRANK CLARK
writer
DEAN SALING
agency producer
JOYCE SCHMIDTBAUER
production company
OBERLENZ FILMS
director
TONY OBER
client
SEATTLE SUPERSONICS
agency
WONGDOODY/SEATTLE

SUPER: The Sonics are coming to your home.
NATE: I heard there was a Tupperware party going on here!
TUPPERWARE LADY: There is a Tupperware party!
NATE: Am I a little late? My name is Nate McMillan and my favorite piece of Tupperware is the Cake Taker. I love making cakes.
TUPPERWARE LADY: And you push and you'll hear a burp. Are you ready? And the thing about the Modular Mate containers is that...
TUPPERWARE LADY: Yes?
NATE: Can you wash these in the dishwasher?
TUPPERWARE LADY: Yes, you can. Thank you for asking.
NATE: Oh, great!
TUPPERWARE LADY: And what's really great about the Remarkabowl is that the outside of it is rubberized. And it feels like a basketball that's been used on the cement.
NATE: Mmm...That's pretty good!
WOMAN: And you play quarterback, right?
NATE: (surprised) I play q...what?
SUPER: See them in your home.
NATE: I appreciate you having me. I really did enjoy myself. I did. Do you have a box or something for me?
SUPER: 56 games on free TV.
TUPPERWARE LADY: Go Sonics!

MERIT AWARD
consumer television
over :30 campaign

art director
LIBBY BROCKHOFF
writers
ROBERT SAVILLE
MARK WAITES
agency producer
ZOE BELL
production company
LIMELIGHT
director
DANIEL KLEINMAN
client
VAN DEN BERGHS FOODS
agency
MOTHER/LONDON

CD2 #54

JULIE: So how are your sweet and sour Super Noodles then?
DAVID: Mmmm.
JULIE: Go on, give us a try.
DAVID: Uh-uh.
JULIE: Oh, come on, I just want a little taste.
DAVID: No.
JULIE: Oh, moody.
DAVID: Look, I hate it when you do this, I offered to make you some and you said no, alright?
JULIE: But I'm not hungry, I just want a little taste.
DAVID: No.
DAVID: Look, you can finish them off if you like.
JULIE: Oh, David are you sure?
DAVID: Yeh.
JULIE: You really love me don't you.
ANNOUNCER: Batchelors Super Noodles, because noodles can be super, can't they?

ANNOUNCER: On the road of life there are passengers and there are drivers. Drivers wanted.

MERIT AWARD
consumer television
:30 single

art director
ALAN PAFENBACH
writers
LANCE JENSEN
RON LAWNER
agency producer
KEITH DEZEN
production company
TATE & PARTNERS
director
BAKER SMITH
client
VOLKSWAGEN
agency
ARNOLD COMMUNICATIONS/ BOSTON

MERIT AWARD
consumer television
:30 single

art directors
GERRY GRAF
DAVID GRAY

writers
GERRY GRAF
DAVID GRAY

agency producer
J.D. WILLIAMS

production company
@RADICAL.MEDIA

directors
BRYAN BUCKLEY
FRANK TODARO

client
MARS/SNICKERS

agency
BBDO/NEW YORK

CD2 #55

ANNOUNCER 1: And it's Dan on the left wing. He passes to Miller, Miller shoots and he scores.
ANNOUNCER 2: Well, there's the first goal, Bob. Just like in Detroit where they throw an octopus on the ice and Florida where they throw rats. Up here in Canada, you guessed it, they throw Canadians.
ANNOUNCERS TOGETHER: Ooh! Ha, ha!
FANS: Haaaa!
VO: Not going anywhere for awhile?
FAN ON ICE: Ooh! Ooh!
VO: Grab a Snickers.
FAN ON ICE: Hey Chuckie!

MERIT AWARD
consumer television
:30 single

art directors
GERRY GRAF
DAVID GRAY

writers
GERRY GRAF
DAVID GRAY

agency producer
J.D. WILLIAMS

production company
@RADICAL.MEDIA

directors
BRYAN BUCKLEY
FRANK TODARO

client
MARS/SNICKERS

agency
BBDO/NEW YORK

CD2 #56

GHEORGHE
MURESAN
cologne QSH

ANNOUNCER: Next up, a very special item for the man.
GHEORGHE MURESAN: You want to smell like me?
ANNOUNCER: Gheorghe Muresan cologne.
HOST OF SHOW: Who wouldn't want to smell like you Gheorghe? I know I would.
GHEORGHE: Ahhh.
ANNOUNCER: Makes a great gift item.
GHEORGHE: I'm waiting for your call.
HOST OF SHOW: Our operators are standing by.
VO: Not going anywhere for a while?
HOST OF SHOW: Is that cabbage Gheorghe?
GHEORGHE: Yeah, chicks dig it.
VO: Grab a Snickers.
GHEORGHE: Call now.

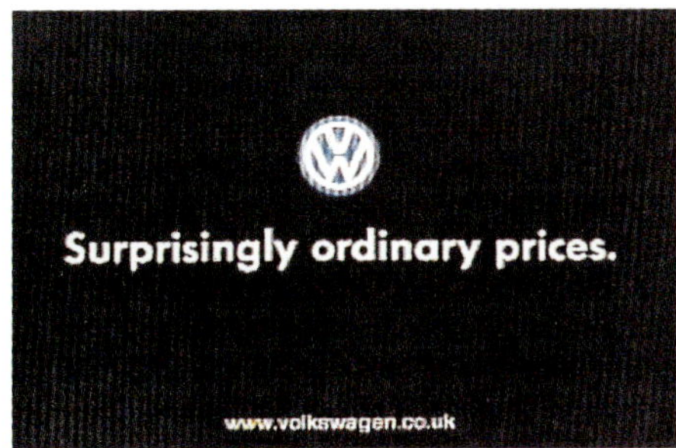

SUPER: Volkswagen.
Surprisingly ordinary prices.

MERIT AWARD
consumer television
:30 single

art director
ANDREW FRASER
writer
ANDREW FRASER
agency producer
HOWARD SPIVEY
production company
OUTSIDER
director
PAUL GAY
client
VOLKSWAGEN
GROUP UK
agency
BMP DDB/LONDON

CD2 #57

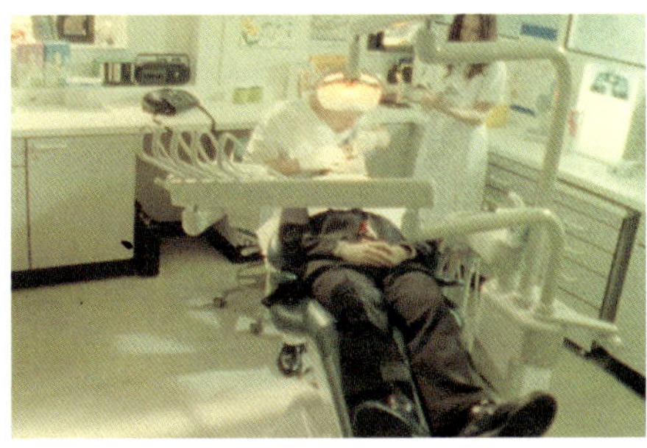

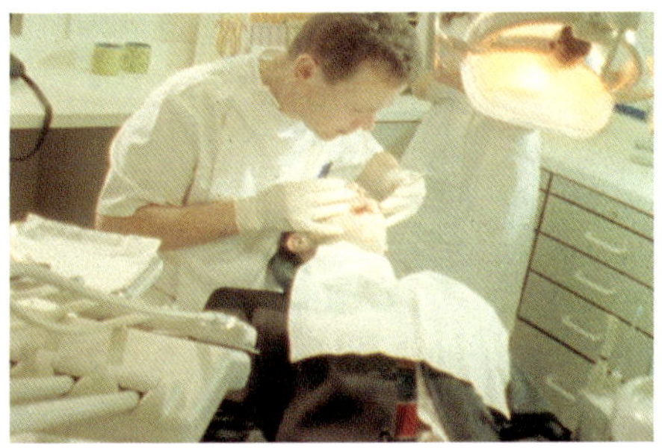

SUPER: Volkswagen.
Surprisingly ordinary prices.

MERIT AWARD
consumer television
:30 single

art director
ANDREW FRASER
writer
ANDREW FRASER
agency producer
HOWARD SPIVEY
production company
OUTSIDER
director
PAUL GAY
client
VOLKSWAGEN
GROUP UK
agency
BMP DDB/LONDON

CD2 #58

MERIT AWARD
consumer television
:30 single

art director
ANDREW FRASER
writer
ANDREW FRASER
agency producer
HOWARD SPIVEY
production company
OUTSIDER
director
PAUL GAY
client
VOLKSWAGEN
GROUP UK
agency
BMP DDB/LONDON

SUPER: Volkswagen.
Surprisingly ordinary prices.

MERIT AWARD
consumer television
:30 single

art director
ANDREW FRASER
writer
ANDREW FRASER
agency producer
HOWARD SPIVEY
production company
OUTSIDER
director
PAUL GAY
client
VOLKSWAGEN
GROUP UK
agency
BMP DDB/LONDON

SUPER: Volkswagen.
Surprisingly ordinary prices.

MERIT AWARD
consumer television
:30 single

art director
RICHARD FLINTHAM
writer
ANDY MCLEOD
agency producer
HOWARD SPIVEY
production company
PARK VILLAGE
director
ROGER WOODBURN
client
SONY
agency
BMP DDB/LONDON

CD2 #59

SUPER: Sony Trinitron.

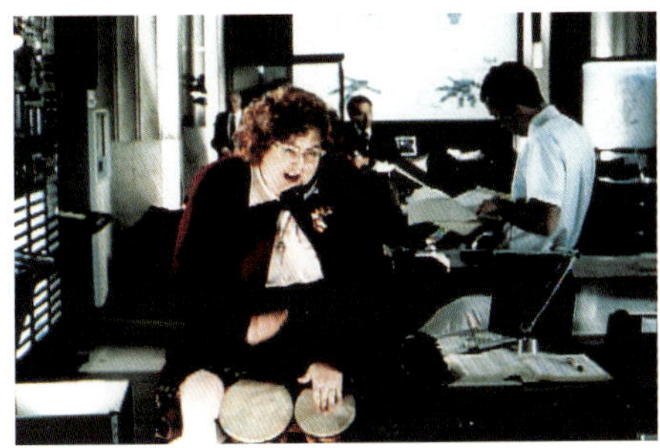

WOMAN: Hello–I need you to get out of there RIGHT NOW! I want you jump up in the air, and hang there...DON'T ARGUE WITH ME, JUST HANG THERE!... Spin your legs very fast...until your legs are making a wheel...Now, come down, hit the ground–and zip out of there.
SUPER: Welcome to Cartoon Network.
DAFFY: Screwy, ain't it?

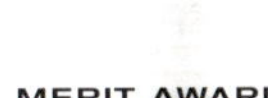

MERIT AWARD
consumer television
:30 single

art director
MICHAEL OUWELEEN
writer
MICHAEL OUWELEEN
agency producer
JENNIFER DAVIDSON
production company
TAYLORMADE
director
BRUCE HURWIT
client
CARTOON NETWORK
agency
CARTOON NETWORK/ ATLANTA

MERIT AWARD
consumer television
:30 single

art director
MICHAEL OUWELEEN
writer
MICHAEL OUWELEEN
agency producer
JENNIFER DAVIDSON
production company
TAYLORMADE
director
BRUCE HURWIT
client
CARTOON NETWORK
agency
CARTOON NETWORK/
ATLANTA

SFX: Phone rings.
WOMAN: (pause) A man's pointing a gun at you? No, don't hang up! No–what I want you to do is reach behind your back. No, I know you don't have anything behind your back. You're just gonna reach behind your back and when you pull your hand out, you're gonna have a reeeally big mallet. Did that work?
DAFFY: Yeth.
SUPER: Welcome to Cartoon Network.
DAFFY: Screwy, ain't it?

MERIT AWARD
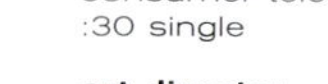
consumer television
:30 single

art director
MICHAEL OUWELEEN
writer
MICHAEL OUWELEEN
agency producer
JENNIFER DAVIDSON
production company
TAYLORMADE
director
BRUCE HURWIT
client
CARTOON NETWORK
agency
CARTOON NETWORK/
ATLANTA

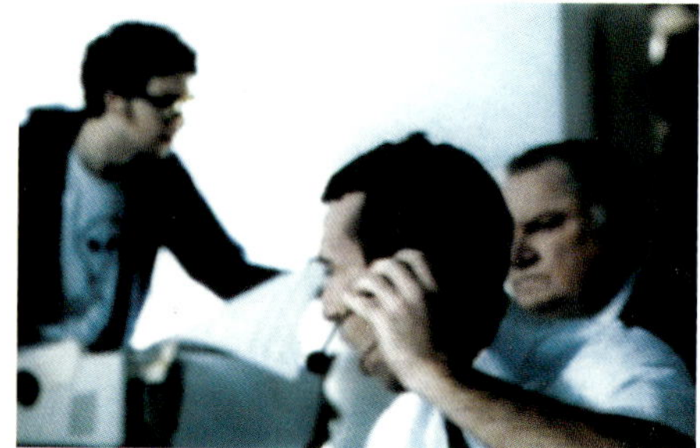

GUY: Got a guy who needs to hide, fast! Let's move! Let's move! Alright! Sir, you gotta stop screaming. Now listen, I need you to look around...is there a rock...a building...a car...anything to hide behind there. Sir?
COMPUTER GUY: What's he got?
GUY: One skinny tree. No, we are going to get you out of there, you hold on. Now sir, for this to work, you're gonna have to tippy-toe behind that tree. And you will disappear.
SUPER: Welcome to the Cartoon Network.
DAFFY: Screwy, ain't it?

MERIT AWARD
consumer television
:30 single

art director
ROGER CAMP
writers
ERIC SILVER
JEFF BITSACK
agency producer
LIZ GRAVES
production company
MOXIE PICTURES
director
CHRISTOPHER GUEST
client
FOX NETWORK
agency
CLIFF FREEMAN & PARTNERS/NEW YORK

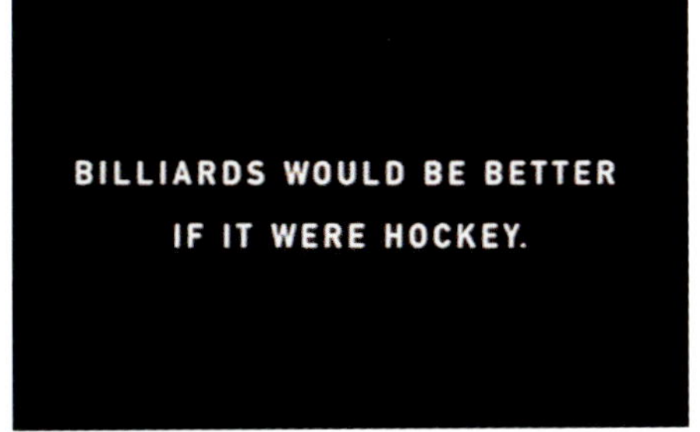

ANNOUNCER 1: Well, he's sweating over there, but not because he's losing. Dan Malloy is leading five to three.
ANNOUNCER 2: He's got to come back up and, hopefully, shoot the five in the same pocket.
ANNOUNCER 1: Well, that shouldn't be a problem. I think that was the toughest thing. It would appear now...uh...the rack is his for the taking.
ANNOUNCER 1: And there it is.
ANNOUNCER 2: Notice the cue ball, center of the table.
SUPER: Billiards would be better if it were hockey. NHL on Fox.
ANNOUNCER 2: Bing.
ANNOUNCER 1: Roddy's lucky to avoid a slashing call. And, as you can see, there's some action on table number one.

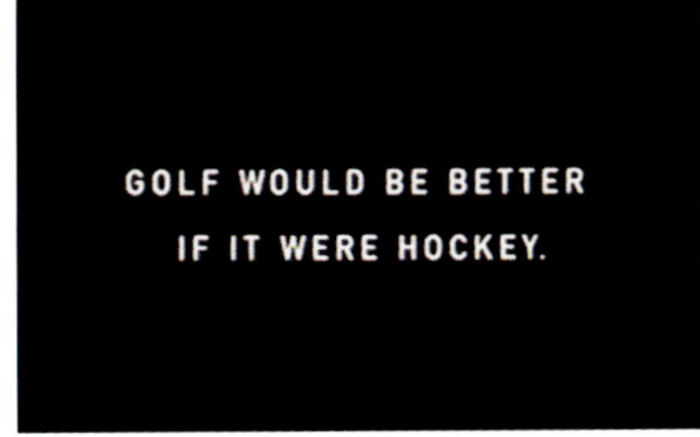

ANNOUNCER 1: Let's go out to 15 now where McDermott has taken a lot of time, Gary, to look at this putt.
ANNOUNCER 1: This would drop him to minus ten.
ANNOUNCER 2: Well, this is downhill, slightly and very fast.
ANNOUNCER 1: There's Davis. He makes the save...and quickly clears.
SUPER: Golf would be better if it were hockey. NHL on Fox.
ANNOUNCER 2: Very smoothly done.
ANNOUNCER 1: Boy, that's a brilliant shot. You don't see that on a scorecard, Gary, but that's the kind of play that wins championships.
ANNOUNCER 2: Splendid effort from the...

MERIT AWARD
consumer television
:30 single

art director
ROGER CAMP
writers
ERIC SILVER
JEFF BITSACK
agency producer
LIZ GRAVES
production company
MOXIE PICTURES
director
CHRISTOPHER GUEST
client
FOX NETWORK
agency
CLIFF FREEMAN & PARTNERS/NEW YORK

MERIT AWARD
consumer television
:30 single

art director
ROGER CAMP
writers
ERIC SILVER
JEFF BITSACK
agency producer
LIZ GRAVES
production company
MOXIE PICTURES
director
CHRISTOPHER GUEST
client
FOX NETWORK
agency
CLIFF FREEMAN
& PARTNERS

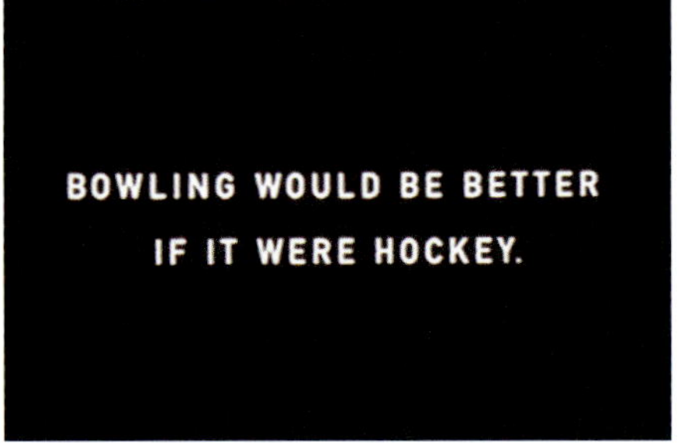

ANNOUNCER 1: Yes, we're here in the Pavilion at Manhattan Beach and you're looking at Christy Ellison. She's up there now in the tenth frame.
ANNOUNCER 2: She needs two strikes to win the match.
ANNOUNCER 1: Just like that. She got a great break–a crossover. But she'd like to have a second strike.
ANNOUNCER 2: And she was striking a bunch in practice.
SUPER: Bowling would be better if it were hockey. NHL on Fox.
ANNOUNCER 1: Well...she has to be disappointed. Did not throw a good shot. And she's left with a very difficult spare.
ANNOUNCER 2: Can you imagine that?

MERIT AWARD
consumer television
:30 single

art directors
ROGER CAMP
MICHELLE ROUFA
writers
MICHELLE ROUFA
ROGER CAMP
agency producer
MARESA WICKHAM
production company
JOHNS + GORMAN FILMS
director
JEFF GORMAN
client
LITTLE CAESARS
agency
CLIFF FREEMAN &
PARTNERS/NEW YORK

CD2 #60

ANNOUNCER: Recently, history was made through the miracle of cloning...
SCIENTIST 1: Pizza.
SCIENTIST 2: Great! How much?
SCIENTIST 1: (Hitting box hard.) $6.99! (Hitting box repeatedly.) Any pizza, any size, any toppings!
SCIENTIST 4: You got two?!?
SCIENTIST 1: (Hitting box.) Any pizza, any size, any toppings, $6.99 each!
SCIENTIST 3: Wow!
ANNOUNCER: Little Caesars–any pizza, any size, unlimited toppings, $6.99 each! Get two and Crazy Bread's free!
LITTLE CAESAR: Pizza! Pizza!

MERIT AWARD
consumer television
:30 single

art directors
ELLEN STEINBERG
writer
DEAN BUCKHORN
agency producer
TOMMY MUROV
production company
COPPOS FILMS
director
MARK COPPOS
client
USA NETWORK
agency
FALLON MCELLIGOTT/
MINNEAPOLIS

CD2 #61

SFX: Wind blowing.
HANGING GUY: Agh! Agh!
ROOF GUY 1: Hang on, Jimmy!!
HANGING GUY: Help me!!
ROOF GUY 1: C'mon, give me your other hand!!
HANGING GUY: I can't!!...I'm slipping.
ROOF GUY: Hey, Jimmy?
HANGING GUY: What??
ROOF GUY 1: Do you ever get the feeling that other shows are filming the same scenes we are??
HANGING GUY: No!! Why do you say that??
ROOF GUY 2: Hang on, Freddy!!
ROOF GUY 3: Hang on, Chuck!!
ROOF GUY 4: Hang on, Tommy!!
ANNOUNCER: Ready for something different? USA Network. The cure for the common show.

MUSIC: Miller Intro Music.
MUSIC: Romantic throughout.
SFX: Chimes.
MUSIC: Ends abruptly.
SFX: Ding.
SFX: Chimes.
SFX: Thump
SFX: Poof.
MUSIC: Romantic music.
SFX: Ppppphttt

MERIT AWARD
consumer television
:30 single

art director
DEAN HANSON
writer
DEAN BUCKHORN
agency producer
HOPE COVINGTON
production company
HOUSE OF USHER
director
KINKA USHER
client
MILLER BREWING
COMPANY/MILLER LITE
agency
FALLON MCELLIGOTT/
MINNEAPOLIS

CD2 #62

MERIT AWARD
consumer television
:30 single

art director
TODD GRANT
writer
STEVE DILDARIAN
agency producer
CINDY EPPS
production company
@RADICAL.MEDIA
directors
FRANK TODARO
BRYAN BUCKLEY
client
ANHEUSER-BUSCH
agency
GOODBY SILVERSTEIN
& PARTNERS/
SAN FRANCISCO

SFX: Crickets chirping in the background.
FROGS: Bud...weis...er. (repeating throughout)
LOUIE: I can't believe they went with the frogs.
LIZARD II: Louie.
LOUIE: Our audition was flawless.
LIZARD II: Louie.
LOUIE: We did the look. Heh?...we did the tongue thing...
LIZARD II: Um-hum.
LOUIE: That was great.
LIZARD II: Louie, frogs sell beer.
LOUIE: Ehh.
LIZARD II: That's it, man, the number one rule of marketing.
LOUIE: The Budweiser Lizards. We could have been huge.
LIZARD II: Hey, there will be other auditions.
LOUIE: Oh yeah, for what. This was Budweiser, buddy. This was big.
SFX: Tongue catching a bug.
LOUIE: Those frogs are gonna pay.
LIZARD II: Let it go, Louie, let it go.

MERIT AWARD
consumer television
:30 single

art director
PAUL HIRSCH
writer
JOSH DENBERG
agency producer
MATTHEW WINKS
production company
PROPAGANDA
director
LLOYD STEIN
client
NIKE
agency
GOODBY SILVERSTEIN
& PARTNERS/
SAN FRANCISCO

CD2 #63

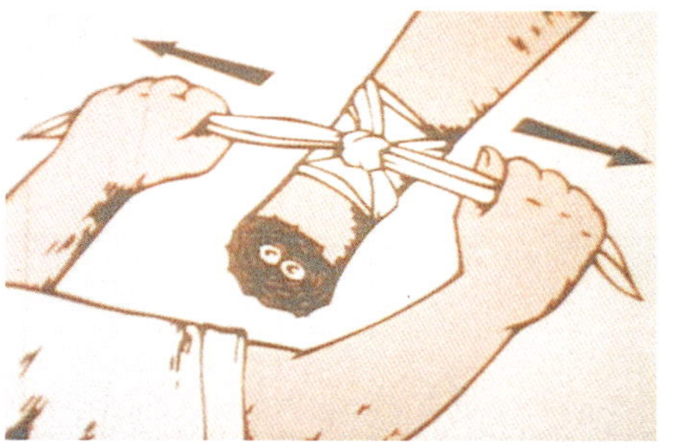

MUSIC: A cappella cowboy-style quartet.
SINGERS: I'll tell you 'bout my troubles on the old Chisolm trail. Come-a tie-yie.
SUPER: Mountain Safety. Part 3. The Tourniquet.
RANGER: The forest is a beautiful place, but it can be dangerous unless you...are prepared. A mountain biker has a bad...accident. Would you know what to do?
SUPER: ?
RANGER: First apply pressure to the wound. Tie tourniquet tight across main artery. Then encourage the victim...to quit his namby–pamby whining. And always make sure...to have a great day.
SINGERS: Come-a tie-yie yippee, yippee-yay yippee-yay, Come-a...
SUPER: Swoosh. Mountain Biking.

MUSIC: A cappella cowboy-style quartet.
SINGERS: And listen to my tale. I'll tell you 'bout my trouble on the old...
SUPER: Mountain Safety. Part 4. Mosquitoes.
RANGER: We share the outdoors with some wonderful creatures...but not everything is friendly. Mosquitoes drink human blood. Protect yourself by wearing insect repellent and by...riding with proper attire. If a...mosquito bites you, don't hit it. Instead...
SUPER: Don't!
RANGER: Get revenge by...squeezing the blood into the mosquito until it explodes. And remember, vengeance is great medicine.
SINGER: Yippee-yay...
SINGERS: Come-a tie-yie yippee, yippee-yay!
SUPER: Swoosh. Mountain Biking.

GOLFER 1: Go, go...
GOLFER 2: He's going for birdie.
GOLFER 1: Go!
GOLFER 2: Going for birdie, one stroke away, one stroke away.
SFX: Police siren.
MAN COP: Hey you guys!
WOMAN COP: Drop the clubs!
GOLFER VO: Where the–did they come from?
GOLFER: There's no problem here!
MAN COP: What do you think you're doing here?
GOLFER 3: Nothin'.
GOLFER 2: I don't know.
GOLFER 3: We found 'em here.
GOLFER 1: Some kids.
MAN COP: Hey, the city didn't build this place so you could come in here with your golf clubs and ruin it.
MAN COP: Now move it let's go. Get your stuff and put it in the car. Come on.
GOLFER 2: Aw, come on.
GOLFER 3: Let us go!
GOLFER 2: This is ridiculous!
GOLFER 3: So can we pick this stuff up at the station?
MAN COP: At the auction.
GOLFER 1: Man, the Man!
GOLFER 2: That's not fair!
GOLFER 3: Good, great, just perfect.
SUPER: What if we treated all athletes, the way we treat skateboarders? Swoosh.

MERIT AWARD
consumer television :30
single

art director
PAUL HIRSCH
writer
JOSH DENBERG
agency producer
MATTHEW WINKS
production company
PROPAGANDA
director
LLOYD STEIN
client
NIKE
agency
GOODBY SILVERSTEIN & PARTNERS/ SAN FRANCISCO

MERIT AWARD
consumer television :30
single

art director
JON SOTO
writer
ALBERT KELLY
agency producer
KRISTIN LOUDIS
production company
TATE & PARTNERS
director
BAKER SMITH
client
NIKE
agency
GOODBY SILVERSTEIN & PARTNERS/ SAN FRANCISCO

MERIT AWARD
consumer television
:30 single

art director
GRANT RICHARDS
writer
SCOTT AAL
agency producer
BARBRO EDDY
production company
HOUSE OF USHER
director
KINKA USHER
client
POLAROID
agency
GOODBY SILVERSTEIN
& PARTNERS/
SAN FRANCISCO

CD2 #64

GIRL: Six months is a long time.
GUY: I wish I could take you with me.
GIRL: Yeah, me too. (sighs).
GUY: Please, for me, all right...for the plane ride? Smile.
MODEL: Your lover?...Oui?
GUY: Um, well, it's my sister...She's sick...um, very sick.

MERIT AWARD
consumer television
:30 single

art director
PAUL RENNER
writer
ROGER BALDACCI
agency producer
LISA SULDA
production company
INTERNATIONAL
ROCKETSHIP
director
DIETER MUELLER
client
CONVERSE
agency
HOUSTON HERSTEK
FAVAT/BOSTON

CD2 #65

MUSIC: Stevie Wonder's Higher Ground.
SUPER: Creator of the Slam Funk.
DOCTOR: Bring Soul to the Hole.
SUPER: Converse. Back in Ball.

MERIT AWARD
consumer television
:30 single

art director
JIM BUCKTIN
writer
DAVE BELL
agency producers
JIM BUCKTIN
DAVE BELL
production company
THE ANNEX FILMS
director
ALASTAIR THAIN
client
NIKON
agency
LANSDOWN
CONQUEST/LONDON

CD2 #66

ANNOUNCER: You're watching a modern day miracle...Because this film was shot on a camera that only takes stills. The Nikon F5. Technically the quickest camera in the world.

MUSIC: Dramatic classical music throughout.
SUPER: Performance. Mercedes.

MERIT AWARD
consumer television
:30 single

art directors
ANDY HIRSCH
RANDY SAITTA
writer
MARTY ORZIO
agency producer
GARY GROSSMAN
production companies
JOY FILMS
CHELSEA PICTURES
director
MEHDI NOROWZIAN
client
MERCEDES-BENZ OF
NORTH AMERICA
agency
LOWE & PARTNERS/
SMS/NEW YORK

CD2 #67

MERIT AWARD
consumer television
:30 single

art director
TOM GIANFAGNA
writer
AMY BORKOWSKY
agency producers
DIANE JEREMIAS
SUSAN DULEPSKI
production company
FIVE UNION SQUARE
director
STOCK
client
COURTYARD BY MARRIOTT
agency
LOWE & PARTNERS/SMS/NEW YORK

NEVER UNDERESTIMATE
THE IMPORTANCE OF
A GOOD NIGHT'S REST.

THE HOTEL DESIGNED

BY BUSINESS TRAVELERS®
Call 800-321-2211

SFX: Crowd murmuring. Horse whinnying.
SUPER: Never underestimate the importance of a good night's rest.
SFX: Crowd applause.
SUPER: The hotel designed by business travelers. Call 800-321-2211.

MERIT AWARD
consumer television
:30 single

art director
JASON GABORIAU
writer
STEVE DOPPELT
agency producer
LIZ HODGE
production companies
SATELLITE PRODUCTIONS
OLIVE JAR
director
SPIKE JONZE
client
THE COCA-COLA COMPANY/SPRITE
agency
LOWE & PARTNERS/SMS/NEW YORK

CD2 #68

KIDS: Mom, we're thirsty.
MOM: Well, I've got two glasses of Sun Fizz coming right up.
KIDS: Sun Fizz. That's our favorite.
SUNNY: That's because there's a delicious ray of sunshine in every drop!
SFX: Kids screaming.
SUNNY: I'm filled with nature's goodness. Hey, what's with you people, I've got vitamins and minerals.
GIRL: Mom!
MOM: Run!
ANNOUNCER: Trust your gut, not some cartoon character.
SUPER: Image is nothing. Thirst is everything. Obey your thirst.

JACK: Excuse me sir, are you looking forward to the Jack Docherty Show on Channel 5?
MAN: I've never heard of it.
JACK: You've heard of Jack Docherty though.
MAN: No.
JACK: So you're saying you wouldn't recognize him if he just walked up to you in the street.
MAN: No.
JACK: No. So you probably wouldn't know if he just hit you in the face with a microphone. (Hits him in the face with microphone.) Eh? So you won't be able to describe him to the police, then.
CAMERAMAN: Jack. Jack.
JACK: Yes, it's Jack. It's been Jack all day. Why would it suddenly change? Would it change to Brian?
SUPER: Watch out for the Jack Docherty Show. Weeknights 11pm.

MERIT AWARD
consumer television
:30 single

art director
LIBBY BROCKHOFF
writer
MARK WAITES
agency producer
ZOE BELL
production company
BLINK
director
TREVOR MELVIN
client
CHANNEL 5
agency
MOTHER/LONDON

CD2 #69

SFX: Television noises.
SFX: Crowd cheering as if someone scored a touchdown
WAITRESS: Are Fridays always like this? This place is nuts.
BARTENDER: Oh, yeah.
WAITRESS: Who are the guys over there?
BARTENDER: Ah, they're here every Friday. They're huge Weekend Outlook Fans. It's on! It's on! Here we go.
CANTORI: Let's take a look at what's on tap for your weekend.
COOL GUY: Stay cool. Stay cool. Stay cool.
WARM GUY: Warm weather. Warm! Yes! Hello, warm weather, right there!
SUPER: The Weather Channel. Weather fans you're not alone.

MERIT AWARD
consumer television
:30 single

art directors
DEB HAGAN
CHRIS GRAVES
writers
MICKEY TAYLOR
ERIK MOE
agency producer
CHERYL CHILDERS
production company
THE A&R GROUP
director
DAVID RAMSER
client
WEATHER CHANNEL
agency
TBWA CHIAT/DAY/
VENICE

CD2 #70

MERIT AWARD
consumer television
:30 single

art directors
RICK MCQUISTON
VINCE ENGEL

writers
JERRY CRONIN
CANICE NEARY

agency producers
BETH HARDING
DAN DUFFY

production company
@RADICAL.MEDIA

directors
RICK LEMOINE
STEVE MILLER

client
ESPN

agency
WIEDEN & KENNEDY/
PORTLAND

DAN: Everyone makes a big deal out of the SportsCenter catch phrases, but honestly, we make this stuff up right on the spot.
EDITOR: Welcome aboard Flight 149 for right field, this is non-chewing flight. It's never iffy if it's Griffey. That blows. It must be a Homer Simpson because the pitcher just went Dhooo!
DAN: And because the catch phrases are so organic, it keeps the show fresh?
EDITOR: Four. I am the most popular player in all the land. Yahtzee!

MERIT AWARD
consumer television
:30 single

art directors
VINCE ENGEL
RICK MCQUISTON

writer
JAMES LEMAITRE

agency producer
DAN DUFFY

production company
@RADICAL.MEDIA

directors
STEVE MILLER
RICK LEMOINE

client
ESPN

agency
WIEDEN & KENNEDY/
PORTLAND

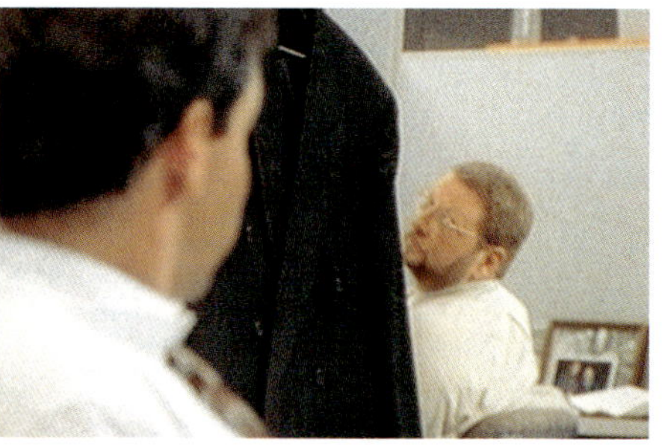

BARRY: People ask me all the time how do you decide which anchors work together? To be honest, it's an awkward process.
LARRY: (reading a note) Dear Larry, do you want to do sports together? If yes, check the box. Charlie.
BARRY: Ultimately, you're looking for a good relationship.
DAN: So I was wondering if you're not doing anything later tonight, would you want to do a show with me?
BARRY: Who ever said all is fair in love and war was probably a broadcaster.
RICH: And we'll be right back with more SportsCenter in a minute.
KENNY: I don't even know who you are anymore.
SUPER: This is SportsCenter.

MERIT AWARD
consumer television
:30 single

art director
KILPATRICK ANDERSON
writer
JAMES LEMAITRE
agency producer
LISA JAKANOVICH
production company
X-RAY
director
JESSE PERETZ
client
NIKE
agency
WIEDEN & KENNEDY/
PORTLAND

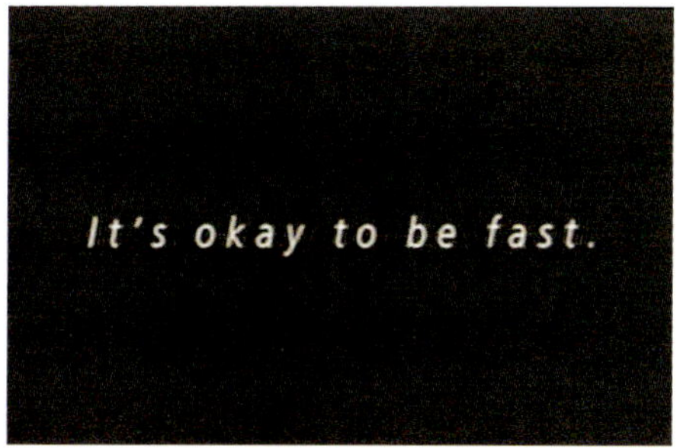

MODERATOR: Michael, before the break you were talking about your nightmare.
MICHAEL JOHNSON: The other night I had this nightmare...I was running in my...Air Zoom Spiridons and everyone was looking...at me,or trying to. I even heard this little girl saying, "Mommy, why is that man all blurry?" And I felt like screaming. Why can't people see the real me? The guy who walks to the mail box. The guy who chews his food slowly so
it digests well. Can I stop now?
MODERATOR: Of course you can...you're gonna make it kiddo...
SUPER: It's okay to be fast.
MODERATOR: ...don't you doubt it for one minute.
SUPER: Thin, light, responsive Zoom Air. Swoosh.

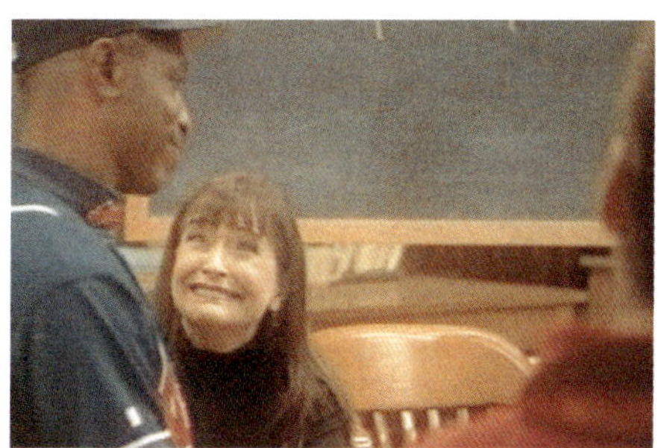

MODERATOR: Let's talk about turning negatives into positives. What's one good thing about wearing shoes that make you faster? Kenny?
KENNY LOFTON: Umm...I don't have to slide into second as much so...it keeps my uniform clean.
MODERATOR: Clean uniform. Good. What else?
KENNY LOFTON: I get around the bases faster, so I'm back on the bench with my teammates, who I enjoy.
MODERATOR: Quality time with friends, right, what else?
KENNY LOFTON: I can cover more of the outfield, so the rest of my teammates can just rest.
MODERATOR: You know what you're doing right now Kenny? You're growing.
SUPER: It's okay to be fast.
ANNOUNCER: Yeah, he's growing, isn't he.
SUPER: Thin, light, responsive Zoom Air. Swoosh.

MERIT AWARD
consumer television
:30 single

art director
KILPATRICK ANDERSON
writer
JAMES LEMAITRE
agency producer
LISA JAKANOVICH
production company
X-RAY
director
JESSE PERETZ
client
NIKE
agency
WIEDEN & KENNEDY/
PORTLAND

MERIT AWARD
consumer television
:30 single

art director
LINDA KNIGHT
writer
MIKE MCCOMMON
agency producer
DONNA LAMAR
production company
HSI PRODUCTIONS
director
ZACH SNYDER
client
NIKE
agency
WIEDEN & KENNEDY/
PORTLAND

CD2 #71

SFX: Ball whizzing by.
SUPER: Swoosh.

MERIT AWARD
consumer television
:30 campaign

art director
ROGER CAMP
writers
ERIC SILVER
JEFF BITSACK
agency producer
LIZ GRAVES
production company
MOXIE PICTURES
director
CHRISTOPHER GUEST
client
FOX NETWORK
agency
CLIFF FREEMAN &
PARTNERS/NEW YORK

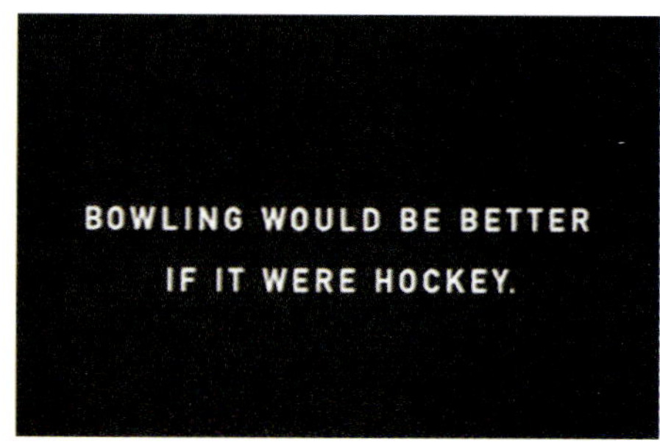

ANNOUNCER 1: Yes, we're here in the Pavilion at Manhattan Beach and you're looking at Christy Ellison. She's up there now in the tenth frame.
ANNOUNCER 2: She needs two strikes to win the match.
ANNOUNCER 1: Just like that. She got a great break–a crossover. But she'd like to have a second strike.
ANNOUNCER 2: And she was striking a bunch in practice.
SUPER: Bowling would be better if it were hockey. NHL on Fox.
ANNOUNCER 1: Well...she has to be disappointed. Did not throw a good shot. And she's left with a very difficult spare.
ANNOUNCER 2: Can you imagine that?

MERIT AWARD
consumer television
:30 campaign

art director
PAUL HIRSCH
writer
JOSH DENBERG
agency producer
MATTHEW WINKS
production company
PROPAGANDA
director
LLOYD STEIN
client
NIKE
agency
GOODBY SILVERSTEIN
& PARTNERS/
SAN FRANCISCO

MUSIC: A cappella cowboy-style quartet.
SINGERS: ...listen to my tale. I'll tell you 'bout my troubles on the old...
SUPER: Mountain Safety. Part 5. Poison Oak.
RANGER: Foliage is a wonderful part of riding in the outdoors...If you know what you're doing. Greg has a disgusting rash. He did a...bitchin' endo and landed in some poison oak. Or was it poison ivy? What's the difference? Both are tree-leafed plants.
SFX: Ding, ding, ding
RANGER: And both.
SUPER: Poison Oak. Poison Ivy.
RANGER: Can be treated with Calamine lotion...or scratched until bloody and infected. So remember if the plant...has three, let it be.
SINGERS: Yippee-yay, Come-a tie-yie yippee, yippee-yay!
SUPER: Swoosh. Mountain Biking.

NEVER UNDERESTIMATE
THE IMPORTANCE OF
A GOOD NIGHT'S REST.

THE HOTEL DESIGNED

BY BUSINESS TRAVELERS®
Call 800-321-2211

SUPER: Never underestimate the importance of a good night's rest.
REPORTER: What? Are we on?
SUPER: The hotel designed by business travelers. Call 800-321-2211.

MERIT AWARD
consumer television
:30 campaign

art director
TOM GIANFAGNA
writer
AMY BORKOWSKY
agency producers
DIANE JEREMIAS
SUSAN DULEPSKI
production company
FIVE UNION SQUARE
director
TOM SCHILLER
client
COURTYARD BY
MARRIOTT
agency
LOWE & PARTNERS/
SMS/NEW YORK

MERIT AWARD
consumer television
:30 campaign

art directors
RICK MCQUISTON
VINCE ENGEL
writers
JAMES LEMAITRE
JERRY CRONIN
CANICE NEARY
agency producers
DAN DUFFY
BETH HARDING
production company
@RADICAL.MEDIA
directors
STEVE MILLER
RICK LEMOINE
client
ESPN
agency
WIEDEN & KENNEDY/
PORTLAND

CD2 #74

DAN: Everyone makes a big deal out of the SportsCenter catch phrases, but honestly, we make this stuff up right on the spot.
EDITOR: Welcome aboard Flight 149 for right field, this is non-chewing flight. It's never iffy if it's Griffey. That blows. It must be a Homer Simpson because the pitcher just went Dhooo!
DAN: And because the catch phrases are so organic, it keeps the show fresh?
EDITOR: Four. I am the most popular player in all the land. Yahtzee!

MERIT AWARD
consumer television
:30 campaign

art directors
RICK MCQUISTON
VINCE ENGEL
writers
CANICE NEARY
JERRY CRONIN
JAMES LEMAITRE
agency producers
DAN DUFFY
BETH HARDING
production company
@RADICAL.MEDIA
directors
RICK LEMOINE
STEVE MILLER
client
ESPN
agency
WIEDEN & KENNEDY/
PORTLAND

CD2 #75

LINDA: What's nice for working mothers here...is the kids center. It fosters a family atmosphere.
EVANDER HOLYFIELD: Today we are going to read Rumble in the Jungle book. See Mohammed? See George? See Muhammad clobber George?
LINDA: And our children learn skills...we don't know how to teach.
EVANDER HOLYFIELD: No, no, no you've got to go to the body, you've got to work the left hook. You understand?
LINDA: They get nutritious meals...and when your teacher is the reigning WBA champ, you're going to listen. Which is nice.
EVANDER HOLYFIELD: It's cold out, don't forget your gloves.
STUDENT: (leaving) Thank you.
SUPER: This is SportsCenter.

MERIT AWARD
consumer television
:30 campaign

art director
KILPATRICK ANDERSON
writer
JAMES LEMAITRE
agency producer
LISA JAKANOVICH
production company
X-RAY
director
JESSE PERETZ
client
NIKE
agency
WIEDEN & KENNEDY/
PORTLAND

CD2 #76

MODERATOR: You are all abnormally fast, and that makes you feel different...Let's start with you...Tell me your name and why you're here.
MICHAEL JOHNSON: My name is Michael, and I'm fast.
FED EX GUY: My name is Randy...and I'm fast.
KENNY LOFTON: My name is Kenny, but I'm not that fast.
MODERATOR: Kenny, you stole 75 bases last year...you've got Zoom Air in your shoes...try it again, OK.
KENNY LOFTON: My name is Kenny, and I'm fast–but not as fast as him.
MODERATOR: Kenny...we can't like you...until you like you.
SUPER: It's okay to be fast.
ANNOUNCER: We're all on your side.
SUPER: Thin, light, responsive, Zoom Air. Swoosh.

MERIT AWARD
consumer television
:20 and under: single

art directors
DAVID ANGELO
CLIFF FREEMAN
ARTHUR BIJUR
writers
ARTHUR BIJUR
CLIFF FREEMAN
DAVID ANGELO
agency producer
MARESA WICKHAM
production company
CROSSROADS FILMS
director
MARK STORY
client
LITTLE CAESARS
agency
CLIFF FREEMAN
& PARTNERS/
NEW YORK

CD2 #77

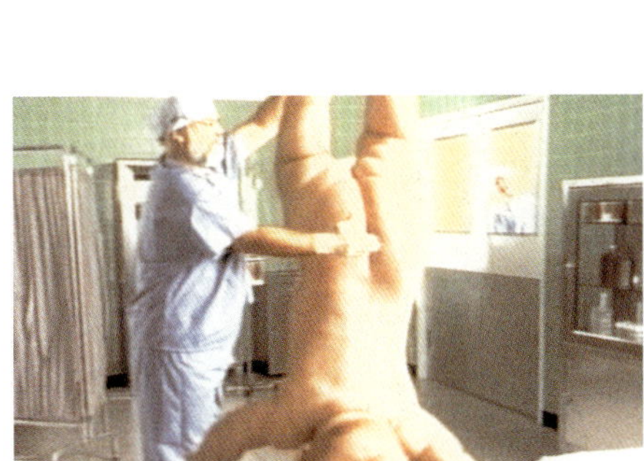

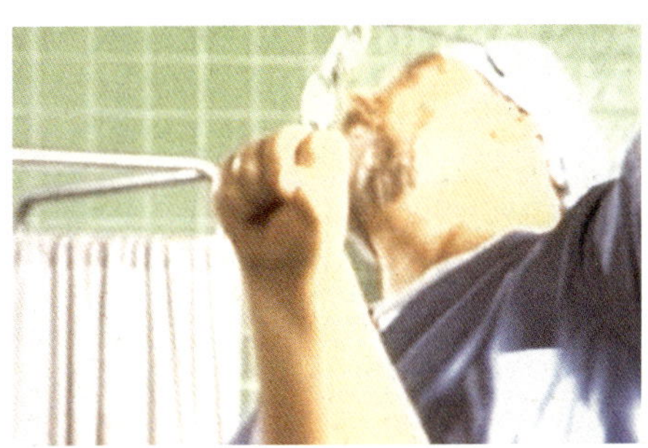

SFX: Computer typing noise.
SFX: Sniffing.
WOMAN: Hello, future people. Something very basic has changed on earth...Up till now. There was a large, medium and small pizza. Now Little Caesars says this...is large, medium, and small!
DOG: Huh?
WOMAN: Does this mean other things will get bigger?
SFX: Whack!
DOCTOR: Oh!
WOMAN: Or does it simply mean Uncle Ed...can come to dinner?
DOG: Bark!
KID: Boy, that's a lot of pizza, Uncle Ed!
UNCLE ED: Yup!
ANNOUNCER: Little Caesars Big! Big! Pizzas! They dwarf the competition! Small $5.99, medium $7.99, large $9.99.
LITTLE CAESAR: Bigger! Bigger!

MERIT AWARD
consumer television
:20 and under: single

art director
TODD GRANT
writer
STEVE DILDARIAN
agency producer
KHRISANA MAYFIELD
production company
@RADICAL.MEDIA
directors
BRYAN BUCKLEY
FRANK TODARO
client
ANHEUSER-BUSCH
agency
GOODBY SILVERSTEIN
& PARTNERS/
SAN FRANCISCO

LOUIE: Enjoy it while you can hot shots. Your days are numbered.
FRANK: Louie.
LOUIE: I know a lot of predators.
FRANK: Lower your voice.
LOUIE: I'm very friendly with the snakes. And I know several very large ferrets. Heh.

MERIT AWARD
consumer television
:20 and under: single

art director
TODD GRANT
writer
STEVE DILDARIAN
agency producer
KHRISANA MAYFIELD
production company
@RADICAL.MEDIA
directors
BRYAN BUCKLEY
FRANK TODARO
client
ANHEUSER-BUSCH
agency
GOODBY SILVERSTEIN
& PARTNERS/
SAN FRANCISCO

LOUIE: Frank, let me ask you a question.
FRANK: Yes.
LOUIE: These frogs.
LOUIE: Do they really taste like chicken?
FRANK: I'm not answering that.
LOUIE: I'm just curious.
FRANK: Stop it.
LOUIE: Come on, it's barbecue season. Would you marinade them? Would you slow cook them? We could toss them over a salad.

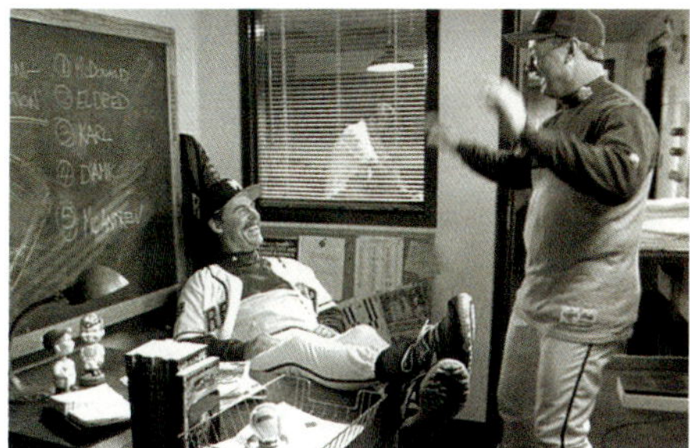

SUPER: The Art of Clubhouse Humor.
SFX: Ambient clubhouse noises.
SUPER: Milwaukee Brewers.
PHIL GARNER: Hee, hee, hee...that's funny.

MERIT AWARD
consumer television
:20 and under: single

art director
RICH KOHNKE
writers
STEVE KOENEKE
KEVIN BRANDT
agency producer
DARLENE STIMAC
production company
RYP FILMWORKS
director
ROBERT PURMAN
client
MILWAUKEE BREWERS
BASEBALL CLUB
agency
KOHNKE HANNEKEN/
MILWAUKEE

CD2 #78

ALI: Back up sucker. Back up. Come get me, sucker. I'm dancin'. I'm dancing. Follow me, son. No, I'm not there. I'm here. Whoa! You out, sucker.
SUPER: Apple. Think Different.

MERIT AWARD
consumer television :20
and under: single

art directors
LEE CLOW
YVONNE SMITH
JENNIFER GOLUB
writer
JENNIFER GOLUB
agency producer
JENNIFER GOLUB
director
JENNIFER GOLUB
client
APPLE COMPUTER
agency
TBWA CHIAT/DAY/
VENICE

MERIT AWARD
consumer television
:20 and under: campaign

art director
GUY SHELMERDINE
writer
STEVE O'BRIEN
agency producer
PATRICIA PHELAN
production company
MOXIE PICTURES
director
CHRISTOPHER GUEST
client
ESPNEWS
agency
GROUND ZERO/
SANTA MONICA

CD2 #79

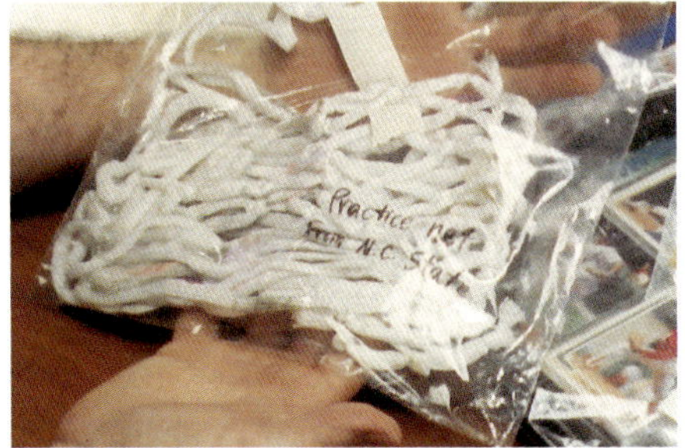

THE RICK: This is a practice net from NC State. I got the guy to cut it down after practice. And I, I sent him like fifteen bucks. He was just a grad student cleaning up there.
SUPER: ESPNEWS is the official channel of The Rick.

MERIT AWARD
consumer television
varying lengths campaign

art directors
JOHN LIEGEY
RICK YAMOKOSHI
BOBBY APPLEBY
writers
ROB MCPHERSON
NANCY NELMS
ERIC SORENSON
agency producers
JULIE HAMPEL
ANDREW WALTON
production companies
PAUL WEILAND COMPANY
STRAWDOGS
directors
FRANK BUDGEN
JESSE DYLAN
client
MILLER BREWING
COMPANY/MILLER LITE
agency
FALLON MCELLIGOTT/
MINNEAPOLIS

CD2 #80

MUSIC: Miller Intro Music.
SFX: Truck motor.
MUSIC: Slow guitar music.
STEER: Stampede. Tomorrow night. Two a.m.
SUPER: Miller Time.
SUPER: Dick. This commercial is made and approved by me. (My Signature.)

COOK: Hey!! That my duck...you.
COP: Follow that guy...Move, I'm a cop!
SFX: Tires screeching.
COP: Slow down! It's just a moped, right? Hey! Hey...you had 'em.
CAB DRIVER: Who loves ya', baby?
COP: What is your deal?...It's just a misdemeanor. You can let him go.
SFX: Tires screeching. Music in. Music out.
SUPER: Levi's. They go on. www.levi.com

MERIT AWARD
consumer television
varying lengths campaign

art directors
KIM SCHOEN
SEAN MULLENS

writers
SUZANNE FINNAMORE
SUSAN TREACY

agency producer
STEVE NEELY

production company
@RADICAL.MEDIA

director
TARSEM

client
LEVI STRAUSS & CO

agency
FOOTE CONE & BELDING/ SAN FRANCISCO

CD2 #81

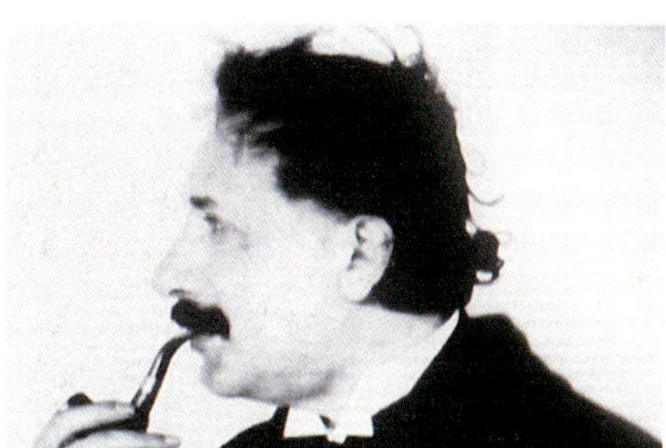

ANNOUNCER: Here's to the crazy ones. The misfits. The rebels. The troublemakers. The round pegs in the square holes. The ones who see things differently. They're not fond of rules. And they have no respect for the status quo. You can quote them, disagree with them, glorify or vilify them. About the only thing you can't do is ignore them. Because they change things. They push the human race forward. And while some may see them as the crazy ones, we see genius. Because the people who are crazy enough to think they can change the world, are the ones who do.
SUPER: Think Different. Apple.

MERIT AWARD
consumer television
varying lengths campaign

art directors
LEE CLOW
YVONNE SMITH
JENNIFER GOLUB

writers
ROB SILTANEN
KEN SEGALL
STEVE JOBS
JENNIFER GOLUB
CRAIG TANIMOTO

agency producer
JENNIFER GOLUB

director
JENNIFER GOLUB

client
APPLE COMPUTER

agency
TBWA CHIAT/DAY
VENICE

CD2 #82

MERIT AWARD
consumer television
varying lengths campaign

art director
CHRIS GRAVES
writer
ERIK MOE
agency producer
MICHELLE BURKE
production company
EPOCH FILMS
director
PHIL MORRISON
client
ENERGIZER
agency
TBWA CHIAT/DAY/
VENICE

CD2 #83

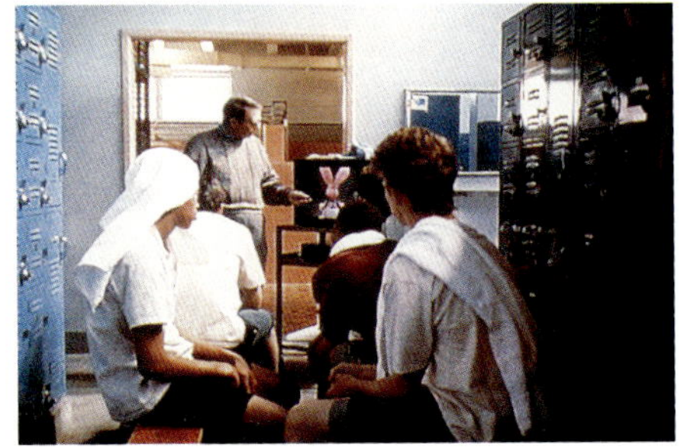

COACH BROWN: Had a real tough early season. They weren't able to finish the races, and...just nothing seemed to work.
MASCOT: We'll win the next time. Don't worry about it.
COACH BROWN VO: Finally, I came up with this.
COACH BROWN: You all know what this is. Each one of you guys has got a battery inside, just like he has, just like it.
SUPER: Simulated demonstration.
RICK: We just think, um, think of the bunny, and we keep going.
CHEERLEADER: That's cool.
RICK: Uh-huh.
COACH BROWN VO: I'm not a great coach. I'm no miracle worker, but yet something inside them has got to keep them going.
SUPER: 1997 Eveready Battery Company.

MERIT AWARD
consumer television
under $50,000 budget
single

art directors
JOHN BUTLER
MIKE SHINE
writer
RYAN EBNER
agency producers
TAMSIN PRIGGE
MEREDITH NORMAN
production company
FAHRENHEIT FILMS
director
NEIL TARDIO, J.R.
client
BORDERS BOOKS
& MUSIC
agency
BUTLER SHINE &
STERN/SAUSALITO

CD2 #84

You can learn a lot from Star Trek.

CELL PHONE GUY: Yeah...I don't care what they're asking for...Look, I said the deal doesn't go unless I authorize it...Just have them fax it.
SUPER: You can learn a lot from Star Trek.
SUPER: The Start Trek Encyclopedia.
SUPER: Borders. Books. Music. Video. And a Cafe. Come inside.

MERIT AWARD
consumer television
under $50,000 budget
single

art director
JON SOTO
writer
ALBERT KELLY
agency producer
KRISTIN LOUDIS
production company
TATE & PARTNERS
director
BAKER SMITH
client
NIKE
agency
GOODBY SILVERSTEIN
& PARTNERS/
SAN FRANCISCO

GOLFER 1: Go, go...
GOLFER 2: He's going for birdie.
GOLFER 1: Go!
GOLFER 2: Going for birdie, one stroke away, one stroke away.
SFX: Police siren.
MAN COP: Hey you guys!
WOMAN COP: Drop the clubs!
GOLFER VO: Where the—did they come from?
GOLFER: There's no problem here!
MAN COP: What do you think you're doing here?
GOLFER 3: Nothin'.
GOLFER 2: I don't know.
GOLFER 3: We found 'em here.
GOLFER 1: Some kids.
MAN COP: Hey, the city didn't build this place so you could come in here with your golf clubs and ruin it.
MAN COP: Now move it let's go. Get your stuff and put it in the car. Come on.
GOLFER 2: Aw, come on.
GOLFER 3: Let us go!
GOLFER 2: This is ridiculous!
GOLFER 3: So can we pick this stuff up at the station?
MAN COP: At the auction.
GOLFER 1: Man, the Man!
GOLFER 2: That's not fair!
GOLFER 3: Good, great, just perfect.
SUPER: What if we treated all athletes, the way we treat skateboarders? Swoosh.

NEVER UNDERESTIMATE
THE IMPORTANCE OF
A GOOD NIGHT'S REST.

THE HOTEL DESIGNED

BY BUSINESS TRAVELERS®
Call 800-321-2211

WOMAN: I need the words.
SUPER: Never underestimate the importance of a good night's rest.
SFX: Crowd reacts.
SUPER: Courtyard by Marriott. The hotel designed by business travelers.
Call 800-321-2211.

MERIT AWARD
consumer television
under $50,000 budget
single

art director
TOM GIANFAGNA
writer
AMY BORKOWSKY
agency producers
DIANE JEREMIAS
SUSAN DULEPSKI
production company
FIVE UNION SQUARE
director
STOCK
client
COURTYARD BY
MARRIOTT
agency
LOWE & PARTNERS/
SMS/NEW YORK

MERIT AWARD
consumer television
under $50,000 budget
single

art director
TOM GIANFAGNA
writer
AMY BORKOWSKY
agency producers
DIANE JEREMIAS
SUSAN DULEPSKI
production company
FIVE UNION SQUARE
director
TOM SCHILLER
client
COURTYARD BY MARRIOTT
agency
LOWE & PARTNERS/
SMS/NEW YORK

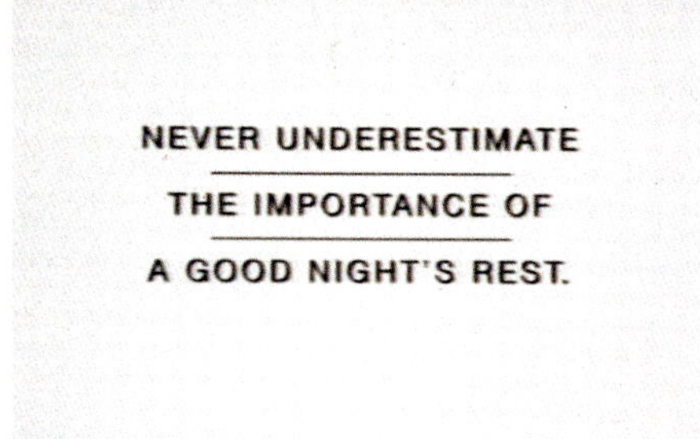

SUPER: Never underestimate the importance of a good night's rest.
REPORTER: What? Are we on?
SUPER: Courtyard by Marriott. The hotel designed by business travelers.
Call 800-321-2211.

MERIT AWARD
non-broadcast: cinema
single

art directors
ROBIN HEISEY
DON EMBREE
writers
DON EMBREE
ROBIN HEISEY
agency producer
JUDY HAMILTON
production company
PLAYERS FILM COMPANY
director
DAVID MCNALLY
client
ROGERS CANTEL
agency
GEE JEFFREY &
PARTNERS/TORONTO

CD2 #85

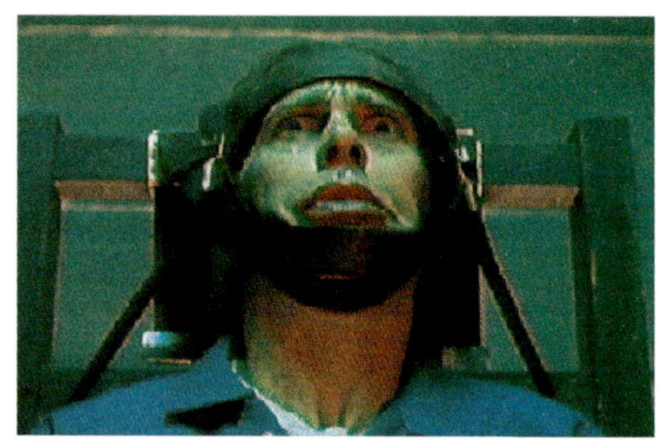

JOHNNY: Mmmm...that was good...you took care of everything, right?
LAWYER: Yeah, the money went through.
GUARD: Alright Johnny...it's time...
SFX: Laughter.
JOHNNY: Hear that? It's time.
SFX: More laughter.
LAWYER: Now don't you worry, the Governor's going to call.
JOHNNY: Of course he's going to call...(whispers) everyone has their price.
LAWYER: Right.
PRIEST: And may God have mercy on your soul...
JOHNNY: See ya in a minute, boys. Evening, Warden.
WARDEN: Jonathan Wayne Braley you have been tried and convicted in the supreme court of this state. The particularly heinous nature of your crimes have dictated that you be sentenced to death by electrocution this 23rd day of January, nineteen hundred and eighty seven. Any last words?
JOHNNY: Yeah. Keep that phone free. I'm expecting an important call.
SFX: Cell phone ringing.
JOHNNY: Ah, that would be for me.
SFX: Another ring.
WARDEN: Yes? Hello?
SFX: Another ring.
GUARD: Wasn't the Governor, just some idiot in the audience with a cell phone...
SUPER: Don't fry the film. Turn off your cell phones and pagers. And please, no talking during the movie. Cineplex Odeon, Cantel AT&T.

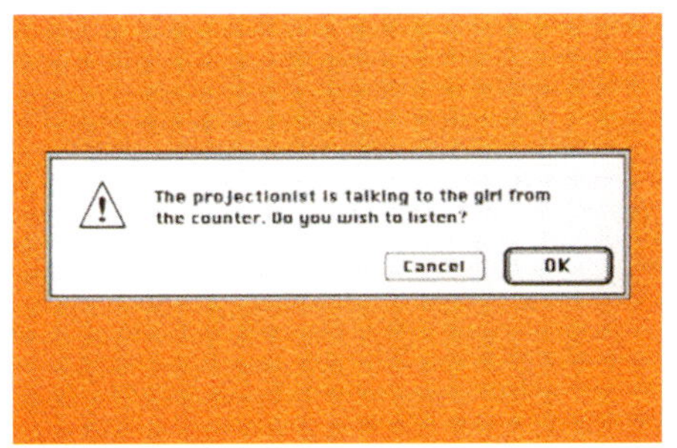

DIALOGUE BOX: Play music in cinema? (OK/Cancel) OK selected.
SFX: Music track played.
DIALOGUE BOX: The gentleman in seat G-17 does not like this song. Increase volume? (OK/Cancel) OK selected.
SFX: Music is played louder.
DIALOGUE BOX: The projectionist is talking to the girl from the counter. Do you wish to listen? (OK/Cancel) OK selected.
SFX: Conversation between the projectionist and the girl overheard.
PROJECTIONIST: Did you work yesterday?
GIRL: Uh-huh...
PROJECTIONIST: And...are you working tomorrow?
GIRL: Yeah.
PROJECTIONIST: Mmmmmm. How's your course going?
GIRL: Oh pretty good you know.
DIALOGUE BOX: Do you wish to hear what the projectionist is thinking instead? (OK/Cancel) OK selected.
SFX: His thoughts overheard.
PROJECTIONIST: You're beautiful!!! Be mine! Be mine! I love you.
DIALOGUE BOX: This cinema was built on a fault line. Cause plates to shift? (OK/Cancel) OK selected.
SFX: Earth rumbling. Screen shaking.
DIALOGUE BOX: It's turning into a major earthquake. Do you wish to continue? (OK/Cancel) Cancel selected.
DIALOGUE BOX: Shutdown? (OK/Cancel) OK selected.
SUPER: Apple. The Apple Rocketbook. So much power, anything is possible.

MERIT AWARD
non-broadcast: cinema single

art director
MIKE O'SULLIVAN
writers
RICHARD MADDOCKS
MURRAY WATT
agency producer
JACKIE CLARK
production company
MOJO PARTNERS AUCKLAND
directors
RICHARD MADDOCKS
MIKE O'SULLIVAN
client
APPLE COMPUTER
agency
MOJO PARTNERS/ AUCKLAND

CD2 #86

MUSIC: Schubert's The Trout.
SUPER: The Starter.
SUPER: The Main Course.
SUPER: The Dessert.
SUPER: P.S. Stay at home. Playstation.

MERIT AWARD
non-broadcast: cinema single

art director
SEAN THOMPSON
writer
ROS SINCLAIR
agency producer
LOUISE FULLER
production company
SERIOUS PICTURES
director
DAN NATHAN
client
SONY PLAYSTATION
agency
TBWA SIMONS PALMER/LONDON

CD2 #87

MERIT AWARD
non-broadcast
out-of-home: single

art director
PETER NICHOLSON
writer
SCOTT WILD
agency producer
BEN LATIMER
production company
SHELTER FILMS
director
JONATHAN DAVID
client
ADIDAS AMERICA
agency
LEAGAS DELANEY/
SAN FRANCISCO

CD2 #88

MUSIC: Throughout.
SFX: Stadium Ambiance.
MR. Y: There.
MR. N: Those guys.
SECURITY GUARD 1: Go check those guys out, huh?
SECURITY GUARD 2: Gentlemen, can I see you over here? C'mon.
SFX: Shirts ripping open.
LEADER OF PREPS: Go Yanks?
SFX: Crowd ambience of game in background. Stadium organ.
SUPER: Only in New York.
SUPER: Adidas.

MERIT AWARD
non-broadcast
out-of-home: single

art director
JOHN CARTER
writer
JAMES BROWN
agency producer
LORA ZARETSKY
production company
CURIOUS PICTURES
director
TOM SCHILLER
client
CURIOUS PICTURES
ANIMATION
agency
PLAN-B/VENICE

CD2 #89

DIRECTOR: You're trying to hide from somebody. So you take this can of invisible ink and put it over your head and become invisible so that only your eyes show.
OK? Action!
Be invisible. Be...no, no, no! C'mon, stand up. Give me invisible. Be invisible.
MUSIC: Cartoon-orchestral.
SUPER: We can do that.
DIRECTOR: Be invisible. Be invisible.
SUPER: Curious Pictures. Animation.
DIRECTOR: Be invisible. And cut.

DENILSON: Gooooooooaaaaaal!
GUGA: C'mon Denilson! You hit the net, bro!
DENILSON: The net's a goal.
SUPER: Pepsi Generation Next.

MERIT AWARD
foreign language television
single

art director
MARCELLO SERPA
writer
EUGENIO MOHALLEM
agency producer
MARIA DO
SOCORRO GOES
production company
O2 FILMES
directors
FERNANDO MEIRELLES
CESAR CHARLONE
client
PEPSI-COLA
agency
ALMAP/BBDO/
SÃO PAULO

CD2 #90

BOY 1: When I grow up, I wanna have a big imported car, convertible...
BOY 2: When I grow up, I wanna have a VW Bus.
SUPER: New VW Bus. Much more space.

MERIT AWARD
foreign language television
single

art director
VALDIR BIANCHI
writers
MIGUEL BEMFICA
SOPHIE SCHOENBURG
agency producer
MARIA DO
SOCORRO GOES
production company
CINE
CINEMATOGRAFICA
director
CLOVIS MELLO
client
VOLKSWAGEN BRAZIL
agency
ALMAP/BBDO/
SAO PAOLO

CD2 #91

MERIT AWARD
foreign language television
single

art director
ELVIO SANCHEZ
writer
JULIO WALLOVITS
production company
GROUP FILMS
director
ANGELES REINE
client
PLANETA
agencies
DELVICO BATES/
BARCELONA

CD2 #92

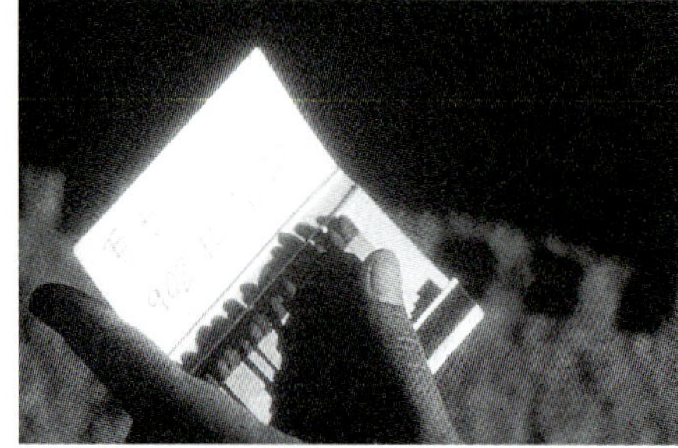

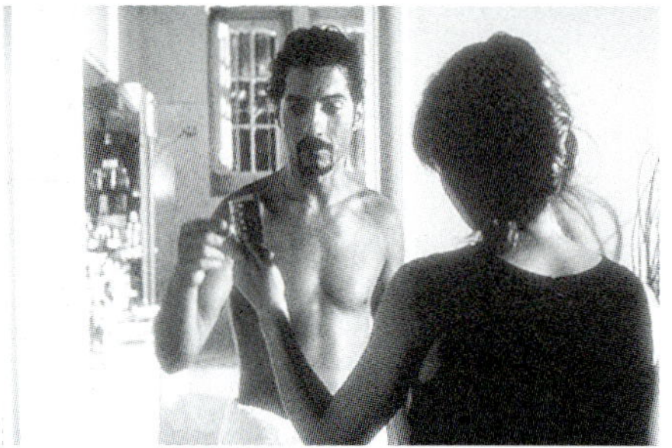

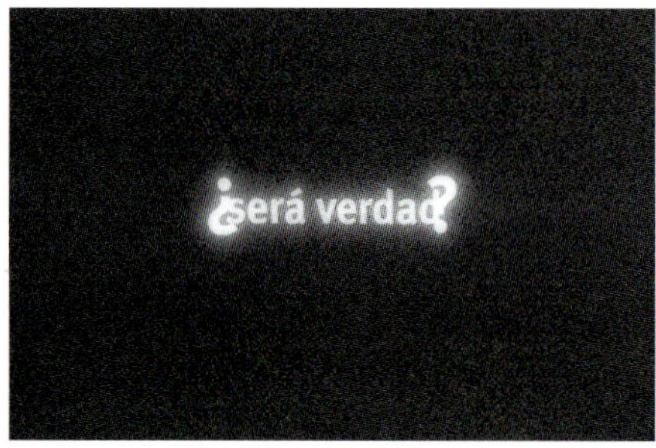

WOMAN: Darling, I didn't know you smoked?
HUSBAND: Smoke? I don't smoke.
WOMAN: Then I can throw away the matches, can't I?
HUSBAND: I wrote down a phone number, um...the phone number of...um, the information of the, um, Planeta Publishing Group. Planeta now pays us 60,000 ptas for our old encyclopedia. It has 30 volumes, completely up-to-date...and we can pay it in easy monthly installments. So I kept their number to..uh, order it..
SUPER: Can this be true?
SUPER: Find out right now by calling the number...

MERIT AWARD
foreign language television
single

writers
FILIP NILSSON
OSCAR ASKELOF
agency producer
MARIA BERGKVIST
production company
TRAKTOR
director
TRAKTOR
client
VOLVO PB SVERIGE/
VOLVO V70 AWD
agency
FORSMAN &
BODENFORS/
GOTHENBURG

CD2 #93

SUPER: The Volvo V70 All Wheel Drive. Not the ordinary 4x4.

MUSIC: Strange Indian pop song throughout.
ANNOUNCER: Thik jaka detha.
SUPER: Always well informed. Berliner Zeitung. Test read it free 0130/735373.

MERIT AWARD
foreign language television single

art director
ROBERT KRAUSE

writer
ROBERT KRAUSE

agency producer
HEIDRUN BÜHRE

production companies
CINEPLUS

directors
SUBODH MUKERIJ
ROBERT KRAUSE

client
BERLINER ZEITUNG

agency
SCHOLZ & FRIENDS/ BERLIN

CD2 #94

MERIT AWARD
foreign language television
single

art director
ARNDT DALLMAN
writer
GUIDO HEFFELS
agency producer
GUIDO HEFFELS
production company
CASPARI FILMS
director
THOMAS CASPARI
client
ARBEITSGEMEINSCHAFT
DERMATOLOGISCHE
PRÄVENTION E.R.
agency
SPRINGER & JACOBY
WERBUNG GMBH/
HAMBURG

CD2 #95

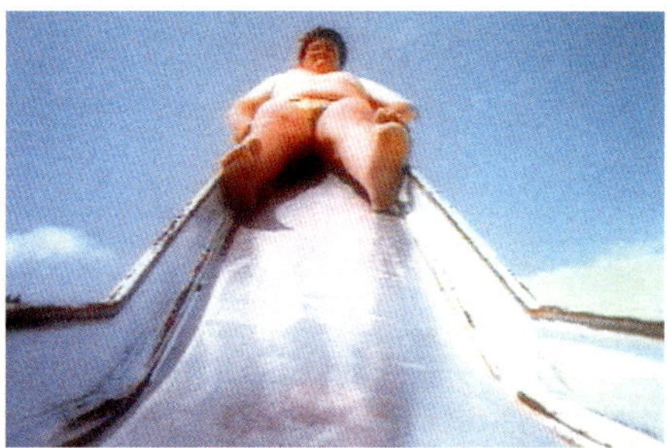

SUPER: Don't forget to use sun cream. Please.

DEPUTY: Captain sir, we have a serious situation here! The beauty queen has been captured.
BEAUTY QUEEN: Help!!
DEPUTY: Captain sir, what are we going to do next?
CAPTAIN: I'll sweet talk him.
SFX: Bang!
DEPUTY: Sir, I think you have shot. What should we do sir?
CAPTAIN: Call Superfarmer.
SUPERFARMER: Music please.
MUSIC: Classical.
DEPUTY: Sir, Superfarmer is here.
BEAUTY QUEEN: (Screams.)
SFX: Popping sound.
SUPER: They're screaming.
ANNOUNCER: Superfarmer uses only Mitsubishi Diesel Engine.
SUPER: Tough! Powerful! Superfarmer. Mitsubishi Diesel Engine.
DEPUTY: Hands up! He won't raise his hands up sir!

MERIT AWARD
foreign language television
single

art directors
SUTHISAK SUCHARITTANONTA
CHANCHAI CHAVANONT

writers
AUSSANEE AUGSORNNUGAL
ANCHALEE SRINUANWONG

agency producer
BRALEE UJJIN

production company
MATCHING STUDIO

director
SUTHON PETCHSUWAN

client
MITSUBISHI DIESEL ENGINE

agency
RESULTS ADVERTISING/ BANGKOK

CD2 #96

MULTIMEDIA MERIT

MERIT AWARD
multimedia campaign

client
TIME MAGAZINE

agency
FALLON MCELLIGOTT/
MINNEAPOLIS

print

art directors
BOB BARRIE
STEVE DRIGGS

writers
DEAN BUCKHORN
DAVE PULLAR

broadcast

art director
BOB BARRIE

writer
DEAN BUCKHORN

agency producer
MONIKA PRINCE

production company
SATELLITE

director
CAITLIN FELTON

CD2 #97

Women are already fighting
in the most dangerous places.
Their barracks, for instance.

The world's most interesting magazine.

We cover the scenes
behind the scenes
behind the scenes.

The world's most interesting magazine.

At what point do science
and morality collide?

At what point do science
and morality collide?

The world's most interesting magazine. **The world's most interesting magazine.**

Life is so unfair.
He can jump farther than you.

Our special issue, "Heroes of Medicine," is dedicated to the men and women who are making our lives healthier and more fulfilling. People who have advanced the science of medicine by leaps and bounds, in a world where there are simply no bounds. **TIME. The world's most interesting magazine.**

MULTIMEDIA MERIT

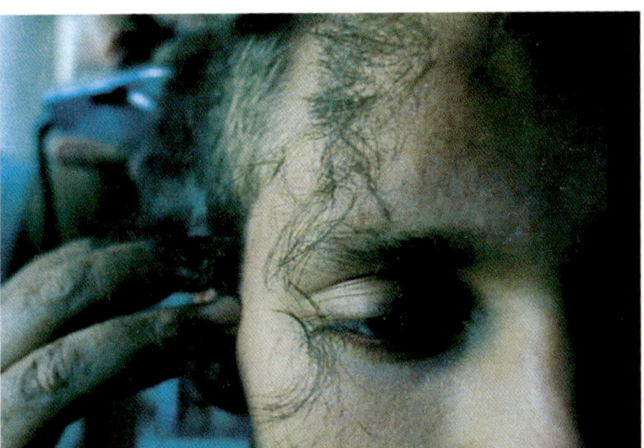

ANNOUNCER: No one who went through boot camp in the '50s or '60s would recognize the place today. Soldiers in training have swapped combat boots for sneakers. On obstacle courses they run around, instead of over some walls. The very phrase "obstacle course" is frowned upon as too harsh. The Navy now prefers "confidence course." But...are they ready for war?
ANNOUNCER and SUPER: Time. The world's most interesting magazine.

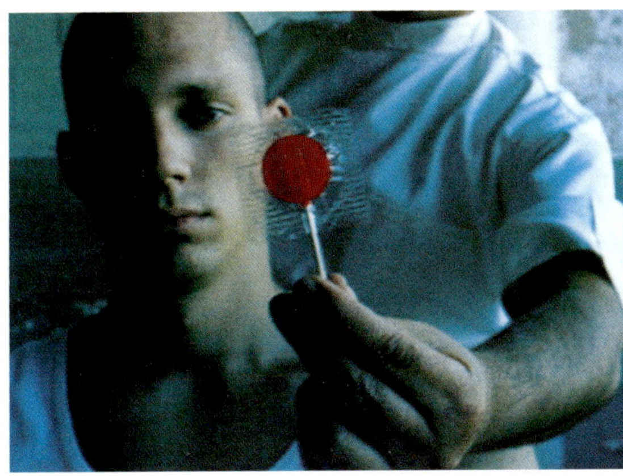

MERIT AWARD
multimedia campaign

client
ADIDAS AMERICA

agency
LEAGAS DELANEY/
SAN FRANCISCO

print

art director
PETER NICHOLSON

writer
SCOTT WILD

photographer
LARS TOPELMANN

broadcast

art director
PETER NICHOLSON

writer
SCOTT WILD

agency producer
BEN LATIMER

production company
SHELTER FILMS

director
JONATHAN DAVID

CD2 #98

Entire subway train had "RESERVED FOR YANKEE FANS" messages.

MULTIMEDIA MERIT

ICE
S

YANKS

MERIT AWARD
multimedia campaign

client
NISSAN

agency
TBWA/CHIAT DAY/
VENICE

print

art director
JOE HEMP

copywriter
ROB SILTANEN

photographers
SMITH-NELSON
JIM ERICKSON

broadcast

art directors
JOE HEMP
CRAIG TANIMOTO

copywriters
ROB SILTANEN
MARK ABELLERA

agency producer
ELAINE HINTON

production company
REACTOR FILMS

director
STEVE CHASE

CD2 #99

MULTIMEDIA MERIT

AGENT 1: Remember, Mr. Pearson. Once you enter the Witness Protection Program, you'll disappear. Here's your new birth certificate, passport, driver's license and keys. Well, good luck, uh–Mr. Symons.
GUY: Mr. Symons?
MUSIC: Happy trails to you.
SECURITY GUARD: Ooh la la.
GARBAGE MAN: Nice car.
TAXI DRIVER: Ooh, yah, nice car. Check it out.
NEWSPAPER MAN: Whoa! Nice car.
AGENT 1: He's not going to make it, is he?
AGENT 2: Uh–no.
SUPER: Nissan. The New Altima. Enjoy the ride.

MULTIMEDIA MERIT

MERIT AWARD
multimedia campaign

client
NIKE

agency
WIEDEN & KENNEDY/
AMSTERDAM

print

art director
OLLIE WATSON

copywriter
BOYD COYNER

illustrator
OLLIE WATSON

photographer
OLLIE WATSON

broadcast

art director
OLLIE WATSON

copywriter
BOYD COYNER

agency producer
CHARLES WOLFORD

production company
NEVE SENTIMENTAL

director
RALF SCHMERBERT

CD2 #100

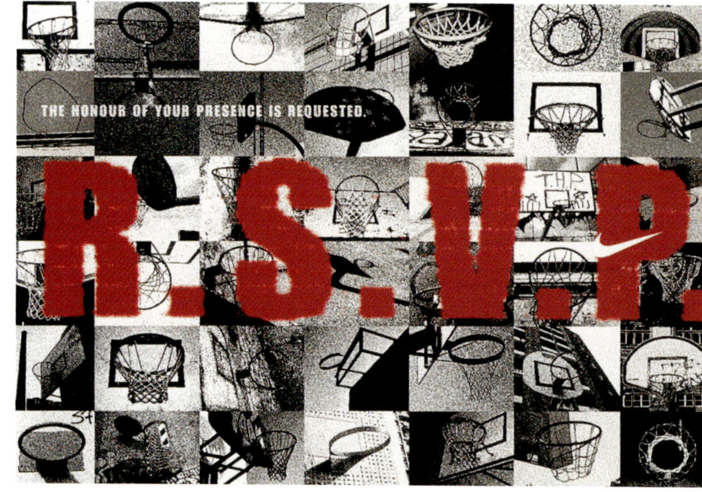

MULTIMEDIA MERIT

MUSIC: Joyous Union, Amber Music, throughout.
SUPER: Please join us for the joyous union.
SUPER: Off ball.
SUPER: And hoop.
SUPER: Everybody's welcome.
SUPER: I will attend, I will not attend.
SUPER: Sincerely.
SUPER: Swoosh.

MUSIC: Amber, Position Available throughout.
SUPER: Position available.
SUPER: No experience necessary.
SUPER: Starting.
SUPER: Now.
SUPER: Apply within.
SUPER: Swoosh.

COLLEGE MERIT

MERIT AWARD
college competition

art director
JOHN CALEY

writer
JOHN CALEY

college
THE ADVERTISING CLUB OF GREATER BOSTON/ BOSTON

MERIT AWARD
college competition

art directors
STEFAN COPIZ
PAM FUJIMOTO

writers
PAM FUJIMOTO
STEFAN COPIZ

college
ART CENTER COLLEGE OF DESIGN/PASADENA

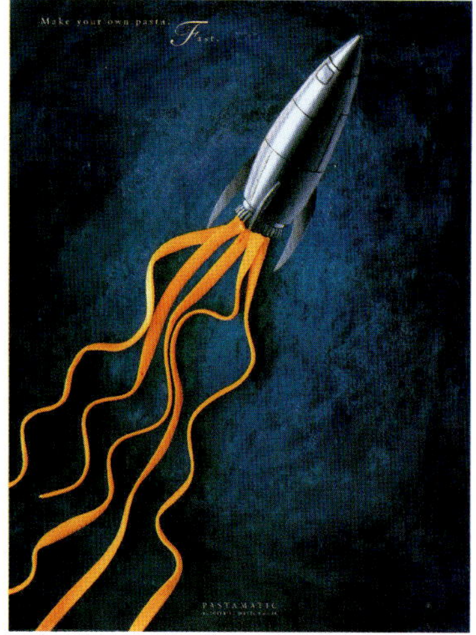

COLLEGE MERIT

MERIT AWARD
college competition

art director
DUSTIN DUKE

writer
DAVID BLACK

photographers
JON BAUCOM
EMILY CARROLL
BRIAN DEUTSCH

college
CREATIVE CIRCUS/ATLANTA

MERIT AWARD
college competition

art director
DUTCH SIERSEMA

writer
MICHAEL GORELIC

colleges
CREATIVE CIRCUS/ATLANTA
PORTFOLIO CENTER/ATLANTA

MERIT AWARD
college competition

art director
JEFF CHURCH

writers
GINGER ROBISON
JOSH FRIEDMAN

photgrapher
DAVID SEIJO

college
CREATIVE CIRCUS/
ATLANTA

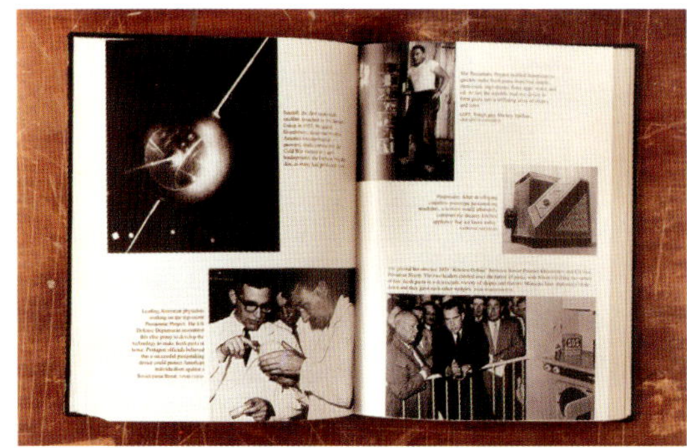

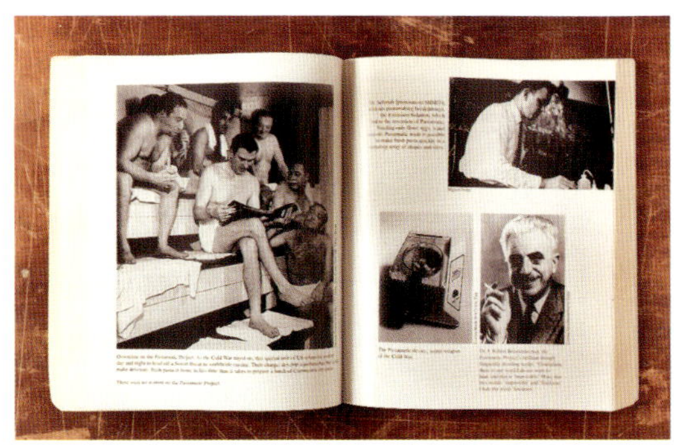

MERIT AWARD
college competition

art directors
MICHELLE LIM YIN YIN
LIEW CHENG MAY

writers
MICHELLE LIM YIN YIN
LIEW CHENG MAY

college
NANYANG
TECHNOLOGICAL
UNIVERSITY/SINGAPORE

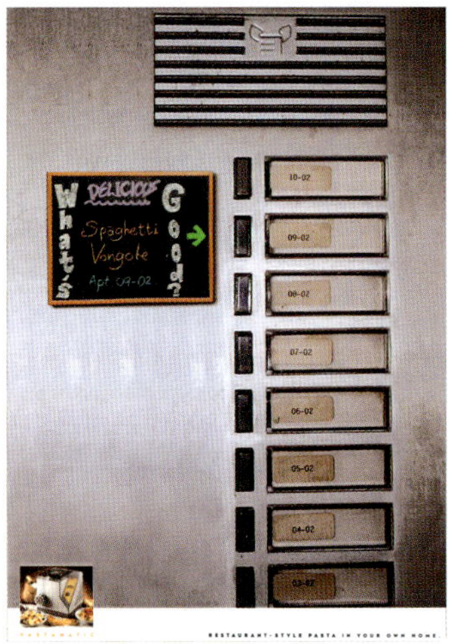

COLLEGE MERIT

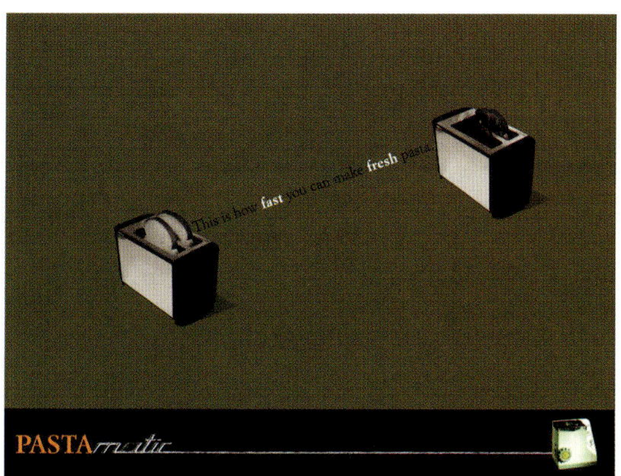

MERIT AWARD
college competition

art directors
JOEL KUNTZ
KARL BACKUS

writers
JOEL KUNTZ
KARL BACKUS

college
PORTFOLIO
CENTER/ATLANTA

MERIT AWARD
college competition

art director
MARCO CEO

writer
BOB MELLETT

college
PORTFOLIO
CENTER/ATLANTA

MERIT AWARD
college competition

art directors
FRANK ANSELMO
DAVID ARNOLD

writers
DAVID ARNOLD
FRANK ANSELMO

college
SCHOOL OF
VISUAL ARTS/NEW YORK

MERIT AWARD
college competition

art director
JESSE COULTER

writer
JESSE COULTER

college
UNIVERSITY OF OREGON/
EUGENE

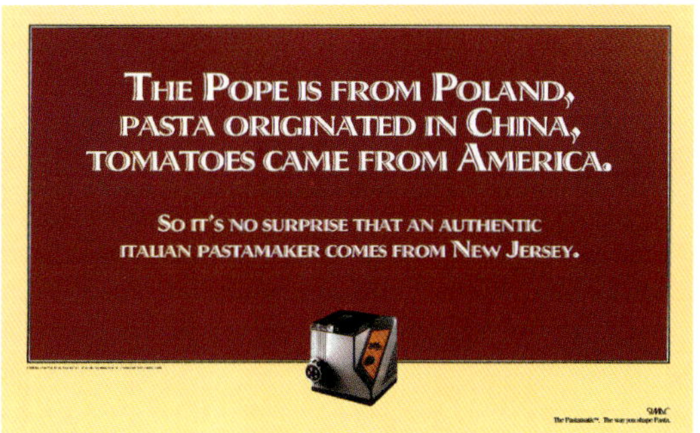

MERIT AWARD
college competition

art director
MICHAEL LANCASTER

writer
ADAM MORGAN

college
UTAH STATE
UNIVERSITY/
MIDVALE

MERIT AWARD
college competition

at director
GRETCHEN CARSWELL

writer
WILL SIMS

college
VCU ADCENTER/
RICHMOND

MERIT AWARD
college competition

art director
SUOSDEY PENN

writers
ADAM SPRINGFELDT
JOHN FIEBKE

college
VCU ADCENTER/
RICHMOND

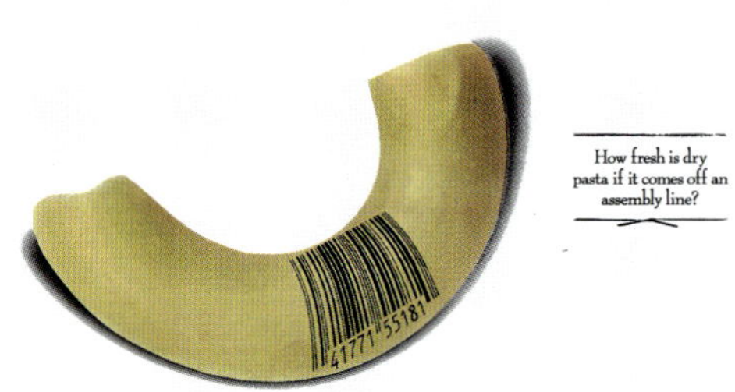

MERIT AWARD
college competition

art director
DONALD VANN

writer
STEVE MCELLIGOTT

college
VCU ADCENTER/
RICHMOND

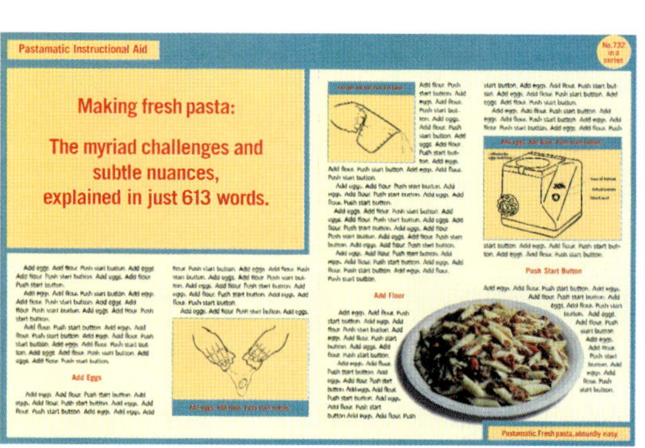

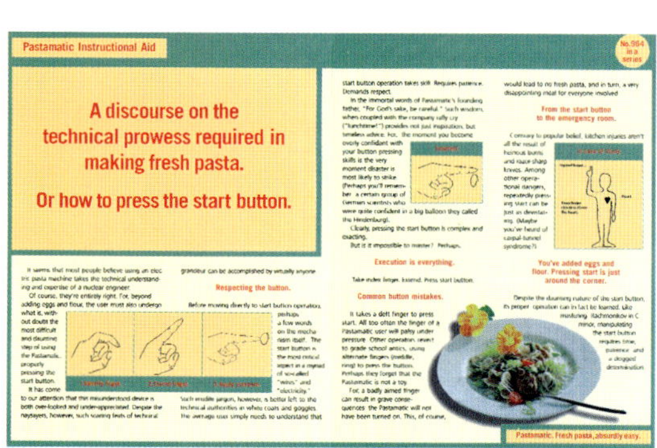

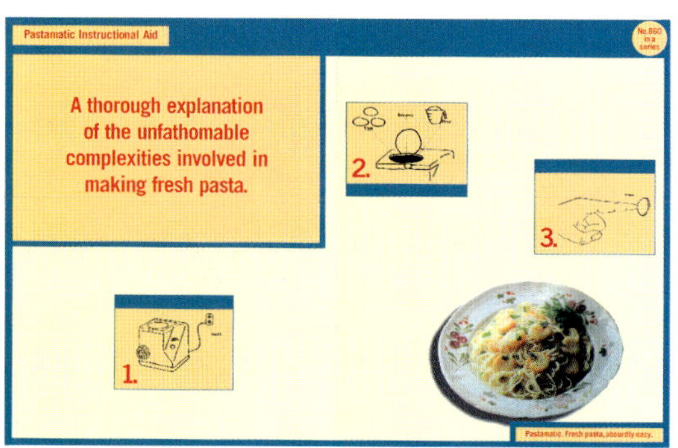

COLLEGE MERIT

MERIT AWARD
college competition

art director
CHRIS SHELDON

writer
JASON BARNES

college
VCU ADCENTER/
RICHMOND

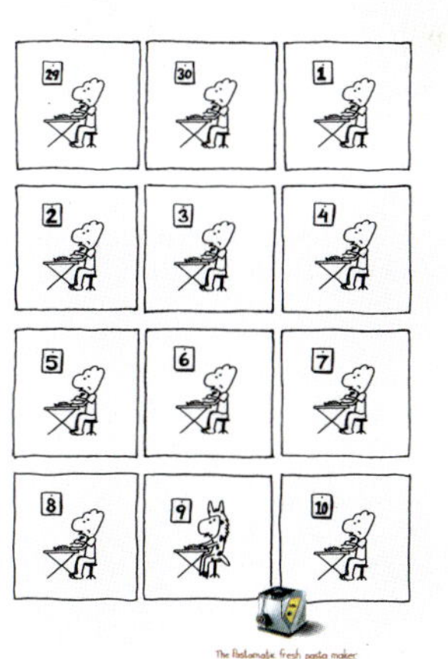

MERIT AWARD
college competition

art director
TOM SCHARPF

writer
SCOTT COONEY

college
VCU ADCENTER/
RICHMOND

INDEX

AGENCIES

AGENCY PRODUCERS

ART DIRECTORS

CLIENTS

COLLEGES

DESIGNERS

DIRECTORS

ILLUSTRATORS

PHOTOGRAPHERS

PRODUCTION COMPANIES

TYPOGRAPHERS

WRITERS